30 DAYS TO THE GMAT CAT

2ND EDITION

TEACHER-TESTED STRATEGIES AND TECHNIQUES FOR SCORING HIGH

MARK ALAN STEWART, J.D.

ARCO

THOMSON LEARNING™

Australia • Canada • Mexico • Singapore • Spain • United Kingdom • United States

An ARCO Book

ARCO is a registered trademark of Thomson Learning, Inc., and is used herein under license by Peterson's.

About Peterson's

Founded in 1966, Peterson's, a division of Thomson Learning, is the nation's largest and most respected provider of lifelong learning online resources, software, reference guides, and books. The Education Supersite^{SM} at petersons.com—the Web's most heavily traveled education resource—has searchable databases and interactive tools for contacting U.S.-accredited institutions and programs. CollegeQuest® (CollegeQuest.com) offers a complete solution for every step of the college decision-making process. GradAdvantage™ (GradAdvantage.org), developed with Educational Testing Service, is the only electronic admissions service capable of sending official graduate test score reports with a candidate's online application. Peterson's serves more than 55 million education consumers annually.

Thomson Learning is among the world's leading providers of lifelong learning, serving the needs of individuals, learning institutions, and corporations with products and services for both traditional classrooms and for online learning. For more information about the products and services offered by Thomson Learning, please visit www.thomsonlearning.com. Headquartered in Stamford, Connecticut, with offices worldwide, Thomson Learning is part of The Thomson Corporation (www.thomson.com), a leading e-information and solutions company in the business, professional, and education marketplaces. The Corporation's common shares are listed on the Toronto and London stock exchanges.

For more information, contact Peterson's, 2000 Lenox Drive, Lawrenceville, NJ 08648; 800-338-3282; or find us on the World Wide Web at: www.petersons.com/about

ISBN: 0-7689-0635-0

Printed in Canada

10 9 8 7 6 5 4 3 2 1   03 02

About The Author

Mark Alan Stewart (B.A., Economics, J.D., University of California at Los Angeles) is an attorney and one of today's preeminent authorities and top-selling authors on the subject of graduate-level entrance exams. For more than a decade, Mr. Stewart served as consultant to schools in the University of California and California State University systems in graduate-level entrance-exam programs. His books on GMAT, LSAT, and GRE preparation continue to be top sellers among aspiring business, law, and graduate students. His other book-length publications for graduate-level admissions include the following:

- *GRE-LSAT-GMAT-MCAT Reading Comprehension Workbook*
- *GMAT CAT—Answers to the Real Essay Questions*
- *Teach Yourself the GMAT CAT in 24 Hours*
- *Teach Yourself the GRE in 24 Hours*
- *30 Days to the LSAT*
- *GRE-LSAT Logic Workbook*
- *GRE—Answers to the Real Essay Questions*
- *Words for Smart Test Takers*
- *Math for Smart Test Takers*
- *Perfect Personal Statements—Law, Business, Medical, Graduate School*

ONLINE UPDATES FOR *30 DAYS TO THE* **GMAT**

At the author's GMAT Web site (www.west.net/~stewart/gmat), you'll find updates and supplements to this book, as well as useful information about other resources for B-school candidates.

THE 30-DAY PROGRAM

CREDITS

Day 1

Get To Know the GMAT

Today's Topics:

1. Five Acronyms You Should Know for Today
2. The GMAT CAT — at a Glance
3. Analysis of an Issue
4. Analysis of an Argument
5. Quantitative Ability
6. Verbal Ability
7. Your Four GMAT Scores
8. Score Reporting
9. How B-Schools Evaluate GMAT Scores
10. Resources for GMAT Preparation
11. DOs and DON'Ts for GMAT Preparation
12. GMAT Availability and Registration

Today you'll familiarize yourself with the structure of the GMAT and learn what abilities each question type is designed to measure. You'll also learn about GMAT scoring and score reporting, how to invest your time and money for GMAT prep, and how and when to register for the exam.

FIVE ACRONYMS YOU SHOULD KNOW FOR TODAY

1. **GMAT** (*Graduate Management Admission Test*): This standardized test provides graduate business schools (as well as vocational counselors and prospective applicants) with predictors of academic performance in MBA programs. Approximately 850 graduate business schools worldwide *require* GMAT scores for admission. Another 450 graduate business schools use—but don't require—GMAT scores to access applicants' qualifications.

2. **GMAC** (*Graduate Management Admission Council*): This organization develops guidelines, policies, and procedures for the graduate business school admission process and provides information about the admission process to the schools and to prospective applicants. The GMAC consists of representatives from more than 100 graduate business schools.

3. **ETS** (*Educational Testing Service*): This organization develops and administers the GMAT in consultation with the GMAC. ETS also conducts ongoing research projects aimed at improving the test.

4. **CAT** (*Computer-Adaptive Test*): Except for some locations outside of North America, the GMAT is now offered only by computer. CAT refers to the computerized version of the GMAT.

5. **AWA** (*Analytical Writing Assessment*): This name applies to the two essay sections of the GMAT. (Each of these two sections has its own name, as well.)

THE GMAT CAT — AT A GLANCE

The GMAT CAT consists of four timed sections. The total testing time (excluding breaks) is 3 hours, 30 minutes. Here's the basic structure of the test:

Structure of the GMAT CAT

SECTION 1 (OR 2): ANALYSIS OF AN ISSUE
(1 essay, 30-minute time limit)

SECTION 2 (OR 1): ANALYSIS OF AN ARGU-MENT
(1 essay, 30-minute time limit)

Optional break (5-minute time limit)

SECTION 3 (OR 4): QUANTITATIVE ABILITY
(37 multiple-choice questions, 75-minute time limit)

- Problem Solving (22–23 questions)
- Data Sufficiency (14–15 questions)

Optional break (5-minute time limit)

SECTION 4 (OR 3): VERBAL ABILITY
(41 multiple-choice questions, 75-minute time limit)

- Sentence Correction (14–15 questions)
- Critical Reasoning (14–15 questions)
- Reading Comprehension (12–13 questions, divided among 4 sets)

Sequence of Exam Sections

The two AWA sections always appear first (in either order), *before* the Quantitative and Verbal sections. The Quantitative and Verbal sections can appear in either order.

Sequence of Questions
(Quantitative and Verbal Sections)

In each of the two multiple-choice sections, question types are interspersed. Here's a typical sequence for each section (on your GMAT, the sequence might be different):

Quantitative Ability
(Typical Sequence of Questions)

Questions 1–2	Problem Solving
Questions 3–7	Data Sufficiency
Questions 8–13	Problem Solving
Question 14	Data Sufficiency
Question 15	Problem Solving
Question 16	Data Sufficiency
Questions 17–21	Problem Solving
Questions 22–27	Data Sufficiency
Questions 28–34	Problem Solving
Question 35	Data Sufficiency
Questions 36–37	Problem Solving

Verbal Ability
(Typical Sequence of Questions)

Questions 1–3	Sentence Correction
Questions 4–5	Critical Reasoning
Questions 6–8	Reading Comprehension
Question 9	Sentence Correction
Questions 10–11	Critical Reasoning
Questions 12–14	Sentence Correction
Questions 15–17	Reading Comprehension
Questions 18–21	Critical Reasoning
Questions 22–24	Sentence Correction
Questions 25–26	Critical Reasoning
Question 27	Sentence Correction
Questions 28–30	Reading Comprehension
Questions 31–33	Critical Reasoning
Questions 34–35	Sentence Correction
Questions 36	Critical Reasoning
Questions 37–39	Reading Comprehension
Question 40	Critical Reasoning
Question 41	Sentence Correction

Ground Rules

Here are some basic procedural rules for the GMAT CAT (during Day 2, I'll cover test-taking procedures in greater detail):

- Once the timed test begins, you cannot stop the testing clock.

- If you finish any section before the time limit expires, you can proceed immediately to the next section, at your option.

- Pencils and "scratch" paper are provided for all exam sections.

- You select a multiple-choice answer by clicking on an oval next to the choice. (All multiple-choice questions include five answer choices.)

- You compose both essays using the word processor built into the GMAT testing system. (Handwritten essays are not permitted.)

ANALYSIS OF AN ISSUE

This 30-minute section tests your ability to present a position on an issue effectively and persuasively. Your task is to compose an essay in which you respond to a brief (1–2 sentence) opinion about an issue of general intellectual interest. You should consider various perspectives, take a position on the issue, and argue for that position.

Here are some key facts about the Issue-Analysis section (during Day 3, I'll cover all these facts in detail):

- There is no "correct" answer; what's important is how effectively you present and support your position, not what your position is.

- Your essay will be evaluated based on (1) content, (2) organization, (3) writing style, and (4) mechanics—grammar, syntax, word usage, etc. (The CAT word processor does not include a grammar-checker.)

- You won't be penalized for errors in spelling and punctuation—unless these errors are frequent and egregious. (The CAT word processor does not include a spell-checker.)

- Your essay will be evaluated by at least one human reader *and* by a computer program called *E-Rater*.

- The CAT will select your topic randomly from a large pool; you won't be able to choose among topics. GMAC has predisclosed its entire pool of Issue-Analysis topics at its Web site (www.gmac.com).

To see what Issue-Analysis topics look like, take a peek at the samples on page 22 (Day 3).

ANALYSIS OF AN ARGUMENT

This 30-minute section is designed to test your critical-reasoning and analytical-writing skills. Your task is to compose an essay in which you critique a paragraph-length argument based on the strength of the evidence presented in support of it and on the argument's logic (line of reasoning). You can also indicate what additional evidence would help you evaluate the argument and how the argument could be improved.

Here are some key facts about the Argument-Analysis section (during Day 4, I'll cover all these facts in detail):

- The argument that you critique will contain at least three major problems in reasoning and logic; to score high on your Argument-Analysis essay, you must identify and discuss each major problem.

- Like your Issue-Analysis essay, your Argument-Analysis essay will be evaluated based on content, organization, writing style, and mechanics.

- Like your Issue-Analysis essay, your Argument-Analysis essay will be evaluated by at least one human reader *and* by a computer program called *E-Rater*.

- The CAT will select your argument randomly from a large pool; you won't be able to choose among arguments. GMAC has predisclosed its entire pool of arguments at its Web site (www.gmac.com).

To see what GMAT arguments look like, take a peek at the samples on page 29 (Day 4).

QUANTITATIVE ABILITY

This 75-minute section is designed to measure your basic mathematical skills, your understanding of basic math concepts, and your ability to reason quantitatively, solve quantitative problems, and interpret graphical data. The Quantitative Ability section covers the following topics:

- Arithmetical operations
- Integers, factors, and multiples
- The number line and ordering
- Decimals, percentages, ratios, and proportion
- Exponents and square roots
- Statistics (mean, median, mode, range, probability, standard deviation)
- Operations with variables
- Algebraic equations and inequalities
- Geometry, including coordinate geometry

Algebraic concepts on the GMAT are those normally covered in a first-year high school algebra course. The GMAT does not cover more advanced areas such as trigonometry and calculus.

Each Quantitative question is multiple-choice (five answer choices) and conforms to one of two formats (any of the topics listed above is fair game for either question format):

Problem Solving questions require you to solve a mathematical problem and then select the correct answer from among five answer choices. About half of these questions will be so-called "story" problems — cast in a real-world setting.

Data Sufficiency problems each consist of a question followed by two statements—labeled (1) and (2). Your task is to analyze each of the two statements to determine whether it provides sufficient data to answer the question and, if neither suffices alone, whether both statements together suffice. *Every Data Sufficiency question includes the same five answer choices.* About half of these questions will be so-called "story" problems — cast in a real-world setting.

To see examples of each format, take a quick peek at the Quantitative Ability practice test (Day 26).

VERBAL ABILITY

This 75-minute section consists of 41 multiple-choice questions. Each question will be one of the following three types (each type covers a distinct set of verbal and verbal-reasoning skills):

Sentence Correction questions measure your command of the English language and of the conventions of standard written English. Areas tested include grammar, diction, usage, and effective expression (but not punctuation). In each question, part (or all) of a sentence is underlined. Your task is to determine which is correct — the original underlined part or one of four alternatives.

Critical Reasoning questions measure your ability to understand, criticize, and draw reasonable conclusions from arguments. Each argument consists of a brief one-paragraph passage.

Reading Comprehension questions measure your ability to read carefully and accurately, to determine the relationships among the various parts of the passage and to draw reasonable inferences from the material in the passage. You'll encounter four sets of questions; all questions in a set pertain to the same passage. The passages are drawn from for a variety of subjects, including the humanities, the social sciences, the physical sciences, ethics, philosophy, and law.

To see examples of each question type, take a quick peek at the Verbal Ability practice test (Day 28).

YOUR FOUR GMAT SCORES

You'll receive four scores for the GMAT:

1. A scaled Quantitative score, on a 0–60 scale
2. A scaled Verbal score, on a 0–60 scale
3. A total score, on a 200–800 scale, based on both your Quantitative and Verbal scores
4. An AWA score, on a 0–6 scale, which averages (to the nearest one-half point) the final scores for each of your two GMAT essays

For each of the four scores, you'll also receive a percentile rank (0–99%). A percentile rank of 60%, for example, indicates that you scored higher than 60% (and lower than 40%) of all other test takers. Percentile ranks reflect your performance relative to the entire GMAT test-taking population during the most recent three-year period.

> NOTE: On pages 280–281 (Day 30), you'll find tables that convert scaled scores to percentile rank.

How the Quantitative and Verbal Sections are Scored

The scoring system for the Quantitative and Verbal sections is a bit tricky. Your score for each of these two sections is based on three factors:

- The *number* of questions you answer correctly
- The *difficulty level* of the questions you answer correctly
- The *range* of question types and topics among the questions you answer correctly

So even if you don't respond to all 37 Quantitative (or 41 Verbal) questions, you can still achieve a high score for the section if a high percentage of your responses are correct—especially if you respond correctly to a wide variety of question types. The CAT system's scoring algorithms are well-guarded ETS secrets; but knowing exactly how the system works wouldn't affect your exam preparation or test-taking strategy, anyway.

> NOTE: Some questions on each of your two multiple-choice sections won't be scored. The test makers include unscored, so-called "pretest" questions on the GMAT in order to assess their integrity, fairness, and difficulty. Some of these questions might show up as scored questions on the GMAT in the future. Pretest questions are mixed in with scored questions, and you won't be able to distinguish them — so don't risk trying.

How GMAT Essays are Evaluated and Scored

The evaluation and scoring system for GMAT essays is also a bit tricky, in its own way. Initially, one person will read and evaluate your Issue-Analysis essay, while a different person reads and evaluates your Argument-Analysis essay. Readers apply a *holistic* scoring approach, meaning that a reader will base his or her evaluation on the overall quality of your writing. In other words, instead of awarding separate sub-scores for content, organization, writing style, and mechanics, the reader will consider how effective your essay is *as a whole*—accounting for all these factors.

All GMAT readers are college or university faculty members; most teach in the field of either English or Communications. Each reader evaluates your writing independently of other readers, and no reader is informed of other readers' scores. All readers are trained by ETS in applying specific scoring criteria. (See Day 3, pages 22–23 and Day 4, page 30 for details about the scoring criteria for each essay.)

A computer program called *E-Rater* will also evaluate each of your essays. E-Rater scrutinizes your essays for problems with grammar, syntax (sentence structure), repetitiveness (repeated use of the same phrases), sentence length, spelling, and punctuation.

Here are the specific steps involved in calculating your AWA score:

1. As mentioned above, one reader will read and score your Issue-Analysis essay, and a different reader will read and score your Argument-Analysis essay. Each reader will award a single score on a scale of 0–6 in whole-point intervals (6 is highest).

2. E-Rater will also evaluate and award a score of 0–6 for each essay.

3. For either essay, if the human reader's score differs from E-Rater's score by more than one point, then a second human reader will read and score the essay (and E-Rater's score is then disregarded).

3. For each essay your final score is the average of the scores awarded by the human reader and E-Rater (or by the second human reader).

4. You final AWA score is the average of your final scores for each essay; AWA scores are rounded up to the nearest half-point.

Here's an example showing how the AWA scoring system works:

4 Reader A's evaluation of the Issue-Analysis essay

2 E-Rater's evaluation of the Issue-Analysis essay

3 Reader B's evaluation of the Issue-Analysis essay

3.5 Final score for the Issue-Analysis essay

3 Reader C's evaluation of the Argument-Analysis essay

3 E-Rater's evaluation of the Argument-Analysis essay

3 Final score for the Argument-Analysis essay

3.5 AWA score

Notice in this example that a second human reader evaluated the Issue-Analysis essay, and that the average of the two final scores has been rounded up.

SCORE REPORTING

Once the GMAT readers have read and scored your two essays, ETS will mail to you an official score report for all four sections. (Expect your score report within ten days after testing.) At the same time, ETS will transmit a score report to each B-school you've designated to receive your score report. (You can send direct reports to as many as five schools without charge.)

At this time, score reports don't include the GMAT essays themselves, although ETS is working on it. Eventually, the CAT system will provide for disclosure of each test taker's complete exam (including the questions). But ETS and GMAC admit that implementation is years away.

> NOTE: GMAT absences and cancellations also appear on your official report, but they will not adversely affect your chances of admission.

HOW B-SCHOOLS EVALUATE GMAT SCORES

Each business school develops and implements its own policies for evaluating GMAT scores. Some schools place equal weight on GMAT scores and GPA, others weigh GMAT scores more heavily,

whereas others weigh GPA more heavily. ETS reports your three most recent GMAT scores to each business school receiving your scores and transcripts. Most schools simply *average* reported scores. (Quantitative, Verbal, Total, and AWA scores are each averaged separately for this purpose.)

A minority of schools have refined this approach by disregarding a score that is sufficiently lower than another score for the same ability — on the basis that the low score unfairly distorts the test taker's ability in this area. Other schools disregard all but your highest score of each type in any event. (This approach is increasingly uncommon, since it discriminates in favor of test takers who can afford to take the GMAT again and again.)

> NOTE: Any B-school will gladly tell you which method it uses among the three mentioned above. But don't expect any school to tell you exactly how much weight it places on each exam section or on different admission criteria (such as GMAT scores, GPA, work experience, and personal statements).

RESOURCES FOR GMAT PREPARATION

How much should you "invest" in your GMAT education—in terms of both time and money? The conventional wisdom is that since the GMAT is one of the most important tests you'll ever take, you should invest as much time and money in it as possible. I disagree; the law of diminishing returns applies to GMAT preparation. This book, along with a few other thoughtfully selected books and online resources, can provide virtually all of the potential benefits of a full-blown GMAT prep course.

GMAT Books

Visit any major brick-and-mortar or online bookstore, and prepare to be overwhelmed by the number of available books for GMAT prep. Here are some suggestions to help you cut through the glut:

- Peruse a book carefully before committing to it. Yes, this means visiting your local brick-and-mortar bookstore.

- Look for a book that emphasizes skill development, not just practice questions.

- Rule out any book that does not include a complete analysis of *all five* answer choices for every Verbal Ability question. You gain just as much from learning why wrong answer choices are wrong as why best answer choices are best.

- Rule out any book that emphasizes so-called "secrets" and "shortcuts," or makes the test out to be easier than it appears. Do you really think the GMAC and ETS would devise a test that can be "cracked" like a cheap safe? If so, think again.

- Limit the number of comprehensive GMAT books you use to two or three altogether. Any more and you'll find yourself reading the same strategies and test-taking tips again.

- Identify your weakest skill area, and supplement this book with a workbook targeted for that area.

- If you must shop for GMAT books at an online bookstore, ignore customer comments and ratings, especially if they are few in number. Laudatory comments are often submitted anonymously by the publishers themselves, while derogatory comments are often factually inaccurate, unfair, and inflammatory.

The bottom line: You don't need to spend more than $40 to $50 on three or four books altogether to be fully prepared for the GMAT.

Online GMAT Resources

The Web is now littered with GMAT advice and practice questions—freely available for public consumption. To separate the wheat from the chaff, limit your GMAT Web surfing to the official GMAC site (**www.gmac.com**) and the sites of test-prep publishers with a time-tested reputation for producing high-quality content, such as Peterson's (**www.petersons.com**). You'll find links to these and other useful GMAT sites at the online supplement for this book (**www.west.net/~stewart/gmat**).

GMAT-Prep Courses

Would it be worthwhile to enroll in a live GMAT-prep course? Well, here are their advantages:

1. The dynamics of a live classroom setting can help you learn difficult concepts by affording different perspectives. (But why not start your own study group? You're just as likely to gain useful insights from your peers as from an GMAT instructor.)

2. Having made a substantial financial investment, you'll probably be motivated to "get your money's worth" out of that investment. (But this is an expensive head game, isn't it? And if you can't afford the course, it doesn't matter anyway.)

3. You're less likely to procrastinate with a set class schedule. (But if you're disciplined enough this is no advantage.)

4. All the materials are provided, so you don't need to decide which books and/or software to buy. (But is this really a significant benefit?)

5. You can commiserate and compare notes with your classmates. In fact, GMAT prep classes typical morph into de facto pre-MBA support groups. (But why not start your own GMAT study/support group?)

Here are some drawbacks and caveats to keep in mind if you're thinking about taking a GMAT prep course:

1. They're expensive; you can easily spend $1,000. (If you're near a university, you might find a course sponsored by the university, perhaps through its extension program, for a fraction of the cost of a private course.)

2. Despite their claims, private test-prep companies pass along no "secrets" to you—nothing at all that you can't find for yourself in test-prep books.

3. The popular test-prep services require each of their GMAT instructors to have taken the real GMAT and attained a high score (typically above the 90th percentile). But this screen hardly ensures that your instructor will be an effective teacher.

4. During peak times of the year, you might have difficulty scheduling out-of-class time in the computer lab, at least during reasonable hours.

5. If you're not located in a major urban area or near a large college or university, the class location might be too remote for you.

If you decide to enroll in an GMAT prep course, keep in mind the following points of advice:

1. Ask about the policy for repeating the course. Insist on an option to repeat the course at least once without charge at any time (not just within the next year).

2. Ask about merit-based or financial-based "scholarships" (fee reductions).

3. If you repeat the course, be sure to arrange for a different instructor; just as with GMAT books, each GMAT instructor has his or her own teaching style.

4. The most significant benefit of a GMAT course is the live classroom; so be sure to attend as many classes as you can.

5. Take full advantage of the chance to meet other students and set up out-of-class study sessions. As I've already noted, you can learn just as much from your peers as from an instructor.

DOs AND DON'Ts FOR GMAT PREPARATION

Regardless of what resources you use to prepare for the GMAT, to maximize your chances of getting the scores you want and getting an acceptance letter from your first-choice B-school, heed the following DOs and DON'Ts for GMAT prep.

DON'T be too confident about your test-taking prowess. Perhaps you think you're a math "wiz" and that the Quantitative GMAT questions won't pose any real challenge; or perhaps you think you have good command of English and believe that Sentence Correction questions will be a breeze. If so, you're already on your way to disappointing GMAT scores. You should prepare diligently for each and every question type on the exam.

DON'T obsess about scores. Perhaps you have a particular B-school in mind as your first choice, and you think that you need a particular GMAT score to gain admission to that school. Setting a goal for your GMAT scores is understandable. But try not to concern yourself as much with your scores as with

what you can constructively do between now and exam day to improve your performance.

DON'T cram for the GMAT, but don't over-prepare either. Preparing for the GMAT is a bit like training for an athletic event. You need to familiarize yourself with the event, learn to be comfortable with it, and build up your endurance. At some point—hopefully around exam day — your motivation, interest, and performance will peak. Cramming for the GMAT makes little sense; it takes time to get comfortable with the exam, to correct poor test-taking habits, to develop an instinct for recognizing wrong-answer choices, and to find your optimal pace.

On the flip side, there's a point beyond which additional study and practice confer little or no additional benefit. Devoting about a month of your attention, energy, and concern to the GMAT is plenty of time. Don't drag out the process by starting several months in advance or by postponing the exam to give yourself more time than you really need for preparation.

DO be realistic in your expectations. You'd love perfect GMAT scores, wouldn't you? And in theory, your capable of attaining them. But in reality, you probably won't score as highly as you'd like to. Accept your limitations. With regular study and practice, you'll perform as well as you can reasonably expect to perform. Also be realistic about the benefits you expect from this or any other GMAT preparation book. There's only so much that you can do in 30 sessions—or even 300 sessions—to boost your GMAT score.

DO practice taking GMAT essays using a word processor. It's particularly crucial that you simulate testing conditions for the two AWA sections. Use a word processor, restrict yourself to the features available on the CAT word processor (see Day 2), and force yourself to adhere to the time limits imposed on the exam.

DO take at least one practice test as you would the real exam—with only a few short breaks between sections. Do not underestimate the role that endurance plays on the GMAT. Half the battle is just making it through the half-day ordeal with your wits intact. Condition yourself by taking full-length sample tests straight through, with only a few short breaks.

DO take the real GMAT once—just for practice. If you have time and can afford it, you should register for and take the real GMAT once as a dress rehearsal — just to get comfortable with the testing environment. You'll rid yourself of a lot of anxiety and nervousness, and if you're like most test takers you'll be far more relaxed yet focused the second time around. In fact, ETS statistics show that among repeaters, more than 90 percent improve their score the second time around. Those are great odds!

DO take the GMAT early to allow yourself the option of retaking it. Most graduate business schools admit new students for the fall term only. Although application deadlines vary widely among the schools, if you take the GMAT no later than the November prior to matriculation, you'll meet almost any application deadline. Ideally, you should take the GMAT early enough so that you can take the exam a second time if necessary and still meet application deadlines. In any event, take the GMAT at a time when you're sure that you have adequate time to prepare for the exam.

DO take certain academic courses beforehand, if you're still in college. The intellectual abilities that the GMAT evaluates are largely developed during your four years of college. So, if you're still in college, consider postponing the GMAT until after you've taken the following types of courses:

- Critical thinking and logic (for GMAT Critical Reasoning questions and the Argument-Analysis essay)

- English composition (for GMAT Sentence Correction questions and for both GMAT essays)

- Courses in the humanities and social sciences (for GMAT Reading Comprehension questions and for the Issue-Analysis essay)

- Basic algebra and basic geometry (for GMAT Quantitative questions)

GMAT AVAILABILITY AND REGISTRATION

If you need to find out when and where the GMAT is available, or how to register for the GMAT, this section is a good starting place. Keep in mind, though, that the following information is only an overview and is current only up to the date this book goes to print.

GMAT Availability

The computer-based GMAT is administered year-round at more than 500 locations, most of which are in North America. Testing centers are located at Prometric Testing Centers, Sylvan Learning Centers, certain colleges and universities, and ETS (Educational Testing Service) field offices. The official GMAT *Bulletin* contains a complete list of GMAT computer-based test centers; an updated list is available at the GMAC Web site (www.gmac.com).

In certain areas outside of North America, the computer-based network is not yet available, so the GMAT is still administered as a paper-based exam. The number of times per year that the paper-based GMAT is administered varies among countries and ranges from one to four. A complete list of international paper-based testing locations and test dates is available at the GMAC Web site (www.gmac.com).

Scheduling a GMAT Appointment

To take the computer-based GMAT you must schedule an appointment by using any of the following four methods:

1. Make an appointment online, via the GMAC Web site (www.gmac.com).

2. Call the test center of your choice directly. A current test-center list is available at the GMAC Web site (www.gmac.com).

3. Call a central registration number: 1-800-GMAT-NOW (1-800-462-8669).

4. Make an appointment by mail. (You'll need to complete and mail the Authorization Voucher Request Form in the official GMAT Bulletin; you should receive your Authorization Voucher about four weeks after you mail the request form, and you cannot schedule a test appointment until you've received your voucher.)

You might be able to sit for the GMAT within a few days after scheduling an appointment. However, keep in mind that popular test centers may experience backlogs up to several weeks. Also, you might find it more difficult to schedule a weekend test date than a weekday test date. So be sure to plan ahead and schedule your GMAT early enough to meet your B-school application deadlines.

Obtaining Up-to-date GMAT Information

For detailed information about GMAT registration procedures, consult the official GMAC Web site (www.gmac.com) or refer to the printed *GMAT Information Bulletin*, published annually by the GMAC. This free bulletin is available directly from ETS and GMAC as well as through career-planning offices at most four-year colleges and universities. You can also download the *Bulletin* from the GMAC Web site. The official GMAC Web site and *Bulletin* both provide detailed and current information about:

- Test center locations, telephone numbers, and hours of operation
- Registration procedures
- Accommodations for disabled test takers
- Requirements for admission to the GMAT
- Registration and reporting fees and refund policies
- Repeating the test
- The paper-based GMAT (availability, registration procedures, etc.)
- Official scoring criteria for the AWA essays
- How GMAT scores should be used by the institutions

The GMAT *Bulletin* is published only once a year, so for the most up-to-date official information, you should check the GMAC Web site.

Contacting the Testing Service

To obtain the *Bulletin*, or for other information about the GMAT, you can contact ETS by any of these methods:

Telephone:
1-609-771-7330
(general inquiries and publications)
1-800-462-8669 (CAT registration only)

E-mail:
gmat@ets.org
World Wide Web:
http://www.gmac.com
http://www.ets.org (the ETS home page)

Mail:
GMAT
Educational Testing Service
P.O. Box 6103
Princeton, NJ 08541-6103

IF YOU HAVE MORE TIME TODAY

Here are three suggestions for supplementing today's lesson:

1. Visit the official GMAC Web site (www.gmac.com); explore the various areas of the site to find out what information is available at the site.

2. To familiarize yourself with the various GMAT question types and with the official directions for each type, log on to the author's GMAT Web site (www.west.net/~stewart/gmat) and try your hand at one question of each type (click on "GMAT Questions—Up Close").

3. Check out the author's online Q&A entitled "Your GMAT Scores: What They Mean to the B-Schools—and for You." Link to it from the "Q&A Corner" of the author's GMAT Web site (www.west.net/~stewart/gmat).

Day 2

The GMAT CAT Testing Experience

Today's Topics:

1. How the Computer-Adaptive GMAT Works

2. The GMAT CAT Interface

3. The CAT Test-Taking Experience

4. DOs and DON'Ts during the Exam

Today you'll familiarize yourself with the GMAT's computerized testing environment and procedures. You'll also learn some basic test-taking strategies that apply to all test sections.

HOW THE COMPUTER-ADAPTIVE GMAT WORKS

The test questions on the computerized GMAT are the same as on the old paper-based version. But procedurally the CAT is an entirely different animal. Let's examine the key features that set the CAT apart from the paper-based GMAT.

During the two multiple-choice sections, the CAT will continually adapt to your ability level. The "A" in CAT stands for "Adaptive," which means that during each of the two multiple-choice sections the testing system tailors its difficulty level to your level of ability. How? The initial few questions *of each type* are average in difficulty level. As you respond *correctly* to questions, the CAT system steps you up to more difficult questions. Conversely, as you respond *incorrectly* to questions, the CAT

steps you down to easier ones. Thus, the CAT builds a customized test for you, drawing on its *very* large pool of multiple-choice questions.

NOTE: Early in an exam section the CAT can shift from the easiest level to a very challenging level (or vice versa) in as few as 3 or 4 successive questions. But later in the section, when your ability level is well established, the difficulty level will not vary as widely.

The CAT does not let you skip questions. Given the adaptive nature of the test, this makes sense. The computer-adaptive algorithm cannot determine the appropriate difficulty level for the next question without a response (correct or incorrect) to each question presented in sequence.

The CAT does not let you return to any question already presented (and answered). Why not? The computer-adaptive algorithm that determines the difficulty of subsequent questions depends on the correctness of prior responses. For example, suppose that you answer question 5 incorrectly. The CAT responds by posing slightly easier questions. Were the CAT to let you return to question 5 and change your response to the correct one, the questions following question 5 would be easier than they should have been, given your amended response. In other words, the process by which the CAT builds your GMAT and determines your score would be undermined.

The CAT does not require you to answer all available questions. The CAT gives you the *opportunity* to respond to a total of 37 Quantitative and 41 Verbal questions. But the CAT does *not* require you to finish either section. The CAT will tabulate a score regardless of the number of available questions you've answered, except that if you don't respond to at least one question during a section, an "NS" (no score) will appear on your score report *for that section only*.

> NOTE: During each of the two essay sections, if you fail to key in (type) at least one character using the CAT word processor, you'll automatically receive a score of 0 (on a scale of 0 to 6) for that section; this score will appear on your report.

Fast, accurate typists have a clear advantage in the AWA section—no doubt about it. But fast-fingered test takers enjoy no advantage for the multiple-choice sections because test takers use only the mouse (not the keyboard) during these sections. And if you're unaccustomed to using a computer, you won't be disadvantaged as a result, because all computerized aspects of the GMAT you'll learn and can easily master during the pretest tutorial. (Later today you'll learn all about the pretest computer tutorial.)

During each section, the CAT automatically provides a 5-minute warning. When 5 minutes remain during each timed section, the on-screen clock (in the upper left corner of the screen) will blink silently several times to warn you. This 5-minute warning will be your only reminder.

> NOTE: Beepers and alarms aren't allowed in the testing room, although silent timing devices are permitted.

THE GMAT CAT INTERFACE

The three simulated screen shots on pages 13–15 show the GMAT CAT interface for the AWA sections,

the Quantitative Ability section, and the Verbal Ability section. Let's first examine the features of the interface that are common to all exam sections.

The CAT Title Bar

A dark title bar will appear across the top of the computer screen at all times during all test sections. (You cannot hide this bar.) The CAT title bar displays three items:

Left corner: The time remaining for the current section (hours and minutes)

Middle: The name of the test (GMAT) and current section number

Right corner: The current question number and total number of questions in the current section

The CAT Toolbar

A series of six buttons appear in a "toolbar" across the bottom of the computer screen at all times during all test sections. (You cannot hide the toolbar.) Here's a description of each button's function:

QUIT TEST

Click on this button to stop the test and cancel your scores for the *entire* test. (Partial score cancellations are not allowed in any event.) If you click here, a dialog box will appear on the screen, asking you to confirm this operation. Stay away from this button unless you're absolutely sure you wish your GMAT score for the day to vaporize and you're willing to throw away your GMAT registration fee.

EXIT SECTION

Click on this button if you finish the section before the allotted time expires and wish to proceed immediately to the next section. A dialog box will appear on the screen, asking you to confirm this operation. Stay away from this button unless you've already answered every question in the current section and don't feel you need a breather before starting the next one!

TIME

Click on this button to display the time remaining to the nearest *second*. By default, the time remaining is displayed (in the upper left corner) in hours and minutes but not to the nearest second.

HELP

Click on this button to access the directions for the current question type (for example, Data Sufficiency or Sentence Correction) as well as the general test directions and the instructions for using the toolbar items.

NEXT and CONFIRM ANSWER

Click on the NEXT button when you're finished with the current question. When you click on NEXT, the current question will remain on the screen until you click on CONFIRM ANSWER. Until you confirm, you can change your answer as often as you wish (by clicking on a different oval). But once you confirm, the question disappears forever and the next one appears in its place. Whenever the NEXT button is enabled (appearing dark gray), the CONFIRM ANSWER button is disabled (appearing light gray), and vice versa.

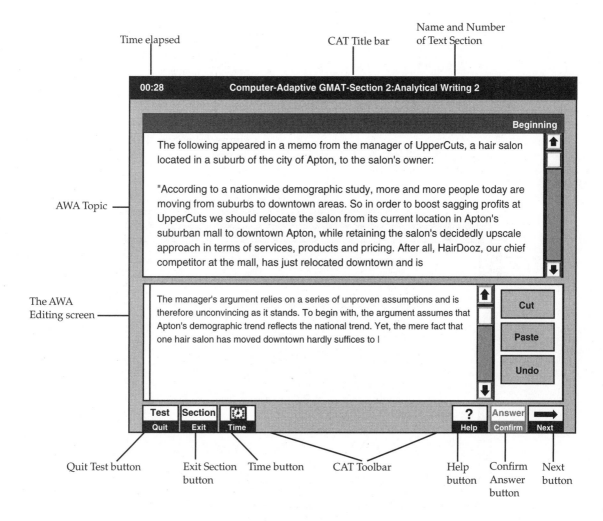

AWA SCREEN (WITH CALLOUTS)

The AWA Screen

As illustrated in the screen shot on page 13, the AWA prompt appears at the top of your screen, and your essay response appears below it as you type your response. (The screen in the figure includes the first several lines of a response.) Notice that you have to scroll down to read the entire topic and question. You compose your essays using the CAT word processor. Just ahead you'll look closely at its features and limitations.

The Quantitative and Verbal Screens

To respond to multiple-choice questions, click on one of the ovals to the left of the answer choices. You can't use the keyboard to select answers. Notice that the answer choices are *not* lettered; you'll click on blank ovals. (In the sample questions throughout this book, the answer choices are lettered for easy reference to corresponding explanations.)

Split screens. For some multiple-choice questions, the screen splits either horizontally or vertically:

- *Reading Comprehension:* The screen splits vertically. The left side displays the passage; the right side displays the question and answer choices.

- *Quantitative questions that include figures:* The screen splits horizontally. The figure appears at the top; the question and answer choices appear at the bottom.

Vertical Scrolling. For some multiple-choice questions, you'll have to scroll up and down (using the vertical scroll bar) to view all the material that pertains to the current question:

- *Reading Comprehension:* Passages are too long for you to see on the screen in their entirety; you'll need to scroll.

- *Quantitative questions that include figures:* Some figures—especially charts and graphs—won't fit on the screen in their entirety; so you might need to scroll.

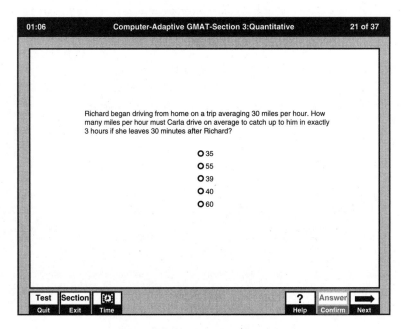

QUANTITATIVE SCREEN

AWA Word-processing Features

During the two GMAT essay sections, you'll use the simple word processor built into the CAT system. The word processor includes some features that are standard in programs like Word and Word Perfect, but it also lacks many features of those programs.

Keyboard Commands for Navigation and Editing

Here are the navigational and editing keys available in the CAT word processor:

Backspace removes the character to the left of the cursor

Delete removes the character to the right of the cursor

Home moves the cursor to the beginning of the line

End moves the cursor to the end of the line

Arrow Keys move the cursor up, down, left, or right

Enter inserts a paragraph break (starts a new line)

Page Up moves the cursor up one page (screen)

Page Down moves the cursor down one page (screen)

Certain often-used features of standard word processing programs are not available in the CAT word processor. For example, no keyboard commands are available for:

- TAB—disabled (does not function)
- Beginning/end of paragraph (not available)
- Beginning/end of document (not available)
- No key combinations (using the CTRL, ALT, or SHIFT keys) or other so-called "macros" are available for editing functions. (You'll use your mouse for cutting and pasting text.)

Mouse-Driven Navigation and Editing Functions

Just as with other word processors, to navigate the editing screen you can simply point the cursor to the position where you want to begin typing, then click. The CAT word processor also includes mouse-driven CUT, PASTE, and UNDO.

Selecting text you wish to cut. You select text the same way as with standard word processing pro-

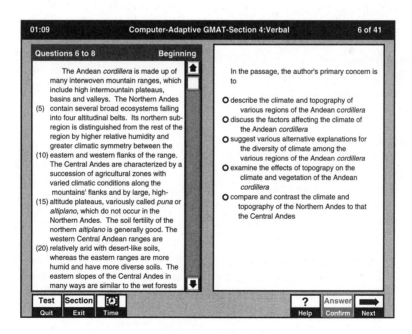

VERBAL SCREEN

grams: either (1) hold down your mouse button while sweeping the I-beam on the screen over the desired text, or (2) hold down the SHIFT key and use the navigation keys to select text.

The CUT Button. If you wish to delete text but want to save it to a temporary clipboard for pasting elsewhere, select that text (see above), then click on the CUT button. Cutting text is not the same as deleting it. When you delete text (using the DELETE key), you cannot paste it elsewhere in your document (but see UNDO below).

The PASTE button. If you wish to move text from one position to another, select and cut the text, then reposition your cursor where you want the text to go, and click on the PASTE button.

The UNDO button. Click on this button to undo the most recent delete, cut, or paste that you performed.

Limitations of CUT and UNDO. The following mouse-driven features are not available:

- DRAG-AND-DROP cut-and-paste (not available)
- COPY (not available; to copy you need to cut, then paste in the same spot)
- MULTIPLE UNDO (The CAT word processor stores *only your most recent* delete, cut, or paste or keyboard entry.)

The vertical scroll bar. Once you key in 10 lines or so, you'll have to scroll to view your entire response. A vertical scroll bar also appears to the right of the AWA prompt. Be sure to scroll all the way down to make sure that you've read the entire prompt.

Spell-checking, grammar-checking, fonts, attributes, hyphenation. The CAT word processor does not include a spell-checker or grammar-checker, nor does it allow you to choose typeface or point size. Neither manual nor automatic hyphenation is available. Attributes such as bold, italics, and underlining are not available.

NOTE: As for words that you would otherwise italicize or underline (such as titles or non-English words), it's okay to leave them as is. The readers understand the limitations of the CAT word processor.

THE CAT TEST-TAKING EXPERIENCE

When you take a test as important as the GMAT, it's a good idea to minimize test anxiety by knowing exactly what to expect on exam day—aside from the timed test itself. For the remainder of today's lesson, I'll walk you through the various pretest and post test procedures and describe the physical testing environment.

When You Arrive at the Test Center

Here's what you can expect when you arrive at the test center:

1. The supervisor will show you a roster, which includes the names of test takers scheduled for that day, and will ask you to initial the roster next to your name and indicate on the roster your arrival time.

2. The supervisor will ask you to read a two-page list of testing procedures and rules. (I'll cover all these rules in the pages immediately ahead.)

3. The supervisor will give you a "Nondisclosure Statement." You're to read the printed statement, then write the statement (in the space provided on the form), and sign it. In the statement, you agree to the testing policies and rules, and you agree not to reproduce or disclose any of the actual test questions. The supervisor will not permit you to enter the exam room until you've written and signed the statement.

4. You'll probably have to sit in a waiting room for a while—until the supervisor calls your name. A 5–10 minute wait beyond your scheduled testing time is not uncommon. (Taking the GMAT CAT is like going to the dentist—in more than one respect!)

5. The supervisor will check your photo identification. (You won't be permitted to take the test unless you have one acceptable form of photo identification with you.)

6. The test center will provide a secure locker (free of charge) for stowing your personal belongings during the test.

7. To help ensure that nobody else takes any part of the exam in your place, the supervisor will take a photograph of you.

8. The supervisor might give you some rudimentary tips about managing your time during the exam. Just ignore the supervisor's tips, because they might not be good advice for you!

9. Before you enter the testing room, you must remove everything from your pockets—except your photo I.D. and locker key.

10. The supervisor will provide you with exactly six pieces of scratch paper (stapled together), along with two pencils. These are the only items you'll have in hand as you enter the testing room.

Testing Procedures and Rules

If you want to exit the testing room for any reason, you must raise your hand and wait for the supervisor to come in and escort you from the room. (You won't be able to pause the testing clock for any reason.)

- No guests are allowed in the waiting room during your test.
- No food or drink is allowed in the testing room.
- No hats are allowed.
- You must sign out whenever you exit the testing room.
- You must sign in whenever you reenter the testing room (the supervisor will ask to see your photo I.D. each time).
- If you need more scratch paper during the exam, just raise your hand and ask for it. The supervisor will happily replace your six-piece bundle with a new batch.
- The supervisor will replace your tired pencils with fresh, sharp ones upon your request anytime during the exam (just raise your hand).

What You Should Know about the CAT Testing Environment

- Individual testing stations are like library carrels; they're separated by half-walls.
- The height of your chair's seat will be adjustable, and the chair will swivel. Chairs at most testing centers have arms.
- Computer monitors are of the 14-inch variety. You can adjust contrast. If you notice any flickering,

ask the supervisor to move you to another station. (You won't be able to tell if your monitor has color capability, because the GMAT is strictly a black-and-white affair.)

NOTE: You can't change the size of the font on the screen, unless you specifically request before the exam begins that a special ZOOMTEXT function be made available to you.

- If your mouse has two buttons, you can use either button to click your way through the exam (both buttons serve the same function). Don't expect that nifty wheel between buttons for easy scrolling, because you're not going to get it. For all you gamers and laptop users, trackballs are available, but only if you request one before you begin the test.
- Testing rooms are not soundproof. During your test, expect to hear talking and other noise from outside the room.
- Expect the supervisor to escort other test takers in and out of the room during your test—and to converse with them while doing so. This can be distracting!
- If the testing room is busy, expect to hear lots of mouse-clicking during your test. Because the room is otherwise fairly quiet, the incessant mouse-clicking can become annoying!
- Earplugs are available upon request.
- Expect anything in terms of room temperature, so dress in layers.
- You'll be under continual audio and video surveillance. To guard against cheating and to record any irregularities or problems in the testing room as they occur, the room is continually audio-taped and videotaped. (Look for the cameras or two-way mirrors, then smile and wave!)

Before You Begin the Test— The Computer Tutorial

Okay, the supervisor has just escorted you into the inner sanctum and to your station and has wished you luck. (My supervisor also encouraged me to "have fun!") Before you begin the test, the CAT System will lead you through a tutorial that includes five sections (each section steps you through a series of "screens"):

1. How to use the mouse (6 screens)

2. How to select and change an answer (6 screens)

3. How to scroll the screen display up and down (6 screens)

4. How to use the toolbars (21 screens); here you'll learn how to

   • Quit the test
   • Exit the current section
   • Access the directions
   • Confirm your response and move to the next question

5. How to use the AWA word processor features (14 screens)

   NOTE: If you want to see what some of the tutorial screens look like, ETS provides a variety of samples in its official GMAT *Bulletin*.

Here's what you need to know about the CAT tutorial:

• You won't be able to skip any section or any screen during the tutorial

• As you progress, the system requires that you demonstrate competency in using the mouse, selecting and confirming answer choices, and accessing the directions. So you can't begin taking the actual test unless you've shown that you know how to use the system. (Don't worry: no test taker has ever flunked the CAT system competency test.)

• At the end of each tutorial section (series of screens), you can repeat that section, at your option. But once you leave a section you can't return to it.

   NOTE: Don't choose to repeat any tutorial section. Why not? If you do, you'll be forced to step through the entire sequence of screens in that section again (an aggravating time-waster, especially for the 21-screen section!)

• The AWA section of the tutorial allows you to practice using the word processor.

• If you carefully read all the information presented to you, expect to spend about 20 minutes on the tutorial.

NOTE: On test day, you'll already know how the CAT system works. So step through the tutorial as quickly as you can, reading as little as possible. You can easily dispense with the tutorial in 5–10 minutes this way. Remember: The less time you spend with the tutorial, the less fatigued you'll be during the exam itself.

Post test CAT Procedures

Okay, it's been about 4 hours since you first entered the testing center, and you've just completed the second of two multiple-choice GMAT sections. You may think you've finished the CAT, but the CAT has not quite finished with you yet! There are a few more hoops to jump through before you're done.

1. **Respond to a brief questionnaire.** The CAT will impose on you a brief questionnaire (a series of screens) about your test-taking experience (believe it or not, these questions are multiple-choice, just like the exam itself). The questionnaire asks you, for example:

   • Whether your supervisor was knowledgeable and helpful

   • Whether the testing environment was comfortable

   • How long you waited after you arrived at the testing site to begin the test

   • Whether you were distracted by noise during your exam

2. **Cancel your test, at your option.** The most important question you'll answer while seated at your testing station is this next one. The CAT will ask you to choose whether to:

   • Cancel your scores (no scores are recorded; partial cancellation is not provided for) *or*

   • See your scores immediately

   Once you elect to see your scores, you can no longer cancel them—ever! So you should take a few minutes to think it over. The CAT gives you 5 minutes to choose. If you haven't decided within 5 minutes, the CAT will automatically show you your scores (and you forfeit your option to cancel).

NOTE: If you click on the CANCEL SCORES button, the CAT will then give you yet another 5 minutes to think over your decision. So you really have 10 minutes altogether to make up your mind.

3. **View and record your scores.** If you elect to see your scores, you should write them down on your scratch paper. When you leave the testing room, the supervisor will allow you to transcribe them onto another sheet of paper (one that you can take home with you), so that you don't have to memorize them.

4. **Direct your scores to the schools of your choice.** Once you've elected to see your scores, the CAT will ask you to select the schools you wish to receive your score report (the CAT provides a complete list of schools).

NOTE: You can select as many as five schools at this time—without incurring an additional fee. This is your last chance for a freebie, so you should take full advantage of it. Compile your list of schools before exam day.

Before You Leave the Testing Center

Upon exiting the testing room for the final time:

- The supervisor will collect your pencils and scratch paper and will count the number of sheets of paper to make sure you aren't trying to sneak out with any. (Then, if you're lucky you'll be allowed to watch while the supervisor ceremoniously rips up your scratch paper and drops it in the trash basket!)

- The supervisor will remind you to collect your belongings from your locker (if you used one) and turn in your locker key.

- The supervisor will provide you with an ETS pamphlet that explains how to interpret your test scores (you can take this home with you).

- The supervisor will provide you with a postcard-sized invitation to "blow the whistle" on anybody you suspect of cheating on the exam (the invitation ends with the assurance: "Confidentiality guaranteed").

DOs AND DON'Ts DURING THE EXAM

Beginning with tomorrow's lesson, I'll be doling out advice for specific GMAT sections and question types. Before I get too specific, here's a list of general dos and don'ts for the GMAT. (Most of these apply only to the multiple-choice sections.) Review this list again prior to taking each mini-test and practice test section in this book.

DON'T resort to random guesses. Instead, always try to eliminate at least one answer choice before you confirm your response.

If you must guess, always try to eliminate obvious wrong-answer choices first, then go with your hunch. Eliminating even one choice improves your odds. If you're out of time on a section, there's no advantage to guessing randomly on the remaining questions. Why? You might luck out and guess correctly. But incorrect responses move you down the ladder of difficulty to easier questions, and correct responses to easier ones aren't worth as much as correct response to more difficult ones. So on balance, there's no net advantage or disadvantage to guessing randomly.

DO find your optimal pace and stay on it.

Time is definitely a factor on every section of the GMAT. On the multiple-choice sections, expect to work at quicker pace than is comfortable for you. Similarly, the 30-minute time limit for each AWA response requires a lively writing pace, allowing little time for editing, revising, and fine-tuning.

During the multiple-choice sections, check your pace after every 10 questions or so (three times during a section), and adjust it accordingly so that you have time to at least consider every question in the section. During each essay section be sure to leave yourself enough time to cover all your main points and to wrap up the essay with a brief concluding paragraph. The best way to avoid the time squeeze is to practice under timed conditions, so that you get a sense for your optimal pace.

DON'T be a perfectionist.

You might find yourself reluctant to leave a question until you're sure your answer is correct. The design of the CAT contributes to this mind set because your reward for correct responses to difficult questions is greater than your reward for easier questions. But a stubborn attitude will only defeat you because it reduces the number of questions that you attempt, which in turn can lower your score. As you attempt the mini-tests and practice test in this book, get comfortable with a quick pace by adhering strictly to the time limits imposed. Set aside your perfectionist tendencies, and remember: You can miss quite a few questions and still score high. Develop a sense of your optimal pace—one that results in the greatest number of correct responses.

DO maintain an active mind set.

During the GMAT it's remarkably easy to fall into a passive mode—one in which you let your eyes simply pass over the words while you hope that the correct response jumps out at you as you scan the answer choices. Fight this tendency by interacting with the test as you read it. Keep in mind that each question on the GMAT is designed to measure a specific ability or skill. So try to adopt an active, investigative approach to each question, in which you ask yourself:

- What skill is the question measuring?
- What is the most direct thought process for determining the correct response?
- How might a careless test taker be tripped up on this type of question?

Answering these three questions is in large part what the rest of this book is all about.

DO use your pencil and scratch paper.

Doing so helps keep you in an active mode. Making brief notes and drawing diagrams and flow charts will help keep your thought process clear and straight.

DO move the keyboard away to the side for the multiple-choice sections.

You won't use the keyboard at all for these sections. So put your scratch paper right in front of you, and get the keyboard out of the way.

DON'T waste time reading directions while the clock is running; make sure you already know them inside and out.

Just before the first question of each type (e.g., Data Sufficiency or Reading Comprehension), the CAT will display the directions for that question type. The clock will be running! So dismiss the direction as quickly as you can by clicking on the DISMISS DI-RECTIONS button—without taking any time to read them. (This advice presupposes that you already know the directions—which of course you will.)

DO take advantage of the two 5-minute breaks, but don't exceed the time limit.

Remember: The GMAT CAT clock is always running, even during the two scheduled 5-minute breaks. By all means, take advantage of these breaks to leave the room, perhaps grab a quick snack from your locker, and do some stretching or relaxing. But don't get too relaxed! Five minutes goes by very quickly, and the test will begin after that time has elapsed—with or without you!

DO read each question in its entirety, and read every answer choice.

You'll discover in the days ahead that the test makers love to bait you with tempting wrong-answer choices. This applies to every type of multiple-choice question on the exam. So unless you're quickly running out of time, never confirm an answer until you've read all the choices! This blunder is one of the leading causes of incorrect responses on the GMAT.

DO take your time with the first few Quantitative and Verbal questions.

The CAT uses your responses to the first few questions to move you either up or down the ladder of difficulty. Of course, you want to move up the ladder, not down. So take great care with the initial questions—perhaps moving at a somewhat slower pace initially. Otherwise, you'll have to answer several questions just to reverse the trend by proving to the CAT that you're smarter than it thinks you are.

IF YOU HAVE MORE TIME TODAY

Reinforce and supplement what you learned in today's lesson with additional pages at the author's GMAT Web site (www.west.net/~stewart/gmat):

- Review a list of DOs and DON'Ts for dealing with the CAT testing environment. (Click on "Taming the CAT.")
- Check out the Q&A entitled "The GMAT CAT's Computer-Adaptive Feature: How to Use it to Your Best Advantage." (You can link to it from the site's "Q&A Corner.")

Day 3

Analytical Writing Assessment (AWA) Lesson 1: Overview and Issue-Analysis Strategies

Today's Topics:

1. Analytical Writing Assessment (AWA)—At a Glance
2. What Issue-Analysis Questions Look Like
3. The Pool of Issue-Analysis Questions
4. Scoring Criteria for the Issue-Analysis Essay
5. Composing Your Issue-Analysis Essay—a 6-Step Strategy
6. A Sample Issue-Analysis Essay
7. Tips for Composing a High-Scoring Issue-Analysis Essay

Today, after a quick glance at both GMAT essay sections, you'll learn how to organize and compose a high-scoring essay for the Issue-Analysis section.

ANALYTICAL WRITING ASSESSMENT (AWA)—AT A GLANCE

HOW MANY: 2 questions (1 question per test section)
WHERE: The two AWA sections appear at the beginning of the GMAT (as Section 1 and Section 2), but they may appear in either order on your exam.
TIME ALLOWED: 60 minutes altogether for two essays—30 minutes per essay
BASIC FORMAT OF EACH SECTION:

Analysis of an Issue. You respond in essay form to a brief (1–2 sentence) statement of opinion on an *Issue* of broad intellectual interest. (The CAT system will randomly select a statement from a large pool.)

Analysis of an Argument. You respond in essay form to a paragraph-length *Argument*, critiquing it in terms of its internal logic and supporting evidence. (The CAT system will randomly select an argument from a large pool.)

SKILLS TESTED:

Content. Your ability to present cogent, persuasive, and relevant ideas and arguments through sound reasoning and supporting examples

Organization. Your ability to present your ideas in an organized and cohesive fashion

Language. Your control of the English language, as demonstrated by your vocabulary and diction (word choice)

Mechanics. Your facility with the conventions of Standard Written English, including grammar, syntax (sentence structure), and word usage

WHAT'S NOT TESTED:

Spelling and punctuation (unless you make many such errors and they interfere with your ability to communicate your ideas effectively)

GROUND RULES:

- No break is provided between the two 30-minute AWA sections

- The CAT system does not allow you to spend more than 30 minutes on either essay.

- The CAT system does not allow you to return to either of the two AWA sections once you've moved on. (But if you've finished an essay early, you can proceed immediately to the next section by clicking on the NEXT button.)

- Scratch paper and pencils are provided (just as for the multiple-choice sections).

- You must use the word processor built into the testing system to compose your essays. (See Day 1 for details about the GMAT word processor's functions and limitations.)

- There is no prescribed or "correct" word length for either essay. The only limitation on word length is the practical one associated with the 30-minute time limit.

SCORING SYSTEM: A different GMAT "reader" reads and scores each of your two essays on a scale of 0–6 (0, 1, 2, 3, 4, 5, or 6), 6 being the highest possible score, based on the four skill areas listed above. A computer program also rates each essay on a 0–6 scale. Average scores for each essay are in turn averaged together to determine your final AWA score. (See Day 1, page X for more details about AWA scoring.)

WHAT ISSUE-ANALYSIS QUESTIONS LOOK LIKE

Your GMAT Issue-Analysis question will consist of two elements:

1. The *topic*—a 1–2 sentence statement of opinion on a particular issue (the statement will appear as a quotation)

2. The *directive*—a brief statement of your task

Here's a sample question, which is similar to some of the ones in the official pool; in fact, it's an amalgam of three or four of the official questions:

"In any large business organization, teamwork is the ultimate key to the organization's success."

Discuss the extent to which you agree or disagree with the foregoing statement. Use reasons and/or examples from your experience, observation, and/or reading to explain your viewpoint.

THE POOL OF ISSUE-ANALYSIS QUESTIONS

GMAT Issue-Analysis topics cover a broad spectrum of issues of intellectual interest, especially those with which graduate-level management students often deal. Although each of the official Issue-Analysis topics is unique, their basic themes cover a lot of common ground. Here's a list of themes that cover most of the official Issue-Analysis topics. The categories here are not mutually exclusive; some topics could fall into more than one category:

- Business—organizational structure/behavior, management
- Business—productivity, efficiency, and teamwork
- Business—advertising and marketing
- Business—labor and employment issues
- Business—ethics
- Business—its overall role and objectives in society
- Government's role in regulating business, commerce, speech
- Government's role in ensuring the welfare of its citizens
- Bureaucracy and "the system"
- "Global village" issues
- Technology and its impact on business and society
- Culture and social mores, attitudes, and values
- Education
- Learning lessons from history
- Keys to individual success
- Individual power and influence
- Personal qualities and values

SCORING CRITERIA FOR THE ISSUE-ANALYSIS ESSAY

Your basic task during the Issue-Analysis section is to analyze the issue presented, considering various perspectives, and to develop your own position on the issue. GMAT readers follow the scoring criteria that are printed in the official *GMAT Bulletin*. Here are the essential requirements for a top-scoring (6) essay (notice that you can attain a top score of 6 even if your essay contains minor errors in grammar, word usage, spelling, and punctuation):

1. The essay develops a position on the issue through the use of incisive reasons and persuasive examples.

2. The essay's ideas are conveyed clearly and articulately.

3. The essay maintains proper focus on the issue and is well organized.

4. The essay demonstrates proficiency, fluency, and maturity in its use of sentence structure, vocabulary, and idiom.

5. The essay demonstrates an excellent command of the elements of standard written English, including grammar, word usage, spelling, and punctuation—but may contain minor flaws in these areas.

The criteria for lower scores are the same as the ones suggested above; the only difference is that the standard for quality decreases for successively lower scores.

COMPOSING YOUR ISSUE-ANALYSIS ESSAY—A 6-STEP STRATEGY

To score high on the Issue-Analysis section, you need to meet the five criteria listed above. To make sure you accomplish this within the 30-minute time limit, follow this 6-step approach:

1. **Brainstorm, and get your pencil moving (1–2 minutes).** Try to come up with a few *reasons* both for and against the stated opinion, as well as a few *examples* supporting each side of the issue. Jot down any idea you can think of, even if it seems far-fetched, trite, insupportable, or unconvincing at the moment; as you compose your essay, it might occur to you how to transform one of your weaker ideas into a strong one. In other words, step 1 is not the time to censor yourself!

2. **Adopt a position, and organize your ideas (1–2 minutes).** Indicate "pro" or "con" next to each one of the reasons and examples you jotted down during step 1. Arrange your ideas into 2–4 body paragraphs, then decide tentatively on a logical order in which to present them. Number the points in your outline accordingly.

3. **Compose the body of your response (15–20 minutes).** Skip any introduction for now. Try to stick to your outline, but be flexible. Start with whichever point is easiest for you to articulate and that seems most insightful or persuasive to you. If you determine later that this point should appear after one or more other points, through the magic of word processing, you can rearrange your paragraphs for logical sense and continuity. During step 3, your chief ambition is to peck away at your keyboard like mad in order to get your ideas onto the screen! Try to devote no more than three or four sentences to any one point in your outline, and don't worry if you don't have time to include every single point from your outline. The readers understand that the 30-minute time constraint prevents most test takers from covering every point they want to make.

4. **Compose a brief concluding (summary) paragraph (1–2 minutes).** Unless your essay has a clear end, the reader might think you didn't finish in time; so be sure to make time to wrap up your essay. Convey the main thrust of your essay in two or three sentences. If an especially insightful concluding point occurs to you, the final sentence of your essay is the place for it.

5. **Compose a brief introductory paragraph (1–2 minutes).** Wait until the end to write your introduction. Why? If your position on the issue evolves as you compose the body of your essay (it could happen), you won't need to rewrite your introduction. Don't begin your introductory paragraph by repeating the topic; this amounts to wasted time, since the reader is already familiar with the topic. Show the reader from the very first sentence that you're thinking for yourself—by

pointing out the complexity of the issue that lies at the heart of your essay. Be sure your introductory and concluding paragraphs are consistent with each other and with the topic.

6. **Proofread for stylistic and mechanical problems (4–5 minutes).** Rework awkward sentences so they flow more naturally. Check for errors in diction, usage, grammar, and spelling. Keep in mind: to score a 6, your essay need not be flawless. GMAT readers won't bring down your mark for the occasional awkward sentence or minor error in punctuation, spelling, grammar, or usage. Don't get hung up on whether each sentence is something Hemingway or Steinbeck, or your high-school English teacher, would be proud of. Use whatever time remains to fix the most glaring mechanical problems.

A SAMPLE ISSUE-ANALYSIS ESSAY

Now take a look at my response to the sample Issue-Analysis question on this page. As you read my response, notice the following:

- I've underlined certain transitional words and phrases—just to help you see how the ideas flow from one to the next. (The stripped-down CAT word processor doesn't allow you to underline or highlight text in any way.)

- I've made it clear at the outset (in the introductory paragraph) that I appreciate the complexity of the issue and that I have a point of view.

- In the final paragraph, I've provided a recapitulation (summary), without introducing additional reasons or examples.

Whether a particular business ultimately succeeds or fails depends, of course, on a myriad of factors— ranging from economic conditions to the extent of competition, even to the charisma and clout of the CEO. Nevertheless, because teamwork is an essential ingredient for the success of any large business, it is, in my view, the pivotal factor in most cases.

First, cooperative interaction is an integral part of nearly all company jobs—including jobs performed in relative isolation and those in which technical knowledge or ability, not the ability to work with others, would seem to be most important. For example, scientists, researchers, and even computer programmers must collaborate to establish common goals and coordinate efforts. Even in businesses where individual tenacity and ambition of salespeople would seem to be the key for a firm's success, sales personnel must coordinate efforts with support staff and managers.

Secondly, in my experience, the kinds of problems that ultimately undermine an organization are those such as low employee morale, attrition, and diminishing productivity. These problems, in turn, almost invariably result from ill-will among co-workers and their unwillingness to communicate, cooperate, and compromise. Thus, problems in working together as a team pose the greatest threat to an organization's success.

Some might argue that the leadership and vision of a company's key executives is of paramount importance. Yet chief executives of our most successful corporations would no doubt admit that without the cooperative efforts of their subordinates, their personal vision would never become reality. Others might cite the heavy manufacturing and natural-resource industries, where the value of tangible assets—raw materials and capital equipment—are often the most significant determinant of business success. However, such industries are diminishing in significance as we move from an industrial society to an information age.

In sum, although leadership, individual ambition, and even the value of tangible assets play crucial roles in the success of many large business organizations, teamwork is the single ingredient common to all such organizations. It is, therefore, the key one.

TIPS FOR COMPOSING A HIGH-SCORING ISSUE-ANALYSIS ESSAY

Here are three checklists of tips—for content, organization, and writing style—to keep you on the right track in organizing and composing your Issue-Analysis essay.

Content—your position on the issue

- There is no "correct" position on any GMAT Issue. So don't waste time second-guessing what the reader might agree (or disagree) with. Instead, just be sure to acknowledge various perspectives on the issue and develop a well-supported position on it.

- Hedge your position by qualifying your viewpoint and acknowledging others. In doing so, you won't appear wishy-washy but rather thoughtful and scholarly!

- It's okay to take a strong stance on an issue; but avoid coming across as fanatical or extreme. Approach the Issue-Analysis essay as an intellectual exercise, not as a forum for sharing your personal belief system.

Content—your supporting reasons and examples

- Its perfectly acceptable to draw on your personal experiences to support your position. Just don't overdo it; try to demonstrate a breadth of both real-world experience and academic knowledge.

- Bolster your position with names and events with which the reader is likely to have at least some familiarity; avoid recounting statistics and quoting obscure sources. At the same time, however, avoid examples that many other test takers are likely to use; dig a bit deeper to set your essay apart from the rest.

- Explain how each example you mention illustrates your point. Anyone can simply list a long string of examples and claim that they illustrate a point. But the reader will be looking for incisive analysis, not fast typing.

- Don't dwell on the details, but don't try to cover everything. Try to cover as many reasons and examples from your outline as you have time for. At the same time, don't worry if you're forced to leave the secondary and more tangential points on your scratch paper. GMAT readers understand your time constraints.

Organization

- Order your paragraphs so your essay flows logically and persuasively from one point to the next. Be sure the first sentence of each paragraph begins a distinct train of thought and clearly conveys to the reader the essence of the paragraph.

- The body of your essay (which excludes the introduction and summary paragraphs) should contain two to four paragraphs, although in my view *three* is optimal given your competing goals of covering the issue and finishing within 30 minutes.

- Your body paragraphs should be balanced in length. If they aren't, perhaps you were overly wordy or repetitive in one area of discussion, while in another you neglected to provide adequate support (reasons and/or examples). Trim back and fill out as needed to achieve a balanced presentation.

- Devote no more than one paragraph to each major point of agreement or disagreement. By doing so, you'll be sure to cover all your key points in 30 minutes.

Writing Style

- Maintain a somewhat formal tone; avoid slang and colloquialisms. Otherwise, instead of hitting a "home run" with your essay, you'll be "out of luck" with the GMAT readers, and you'll have to "snake" your way in to a "bottom-barrel" B-school. Get the idea?

- Don't try to make your point with humor or sarcasm. Not that the GMAT readers don't have a sense of humor; it's just that they leave it at the door when they go to work for the testing service.

- The occasional use of Latin terms and acronyms—such as *per se*, *i.e.*, and *e.g.*—is perfectly acceptable.

Non-English words used commonly in academic writing—such as *vis-à-vis*, *caveat*, and *laissez faire*—are also acceptable. Just don't overdo it.

NOTE: The GMAT word processor won't allow you to include diacritical marks, like the one above the "a" in "*vis-à-vis*." But don't worry about it; again, the GMAT readers understand the exam's constraints.

- There's nothing wrong with demonstrating a strong vocabulary in your Issue-Analysis essay. (Notice the words "tenacity," "paramount," and "myriad" in the sample essay earlier in today's lesson.) Just don't overdo it; otherwise the reader will suspect you're using impressive words to mask an otherwise weak essay. Also, avoid technical terminology that only specialists and scholars in a specific field can understand.

- Use transition words and phrases that help your essay flow naturally from one idea to the next. Look again at the underlined words in my sample essay earlier in this lesson. Make sure to connect your ideas with words such as these, to convince the reader that you can organize your thoughts under time pressure.

- Self-references are perfectly acceptable—for example, "In my view..." and "I agree only in part...." Just don't overdo it; limit self-references to one each in your introductory and summary paragraph.

- Don't worry too much about the word length of your essay. An essay that is concise and to the point can be more effective than a long-winded, rambling one. Rest assured: You can score a 6 with an essay as brief as my 330-word sample in this lesson.

IF YOU HAVE MORE TIME TODAY

Here are three ways to supplement what you've learned in today's lesson:

1. Read through the entire list of official Issue-Analysis questions. You can link to them quickly via the "Downloads" area of my GMAT website (www.west.net/~stewart/gmat).

2. Randomly select two or three of the official questions. For each one, perform steps 1 and 2 (brainstorming and outlining) of the 6-step approach your learned today.

3. Read my other essay response to this lesson's question about leadership; you'll find the response online (www.west.net/~stewart/awaissue.htm). Notice that the response presents a contrary position to the one in this lesson.

ADDITIONAL PREPARATION FOR THE ISSUE-ANALYSIS SECTION

Perhaps your verbal and writing skills are particularly weak. Or perhaps English is your second language. Or perhaps you just want a leg up on the competition when it comes to your AWA score. To prepare further for the Issue-Analysis essay, follow the suggestions in this section.

Practice, practice, and practice!

There's no substitute for putting yourself to the task under simulated exam conditions, especially under the pressure of time. Compose as many practice essays as you reasonably have time for, responding to the official questions. As you do so:

- Always practice under timed conditions. I cannot overemphasize this point. Unless you are put under the pressure of time, you really won't be ready for the Issue-Analysis section.

- Always use a word processor for your practice tests. Restrict your use of editing functions to the ones provided on the real exam.

- Evaluate your practice essays. Practicing isn't all that helpful if you make the same strategic mistakes again and again. After composing an essay, use the official scoring criteria to evaluate it. (Better yet, ask a colleague, friend, or professor to evaluate it for you using these criteria.) Then reflect on your weaknesses, and concentrate on improving in those areas next time. Don't worry if your essays don't turn out as polished as my samples in this book. Instead, concentrate on improving your own performance.

Do some serious brainstorming.

To beat the competition, brainstorm for as many of the official Issue-Analysis topics as you reasonably have time for. After downloading and generating a printout of the official topics list, follow these steps:

1. Earmark two or three questions from each thematic category (see page 22).

2. Read each question, and ponder the issue at hand. Jot down whatever points and examples pop into your mind—either in support of or in opposition to the statement. Don't try to organize your thoughts or commit to a position. Just make some quick shorthand notes, then move on to the next question. Keep both your mind and your pencil moving!

3. Save your notes and review them shortly before exam day.

Read my model essays for substantive, organizational, and writing-style ideas.

In the 2nd edition of my book *GMAT CAT: Answers to the Real Essay Questions*, I've provided model re-sponses to 115 of the official Issue-Analysis questions. Here are three suggestions for using this resource to further prepare yourself for the Issue-Analysis section:

1. Read the *first* and *last* paragraphs of all 115 essays, alongside your list of Issue-Analysis questions. You'll learn by osmosis what makes effective bookends for an Issue-Analysis essay.

2. Read a sampling of the essays (perhaps 15 or 20). As you read, highlight transitional and rhetorical phrases, which lend persuasiveness and continuity to an essay. Review the phrases, then try composing some essays yourself, making a special effort to incorporate similar phrases into your essays; keep practicing until they become part of your own natural writing style.

3. Identify the two or three thematic areas from my list (see page 22) for which you anticipate having the most trouble conjuring up ideas. Then read the corresponding essays in my book. Jot down the points you find clearest and most convincing. Review your notes shortly before exam day.

Day 4

Analytical Writing Assessment (AWA) Lesson 2: Argument-Analysis Strategies

Today's Topics:

1. What Argument-Analysis Questions Look Like
2. Scoring Criteria for the Argument-Analysis Essay
3. Composing Your Argument-Analysis Essay—a 7-Step Strategy
4. A Sample Argument-Analysis Essay
5. Tips for Composing a High-Scoring Argument-Analysis Essay
6. Recognizing and Responding to Flaws in GMAT Arguments

Today you'll learn how to organize and compose a high-scoring Argument-Analysis essay.

WHAT ARGUMENT-ANALYSIS QUESTIONS LOOK LIKE

The Argument-Analysis section is designed to test your critical-reasoning skills as well as your writing skills. Each Argument in the official pool consists of a paragraph-length passage, which presents an *Argument*, followed by a *directive* (statement of your task). The Argument will contain numerous *logical problems and flaws*.

The Argument

The Argument itself will appear as a quotation from some fictitious source. Here's a sample, which is similar to the ones in the official pool—although you won't see this one on your exam.

The following appeared in a memo from the manager of UpperCuts, a hair salon located in a suburb of the city of Apton, to the salon's owner:

"According to a nationwide demographic study, more and more people today are moving from suburbs to downtown areas. So in order to boost sagging profits at UpperCuts, we should relocate the salon from its current location in Apton's suburban mall to downtown Apton, while retaining the salon's decidedly upscale approach in terms of services, products, and pricing. After all, Hair-Dooz, our chief competitor at the mall, has just relocated downtown and is thriving at its new location. Moreover, the most prosperous hair salon in nearby Brainard is located in that city's downtown area. By emulating these two successful salons, UpperCuts is sure to become more profitable."

The Directive

The directive is the same for every Argument in the official pool:

Discuss how well reasoned you find this argument. In your discussion be sure to analyze the line of reasoning and the use of evidence in the argument. For example, you may need to consider what questionable assumptions underlie the thinking and what alternative explanations or counterexamples might weaken the conclusion. You can also discuss what sort of evidence would strengthen or refute the argument, what changes in the argument would make it more logically sound, and what, if anything, would help you better evaluate its conclusion.

Logical problems and flaws

The test makers have intentionally loaded each argument with numerous flaws for you to identify and address in your essay. That's what your task is all about during this test section. A typical GMAT Argument will contain three or four discrete logical flaws. Here's a list of the seven types of flaws that appear most frequently in GMAT Arguments:

1. Drawing a weak analogy between two things

2. Confusing a cause-and-effect relationship with a mere correlation or temporal sequence

3. Assuming that characteristics of a group apply to each group member

4. Assuming that a certain condition is necessary and/or sufficient for a certain outcome

5. Relying on potentially unrepresentative statistical results

6. Assuming that all things remain unchanged over time

7. Making a recommendation based on narrow "either/or" reasoning

Later in today's lesson you'll find detailed explanations and illustrations of these flaws.

SCORING CRITERIA FOR THE ARGUMENT-ANALYSIS ESSAY

Your basic task during the Argument-Analysis section is to critique the stated argument in terms of its cogency (logical soundness) and in terms of the strength of the evidence offered in support of the argument. GMAT readers follow the scoring criteria that are printed in the official *GMAT Bulletin*. Here are the essential requirements for a top-scoring (6) essay (notice that you can attain a top score of 6 even if your essay contains minor errors in grammar, word usage, spelling, and punctuation):

1. The essay identifies the key features of the argument and analyzes each one in a thoughtful manner.

2. The essay supports each point of critique with insightful reasons and examples.

3. The essay develops its ideas in a clear, organized manner, with appropriate transitions to help connect ideas together.

4. The essay demonstrates proficiency, fluency, and maturity in its use of sentence structure, vocabulary, and idiom.

5. The essay demonstrates an excellent command of the elements of Standard Written English, including grammar, word usage, spelling, and punctuation—but may contain minor flaws in these areas.

The criteria for lower scores are the same as the ones above; the only difference is that the standard for quality decreases for successively lower scores.

The directive for your Argument-Analysis essay (page 29) provides more specific guidelines for meeting criterion 1 above. According to the directive, to score high on your Argument-Analysis essay you should:

• Analyze the argument's line of reasoning

• Consider questionable assumptions underlying the argument

• Consider the extent to which the evidence presented supports the argument's conclusion

• Discuss what additional evidence would help strengthen or refute the argument

• Discuss what additional information, if any, would help you to evaluate the argument's conclusion

COMPOSING YOUR ARGUMENT-ANALYSIS ESSAY—A 7-STEP STRATEGY

For a top scoring Argument-Analysis essay, you need to meet all the requirements listed above. To make sure you meet these requirements within the 30-minute time limit, follow this 7-step approach:

1. **Read the Argument; as you do so, identify its conclusion and its supporting evidence (1 minute).** As you read the Argument for the first time, be sure you identify its final conclusion. (You'll probably find it in either the first or last sentence of the Argument.) Jot it down on your scratch paper! In the Argument it might be called a "claim," a "recommendation," or a "contention." Why is Step 1 important? Unless you are clear about the Argument's final conclusion, it's impossible to evaluate the author's reasoning or the strength of the evidence offered in support of the argument's conclusion.

2. **Brainstorm, and get your pencil moving (2–3 minutes).** Try to identify at least three or four discrete flaws in the Argument. For ideas, start with my list of seven. If additional logical problems jump out at you, by all means jot them down. Be on special lookout for any unsubstantiated or unreasonable assumptions upon which the Argument's conclusion depends. Don't worry at this point if some flaws you identified overlap. You can sort them out during the next step.

3. **Organize your essay (2–3 minutes).** Using your notes from step 2 as a guide, arrange your ideas into paragraphs (probably three or four, depending on the number of flaws built into the argument). Take a minute to consider whether any of the flaws you identified overlap, and whether any can be separated into two distinct flaws. In many cases the best sequence in which to present your points of critique is the same order in which they appear in the Argument.

4. **Type the body of your response (15–20 minutes).** Skip any introduction for now. Try to stick to your outline, but be flexible. Start with whichever points of critique strike you as the most important, are clearest in your mind, and are easiest to articulate. (You can always rearrange your points later.) As in the Issue-Analysis essay, during this step your chief aim is to peck madly at your keyboard in order to get your ideas onto the screen!

5. **Compose a concluding paragraph (3–4 minutes).** In this final paragraph you should sum up the points of your critique but from a different angle. Review each point in terms of:

   1.   How the Argument can be strengthened

   2.   What additional information would be helpful in evaluating the Argument's conclusion

6. **Revise and proofread your essay (3–5 minutes).** Check for errors in diction, usage, and grammar. Check the flow of your essay, paying particular attention to transitions. If you have time, rearrange paragraphs so they appear in a logical sequence, and rework awkward sentences so they flow more naturally.

7. **Write a brief introductory paragraph (1–2 minutes).** Postpone composing your introduction until the last minute or two. The introduction is not as crucial as the points of your critique. Here's all you should try to accomplish in an introductory paragraph:

   •   Indicate the Argument's final conclusion.

   •   Allude to the sort of evidence offered to support the conclusion.

   •   Assert that the Argument suffers from various flaws or logical problems.

Don't waste time repeating the entire Argument in an introductory paragraph. The reader, whom you can assume is already well familiar with the Argument, is interested in your critique—not in your transcription skills.

A SAMPLE ARGUMENT-ANALYSIS ESSAY

Now take a look at my response to the sample Argument you encountered earlier in this lesson. In this response I've underlined certain transitional words and phrases to help you see how I formulated my introductory and concluding paragraphs and how I organized and presented points of critique so that they flow logically from one to the next. (On the real exam you won't be able to underline, italicize, or otherwise highlight text.)

Citing a general demographic trend and certain evidence about two other hair salons, the manager of UpperCuts (UC) concludes here that UC should relocate from suburban to downtown Apton. However, the manager's argument relies on a series of unproven assumptions and is therefore unconvincing as it stands.

To begin with, the argument assumes that Apton's demographic trend reflects the national trend. Yet, the mere fact that one hair salon has moved downtown hardly suffices to infer any such trend in Apton; Hair-Dooz might owe its success at its new location to factors unrelated to Apton's demographics. Without better evidence of a demographic shift toward downtown Apton, it is just as likely that there is no such trend in Apton. For that matter, the trend might be in the opposite direction, in which event the manager's recommendation would amount to especially poor advice.

Even if Apton's demographics do reflect the national trend, it is unfair to assume that UC will become more profitable simply by relocating downtown. It is entirely possible that the types of people who prefer living in downtown areas tend not to patronize upscale salons. It is also possible that Hair-Dooz will continue to impede UC's profitability downtown, just as it might have at the mall. Moreover, UC's sagging profits might have resulted from mismanagement or other problems unrelated to location. Without ruling out these and other reasons why UC might not benefit from the demographic trend, the manager cannot convince me that UC would increase its profits by moving downtown.

Nor can the manager justify the recommended course of action on the basis of the Brainard salon's success. Perhaps hair salons generally fare better in downtown Brainard than downtown Apton, due to demographic differences between the two areas. Or perhaps the Brainard salon owes its success not to its location but rather to savvy marketing or especially talented stylists. Or perhaps the salon thrives only because it is long-established in downtown Brainard—an advantage that UC clearly would not have in its new location. In short, the manager cannot defend the recommended course of action on the basis of what might be a false analogy between two hair salons.

In sum, the argument is dubious at best. To strengthen it the manager should provide better evidence of a demographic shift in Apton toward the downtown area, and clear evidence that those demographics portend success there for an upscale hair salon. To better evaluate the argument I would need to know why Hair-Dooz relocated, what factors have contributed to the Brainard salon's success, and what factors other than location might have contributed to UC's sagging profits at the mall.

TIPS FOR COMPOSING A HIGH-SCORING ARGUMENT-ANALYSIS ESSAY

Here are three checklists of tips—for content, organization, and writing style—to keep you on the right track in organizing and composing your Argument-Analysis essay.

Content—your critique of the Argument

- Don't merely restate or rehash the stated Argument. The only way to score points is to tell the reader what's wrong with the Argument.

- Analyze the Argument with an eye for uncovering three or four flaws—in the author's line of reasoning and use of evidence. The seven flaws in my list are the ones you're most likely to encounter, so memorize the list! Unless you've recognized and discussed at least *three* flaws, you've missed something—and you won't score a 5 or 6.

- Support each point of your critique with realistic examples; two examples per point should suffice. Notice in my hair-salon essay that in each body paragraph I've included at least two examples (signaled by connecting phrases such as "It is possible that..." and "Or perhaps....") to illuminate my point of critique in the paragraph.

- Don't stray from the argument at hand. Your personal opinions about the issue discussed in the argument are irrelevant to the Argument writing task.

- Discuss what is required to make the Argument more persuasive and/or what would help you better evaluate its conclusion.

Organization

- Organize your points of critique in a logical order, one per paragraph. The sequence in which the flaws appear in the Argument itself is often as good a sequence as any for these points.

- Don't introduce any new points of critique in the concluding paragraph. Your job here is simply to reiterate the Argument's main problems and indicate what is required to make the Argument more convincing.

- The introduction is the least important element of your Argument-Analysis essay. If you don't have time for a full paragraph like the one in my sample essay, begin your essay with a sentence like one of the following two, then delve right into your first point of critique—without a paragraph break:

  "This argument suffers from numerous flaws that, considered together, render untenable the conclusion that UpperCuts should relocate to downtown Apton. One such flaw involves..."

  "I find the argument for moving UpperCuts salon downtown specious at best, because it relies on a series of unproven, and doubtful, assumptions. One such assumption is that..."

Writing Style

- Use transition words and phrases that connect the various points of your critique in a way that helps your ideas flow naturally and logically from one to the next. Look again at the underlined words in my sample essay earlier in this lesson. Make sure

to connect your ideas with words such as these to help the reader follow your line of reasoning.

- To save time it's okay to use shorthand names or acronyms for proper nouns. If you use an acronym, be sure to identify it the first time you use it—for example, "UpperCuts (UC)."

- The length of your Argument-Analysis essay is limited only by the 30-minute time limit and the number of logical flaws that are available to discuss. 400 words (the approximate length of my essay in this lesson) will suffice for a top-scoring response to any GMAT Argument.

RECOGNIZING AND RESPONDING TO FLAWS IN GMAT ARGUMENTS

The test makers intentionally incorporate into each GMAT Argument numerous flaws in logic that render the Argument vulnerable to criticism. In a typical Argument you can find three or four distinct areas for critique.

In this section, you'll explore the seven logical fallacies and other problems that appear most frequently in GMAT Arguments. I've presented them here in order—from most frequent to less frequent. For each problem you'll find a simulated Argument that illustrates the problem, along with an effective essay response. Each response also includes a model for how you might sum up the analysis in your final paragraph.

> NOTE: These examples are a bit briefer than real GMAT Arguments—because each one is intended to isolate one particular problem.

1. Drawing a weak analogy between two things

A GMAT Argument might draw a conclusion about one thing (perhaps a city, school, or company) on the basis of an observation about a similar thing. However, in doing so the Argument assumes that because the two things are similar in certain respects they are similar in all respects, at least as far as the Argument is concerned. Unless the Argument provides sufficient evidence to substantiate this assumption (by the way, it won't), the Argument is vulnerable to criticism.

> *Example:* The Argument you encountered earlier in today's lesson—involving UpperCuts hair salon—relies on a weak analogy between UpperCuts and the Brainard salon. Read again the *fourth* paragraph of my response to that Argument.

2. Confusing a cause-and-effect relationship with a mere correlation or temporal sequence

Many GMAT Arguments rely on the claim that certain events cause other certain events. A cause-and-effect claim might be based on:

1. a significant *correlation* between the occurrence of two phenomena (both phenomena generally occur together), or
2. a *temporal relationship* between the two (one event occurred after another).

A significant correlation or a temporal relationship between two phenomena is one indication of a cause-and-effect relationship between them. However, neither in itself suffices to prove such a relationship. Unless the Argument also considers and eliminates all other plausible causes of the presumed "result" (by the way, it won't), the Argument is vulnerable to criticism. The following example incorporates both claims (1 and 2) listed above.

> *Argument:*
>
> The following appeared in the editorial section of a newspaper:
>
> "Many states have enacted laws prohibiting environmental emissions of nitrocarbon byproducts on the basis that these byproducts have been shown to cause Urkin's Disease in humans. These laws have clearly been effective in preventing the disease. After all, in every state that has enacted such a law the incidence of Urkin's disease is lower than in any state that has not enacted a similar law....
>
> *Response:*
>
> The argument concludes that, based on a known correlation between laws prohibiting certain emissions and the low incidence of Urkin's Disease, the

latter is attributable, at least partly, to the former. Yet the correlation alone amounts to scant evidence of the claimed cause-and-effect relationship. Perhaps Urkin's disease can be caused by other factors as well, which are absent in these particular states but present in all others. Moreover, the argument overlooks the fact that it is the level of compliance with a law, not its enactment, that determines its effectiveness. The editorial's author has not accounted for the possibility that the laws prohibiting the emissions were never enforced or complied with and that the emissions have continued unabated. If this is the case, then the conclusion that the laws are effective in preventing Urkin's Disease would lack any merit whatsoever.

> *[Final paragraph]*
>
> ...To strengthen the argument, the editorial's author must rule out other possible explanations for the comparatively high incidence of Urkin's disease in states that allow nitrocarbon emissions.... To better evaluate the strength of the author's claim I would need to know the extent of compliance with the laws prohibiting these emissions....

3. Assuming that characteristics of a group apply to every member of that group

A GMAT Argument might point out some fact about a general group—such as students, employees, or cities—to support a claim about one particular member of that group. Unless the Argument supplies clear evidence that the member is representative of the group as a whole (by the way, it won't), the Argument is vulnerable to criticism.

> *Example:* The Argument you encountered earlier in today's lesson—involving UpperCuts hair salon—suffers from this flaw. Read again the *second* paragraph of my response to that Argument.

4. Assuming that a certain condition is necessary and/or sufficient for a certain outcome

A GMAT Argument might recommend a certain course of action, based on one or both of the following claims:

1. The course of action is necessary to achieve a desired result.

2. The course of action is sufficient to achieve the desired result.

Both claims often occur in the same Argument, and both are potentially vulnerable to criticism. With respect to claim 1, the Argument must provide evidence that no other means of achieving the same result are available (by the way, it won't). With respect to claim 2, the Argument must provide strong evidence that the proposed course of action by itself would be sufficient to bring about the desired result (by the way, it won't). Lacking this sort of evidence, the Argument cannot rely on these claims to support its recommendation.

Example: The Argument you encountered earlier in today's lesson—involving UpperCuts hair salon—relies on claim 2. Read again the *third* paragraph of my response to that Argument.

In the following additional example, the response includes two paragraphs; the first challenges claim 1, while the second challenges claim 2.

Argument:

The following appeared in a memo from the superintendent of the Harper County school district:

"In order to raise the level of reading skills of our district's elementary-school students to a level that at least represents the national average, we should adopt the 'Back to Basics' reading program. After all, this reading program has a superior record for improving reading skills among youngsters nationwide. By adopting Back to Basics, the parents of our young students would be assured that their children will develop the reading skills they will need throughout their lives...."

Response:

The recommendation depends on the assumption that no alternative means of improving the students' reading skills are available. Yet no evidence is offered to substantiate this assumption. Admittedly, the superior record of the Back to Basics (BTB) program is some evidence that no other program is as likely to achieve the desired result. However, it is entirely possible that means other than this or any other reading program would also achieve the desired result. Perhaps the desired improvement could be achieved if the schools instead hired special reading instructors, or encouraged parents to read with their children, or simply devoted more time during school to reading. Without considering and ruling out these and other alternative means of improving reading skills, the superintendent cannot confidently conclude that the schools must adopt the BTB program—or for that matter any reading program—in order to achieve the district's goal.

The recommendation depends on the additional unsubstantiated assumption that adopting BTB would by itself improve students' reading skills to the desired extent. Absent evidence that this is the case, it is equally possible that adopting the program would not suffice by itself. Students must be sufficiently attentive and motivated, and teachers must be sufficiently competent; otherwise, the program will not be effective. In short, unless the superintendent can show that the program will be effectively implemented and received, I cannot accept the recommendation.

[Final paragraph]

...To strengthen the argument, the superintendent must provide clear evidence that BTB is both a necessary and sufficient means of achieving the desired level of reading skill among the district's elementary-school students....

5. Relying on potentially unrepresentative statistical results

A GMAT Argument might cite statistical evidence from a study, survey, or poll involving a "sample" group or population, then draw a conclusion about a larger group or population that the sample supposedly represents. But in order for a statistical sample to reliably represent a larger population, the sample must meet two requirements:

1. The sample must be significant in size (number), as a portion of the overall population.

2. The sample must be *representative* of the overall population in terms of relevant characteristics.

GMAT Arguments that cite statistics from studies, surveys, and polls often fail to establish either of these two requirements. Of course this failure is by design of the test makers, who are inviting you to call into question the reliability of the evidence. The following example shows how you can handle both problems together, in one paragraph of your response.

Argument:

The following recommendation was recently made by the president of Kidco Toy Company:

"Our latest Kidco customer survey indicates that parents are becoming increasingly concerned that too much exposure to depictions of violence early in life might have a detrimental long-term impact on their children. Thus in order to increase our market share and, in turn, our profitability, Kidco should discontinue its line of military action toys and expand its line of educational toys...."

Response:

The results of Kidco's customer survey might not be representative of the overall population of potential toy buyers, especially if the survey's respondents constitute only a small percentage of Kidco's customers and of the entire target market. If it turns out that Kidco's current customers are more concerned about youth violence and education than most parents, then a substantial portion of Kidco's target market might not react favorably to the proposed changes, which in turn might result in a shrinking market share for Kidco.

[Final paragraph]

...To better assess the argument I would need to determine the extent to which the Kidco customers responding to the survey are representative of toy-buying parents generally. At a minimum I would need to know the total number of survey respondents as a percentage of current Kidco customers and as a percentage of the target market.

6. Assuming that all things remain unchanged over time

A GMAT Argument might rely on evidence collected in the past in order to draw some conclusion about (or make a recommendation for) the present or the future. But unless the Argument provides clear evidence that key circumstances are similar now as they were at the time past, the Argument is vulnerable to criticism. Following is an example.

Argument:

The following appeared in a recent report by the sanitation district of Blackburn County:

"During the last five years the volume of recyclable materials produced in Blackburn County has increased steadily, while the volume of non-recyclable refuse has been declining. Since our current resources for accommodating refuse are ample, the county should reduce spending in this area and apply the savings to subsidies for businesses willing to collect, recycle, and resell recyclable materials...."

Response:

The district assumes that the current decline in refuse volume will continue, or at least not reverse itself, in the foreseeable future. However, the district fails to account for possible future developments that might prove this assumption erroneous. For example, the county might experience an influx of new residents, or its residents' willingness to recycle might wane. In either case the volume of refuse is likely to increase, and the district's proposed course of action might result in a shortage of resources for handling refuse.

[Final paragraph]

...To bolster its recommendation the district should provide better evidence, perhaps in the form of population projections and county-resident surveys, that the volume of refuse in Blackburn County will not increase in the foreseeable future....

7. Making a recommendation based on narrow "either–or" reasoning

A GMAT Argument might recommend one course of action over another in order to achieve a desired result, without considering one or both of the following:

1. It is possible to pursue both courses of action, thereby increasing the likelihood of achieving the desired result. (In other words, they are not mutually exclusive alternatives.)

2. Other courses of action that might bring about the desired result are also available. (In other words, neither course of action is a necessary condition.)

Both problems usually occur in the same Argument, and you should discuss both in your essay. You'll probably be able to address both in the same paragraph, as in the following example.

Argument:

The following appeared in a memo from the superintendent of the Harper County school district:

"Over the past decade the reading skills of our district's elementary school students have diminished considerably. To reverse this undesirable trend, many parents suggest that our teachers devote more school time to reading. Nevertheless, we should adopt the "Back to Basics" reading program instead. This program involves an innovative approach to reading but does not necessarily require more school-time than our teachers currently devote to reading. Moreover, the Back to Basics program has a proven record for improving reading skills among youngsters nationwide...."

Response:

The superintendent assumes without justification that the two proposals are mutually exclusive alternatives. The memo provides no reason why the district cannot adopt both polices at the same time. By doing so the district might improve its chances of achieving its objectives. Moreover, the memo unfairly assumes that these are the only two possible means of achieving the stated objective. Per-

haps the objective could be achieved if the schools hired special reading instructors, enhanced the reading materials available to the students, or encouraged parents to read with their children at home. In short, without showing that the district must choose only one of these two proposals, and no others, the superintendent cannot confidently conclude that adopting Back to Basics alone would be the district's wisest course of action.

[Final paragraph]

...To strengthen the argument the superintendent must explain why both proposals cannot be implemented at the same time.... To better evaluate the argument I would need to know what other alternatives are available for the purpose of improving the students' reading skills, and the comparative merits of the various alternatives, including both of the proposals.

IF YOU HAVE MORE TIME TODAY

Here are three ways to supplement what you've learned in today's lesson:

1. Read a sampling (perhaps a dozen) of Arguments in the official pool. You can link to them via the "Downloads" area of my GMAT Web site (www.west.net/~stewart/gmat).

2. Randomly select two or three Arguments from the official pool. For each one perform steps 1–3 (the prewriting steps) from the 7-step strategy you learned today.

3. Study my essay response to another simulated Argument; you'll find the Argument and response on line (www.west.net/~stewart/awaargum.htm). Try to identify which flaws among the list of seven from today's lesson weaken the Argument and are discussed in my response. Also notice the sequence in which I discuss the flaws and the words and phrases I've used to connect my points of critique.

ADDITIONAL PREPARATION FOR THE ARGUMENT-ANALYSIS SECTION

Here are three suggestions for additional Argument-Analysis preparation—if you have more time before exam day:

1. Randomly select up to fifteen Arguments from the official pool. For each one perform steps 1–3 (the prewriting steps) of the 7-step strategy you learned today.

2. In my book *GMAT CAT: Answers to the Real Essay Questions (2d Edition)*, I've provided model responses to 115 of the official Argument-Analysis questions. Read a sampling of the essays (perhaps 15 or 20). As you read, highlight transitional phrases, which connect the essay's points of critique. Review the phrases, then try composing several essays yourself (see 3 below), making a special effort to incorporate similar phrases into your essays.

3. Compose as many practice essays as you reasonably have time for, responding to the official questions. Be sure to practice under timed conditions with a word processor; restricting your use of editing functions to the ones provided on the real exam. Evaluate your practice essays, referring to the official scoring criteria; reflect on your weaknesses, and concentrate on improving in those areas next time.

Day 5

Analytical Writing Assessment (AWA) Lesson 3: Mini-Test and Review

Today you apply what you learned on Days 3 and 4 to either an Issue-Analysis or Argument-Analysis question. If you have more time, take *both* Mini-Tests.

ISSUE-ANALYSIS MINI-TEST

Number of questions: 1
Time Limit: 30 Minutes
Directions: Using a word processor, compose a response to the following topic and question. Do not use any spell-checking or grammar-checking functions.

"The only way to ensure that our natural environment will be protected and preserved is through government penalties and other regulatory measures. No society can rely on the voluntary efforts of its individuals and private businesses to achieve these objectives."

In your view, how accurate is the statement above? Use relevant reasons and/or examples to support you viewpoint.

ARGUMENT-ANALYSIS MINI-TEST

Number of questions: 1
Time Limit: 30 Minutes
Directions: Using a word processor, compose an essay for the following argument and directive. Do not use any spell-checking or grammar-checking functions.

The following appeared in an advertisement for United Motors trucks:

"Last year the local television-news program *In Focus* reported in its annual car-and-truck safety survey that over the course of the last ten years United Motors vehicles were involved in at least 30 percent fewer fatal accidents to drivers than vehicles built by any other single manufacturer. Now United is developing a one-of-a-kind computerized crash warning system for all its trucks. Clearly, anyone concerned with safety who is in the market for a new truck this year should buy a United Motors truck."

Discuss how well reasoned you find this argument. In your discussion, be sure to analyze the line of reasoning and the use of evidence in the argument. For example, you may need to consider what questionable assumptions underlie the thinking and what alternative explanations or counterexamples might weaken the conclusion. You can also discuss what sort of evidence would strengthen or refute the argument, what changes in the argument would make it more logically sound, and what, if anything, would help you better evaluate its conclusion.

ISSUE-ANALYSIS MINI-TEST: REVIEW AND SAMPLE RESPONSE

Evaluate your Issue-Analysis essay according to the criteria listed on page 23 (Day 3). Following is my response to this question. As you read it, keep in mind:

- This response is relatively simple in style and language and brief enough (400 words) to compose and type in 30 minutes. Nevertheless, a top-scoring essay need not be as long or contain as many paragraphs as mine.

- I've underlined certain words and phrases to help you see how I've organized my essay and how I've connected my ideas together. (The exam's word-processor will not allow you to underline, italicize, or otherwise highlight text.)

- There is no "correct" answer, so don't worry if your position on the issue differed from mine. What's important is how effectively you present and support your position.

- I didn't compose this response under time pressure, so don't worry if your essay isn't as finely tuned as mine is. You can attain a top score of 6 with a less polished essay.

<u>While nearly everyone would agree</u> in principle that certain efforts to preserve the natural environment are in humankind's best interests, exclusive reliance on volunteerism would be naive and imprudent, especially considering the stakes involved. <u>For this reason, and because</u> serious environmental problems are generally large in scale, <u>I agree that</u> government participation is needed to ensure environmental preservation.

<u>Experience tells us</u> that individuals and private corporations tend to act in their own short-term economic and political interest, not on behalf of the environment or the public at large. <u>For example</u>, current technology makes possible the complete elimination of polluting emissions from automobiles. Nevertheless, neither automobile manufacturers nor consumers are willing or able to voluntarily make the short-term sacrifices necessary to accomplish this goal. Only the government holds the regulatory and enforcement power to impose the necessary standards and to ensure that we achieve such goals.

<u>Admittedly</u>, government penalties do not guarantee compliance with environmental regulations. Businesses often attempt to avoid compliance by concealing their activities, lobbying legislators to modify regulations, or moving operations to jurisdictions that allow their environmentally harmful activities. Others calculate the cost of polluting, in terms of punishment, then budget in advance for anticipated penalties and openly violate the law. <u>However</u>, this behavior only serves to underscore the need for government intervention, because left unfettered this type of behavior would only exacerbate environmental problems.

<u>One must admit as well</u> that government regulation, environmental or otherwise, is fraught with bureaucratic and enforcement problems. Regulatory systems inherently call for legislative committees, investigations, and enforcement agencies, all of which add to the tax burden on the citizens whom these regulations are designed to protect. <u>Also</u>, delays typically associated with bureaucratic regulation can thwart the purpose of the regulations, because environmental problems can quickly become grave indeed. <u>However</u>, given that the only alternative is to rely on volunteerism, government regulation seems necessary.

Finally, environmental issues inherently involve public health and are far too pandemic in nature for individuals to solve on their own. Many of the most egregious environmental violations traverse state, and sometimes national, borders. Individuals have neither the power nor the resources to address these widespread hazards.

In the final analysis, only the authority and scope of power that a government possesses can ensure the attainment of agreed-upon environmental goals. Because individuals are unable and businesses are by nature unwilling to assume this responsibility, government must do so.

ARGUMENT-ANALYSIS MINI-TEST: REVIEW AND SAMPLE RESPONSE

Evaluate your Argument-Analysis essay according to the criteria listed on page 30 (Day 4). To further evaluate your essay, here's a list of the major flaws in the Argument. For a top score of 6, your essay must recognize and discuss each of these four flaws:

1. The Argument relies on an insufficiently small and potentially unrepresentative statistical sample (see the *second* paragraph of my response).

2. The Argument assumes that characteristics of a large group apply to a subset of that group, and vice versa (see the *third* paragraph of my response).

3. The Argument assumes that certain past conditions have remained unchanged up to the present time (see the *fourth* paragraph of my response).

4. The Argument attributes a potentially false cause to a certain phenomenon (see the *fifth* paragraph of my response).

As you read my response below, keep in mind:

5. This response is longer (650 words) than you need for a high-scoring Argument-Analysis essay.

6. I've underlined certain words and phrases to help you see how I've organized my essay and how I've connected my ideas together. (The exam's

word-processor will not allow you to underline, italicize, or otherwise highlight text.)

7. I didn't compose this response under time pressure, so don't worry if your essay isn't as finely tuned as mine. You can attain a top score of 6 with a less polished essay.

This advertisement claims that truck buyers should favor new United Motors trucks over other new trucks. To support this claim, the ad cites United's overall fatality record over a 10-year period, and the development of new safety features for United trucks. On several grounds, this evidence provides little credible support for the ad's claim.

To begin with, the ad provides no information about the scope of the survey upon which it depends. For the purpose of drawing any reliable conclusions about the comparative safety of United Motors vehicles, the number of fatal vehicle accidents accounted for by the survey might have constituted an insufficiently small portion of all fatal vehicle accidents. The survey's reliability might also depend on its geographic scope. For example, if the survey was conducted in a region where United vehicles are not readily available for purchase, then the fact that comparatively few such vehicles are involved in fatal accidents in that region would be scant evidence of the comparative safety of United vehicles. In fact, since *In Focus* is a local production it is quite possible that the scope of the survey was only local.

The survey results are problematic in two additional respects as well. First, the results reflect accidents involving all types of road vehicles, not just trucks—allowing for the possibility that while United cars were involved in fewer fatal accidents than other cars, United trucks were actually involved in a greater number of such accidents. Second, the results reflect fatal accidents but exclude non-fatal accidents. However, non-fatal accidents are also relevant to a truck's safety. In short, without more specific information about the comparative safety records of various trucks in both fatal and nonfatal accidents, the ad's claim is indefensible.

Even assuming that the overall safety record of United trucks during the cited ten-year period is comparatively good, the ad assumes without justification that United's new trucks this year are also comparatively safe. Absent evidence to substantiate this assumption, it is just as possible that the safety of competing trucks has improved recently, or that the safety of United trucks has diminished recently. For that matter, perhaps United's truck-fatality record during the most recent few years is no better or perhaps even worse than those of its competitors. In fact, this scenario might explain why United is currently developing additional safety features for its trucks.

The ad's claim relies on yet another unsubstantiated assumption: that it was the safety of United vehicles, and not some other factor, that was responsible for United's stellar fatality record over the ten-year period. However, this isn't necessarily the case. Perhaps there were far fewer United vehicles than other vehicles on the road during this period. Or, perhaps the people who drive United trucks are generally better drivers than drivers of other trucks. Without considering and ruling out these and other alternative explanations for United's fatality record, United cannot convince me that its trucks are any safer than other trucks.

A final problem with the ad involves its point that United is currently developing a new safety feature for its trucks. While this evidence might help show that in future years new United trucks will be relatively safe, this additional feature is presumably not included in United's current line of trucks. Accordingly, this evidence accomplishes nothing toward showing that consumers should favor a new United truck over other new trucks this year.

In conclusion, the ad is unpersuasive as it stands. To strengthen its truck-safety claim United must show that the survey's sample of vehicle-related fatalities is sufficiently representative of all fatalities involving truck occupants. United must also provide additional evidence that its safety record over a ten-year period applies to nonfatal accidents as well, and that this record reflects United's current truck-safety record. Finally, to better evaluate the argument I would need to know whether the new safety features which the ad mentions are included in United's new trucks this year and, if so, to what extent these features are effective.

Day 6

Quantitative Ability Lesson 1: Overview and Strategies

Today's Topics:

1. The Problem-Solving Format
2. The Data Sufficiency Format

Today you'll learn the basics for the Quantitative Ability section. For each of the two question formats—Problem Solving and Data Sufficiency—you'll examine sample questions and learn strategies for handling test questions.

THE PROBLEM-SOLVING FORMAT

Problem Solving questions require you to work to a solution (a numerical value or other expression), then find that solution among the five answer choices.

HOW MANY: 23–24 questions (out of 37 Quantitative questions altogether)

WHERE: Interspersed with Data Sufficiency questions (see Day 1, page 2 for a typical sequence)

WHAT'S COVERED: Any of the Quantitative areas listed on page 4 is fair game for a Problem Solving question.

DIRECTIONS: Whenever you encounter a Problem Solving question, you'll access the following directions by clicking on the HELP button:

Solve this problem and indicate the best of the answer choices given.

<u>Numbers:</u> All numbers used are real numbers.

<u>Figures:</u> A figure accompanying a problem solving question is intended to provide information useful in solving the problem. Figures are drawn as accurately as possible EXCEPT when it is stated in a specific problem that its figure is not drawn to scale. Straight lines may sometimes appear jagged. All figures lie on a plane unless otherwise indicated.

To review these directions for subsequent questions of this type, click on HELP.

What Problem Solving Questions Look Like

Each Problem Solving question includes a question or other prompt along with five answer choices; this conventional format should already be familiar to you and comfortable for you. Let's look at three typical examples. (I'll analyze all three beginning on page 44.) Question 1 involves *sets* (one of the topics for Day 7) and is easier than average. Take 1–2 minutes to solve this problem. Here are a few tips to help you along:

- Drawing a comparison between totals does not necessarily require calculating the totals.

- When adding or subtracting negative numbers be careful to keep the signs straight.

1. What is the difference between the sum of the integers –15 through 33, inclusive, and the sum of the integers –10 through 31, inclusive?

   (A) 0

   (B) 3

   (C) 21

   (D) 65

   (E) 130

Question 2 (below) involves the concept of *weighted average* (one of the topics for Day 16) and is moderate in difficulty level. Take 1–2 minutes to solve this problem. Here are a few tips to help you along:

- The problem calls for a more complex task than calculating a simple average (arithmetic mean).

- You can increase your odds of responding correctly by making a common-sense estimate, then narrowing down the answer choices.

2. Of nine executives at ABC Corporation, five earn $150,000 each per year, three earn $170,000 each per year, and one earns $180,000 per year. To the nearest dollar, what is the average annual salary of these executives?

   (A) $158,000

   (B) $160,000

   (C) $162,500

   (D) $165,000

   (E) $166,666

Question 3 (below) is a bit more difficult than average and involves the concepts of *proportion* and *linear equations*—topics for Days 7 and 16, respectively. Notice that instead of performing a numerical computation, your task in this question is to *express a*

computational process in terms of letters. On the GMAT, expect to encounter at least three Problem Solving questions of this type. Take 1–2 minutes to solve this problem. Here are a few tips to help you along:

- Solving it requires converting one type of unit to another.

- What the answer choices all have in common must be features of your solution.

3. If one dollar can buy m pieces of paper, how many dollars are needed to buy p reams of paper? [*Note:* 1 ream = 500 pieces of paper.]

   (A) $\dfrac{p}{500m}$

   (B) $\dfrac{m}{500p}$

   (C) $\dfrac{500}{p+m}$

   (D) $\dfrac{500p}{m}$

   (E) $\dfrac{500m}{p}$

Analysis of Sample Questions

Analysis of Question 1
You don't need to add together the terms of either sequence. Instead, notice that the two sequences have in common integers –10 through 31, inclusive. So those integers cancel out, leaving 32 and 33 (which total 65) in the first sequence and –10,–11,–12,–13, and –14 (which total –65) in the second sequence. The *difference* between the two totals is 130. Thus, the correct response is (E).

Analysis of Question 2
The salaries range from $150,000 to $180,000. Since five of the nine executives earn the lowest salary in the range, common sense should tell you that the average salary is *probably* a bit below the midway point between these two figures ($165,000). Common sense should also tell you that the problem is too

complex to solve simply by calculating the average of three numbers, which is $166,666. So, you can eliminate choice (E) and probably choice (D). Now, here's how to solve the problem. First assign a "weight" to each of the three salary figures (to minimize pencil-work omit dollar signs and extraneous zeros):

$$5(15) = 75$$
$$3(17) = 51$$
$$1(18) = 18$$

Then determine the weighted average of the nine salaries:

$$75 + 51 + 18 = 144$$

$$\frac{144}{9} = 16$$

There's no need to add back those extraneous zeros. It's clear enough from the number we've calculated (16) that the correct response to question 1 is choice (B).

Analysis of Question 3
Notice that each answer choice is a fraction containing the number 500. This is an important clue about how you should set up the problem. The question is essentially asking: "1 is to m as what is to p?" First, set up a proportion (equate two fractions). Then convert either pieces of paper to reams (divide m by 500) or reams to pieces (multiply p by 500). Then solve for x (I'll use the second conversion method):

$$\frac{1}{m} = \frac{x}{500p}$$

$$mx = 500p$$

$$x = \frac{500p}{m}$$

This solution corresponds to answer choice (D). If you're not confident that your solution is correct, ask yourself what the correct answer should look like, generally speaking. It should represent a relatively large value, because the question asks for a price in terms of a unit (ream) that is *500 times greater* than

the price of another unit (a piece of paper). Accordingly, would it make far more sense if the number 500 were to appear in the numerator of the fraction (resulting in a large value) than in its denominator (which would yield a very small value). Choice (D) is one of the three choices that fits the bill. [If you needed to resort to guesswork on Question 3, by using this common-sense approach, you could have at least eliminated choices(A) and (B), thereby improving your odds.]

Key Features of Problem Solving Questions

- **Numerical answer choices are listed in order—from smallest in value to greatest in value.** But there is an exception to this pattern: if a question asks which answer choice is greatest (or smallest) in value, the answer choices will not necessarily be listed in ascending order of value, for obvious reasons.

- **Expect story problems to account for about half of you Problem Solving questions.** This will be true regardless of the overall difficulty level of your particular GMAT, since story problems are not necessarily more difficult than other Problem Solving questions.

- **Figures are drawn accurately unless the problem indicates otherwise.** Some Problem Solving questions will include figures (geometry figures, graphs, and charts) that are intended to provide information useful in solving the problems. Figures are intended to help you, not to mislead or trick you by their visual appearance. If a figure is not drawn to scale, you'll see this warning near the figure: "<u>Note:</u> Figure not drawn to scale."

  NOTE: It's a whole different ball game when it comes to Data Sufficiency questions, in which figures are *not* necessarily drawn to scale. (You'll look at the Data Sufficiency format just ahead.)

Tips for Tackling Problem Solving Questions

  Use your pencil and scratch paper. Carelessness, *not* lack of knowledge or ability, is the leading cause of incorrect responses when it comes to Problem Solving questions. Use your pencil and scratch paper for all but the most simple mathematical or algebraic steps.

Don't split hairs with story problems; instead, accept the premise at face value. Story problems simulate "real-life" scenarios, but in a simplified fashion. Don't second-guess the premise or look for subtle ambiguities in the meaning of particular words or phrases. Otherwise, you might convince yourself that the problem at hand is not solvable as it stands. Don't waste your time or your "genius" this way; by fighting the test you'll only defeat yourself.

Narrow down answer choices by sizing up the question. If the question asks for a numerical value, you can probably narrow down the answer choices by estimating the size and type of number you're looking for. Use your common sense and real-world experience to formulate "ballpark" estimates for story problems. (You can also use common-sense estimates to check your solution.)

Check the answer choices for clues. Always scan the answer choices after reading the question — but *before* solving the problem. Check the answer choices for variables, radical signs (roots), fractions, and so forth. Characteristics such as these often provide clues for how you should set up the problem and what kind of solution you should be working toward.

If you're stuck, work backwards by "plugging in" answer choices. If a Problem Solving question asks for a number value, and if you draw a blank as far as how to set up and solve the problem, don't panic. You might be able to test each answer choice one at a time to see if it works with the information provided in the question. This may take a bit of time, but it's better than random guessing.

Answer the precise question being asked. One of the most common Problem Solving blunders is simply forgetting what the question asks. After solving any problem, check the question itself one more time. For example, does the question ask for:

- a sum or a difference?
- a total or an average?

- a circumference or an area?
- a perimeter or a length of one side only?

Don't get sucked in by "sucker bait" answer choices. The test-makers will intentionally "bait" you with wrong choices that result from making specific common errors in calculation and in setting up and solving equations. Don't assume that your response is correct just because your solution appears among the five answer choices! Rely instead on your sense for whether you understood what the question calls for and performed the calculations and other steps carefully and accurately.

Do NOT rely on diagrams to solve geometry problems. Even though diagrams will be drawn to scale (unless otherwise noted), don't use figures to estimate or measure values (distances, lengths, areas). Rely instead on you knowledge of mathematics and on the numbers and other information in the question itself.

THE DATA SUFFICIENCY FORMAT

The other type of Quantitative question format is called *Data Sufficiency*. This format is unique to the GMAT; you won't find it on any other standardized test! Each Data Sufficiency question includes a question followed by two statements (labeled 1 and 2). Your job is to analyze each of the two statements to determine whether it provides sufficient data to answer the question.

HOW MANY: 13–14 questions (out of 37 Quantitative questions altogether)

WHERE: Interspersed with Problem Solving questions (see page 2 for a typical sequence)

WHAT'S COVERED: Data Sufficiency questions cover the same mix of arithmetic, algebra, and geometry as Problem Solving questions.

DIRECTIONS: Here are the directions for Data Sufficiency questions. (You access these directions when you click on the HELP button). Notice that some of the directions are new—in other words, they don't apply to Problem Solving questions.

This data sufficiency problem consists of a question and two statements, labeled (1) and (2), in which certain data are given. You have to decide whether the data given in the statements are <u>sufficient</u> for answering the question. Using the data given in the statements <u>plus</u> your knowledge of mathematics and everyday facts (such as the number of days in July or the meaning of *counterclockwise*), you must indicate whether:

- statement 1 ALONE is sufficient, but statement 2 alone is not sufficient to answer the question asked;
- statement 2 ALONE is sufficient, but statement 1 alone is not sufficient to answer the question asked;
- BOTH statements 1 and 2 TOGETHER are sufficient to answer the question asked; but NEITHER statement ALONE is sufficient;
- EACH statement ALONE is sufficient to answer the question asked;
- statements (1) and (2) TOGETHER are NOT sufficient to answer the question asked, and additional data specific to the problem are needed.

<u>Numbers:</u> All numbers used are real numbers.

<u>Figures:</u> A figure accompanying a data sufficiency problem will conform to the information given in the question. but will not necessarily conform to the additional information in statements (1 and 2).

Lines shown as straight can be assumed to be straight and lines that appear jagged can also be assumed to be straight.

You may assume that positions of points, angles, regions, etc., exist in the order shown and that angle measures are greater than zero. All figures lie in a plane unless otherwise indicated.

<u>Note:</u> In data sufficiency problems that ask you for the value of a quantity the data given in the statements are sufficient only when it is possible to determine exactly one numerical value for the quantity.

To review these directions for subsequent questions of this type, click on HELP.

What Data Sufficiency Questions Look Like

Each Data Sufficiency question consists of three elements:

- A question
- Two statements (labeled 1 and 2)
- The same five answer choices listed in the directions (see above)

Let's look at three typical examples. (I'll analyze all three beginning on page 48.) Question 1 involves the concept of *percent* (one of the topics for Day 7) and is easier than average. Take 1–2 minutes to solve this problem. Here are a few tips to help you along:

- Before reading statements 1 and 2, ask yourself what information you need to answer the question, then check whether the two statements supply it.
- You don't need to calculate numbers or percentages; in other words, you don't need to answer the question itself.

1. The storage capacity of computer disk A is 85 percent that of disk B. What percentage of disk B's storage capacity is currently in use?

    (1) Disk B holds 3 more gigabytes than disk A.

    (2) 8.5 gigabytes of disk B's storage capacity is currently in use.

    (A) Statement 1 ALONE is sufficient, but statement 2 alone is NOT sufficient to answer the question asked.

    (B) Statement 2 ALONE is sufficient, but statement 1 alone is NOT sufficient to answer the question.

    (C) BOTH statements (1) and (2) TOGETHER are sufficient to answer the question asked, but NEITHER statement ALONE is sufficient.

    (D) Each statement ALONE is sufficient to answer the question asked.

    (E) Statements (1) and (2) TOGETHER are NOT sufficient to answer the question asked, and additional data specific to the problem are needed.

Question 2 (below) involves the concept of *absolute value* (another topic for Day 7) and is moderate in difficulty level. Take 1–2 minutes to solve this problem. Here are a few tips to help you along:

- Consider negative as well as positive values for each of the two variables p and q.

- If you're stuck, try substituting some simple numbers for p and q.

2. If $pq \neq 0$, is $p > q$?

  (1) $|p| > |q|$

  (2) $p = 2q$

  (A) Statement 1 ALONE is sufficient, but statement 2 alone is NOT sufficient to answer the question asked.

  (B) Statement 2 ALONE is sufficient, but statement 1 alone is NOT sufficient to answer the question.

  (C) BOTH statements (1) and (2) TOGETHER are sufficient to answer the question asked, but NEITHER statement ALONE is sufficient.

  (D) Each statement ALONE is sufficient to answer the question asked.

  (E) Statements (1) and (2) TOGETHER are NOT sufficient to answer the question asked, and additional data specific to the problem are needed.

Question 3 involves the *properties of triangles* (a topic for Day 21) and is more difficult than average. Take 1–2 minutes to solve this problem. Here are a few tips to help you along:

- Do not rely on the visual size of the angles; rely instead on the information in the question and the two statements.

- For a reasoned response, you'll need to know certain rules about the interior angles of triangles.

- If you're stuck, use your intuition to guess whether each statement provides sufficient information, then narrow down your answer choices based on your intuition.

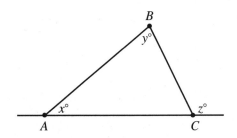

3. In the figure above, is AB equal in length to AC ?

  (1) $x + y = z$

  (2) $y = 180 - z$

  (A) Statement 1 ALONE is sufficient, but statement 2 alone is NOT sufficient to answer the question asked.

  (B) Statement 2 ALONE is sufficient, but statement 1 alone is NOT sufficient to answer the question.

  (C) BOTH statements (1) and (2) TOGETHER are sufficient to answer the question asked, but NEITHER statement ALONE is sufficient.

  (D) Each statement ALONE is sufficient to answer the question asked.

  (E) Statements (1) and (2) TOGETHER are NOT sufficient to answer the question asked, and additional data specific to the problem are needed.

Analysis of Sample Questions

Analysis of Question 1
To answer the question you need to know disk B's *total* capacity as well as the amount (number of gigabytes) *in current use*. Statement 1, together with the information given in the question stem, provides the former while statement 2 provides the latter. Thus, the correct response is choice (C). (There's no need for any calculations. For the record, though, the storage capacities of disks A and B are 17 and 20, respectively. Of disk B's 20 gigabyte capacity, 42.5%, or 8.5 gigabytes, is in current use.)

Analysis of Question 2

In Data Sufficiency questions, whenever you see inequalities and variables but no numbers, that's a clue that to determine the correct answer choice you'll need to consider various value *ranges*—such as negative numbers, positive numbers, and fractional values between –1 and 1. In question 2, consider positive as well as negative values for p and q. Given $|p| > |q|$, a p-value of either 4 or –4 and a q-value of 2, for example, satisfies the inequality but results in two different answers to the question. Thus statement 1 alone is insufficient to answer the question. Eliminate choices (A) and (D).

Now consider statement 2 alone. (Disregard statement 1 for now.) Given $p = 2q$, if you use negative values for both p and q (for example, $p = -4$ and $q = -2$), then the answer to the question is *no*; but if you use positive values (for example, $p = 4$ and $q = 2$), then the answer to the question is *yes*. Thus, statement 2 alone is insufficient. Eliminate choice (B).

Statements 1 and 2 together are still insufficient. For example, if $p = -4$ and $q = -2$, both statements 1 and 2 are satisfied, $p < q$, and the answer to the question is *no*. However, if $p = 4$ and $q = 2$, both statements 1 and 2 are satisfied, but $p > q$, and the answer to the question is *yes*. Eliminate choice (C). The correct answer choice must be choice (E).

Analysis of Question 3

This question involves three distinct rules of geometry. Two of these rules (A and C below) apply specifically to triangles:

Rule A: If two angles of a triangle are equal in size, then the two sides opposite those angles are equal in length.

Rule B: If angles formed from the same vertex form a straight line, their degree measures total 180 (and they are known as "supplementary" angles)

Rule C: In any triangle, the sum of the degree measures of the three interior angles is 180.

Given Rule A, to answer the question you need to know whether angle y is equal in size to the triangle's unidentified angle—the interior angle at point C. Let's call this angle a. If $a = y$, then the answer to the question is *yes*. Otherwise, the answer is *no*. In either case, you need to know whether $a = y$ in order to answer the question.

Notice that angles a and z together form a straight line—the line passing through points A and C. Thus given Rule B:

$$a + z = 180$$
$$a = 180 - z$$

Notice that this equation, together with statement 2, establishes that $a = y$, and hence that the answer to the question is *yes*. Since statement 2 alone suffices to answer the question, the correct response must be either choice (B) or choice (D).

Now consider statement 1 alone. (Disregard statement 2 for now.) The sum of x, y, and a is 180 (Rule C). You can substitute $(180 - z)$ for a in this equation, and manipulate the result so that it is identical to statement 1:

$$x + y + a = 180$$
$$x + y + (180 - z) = 180$$
$$x + y - z = 0$$
$$x + y = z$$

Statement 1 essentially restates a rule that is true for any triangle, so it is insufficient alone to determine whether $a = z$. Since statement 1 alone is insufficient to answer the question while 2 alone is sufficient, the correct response is choice (B).

Key Features of Data Sufficiency Questions

- **The five answer choices are the same for each and every Data Sufficiency question.** And they'll always appear in the same sequence you've seen in this lesson. [Throughout this book they're marked (A) through (E) in this sequence; on the actual GMAT they'll appear in the same sequence but they won't be lettered.]

- **Data Sufficiency questions can vary widely in difficulty level.** Assuming you're familiar with their unique format, these questions are not inherently easier or tougher than Problem Solving questions. The level of difficulty and complexity can vary widely (depending on the correctness of your responses to earlier questions).

- **A Data Sufficiency question that asks for a specific numerical value is answerable only if one and only one value results.** Some, but not all, Data Sufficiency questions will ask for a particular numerical value—for example:

This question asks for a numerical value:

What percentage of disk B's storage capacity is currently in use?

These questions do not ask for a numerical value:

Is $p > q$?

Is AB equal in length to AC ?

If a question asks for a numerical value, and the statement (1 or 2) allows for *two or more* possible values, then the statement does not suffice to answer the question.

- **The two statements (1 and 2) will not conflict with each other.** Perhaps you're wondering which response you should choose—(D) or (E)—if you can answer the question with either statement alone but where you get two conflicting answers. Don't worry; this won't happen. If you can answer the question given either statement alone, *the answer will be the same in both cases.* In other words, statements 1 and 2 will never conflict with each other. Why? The test makers design Data Sufficiency questions this way in order to avoid the "D vs. E" conundrum.

- **Expect story problems to account for at least half of you Data Sufficiency questions.** This will be true regardless of the overall difficulty level of your particular GMAT, since story problems are not necessarily more difficult than other Data Sufficiency questions.

- **Figures are not necessarily drawn to scale, unless noted otherwise.** Any figure accompanying a Data Sufficiency question will conform to the information in the question itself, but it will not necessarily conform to either statement 1 or 2. So, although the figures are not designed to mislead you, they are not necessarily drawn to scale. Rely on the information in the question and statements, not on a figure's appearance.

- **Calculating is not what Data Sufficiency is primarily about.** Expect to do far less number crunching and equation solving for Data Sufficiency questions than for Problem Solving questions. What's being tested here is your ability to recognize and understand *principles*, not to work step-by-step toward a solution. (That's what Problem Solving is about.)

Tips for Tackling Data Sufficiency Questions

Memorize the five answer choices. They're exactly the same, and appear in the same sequence, for each and every Data Sufficiency question. Don't waste a second of your exam time reading any Data Sufficiency answer choice.

Accept story problems at face value. Just like story problems in the Problem Solving format, Data Sufficiency story problems depend on assumptions that enable you to respond to the question posed. Accept story problems for what they are: simplified "real-world" scenarios. Don't second-guess the premise, split hairs as to what particular words or phrases mean, or read anything into the information provided that isn't there. You'll only defeat yourself.

Be sure to consider each statement by itself. After analyzing statement 1, you'll be surprised how difficult it can be to purge the information in Statement 1 from your mind and start with a clean slate in considering Statement 2. Be alert at all times to this potential pitfall.

Do only as much work as you need to select the correct response. The Data Sufficiency format does not require you to answer the questions posed. So once you've convinced yourself that a statement (1 or 2) suffices to answer the question, stop right there! You'd only be wasting your precious time by figuring out the answer itself.

Resist performing many calculations. A few simple calculations or other scribbles may be appropriate; but if you're doing a lot of number crunching, you're probably missing the mathematical principle the question is testing you on.

Don't rely on diagrams (figures) to analyze Data Sufficiency questions. Although any figure will conform to the information in the question, it won't necessarily conform to either statement 1 or 2. So, don't use a Data Sufficiency figure to estimate or measure values, shapes, lengths, or other sizes. Rely instead on the numbers and other information provided in the question and statements.

Consider all the possibilities when it comes to unknowns. When analyzing a Data Sufficiency question involving unknowns (variables such as x and y), unless the question explicitly restricts their value, consider positive *and* negative values, as well as fractions and the numbers zero (0) and 1. If the answer to the question depends on what kind of value you plug in, then the statement (1 or 2) does not suffice to answer it.

Don't feel compelled to handle statements 1 and 2 in that order. If you're having trouble analyzing statement 1, *tentatively* earmark it as "insufficient alone" and move on to statement 2. After analyzing statement 2, you might find that statement 1 makes a lot more sense to you—that the puzzle's pieces fall into place. For example, you might realize that statement 2 provides all but one piece of information needed to answer the question, and that statement 1 supplies that needed piece.

Make reasoned guesses—if you're running out of time—by eliminating answer choices. If statement 1 alone is insufficient to answer the question, you can eliminate both choices (A) and (D). On the other hand, once you've determined that one of the statements alone is sufficient, you can eliminate choices (C) and (E). At this point, you're odds of guessing correctly are about 33 percent, which is a lot better than 20 percent for compete random guess. So if you're having trouble analyzing one statement, but you're confident about whether the other statement is sufficient alone, go with a reasoned guess—and move on to the next question.

Be on the lookout for two statements that say essentially the same thing. Check to see if the two statements provide essentially the same information—just in a slightly different form. If they're the same, you know the correct answer must be either choice (D) or choice (E).

Check each statement to see if it provides numbers needed to answer the question. A Data Sufficiency question might cover a particular formula (*e.g.*, for arithmetic mean, for rate of work or motion, or for the area, perimeter, or volume of a geometric figure). If the question asks for a numerical value, rule out a statement (1 or 2) as sufficient if it fails to supply the missing ingredient of the formula.

Make reasoned guesses based on the quality of information in the two statements. If you're having trouble analyzing a particular question and have decided to take a guess and move on, first ask yourself what kind of information each statement provides. A statement (1 or 2) is more likely to be *sufficient* to answer the question:

- If it provides specific numerical values not given in the premise
- If it adds something new to the premise
- If it provides information that strikes you as relevant to the question

On the other hand, a statement (1 or 2) is more likely to be *insufficient* to answer the question

- If it does not provide any specific numerical values that the premise leaves unknown
- If it seems redundant—simply paraphrasing the premise (or some part of it)
- If the information strikes you as irrelevant to the premise or question

---

IF YOU HAVE MORE TIME TODAY

Here are two suggestions for supplementing what you've learned today:

1. Put into practice the tips you've learned in today's lesson. Log on to the GMAT area of Peterson's Web site (www.petersons.com); there you'll find a variety of Quantitative questions in both the Problem Solving and Data Sufficiency formats. This practice will also help you diagnosis your strong and weak areas (for example, algebra, geometry, or roots and exponents), so you can bet-

ter prepare for the GMAT with the remaining Quantitative Ability lessons in this book.

2. For additional insight about maximizing your accuracy and efficiency in handling Quantitative Ability questions, link to the following article from the "Q&A Corner" of the author's GMAT Web site (www.west.net/~stewart/gmat): "The GMAT Quantitative Ability Section—Estimation, Rounding, Process-of-Elimination, and other Time-saving Shortcuts." (This Q&A also serves as a perfect prelude to tomorrow's lesson.)

Day 7

Quantitative Ability Lesson 2: Arithmetic and Number Theory

Today's Topics:

1. Real numbers
2. Absolute values
3. Integers
4. Laws of arithmetic
5. Fractions
6. Ratios and proportion
7. Decimals
8. Percent
9. Exponents (powers)
10. Roots
11. Descriptive Statistics
12. Statistical Probability

Today you will review basic terminology, concepts, and rules of arithmetic and number theory, focusing on particular areas that bear most directly on GMAT Quantitative questions.

ABOUT TODAY'S LESSON

The topics covered today are basic building blocks for more complex GMAT quantitative problems. Most of what you read here should be review. Nevertheless, pay close attention, because any misunderstanding or confusion about a basic concept might have an adverse effect on your Quantitative score. Moreover, some GMAT questions involving only the basic concepts examined here can be surprisingly difficult.

REAL NUMBERS

A *real number* is any number on the real number line (see figure below). All real numbers except zero are either positive or negative.

A real number x is less than another real number y if x appears to the left of y on the real number line.

If $x < y < z$, then x is to the left of both y and z on the number line, whereas y is to the left of z on the number line. In other words, y is between x and z.

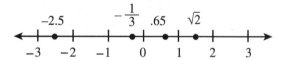

ABSOLUTE VALUE

The *absolute value* of a real number refers to the number's distance from zero (the origin) on the number line. The absolute value of x is indicated as $|x|$. Although any negative number is less than any positive number, the absolute value of a negative number can either be less than (example 1), equal to (example 2), or greater than (example 3) a positive number:

1. $|-7| = 7 < |8|$
2. $|-7| = 7 = |7|$
3. $|-7| = 7 > |6|$

INTEGERS

Integers include the set of all "counting" numbers on the number line: {... -3, -2, -1, 0, 1, 2, 3... }. *Even* integers are divisible by 2 (an even integer divided by 2 yields an integer quotient), whereas *odd* integers are not divisible by 2 (the quotient is not an integer). Zero is an integer, but it is neither even nor odd.

Operations on Integers

Here are some observations about the results of operations (addition, subtraction, multiplication, and division) on integers:

Addition and subtraction

- (integer) ± (integer) = integer
- (even) ± (even) = even (or zero, if the two integers are the same)
- (even) ± (odd) = odd
- (odd) ± (odd) = even (or zero, if the two integers are the same)

Multiplication and division

- (integer) x (integer) = integer
- (nonzero integer) ÷ (nonzero integer) = integer, but only if the numerator is divisible by the denominator
- (odd) x (odd) = odd
- (even) x (nonzero integer) = even
- $\dfrac{even}{2}$ = integer

- $\dfrac{odd}{2}$ = noninteger

Properties of the integer 1

If n is a nonzero real number:

- $n \times 1 = n$

- $\dfrac{n}{1} = n$

- $\dfrac{n}{n} = 1$

Properties of the integer 0 (zero)

If n is a real number:

- $n \pm 0 = n$

- $n \times 0 = 0$

- $\dfrac{0}{n} = 0$

- $\dfrac{n}{0}$ = undefined

- $\dfrac{0}{0}$ = indeterminate

You will not encounter undefined or indeterminate numbers on the GMAT; questions explicitly restrict denominators to nonzero values wherever necessary to avoid these numbers.

Factors, Multiples, and Prime Numbers

Factors and multiples. Where the product of a nonzero integer x and another integer is an integer y, x is said to be a *divisor* or *factor* of y. In other words, if y is divisible by x, x is a factor of y (and, conversely, y is said to be a *multiple* of x). By definition, the absolute value of an integer is greater than or equal to that of any of its factors. Consider the integer 30:

- There are 16 factors (8 positive, 8 negative) of 30: {1, -1, 2, -2, 3, -3, 5, -5, 6, -6, 10, -10, 15, -15, 30, and -30}.

- The number 30 is a multiple of (divisible by) 16 different integers.

Remember these important points about factors:

- Any integer is a factor of itself.
- The number 1 is a factor of all integers.
- The integer zero has no factors and is not a factor of any integer.
- A positive integer's largest factor (other than itself) is never greater than half the integer's value.

Prime numbers. A *prime number* is a positive integer having only two factors: 1 and the number itself. In other words, a prime number is not divisible by any integer other than itself and 1. The set of prime numbers up to and including 31 includes 2, 3, 5, 7, 11, 13,

17, 19, 23, 29, and 31. One and zero are not prime numbers.

Shortcuts to determining factors (divisibility). Determining factors of large integers can be difficult. Keep in mind the following rules to help you determine quickly whether one integer is a multiple of (is divisible by) another integer:

- If the integer ends in 0, 2, 4, 6, or 8, the number is divisible by 2.

- If the sum of the digits is divisible by 3, the number is divisible by 3.

- If the number formed by the last two digits is divisible by 4, the number is divisible by 4.

- If the number ends in 5 or 0, the number is divisible by 5.

- If the number meets the tests for divisibility by 2 and 3, the number is divisible by 6.

- If the number formed by the last three digits is divisible by 8, the number is divisible by 8.

- If the sum of the digits is divisible by 9, the number is divisible by 9.

LAWS OF ARITHMETIC

The laws of arithmetic are the fundamental tools to use in combining and simplifying mathematical expressions. Keep in mind the following basic laws of arithmetic, which you will put to use repeatedly in GMAT quantitative problems.

Commutative laws

- $a + b = b + a$

- But $a - b \neq b - a$ (unless $a = b$)

- $ab = ba$

- But $\dfrac{a}{b} \neq \dfrac{b}{a}$ (unless $a = b$)

Associative laws

- $a + (b + c) = (a + b) + c$

- But $a - (b + c) \neq (a - b) + c$

- $a(bc) = (ab)c$

- But $\dfrac{ab}{c} \neq \dfrac{ac}{b}$ or $\dfrac{a}{bc}$

Distributive laws

- $a(b + c) = ab + ac$

- $a - (b + c) = a - b - c$

- $\dfrac{a+b}{c} = \dfrac{a}{c} + \dfrac{b}{c}$

- But $\dfrac{a}{b+c} \neq \dfrac{a}{b} + \dfrac{a}{c}$

FRACTIONS

A fraction is a number of the form $\quad$ ($y \neq 0$). x is referred to as the *numerator*, and y is referred to as the *denominator*. A *mixed number* includes an integer and a proper fraction (for example, $7\frac{5}{6}$). To convert a mixed number to proper fraction, multiply the denominator by the integer, add the product to the numerator, then place the sum over the original denominator:

$$7\frac{5}{6} = \frac{(6)(7)+5}{6} + \frac{47}{6}$$

Addition and Subtraction of Fractions

To add or subtract two fractions having the same denominator, combine only the two numerators:

$$\frac{3}{7} + \frac{5}{7} = \frac{8}{7}$$

$$\frac{8}{5} - \frac{11}{5} = -\frac{3}{5}$$

To add or subtract two fractions having *different denominators*, determine a multiple common to both denominators. For each fraction, multiply the numerator and denominator by an integer that results in that common denominator. In the following example, 12 is the lowest common multiple of 4 and 3, and is referred to in the context of the fraction as the *lowest common denominator*:

$$-\frac{13}{4}+\frac{8}{3}=$$

$$-\frac{(13)(3)}{(4)(3)}+\frac{(8)(4)}{(3)(4)}=$$

$$-\frac{39}{12}+\frac{32}{12}=-\frac{7}{12}$$

Multiplication of Fractions

To multiply one fraction by another, multiply the two numerators and multiply the two denominators (the denominators need not be the same):

$$\left(\frac{13}{2}\right)\left(-\frac{3}{7}\right)=-\frac{39}{14}$$

To simplify the multiplication, always look for the possibility of canceling factors common to either numerator and either denominator:

$$\frac{18}{7}\cdot\frac{7}{12}=\frac{{}^{3}\cancel{18}}{{}^{1}\cancel{7}}\cdot\frac{{}^{1}\cancel{7}}{{}^{2}\cancel{12}}=\frac{3}{2}$$

Division of Fractions

On the GMAT, problems involving operations with fractions typically involve *complex fractions*, which express either the numerator or denominator (or both) as a fraction and/or as a sum or difference of two terms. To simplify complex fractions, try the following four steps:

1. Combine terms within the numerator and within the denominator (canceling common factors wherever possible).

2. If the denominator is not already a fraction itself, express it as such by placing it in a numerator over the denominator 1.

3. Invert (switch) the terms of the fraction by which you are dividing. (The inverted fraction is called the *reciprocal* of the original fraction.)

4. Multiply the two resulting simple fractions, canceling common factors, if possible.

Here is an example:

$$\frac{\dfrac{5}{3}-1}{\dfrac{1}{5}+2}=\frac{\dfrac{2}{3}}{\dfrac{11}{5}}=\frac{2}{3}\cdot\frac{5}{11}=\frac{10}{33}$$

Here is another example:

$$\frac{\dfrac{5}{9}}{15}=\frac{\dfrac{5}{9}}{\dfrac{15}{1}}=\frac{5}{9}\cdot\frac{1}{15}=\frac{{}^{1}\cancel{5}}{9}\cdot\frac{1}{\cancel{15}^{3}}=\frac{1}{27}$$

RATIOS AND PROPORTION

Ratios are used to express proportion or comparative size. You can express the size of a number *x* relative *to* the size of a number *y* in any of these three ways:

$x:y$ (ratio) x to y (verbal) $\dfrac{x}{y}$ (fraction)

    As with fractions, you can reduce ratios to lowest terms—by canceling common factors. Let's put all of this in a verbal context. Given 12 male students and 16 female students in a certain class:

The ratio of males to females is:

    12 to 16, or 3 to 4

    12:16, or 3:4

    $\dfrac{12}{16}$, or $\dfrac{3}{4}$

The ratio of females to males is:

    16 to 12, or 4 to 3

    16:12, or 4:3

    $\dfrac{16}{12}$, or $\dfrac{4}{3}$

Comparing Parts of a Whole

Think about a ratio as a whole made up of different parts—like a whole pie divided into pieces. For example, given a male-female ratio of 12:16 (3:4), the "whole pie" consists of 28 equal slices—the total number of students. The whole equals the sum of its slices:

16 slices + 12 slices = the whole pie
(males)   (females)   (28 students)

$$\frac{16}{28} + \frac{12}{28} = \frac{28}{28} \text{ (the whole pie)}$$

Setting Up Proportions (Equal Ratios)

A proportion is simply a statement that two ratios are equal. Since you can express ratios as fractions, you can express a proportion as an equation—for example, $\frac{16}{28} = \frac{4}{7}$. If one of the four terms is missing from the proportion, you can solve for the missing term using algebra. For example, if $\frac{3}{4} = \frac{4}{x}$, you can equate the product of numerator and denominator across the equation, then solve for x:

$$(3)(x) = (4)(4)$$
$$3x = 16$$
$$x = \frac{16}{3}, \text{ or } 5\frac{1}{3}$$

Altering a Ratio

When you add (or subtract) the same number to (or from) each term in a ratio, in most cases you alter the ratio. For example:

Does 4:7 equal 5:8? You're asking:

Does $\frac{4}{7}$ equal $\frac{4+1}{7+1}$?   No! $\frac{4}{7} < \frac{5}{8}$.

Does 9:5 equal 7:3? You're asking:

Does $\frac{9}{5}$ equal $\frac{9-2}{5-2}$?   No! $\frac{9}{5} < \frac{7}{3}$.

OPERATIONS WITH DECIMAL NUMBERS

In a *decimal number* one or more non-zero digits appears to the right of a decimal point, indicating fractional amounts. Adding and subtracting decimal numbers is straightforward; align the numbers vertically at the decimal point, then add (or subtract) one column (place) at a time. Multiplication and division of decimal numbers is more complex, but certain techniques can help simplify the process.

Multiplying Decimal Numbers

The number of decimal places (digits to the right of the decimal point) in a product should be the same as the total number of decimal places in the numbers you multiply. So to multiply decimal numbers quickly:

1. Multiply, but ignore the decimal points.

2. Count the total number of decimal places (digits to the right of a decimal point) among the numbers you multiplied.

3. Include that number of decimal places in your product.

Here's an example:

(23.6)(.07)	3 decimal places altogether
(236)(7) = 1652	Decimals temporarily ignored
(23.6)(.07) = 1.652	Decimal point inserted

Here's another example:

(.01)(.02)(.03)	6 decimal places altogether
(1)(2)(3) = 6	Decimals temporarily ignored
(.01)(.02)(.03) = .000006	Decimal point inserted

Dividing Decimal Numbers

When you divide (or compute a fraction), you can move the decimal point in both numbers by the same number of places either to the left or right without altering the quotient (value of the fraction). Here are three related examples:

$$11.4 \div .3 \text{ (or } \frac{11.4}{3}) = \frac{114}{3} = 38$$

$$1.14 \div 3 \text{ (or } \frac{1.14}{3}) = \frac{114}{300} = .38$$

$$114 \div .03 \text{ (or } \frac{114}{.03}) = \frac{11,400}{3} = 3800$$

As you can see, removing decimal points from a fraction helps you to see the general size (value) of the fraction you're dealing with.

PERCENT

Percent means *per hundred*. Percents are usually less than 100, but they can be 100 or greater as well. Any percent can also be expressed as a fraction or in decimal form. Here are some examples:

- $37\% = 37$ out of $100 = \dfrac{37}{100} = .37$

- $284\% = \dfrac{284}{100} = 2.84$

- $5\% = 5$ out of $100 = \dfrac{5}{100} = .05$

- $3.4\% = 3.4$ out of $100 = \dfrac{3.4}{100} = \dfrac{34}{1000} = .034$

- $x\% = x$ out of $100 = \dfrac{x}{100} = \dfrac{1}{100}(x) = .01x$

- $\dfrac{1}{4}\% = \dfrac{1}{4}$ out of $100 = \dfrac{\frac{1}{4}}{100} = \left(\dfrac{1}{100}\right)(.25) = .0025$

A percentage expressed as a negative number indicates decrease. Otherwise, the number system includes no such thing as a negative portion or percentage.

Fractional and Decimal Equivalents of Percents

Changing a percent to a decimal (and vice versa). To change a percent to a decimal, simply move the decimal point two places to the left and remove the percent sign. Conversely, to change a decimal to a percent, move the decimal point two places to the right and add the percent sign. Here are some examples:

- $9.5\% = .095$

- $.4\% = .004$

- $123\% = 1.23$

- $.003 = .3\%$

- $.704 = 70.4\%$

- $13.661 = 1,366.1\%$

Changing a percent to a fraction (and vice versa). To change a percent to a fraction, simply remove the percent sign and divide by 100 (simplify by canceling common factors). Reverse the process to change a fraction to a percent (simplify by canceling common factors). Here are some examples:

- $23\% = \dfrac{23}{100}$

- $2.891\% = \dfrac{2.891}{100} = \dfrac{2,891}{100,000}$

- $810\% = \dfrac{810}{100} = \dfrac{81}{10} = 8\dfrac{1}{10}$

- $\dfrac{4}{5} = \dfrac{4}{5}(100\%) = \dfrac{400}{5}\% = 80\%$

- $\dfrac{3}{8} = \dfrac{3}{8}(100\%) = \dfrac{300}{8}\% = \dfrac{75}{2}\% = 37\dfrac{1}{2}\%$

Guarding against errors in converting one form to another. To avoid conversion errors, keep in mind the general size of the number with which you are working. For example, a test taker in a hurry might carelessly (and incorrectly) express

- $.09\%$ as $.9$ or $\dfrac{9}{100}$

- $\dfrac{.4}{5}$ as $.8\%$

- 668% as 66.8 or $.668$

One good way to check your conversion is to verbalize the original expression, perhaps rounding off the original number to a more familiar one. In the first of the preceding examples, think of $.09\%$ as just under $.1\%$, which is one-tenth of a percent, or a thousandth (a pretty small number). In the second example, think of $\dfrac{.4}{5}$ as just under $\dfrac{.5}{5}$, which is $\dfrac{1}{10}$, or 10%. Think of 668% as more than six times a complete 100% or between 6 and 7.

Common (Testworthy) Fraction, Decimal, and Percent Equivalents

Certain fractional and decimal equivalents of common percents occur frequently enough on the GMAT that you should memorize them. These fractions, percentages, and decimals are favorites of the testing service because they reward test takers who recognize quicker ways to determine answers to questions. The equivalents in the table below should make your work with percent problems much easier.

PERCENT	DECIMAL	FRACTION
50%	.5	$\frac{1}{2}$
25%	.25	$\frac{1}{4}$
75%	.75	$\frac{3}{4}$
10%	.1	$\frac{1}{10}$
30%	.3	$\frac{3}{10}$
70%	.7	$\frac{7}{10}$
90%	.9	$\frac{9}{10}$
$33\frac{1}{3}\%$	$.33\frac{1}{3}$	$\frac{1}{3}$
$66\frac{2}{3}\%$	$.66\frac{2}{3}$	$\frac{2}{3}$
$16\frac{2}{3}\%$	$16\frac{2}{3}$	$\frac{1}{6}$
$83\frac{1}{3}\%$	$.83\frac{1}{3}$	$\frac{5}{6}$
20%	.2	$\frac{1}{5}$
40%	.4	$\frac{2}{5}$
60%	.6	$\frac{3}{5}$
80%	.8	$\frac{4}{5}$
$12\frac{1}{2}\%$	.125	$\frac{1}{8}$
$37\frac{1}{2}\%$	.375	$\frac{3}{8}$
$62\frac{1}{2}\%$	.625	$\frac{5}{8}$
$87\frac{1}{2}\%$	.875	$\frac{7}{8}$

Finding a Percent of a Number

Consider the following question: *What is 35% of 65?* There are three methods of finding a percent of a given number:
(1) Proportion, (2) Decimal, (3) Fractional

Proportion method. Equate $\frac{35}{100}$ with the unknown number divided by 65:

$$\frac{x}{65} = \frac{35}{100}$$

$$\frac{x}{65} = \frac{7}{20}$$

$$x = \frac{455}{20}$$

$$x = \frac{91}{4}$$

$$x = 22\frac{3}{4}$$

Decimal method. Change 35% to .35:
$$(.35)(65) = 22.75$$

Fractional method. Change 35% to $\frac{35}{100}$:

$$\left(\frac{35}{100}\right)(65) = \left(\frac{7}{20}\right)(65) = \frac{(7)(13)}{4} = \frac{91}{4} = 22\frac{3}{4}$$

Finding a Number When Percent of the Number is Given

Consider the following question: *7 is 5% of what number?* You can use the proportion method to find a number when a problem gives a percent. Or you can set up a different equation—one that states algebraically exactly what the question asks verbally. The proportion method is as follows:

$$\frac{5}{100} = \frac{7}{x}$$

$$5x = 700$$

$$x = 140$$

Compare the verbal equation method:
$$7 = .05x \ (7 \text{ is } .05 \text{ of } x)$$
$$700 = 5x$$
$$x = 140$$

Finding What Percent One Number Is of Another

Consider the following question: *12 is what percent of 72?* You can use the proportion method to solve this problem, but you will probably find the fractional method easier and more intuitive. The proportion method is as follows:

$$\frac{x}{100} = \frac{12}{72}$$

$$x = \frac{1,200}{72}$$

$$x = \frac{50}{3}$$

$$x = 16\frac{2}{3}\%$$

You can solve the same problem using the fractional method:

$$\frac{12}{72} = \frac{1}{6} = 16\frac{2}{3}\%$$

Finding the Percent of Increase or Decrease

Consider the following question:

10 increased by what percent is 12? In handling such questions, keep in mind that the percent change always relates to the value *before* the change. First, determine the amount of the increase—2 in this case. Next, compare that increase to the original number (before the change) by a fraction—$\frac{2}{10}$ in this case. Ten increased by $\frac{2}{10}$ (or 20%) is 12.

You can use the same procedure for percent decrease. Consider the following question:

12 decreased by what percent is 10? As before, first determine the amount of the change (2), then compare the change with the original amount (before the decrease)—12 in this case. The fractional decrease is $\frac{2}{12}$. Twelve decreased by $\frac{2}{12}$ (or $\frac{1}{6}$ or $16\frac{2}{3}$) is 10. (Did you remember $16\frac{2}{3}\%$ from the conversion table on page 59?)

Notice that the percent increase from 10 to 12 (20%) differs from the percent decrease from 12 to 10 ($16\frac{2}{3}\%$). The reason for this is that you determine the change based on the original number (before the change), and that number is different in the two questions.

EXPONENTS (POWERS)

An *exponent* (or *power*) refers to the number of times that a number (called the base number) is multiplied by itself. For example, $n3 = (n)(n)(n)$; *n* is said to be raised to the third power or "cubed." An exponent can be an integer or a fraction, a positive number or a negative number.

Exponents and Ordering

Raising numbers to powers can have surprising effects on the *size* and *sign* (negative or positive) of the base number. Here are some useful observations about the impact of exponents on ordering (the position along the real number line):

- (positive base) raised to (any exponent) = (positive number)
- (negative base) raised to (even integer) = (positive number)
- (negative base) raised to (odd integer) = (negative number)
- (base number >1) raised to (exponent greater than 1) increases the number
- (base number between 0 and 1) raised to (exponent greater than 1) decreases the number toward 0
- (base number between -1 and 0) raised to (odd exponent greater than 1) increases the number toward 0
- (base number less than -1) raised to (odd exponent >1) decreases the number

Combining (Simplifying) Terms That Include Exponents

The rules relating to combining base numbers and exponents can be quite confusing. Here are some observations about the results of operations (addition, subtraction, multiplication, and division) on terms (numbers and variables) that include exponents. Keep in mind that most forms of combining are prohibited.

Addition and subtraction. You can't combine base numbers or exponents when adding or subtracting two terms unless base numbers are the same and exponents are the same.

$a^x + a^x = 2a^x$ *(okay to combine)*

$a^x + b^x$ *(cannot be combined)*

$a^x + a^y$ *(cannot be combined)*

Multiplication and division. When multiplying or dividing, you can combine different base numbers, but only if the exponents are the same:

$$a^x \bullet b^x = (ab)^x$$

$$\frac{a^x}{b^x} = \left(\frac{a}{b}\right)^x$$

You can combine exponents, but only if base numbers are the same. When multiplying terms, add the exponents. When dividing terms, subtract the denominator exponent from the numerator exponent.

$$a^x \bullet a^y = a^{(x+y)}$$

$$\frac{a^x}{a^y} = a^{x-y}$$

Additional Exponent Rules

Here are some more exponent rules that you should know.

$$\left(a^x\right)^y = a^{x \bullet y}$$

$$a^{x/y} = \sqrt[y]{a^x}$$

$$a^{-x} = \frac{1}{a^x}$$

$$a^{-x/y} = \frac{1}{a^{x/y}} = \frac{1}{\sqrt[y]{a^x}}$$

$$a^0 = 1 \quad (a \neq 0)$$

Common (Testworthy) Exponential Values

The exponential values (numbers) indicated in the table below occur frequently on the GMAT, so you should memorize them.

	POWER & CORRESPONDING VALUE						
BASE	2	3	4	5	6	7	8
2	4	8	16	32	64	128	256
3	9	27	81	243			
4	16	64	256				
5	25	125	625				
6	36	216					

ROOTS

A *square root* of a number n is a number that multiplied by itself equals *n*. (Roots are denoted by *radical* signs, as in $\sqrt{n}$ and $\sqrt[3]{n}$.) The rules for roots (examined below) are quite similar to those for exponents.

Roots and Ordering

As with exponents, the root of a number can bear a surprising relationship on the *size* and *sign* (negative versus positive) of the number. Here are some useful observations:

- If $n > 1$, then $1 < \sqrt[3]{n} < \sqrt{n} < n$.

- If $0 < n < 1$, then $0 < n <$ (notice that the square root is larger than its square, and the cube root is even larger).

- The *square* root of any negative number is an imaginary number (not a real number). You will not encounter imaginary numbers on the GMAT.

- Every negative number has exactly one cube root, and that root is a negative number [(-)(-)(-)= (-)]. The same holds true for all other *odd*-numbered roots of negative numbers.

- Every positive number has two square roots: a negative number and a positive number (with the same absolute value). The same holds true for all other *even*-numbered roots.

- Every positive number has only one cube root (a positive number). The same holds true for all other *odd*-numbered roots.

Combining and Simplifying Terms That Include Roots

The GMAT also covers the rules for combining terms that include roots. Terms under different radicals cannot be combined under a common radical if you are *adding* or *subtracting* them:

$$\sqrt{x}\sqrt{y} \neq \sqrt{x+y}$$

$$\sqrt{x} - \sqrt{y} \neq \sqrt{x-y}$$

$$\sqrt{x} + \sqrt{x} = 2\sqrt{x} \quad \left(\text{not } \sqrt{2x}\right)$$

However, terms under different radicals can be combined under a common radical if you are *multiplying* or *dividing* them (as long as the root is the same—for example, two square roots):

$$\sqrt{x}\sqrt{y} = \sqrt{xy}$$

$$\frac{\sqrt{x}}{\sqrt{y}} = \sqrt{\frac{x}{y}}$$

$$\sqrt{x}\sqrt{x} = x$$

On the GMAT, radicals and roots often occur in equations. To simplify such an equation, squaring both sides of the equation is often a good idea, as in the following example:

$$\sqrt{x+2y} = 7$$

$$x + 2y = 49$$

Calculating and Estimating Roots

The GMAT does not require that you calculate exact roots (square or otherwise) of large numbers. The exam might, however, ask you to *approximate* or determine parameters of square roots (or other roots). For example, $\sqrt[3]{50}$ lies somewhere between 3 and 4 ($3^3 = 27$, $4^3 = 64$). This range will probably suffice to respond to a GMAT question.

Common (Testworthy) Roots

Some square and cube roots occur frequently enough on the GMAT that you should memorize them. The numbers in the table below should make your work with roots much easier.

Common square roots >10:

$\sqrt{121} = 11$
$\sqrt{144} = 12$
$\sqrt{169} = 13$
$\sqrt{196} = 14$
$\sqrt{225} = 15$
$\sqrt{625} = 25$

Cube roots from 2 to 10:

$\sqrt[3]{8} = 2$
$\sqrt[3]{27} = 3$
$\sqrt[3]{64} = 4$
$\sqrt[3]{125} = 5$
$\sqrt[3]{216} = 6$
$\sqrt[3]{343} = 7$
$\sqrt[3]{512} = 8$
$\sqrt[3]{729} = 9$
$\sqrt[3]{1,000} = 10$

DESCRIPTIVE STATISTICS

The area of *descriptive statistics* includes many concepts, but here are the only five you need to know for the GMAT (the first is covered on the exam more frequently than the others):

1. **Arithmetic mean (simple average):** In a set of n measurements, the sum of the measurements divided by n

2. **Median:** The middle measurement after the measurements are ordered by size (or the average of the two middle measurements if the number of measurements is odd)

3. **Mode:** The measurement that appears most frequently in a set

4. **Range:** The difference between the greatest measurement and the least measurement

5. **Standard deviation:** A measure of dispersion among members of a set

Here's a simple example that illustrates each of the five concepts:

Given a set of six measurements {8, –4, 8, 3, 2, 7}:

Mean = 4	$(8 - 4 + 8 - 3 + 2 + 7) \div 6 =$ $24 \div 6 = 4$
Median = 5	The average of 3 and 7—the two middle measurements in the set ordered in this way: {–4, 2, 3, 7, 8, 8}
Mode = 8	8 appears twice (more frequently than any other measurement)
Range = 12	The difference between –4 and 8
Standard deviation = 4+	Determining standard deviation involves five steps:

1. Calculate the arithmetic mean (simple average) of all terms in the set: $24 \div 6 = 4$

2. Calculate the difference between the mean and each term: {4, 8, 4, 1, 2, 3}

3. Square each difference you computed in step 2:
{16, 64, 16, 1, 4, 9}

4. Calculate the mean of the squares you computed in step 3: $110 \div 6 = 18 - \dfrac{1}{3}$

5. Calculate the nonnegative square root of the mean you computed in step 4: 4^+ (just over 4)

STATISTICAL PROBABILITY

Statistical probability refers to the mathematical likelihood of an event occurring (or not occurring). By definition, the probability of an event occurring ranges from 0 (0% possibility) to 1 (100% certainty). For the GMAT, you need to know only the most basic aspects of probability. A GMAT probability question might ask for either:

• Possible combinations of members in one or more sets

• The probability of selecting a certain combination of members from one or more sets

You can use the same informal approach for both question types: tally up the possibilities, working methodically from left to right *only* (to avoid double-counting). Here's a simple illustration of this approach:

The set {A, B, C, D, E} contains 10 distinct pairs:

A with B, C, D or E (4 pairs)
B with C, D or E (3 pairs)
C with D or E (2 pairs)
D with E (1 pair)

The probability of selecting any one pair is 1 in 10, or $\dfrac{1}{10}$.

Here's another illustration of this approach. This one involves two distinct sets:

Selecting one member from set 1 {A, B} and two members from set 2 {C, D, E} might result in any of six possible combinations:

A with CD, CE, or DE (3 combinations)
B with CD, CE, or DE (3 combinations)

The probability of selecting any one combination is 1 in 6, or $\dfrac{1}{6}$.

When combining terms from more than one set, another way to determine probability is to multiply together the probabilities from each individual set. Here's an example:

Selecting two members from set 1 {A, B, C} and two members from set 2 {D, E, F, G} might result in any of these combinations from each set:

Set 1 contains 3 pairs: AB, AC, BC (the probability of selecting any one pair is $\dfrac{1}{3}$).

Set 2 contains 6 pairs: DE, DF, DG, EF, EG, FG (the probability of selecting any one is $\dfrac{1}{6}$).

The probability of selecting any distinct two-pair combination (for example, AB together with DE) is $\dfrac{1}{3} \times \dfrac{1}{6}$, or $\dfrac{1}{18}$.

IF YOU HAVE MORE TIME TODAY

Here are two suggestions for supplementing today's lesson:

1. To apply the principles you've reviewed today to some GMAT-style questions, log on to the author's GMAT Web site (www.west.net/~stewart/gmat) and attempt an Arithmetic and Number Theory mini-test, which covers all of today's topics in both formats: Problem Solving and Data Sufficiency. (To find the mini-test click on "Quantitative Ability" in the "Test Yourself" area.)

2. For special insight about how the GMAT test makers design descriptive-statistics questions—and how to handle these questions—check out

the Q&A entitled "GMAT Descriptive-Statistics Questions—Why Simple Average Isn't Always so Simple." You can link to it from the "Q&A Corner" of the author's GMAT website (www.west.net/~stewart/gmat).

Day 8

Quantitative Ability Lesson 3:
Mini-Test and Review (Arithmetic and Number Theory)

Today you will apply what you learned from the previous two lessons (Days 6 and 7) to a 20-question mini-test, which includes both Problem Solving and Data Sufficiency questions.

INSTRUCTIONS

Attempt the following 20 Quantitative questions under simulated exam conditions. After completing the mini-test, review the explanations that follow. Preceding the explanation for each question, the question type and difficulty level are indicated. Refer to Day 6 for complete Quantitative directions.

MINI-TEST (QUANTITATIVE ABILITY)

Number of questions: 20
Suggested Time: 35 minutes

1. A clerk's salary is $320 after a 25% raise. Before the clerk's raise, the supervisor's salary was 50% greater than the clerk's salary. If the supervisor also receives a raise in the same dollar amount as the clerk's raise, what is the supervisor's salary after the raise?

(A) $370
(B) $424
(C) $448
(D) $480
(E) $576

2. Which of the following has the largest numerical value?

(A) $\frac{7}{5} - \frac{5}{7}$

(B) $.5 \times .7$

(C) $.57 + .075$

(D) $(.57)^2$

(E) $\frac{.5}{.7}$

3. If $abc \neq 0$, and if $0 < c < b < a < 1$, is $\dfrac{a^4 b^3 c^2}{b^2 c d^2} < 1$?

    (1) $a = \sqrt{d}$

    (2) $d > 0$

    (A) Statement 1 ALONE is sufficient, but statement 2 alone is not sufficient to answer the question asked.

    (B) Statement 2 ALONE is sufficient, but statement 1 alone is not sufficient to answer the question asked.

    (C) BOTH statements 1 and 2 TOGETHER are sufficient to answer the question asked; but NEITHER statement ALONE is sufficient.

    (D) EACH statement ALONE is sufficient to answer the question asked.

    (E) Statements 1 and 2 TOGETHER are NOT sufficient to answer the question asked, and additional data specific to the problem are needed.

4. If $<x> = (x + 2) - (x + 1) - (x - 1) - (x - 2)$, what is the value of $<-100> - <100>$?

    (A) –196

    (B) –1

    (C) 6

    (D) 202

    (E) 400

5. If ☐ represents a digit in the five-digit number 62,☐79, what is the value of ☐?

    (1) 62,☐79 is a multiple of 3.

    (2) The sum of the digits of 62, ☐79 is divisible by 4.

    (A) Statement 1 ALONE is sufficient, but statement 2 alone is not sufficient to answer the question asked.

    (B) Statement 2 ALONE is sufficient, but statement 1 alone is not sufficient to answer the question asked.

    (C) BOTH statements 1 and 2 TOGETHER are sufficient to answer the question asked; but NEITHER statement ALONE is sufficient.

    (D) EACH statement ALONE is sufficient to answer the question asked.

    (E) Statements 1 and 2 TOGETHER are NOT sufficient to answer the question asked, and additional data specific to the problem are needed.

6. If x and y are negative integers, and $x - y = 1$, what is the least possible value of xy?

    (A) 0

    (B) 1

    (C) 2

    (D) 3

    (E) 4

7. Diane receives a base weekly salary of $800 plus a 5% commission on sales. In a week in which her sales totaled $8,000, what was the ratio of her total weekly earnings to her commission?

    (A) 2:1

    (B) 3:1

    (C) 3:2

    (D) 5:2

    (E) 8:5

8. Susan has selected exactly three crayons, each a different color, from a crayon box. How many crayon colors were represented in the box before her selection?

    (1) Exactly four distinct three-crayon color combinations were represented in the box before Susan selected three crayons.

    (2) Just before Susan's selections, the box contained exactly five crayons.

    (A) Statement 1 ALONE is sufficient, but statement 2 alone is not sufficient to answer the question asked.

    (B) Statement 2 ALONE is sufficient, but statement 1 alone is not sufficient to answer the question asked.

    (C) BOTH statements 1 and 2 TOGETHER are sufficient to answer the question asked; but NEITHER statement ALONE is sufficient.

(D) EACH statement ALONE is sufficient to answer the question asked.

(E) Statements 1 and 2 TOGETHER are NOT sufficient to answer the question asked, and additional data specific to the problem are needed.

9. $\dfrac{\dfrac{3a^2c^4}{4b^2}}{6ac^2}$ =

(A) $\dfrac{ac^2}{8b^2}$

(B) $\dfrac{ac^2}{4b^2}$

(C) $\dfrac{4b^2}{ac^2}$

(D) $\dfrac{8b^2}{ac^2}$

(E) $\dfrac{ac^2}{6b^2}$

10. If the product of two integers x and y is negative, what is their difference?

(1) $x + y = 2$

(2) $-3 < x < y$

(A) Statement 1 ALONE is sufficient, but statement 2 alone is not sufficient to answer the question asked.

(B) Statement 2 ALONE is sufficient, but statement 1 alone is not sufficient to answer the question asked.

(C) BOTH statements 1 and 2 TOGETHER are sufficient to answer the question asked; but NEITHER statement ALONE is sufficient.

(D) EACH statement ALONE is sufficient to answer the question asked.

(E) Statements 1 and 2 TOGETHER are NOT sufficient to answer the question asked, and additional data specific to the problem are needed.

11. Which of the following is nearest in value to $\sqrt{664} + \sqrt{414}$?

(A) 16

(B) 46

(C) 68

(D) 126

(E) 252

12. The average of six numbers is 19. When one of those numbers is taken away, the average of the remaining five numbers is 21. What number was taken away?

(A) 2

(B) 8

(C) 9

(D) 11

(E) 20

13. If $xy \neq 0$, is $x > y$?

(1) $|x| > |y|$

(2) $x = 2y$

(A) Statement 1 ALONE is sufficient, but statement 2 alone is not sufficient to answer the question asked.

(B) Statement 2 ALONE is sufficient, but statement 1 alone is not sufficient to answer the question asked.

(C) BOTH statements 1 and 2 TOGETHER are sufficient to answer the question asked; but NEITHER statement ALONE is sufficient.

(D) EACH statement ALONE is sufficient to answer the question asked.

(E) Statements 1 and 2 TOGETHER are NOT sufficient to answer the question asked, and additional data specific to the problem are needed.

14. Which of the following distributions of numbers has the largest standard deviation?

(A) {-3, 1, 2}

(B) {-2, -1, 1, 2}

(C) {3, 5, 7}

(D) {-1, 2, 3, 4}

(E) {0, 2, 4}

15. If x, y, and z are consecutive negative integers, and if $x > y > z$, which of the following must be a positive odd integer?

(A) xyz

(B) $x + y + z$

(C) $x - yz$

(D) $x(y + z)$

(E) $(x - y)(y - z)$

16. Three salespeople—A, B, and C—sold a total of 500 products among them during a particular month. During the month, did A sell more products than B sold as well as more products than C sold?

(1)   A sold 166 products during the month.

(2)   C sold 249 products during the month.

(A) Statement 1 ALONE is sufficient, but statement 2 alone is not sufficient to answer the question asked.

(B) Statement 2 ALONE is sufficient, but statement 1 alone is not sufficient to answer the question asked.

(C) BOTH statements 1 and 2 TOGETHER are sufficient to answer the question asked; but NEITHER statement ALONE is sufficient.

(D) EACH statement ALONE is sufficient to answer the question asked.

(E) Statements 1 and 2 TOGETHER are NOT sufficient to answer the question asked, and additional data specific to the problem are needed.

17. If $x = -1$, then $x^{-3} + x^{-2} + x^2 + x^3 =$

(A) -2

(B) -1

(C) 0

(D) 1

(E) 2

18. Machine X, Machine Y, and Machine Z each produce widgets. Machine Y's rate of production is one-third that of Machine X, and Machine Z's production rate is twice that of Machine Y. If Machine Y can produce 35 widgets per day, how many widgets can the three machines produce per day working simultaneously?

(A) 105

(B) 164

(C) 180

(D) 210

(E) 224

19. At a particular ice cream parlor, customers can choose among five different ice cream flavors and can choose either a sugar cone or a waffle cone. Considering both ice cream flavor and cone type, how many distinct triple-scoop cones with three different flavors are available?

(A) 10

(B) 15

(C) 20

(D) 30

(E) 35

20. There is enough food at a picnic to feed either 20 adults or 32 children. All adults eat the same amount, and all children eat the same amount. If 15 adults are fed, how many children can still be fed?

(A) 4

(B) 6

(C) 8

(D) 9

(E) 10

Quick Answer Guide

Mini-Test: Arithmetic

1. C
2. E
3. A
4. E
5. C
6. C
7. B
8. C
9. A
10. E

11. B
12. C
13. E
14. A
15. E
16. A
17. C
18. D
19. C
20. C

EXPLANATIONS

1. The correct answer is (C). Percent (moderate).

$320 is 125% of the clerk's former salary. Expressed algebraically:

$320 = 1.25x$

$32,000 = 125x$

$256 = x$ (clerk's salary before the raise)

Thus, the clerk received a raise of $64 ($320 – $256). The supervisor's salary before the raise was as follows:

$256 + 50% of $256 =

$256 + $128 =

$384

The supervisor received a $64 raise. Thus, the supervisor's salary after the raise is $448 ($384 + $64).

2. The correct answer is (E). Equivalent forms of numbers (easier).

As shown below, only choices (A) and (E) are viable choices. Since $\frac{25}{35} = \frac{5}{7}$, quantity (A) must be less than quantity (E).

(A) $\frac{7}{5} - \frac{5}{7} = \frac{49}{35} - \frac{25}{35} = \frac{24}{35}$ $(< \frac{5}{7})$

(B) $.5 \times .7 = .35$

(C) $.57 + .075 = .645$

(D) $(.57)^2 \approx (.6)^2 = .36$

(E) $\frac{.5}{.7} = \frac{5}{7}$ $(>.7)$

3. The correct answer is (A). Exponents (moderate).

Before analyzing the two statements, simplify the fractional expression by canceling b^2 and c from both numerator and denominator. The simplified fraction is $\frac{a^4 bc}{d^2}$. Given statement 1, $a^2 = d$. Substituting a^2 for d in the fraction: $\frac{a^4 bc}{d^2} = bc$. Given that b and c are both positive but less than 1, $bc < 1$, and the answer to the question is *yes*. Statement 1 alone suffices to answer the question. However, statement 2 alone is insufficient to answer the question. Even if d is greater than zero, statement 2 fails to provide sufficient information to determine the relative values of the numerator and denominator. A sufficiently small d-value relative to the values of a, b, and c results in a quotient greater than 1, whereas a sufficiently large relative d-value results in a quotient less than 1.

4. The correct answer is (E). Integers/signs (easier).

Apply the defined operation to -100 and to 100 in turn, by substituting each value for x in the operation:

$$<-100> = -98 - (-99) - (-101) - (-102) =$$
$$-98 + 99 + 101 + 102 = 204$$
$$<100> = 102 - 101 - 99 - 98 = -196$$

Then combine the two results:

$$<-100> - <100> = 204 - (-196) = 204 + 196 = 400$$

5. The correct answer is (C). Integers (moderate).

If the sum of the digits of a number is divisible by 3, the number is also divisible by 3. The sum of the digits in the number $62,\square 79$, excluding $\square$, is 24. Thus, if the number is a multiple of (divisible by) 3, $\square = 0, 3, 6,$ or 9. Thus, statement 1 alone is insufficient to answer the question. Given statement 2, $\square = 0, 4,$ or 8. Thus, statement 2 alone is insufficient to answer the question. Statements 1 and 2 together establish that $\square = 0$, and so both statements together suffice to answer the question.

6. The correct answer is (C). Integers (easier).

The first step is to solve for x: $x = y + 1$. Using negative integers with the smallest absolute value yields

the smallest product: $y = -2$, and $x = -1$. Accordingly, $xy = 2$.

7. The correct answer is (B). Percent and ratio (moderate).

You can express Diane's commission as $(.05)(8,000) = \$400$. You can add her commission to her base salary as follows: $\$800 + \$400 = \$1,200$ (total earnings). The ratio of $\$1,200$ to $\$400$ is 3:1.

8. The correct answer is (C). Sets (challenging).

Statement 1 alone is insufficient to answer the question. For example, letting letters represent colors, the box could include four crayons and four different colors—A, B, C, and D—offering four distinct three-crayon combinations: {ABC}, {ABD}, {ACD}, and {BCD}. As an alternative, the box could include five crayons but only three different colors—{A,A,A,B,C}—offering four distinct three-crayon combinations: {ABC}, {AAA}, {AAB}, and {AAC}. Statement 2 alone is also insufficient to answer the question. Prior to Susan's selection, the box could have represented anywhere from three to five colors. Again, using letters to represent colors, possible combinations include {AAABC}, {AABCD}, and {ABCDE}, to list just a few. Together, statements 1 and 2 suffice to answer the question. Exactly three colors must be represented in a box of five crayons offering exactly four three-crayon combinations. Again, using letters to represent colors, the configuration must be {AAABD}. All other five-crayon configurations of three or more colors offer too many three-crayon color combinations. The closest is {A,A,B,C}, which offers five combinations: {AAB}, {AAC}, {ABC}, {ABB}, and {BBC}.

9. The correct answer is (A). Exponents (easier).

You can simplify by multiplying the numerator fraction by the reciprocal of the denominator:

$$\frac{3a^2 c^4}{4b^2} \times \frac{1}{6ac^2}$$

Factor out 3, *a*, and c^2 from both numerator and denominator:

$$\frac{ac^2}{4b^2} \times \frac{1}{2} = \frac{ac^2}{8b^2}$$

10. The correct answer is (E). Integers (moderate).

Given $xy < 0$, either x or y (but not both) must be negative. Despite this restriction, statement 1 alone is insufficient to answer the question because it specifies one equation in two variables. Statement 2 alone is also insufficient. Although x must equal either −2 or −1 (x must be a negative integer), y could be any positive integer. Considering statements 1 and 2 together, because there are two possible values of x (−2 and −1) in the equation $x + y = 2$, the difference between x and y could be either 4 or 6. Thus, statements 1 and 2 together are insufficient to answer the question.

11. The correct answer is (B). Roots (easier).

You need not calculate either root because the question asks for an approximation. The number 664 is slightly greater than 625, which is 25^2. The number 414 is slightly greater than 400, which is equal to 20^2. Thus, the sum of the terms is just over 45 (approximately 46).

12. The correct answer is (C). Arithmetic mean (moderate).

You can solve this problem quickly if you simply compare the sums. Before you take away the sixth number, the sum of the numbers is 114 (6×19). After you take away the sixth number, the sum of the remaining numbers is 105 (5×21). The difference between the two sums is 9, which is the value of the number that you took away.

13. The correct answer is (E). Absolute value (moderate).

You must consider both positive and negative values for x and y. Given $|x| > |y|$, an x-value of either 4 or −4 and a y-value of 2, for example, satisfies the

inequality but results in two different answers to the question. Thus, statement 1 alone is insufficient to answer the question. Similarly, given $x = 2y$, if you use negative values for both x and y (for example, $x = -4$ and $y = -2$), the answer to the question is *no*; however, if you use positive values (for example, $x = 4$ and $y = 2$), the answer to the question is *yes*. Thus, statement 2 alone is insufficient. Statements 1 and 2 together are still insufficient. For example, if $x = -4$ and $y = -2$, both statements 1 and 2 are satisfied, $x < y$, and the answer to the question is *no*. However, if $x = 4$ and $y = 2$, both statements 1 and 2 are satisfied, but $x > y$, and the answer to the question is *yes*.

14. The correct answer is (A). Standard deviation (challenging).

Computing standard deviation involves these steps:
(1) compute the arithmetic mean (simple average) of all terms in the set
(2) compute the difference between the mean and each term
(3) square each difference you computed in step (2)
(4) compute the mean of the squares you computed in step (3)
(5) compute the non–negative square root of the mean you computed in step (4)

Applying steps 1–4 to each of the five answer choices yields the following results:

(A) $\dfrac{14}{3}$

(B) $\dfrac{5}{2}$

(C) $\dfrac{8}{3}$

(D) $\dfrac{7}{2}$

(E) $\dfrac{8}{3}$

Choice (A) is the only fraction that exceeds 4. There's no need to compute the square roots of any of these fractions (step 5), since their relative sizes would remain the same. [Notice that in distributions (A) and (D) the range is 5, compared with a range of 4 in each of the other three distributions. This is a strong indication that the correct answer is probably either choice (A) or (D), especially given the small number of terms in each distribution.]

15. The correct answer is (E). Integers (moderate).

Given that x, y, and z are consecutive negative integers, either one integer is odd or two integers are odd. Also, a negative number multiplied by a negative number yields a positive number. With this in mind, consider each answer choice in turn:

(A) xyz must be negative and even.

(B) $x + y + z$ must be negative; however, whether answer B is odd or even depends on whether one or two of the three integers are odd.

(C) $x - yz$ must be negative (because yz, a positive number, is subtracted from the negative number x). However, whether answer C is odd or even depends on whether one or two of the three integers are odd. yz must be even; however, x could either be even or odd.

(D) $(y + z)$ must be negative and odd. Thus, the product of x and $(y + z)$ must be positive (either odd or even).

(E) $(x - y)$ must be odd and positive. $(y - z)$ must be odd and positive, because $y > z$. The product of the terms must therefore be odd and positive.

16. The correct answer is (A). Proportion (easier).

Given that a total of 500 products were sold, statement 1 alone suffices to answer the question. If A sold 166 products, A sold just less than one-third of the total number. Either B or C must sell more than one-third, and the answer to the question is *no*. Statement 2 alone is insufficient to answer the question. If C sold 249 products, A could have sold anywhere from 0 to 251 products; if A sold either 250 or 251 products, A also sold more products than either B or C. However, if A sold 0–249 products, A did not sell more products than B or C.

17. The correct answer is (C). Exponents (moderate)

The key here is to recognize that any term raised to a negative power is the same as "one over" the term, but raised to the *positive* power. Also, remember that a negative number raised to a power is negative if the exponent is *odd*, yet positive if the exponent is *even*:

$$-1^{(-3)} + \left[-1^{(-2)}\right] + \left[-1^2\right] + \left[-1^3\right] =$$

$$-\left(\frac{1}{1}\right) + \frac{1}{1} + 1 - 1 = 0$$

18. The correct answer is (D). Ratio (moderate).

The ratio of X's rate to Y's rate is 3 to 1, and the ratio of Y's rate to Z's rate is 1 to 2. You can express the ratio among all three as 3:1:2 (x:y:z). Accordingly, Y's production accounts for one-sixth of the total widgets that all three machines can produce per day. Given that Y can produce 35 widgets per day, all three machines can produce $(35)(6) = 210$ widgets per day.

19. The correct answer is (C). Sets (moderate).

{A, B, C, D, E} represents the set of ice cream flavors. Ten triple-scoop combinations are available: {ABC}, {ABD}, {ABE}, {ACD}, {ACE}, {ADE}, {BCD}, {BCE}, {BDE}, and {CDE}. Each of these combinations is available on either of the two cone types. Thus, the total number of distinct ice cream cones is 20.

20. The correct answer is (C). Proportion (moderate).

If 15 adults are fed, three-fourths of the food is gone. One-fourth of the food will feed $\left(\frac{1}{4}\right)(32)$, or 8, children.

Day 9

Sentence Correction Lesson 1: Format, Strategies, Grammar Review

Today's Topics:

1. Sentence Correction—At a Glance

2. What Sentence Correction Questions Look Like

3. Analysis of Sample Question

4. Tips for Tackling Sentence Correction Questions

5. Grammatical Errors Involving Adjectives and Adverbs

6. Grammatical Errors Involving Pronouns

7. Grammatical Errors in Subject-Verb Agreement

Today you'll learn what Sentence Correction questions look like, and you'll learn some tips for avoiding common pitfalls in answering them. You'll also learn to recognize and fix grammatical problems involving parts of speech and pronouns. (Tomorrow you'll examine other types of grammatical errors.)

SENTENCE CORRECTION— AT A GLANCE

HOW MANY: 14–15 out the 41 questions in the Verbal section

WHERE: In the GMAT CAT Verbal section, mixed in with Reading Comprehension and Critical Reasoning questions

WHAT'S COVERED: Two areas of English language proficiency:

1. *Correct expression*, measured by your ability to recognize errors in grammar and usage

2. *Effective expression*, measured by your ability to improve sentences that are poorly worded or structured

WHAT'S NOT COVERED: Other areas of English language proficiency:

1. *Punctuation* (except that comma placement can come into play if it affects the meaning of a sentence)

2. *Vocabulary* (you won't need to memorize long lists of obscure and erudite words just for GMAT Sentence Correction)

3. *Slang and colloquialisms* (informal expressions don't appear at all in Sentence Correction questions)

DIRECTIONS: These directions will appear on your screen before your first Sentence Correction question:

This question presents a sentence, all or part of which is underlined. Beneath the sentence, you will find five ways of phrasing the underlined part. The first of these repeats the original; the other four are different. If you think the original is best, choose the first answer; otherwise choose one of the others.

This question tests correctness and effectiveness of expression. In choosing your answer, follow the requirements of standard written English; that is, pay attention to grammar, choice of words, and sentence construction. Choose the answer that produces the most effective sentence; this answer should be clear and exact, without awkwardness, ambiguity, redundancy, or grammatical error.

To review these directions for subsequent questions of this type, click on HELP.

WHAT SENTENCE CORRECTION QUESTIONS LOOK LIKE

For each Sentence Correction question, part of a sentence (or the whole sentence) will be underlined. Answer choice (A) will simply restate the underlined part "as is." The other four choices will provide alternatives to the original underlined phrase. Here's a typical Sentence Correction question (I'll analyze it just ahead):

Q: Despite sophisticated computer models for assessing risk, such a model is nevertheless limited in their ability to define what risk is.

(A) Despite sophisticated computer models for assessing risk, such a model is nevertheless

(B) Sophisticated computer models, which assess risk, are nevertheless

(C) Despite their sophistication, computer models for assessing risk are

(D) Assessment of risk can be achieved with sophisticated computer models, but these sophisticated computer models are

(E) Assessing risk with sophisticated computer models is limited because such models are

Here are some features of GMAT Sentence Correction that you should know about:

- **The sentences are somewhat formal in tone, and most involve academic topics.** Don't worry: You won't need any knowledge of the topic at hand in order to handle a question. (Experts in computer modeling or risk assessment wouldn't hold any advantage in the sample question above, would they?)

- **Any portion of the sentence might be underlined.** The underlined part may appear at the beginning, middle, or end of the sentence. Also, in some cases, the entire sentence will be underlined.

- **The first answer choice simply restates the underlined part "as is."** The other four choices present alternatives to the original underlined phrase.

- **The best answer choice isn't always perfect.** In some cases, the best choice among the five may be a bit awkward or wordy—but nevertheless the only choice that is free of grammatical errors. Don't be stubborn and insist on finding an answer choice that makes for an ideal sentence that your high-school English teacher would be proud of. You're looking for the best version of the five, not the perfect version.

- **More than one answer choice may be grammatically correct.** These questions cover not just grammar, but also effective expression. So, don't select an answer choice just because it results in a grammatically correct sentence. Another answer choice may be clearer, more concise, or less awkward—and therefore better.

- **Punctuation doesn't matter.** You won't find errors in punctuation in these sentences (except as part of larger errors involving sentence structure). The test-makers rely instead on your two GMAT essays to demonstrate your punctuation prowess.

ANALYSIS OF SAMPLE QUESTION

Let's go back to the sample question. Upon a first reading, the phrase *such a model* sounds a bit awkward, doesn't it? That's a good clue that (A) is not the correct response. In fact, the original sentence contains two flaws. One is a grammatical error: the plural pronoun *their* is used to refer to the singular noun *model*. Either both should be plural or both should be singular; but they must match! The word *their* in not part of the underlined phrase, so look for an answer choice that uses *models* instead of *model*. (In grammatical terminology, the original sentence contains an error in "pronoun-antecedent agreement.") The other flaw is one of ineffective expression: the first clause (before the comma) is structured differently from the second clause, and the result is an awkward and confusing sentence. So you should look for an answer choice that renders the sentence clearer and perhaps a bit more concise—one that helps the sentence sound a bit sweeter and "flow" a bit more smoothly. Eliminate choice (A).

Choice (B) does not contain any grammatical errors. But the phrase *which assess risk* appears to describe computer models in general rather than models for assessing risk. Surely, this isn't the intended meaning of the sentence. Choice (B) is a perfect example of an answer choice that is wrong because it either distorts, confuses, or obscures the intended meaning of the sentence. Eliminate choice (B).

Choice (C) takes care of both problems with the original sentence. The plural noun *models* matches the plural pronoun *their*, and both clauses are now constructed to provide a more clear and brief sentence. Choice (C) is probably the correct answer, but read the remaining choices anyway.

Choice (D) sounds pretty good when you read it as part of the sentence, doesn't it? No grammatical errors jump out at you. So, is it a toss-up between choices (B) and (D)? Well, go on to choice (E) for now, then come back to the choice (B) versus choice (D) debate.

Choice (E) incorrectly uses the phrase *is limited* to describe *assessing risk*. It is the computer models' ability, *not* assessing risk, that is limited. Eliminate choice (E).

Go back to choices (C) and (D). Is one less awkward than the other? More concise? Closer in meaning to the original version? Perhaps you noticed that the first clause in choice (D) (*assessment of risk can be*

achieved) sounds a bit awkward. (The clause employs the so-called "passive" voice, an awkward construction that you'll learn more about tomorrow.) So, you should choose choice (C) over (D). Check choice (C) one more time by plugging it into the sentence: *Despite their sophistication, computer models for assessing risk are limited in their ability to define what risk is.* Sounds great! Confirm your response, and move on to the next question.

NOTE: Don't worry if you just encountered a few unfamiliar grammatical terms; when you look at the rules of English grammar later today and tomorrow, you'll learn what those terms mean.

TIPS FOR TACKLING SENTENCE CORRECTION QUESTIONS

Read the entire sentence with each version, in turn. GMAT Sentence Correction questions are not nearly as time-consuming as other Verbal questions. So take your time; plug each version into the sentence, then read the entire sentence. Sure, you'll see the occasional answer choice that's grammatically incorrect apart from the rest of the sentence. But such cases are the exceptions, not the rule.

Don't just skim the answer choices; one little word can make all the difference! The difference between answer choices can be extremely subtle: perhaps one extra little word, or perhaps a word replaced by a different one. It's easy to overlook these differences if you rush through a question. Take your time, and read carefully.

Trust your ear. If any version sounds wrong or odd to your ear as you read it, or if the version seems a bit confusing, eliminate it, even if you're not sure why it's wrong. There's no need to analyze it any further.

Eliminate answer choices that change the meaning of the original sentence. If an answer choice alters, distorts, or confuses the meaning of the original sentence, it cannot be the best choice, even if it is grammatically correct.

Don't choose an answer just because it fixes every flaw in the original version. If the original version is flawed, it's a sure bet that at least one answer choice will fix the flaw but at the same time create a new flaw!

Resolve close judgment calls in favor of clearer, more concise expression. If it comes down to a coin flip between two answer choices, select:

- a briefer, more concise version
- a version that more accurately conveys the intended meaning of the sentence
- a less awkward version

But don't assume that shorter choices are automatically better than longer ones. Apply this technique only when your decision comes down to that coin flip.

Don't presume the original sentence is wrong. During Sentence Correction, GMAT test takers tend to "hyper-correct"—in other words, they presume that among choices (B) through (E) there is a better version than the original one. But keep in mind that in about one out of five Sentence Correction questions, the original sentence will be the best of the five choices.

Verify your selection before confirming your response. Check your selection one more time by plugging it into the sentence. If it sounds right, confirm your response, and move on.

GRAMMATICAL ERRORS INVOLVING ADJECTIVES AND ADVERBS

For the rest of today's lesson, you'll examine grammatical errors involving parts of speech (adjectives, adverbs, pronouns, and verbs). The error types covered here are the ones that appear most frequently in GMAT Sentence Correction. We'll start with adjectives and adverbs.

Error in Choice between Adjective and Adverb

Adjectives describe nouns, while *adverbs* describe verbs, adjectives, and other adverbs. Adverbs generally end with *-ly*, while adjectives don't. In GMAT Sentence Correction, be on the lookout for adjectives incorrectly used as adverbs (and vice versa).

INCORRECT: The movie ended *sudden*.
CORRECT: The movie ended *suddenly*. (The adverb *suddenly* describes the verb *ended*.)

Although adverbs generally end with *-ly*, some adverbs don't. Also, if you're dealing with two adverbs in a row, sometimes the *-ly* is dropped from the second adverb. There are no hard-and-fast rules here. Trust your ear as to what sounds correct.

INCORRECT: Risk-takers drive *fastly*, play *hardly*, and arrive *lately* for their appointments.
CORRECT: Risk-takers drive *fast*, play *hard*, and arrive *late* for their appointments.
INCORRECT: The Canadian skater jumps *particularly highly*.
CORRECT: The Canadian skater jumps *particularly high*.

Now look at how the test makers might try to slip one of these errors past you in a GMAT sentence. In the question below, the original sentence is flawed, so choice (A) is incorrect. Your choice is between (C) and (D).

NOTE: To help you focus on the specific grammatical error at hand, I'll be simplifying the Sentence Correction format by listing just *three* answer choices, and by limiting the different kinds of errors altogether to only a few. Actual GMAT questions include five answer choices, of course.

Q: A recent report from the Department of Energy suggests that over the next two decades demand for crude oil will <u>increase at an alarming fast rate, and greatly exceeds</u> most economists' previous forecasts.

   (A) increase at an alarming fast rate, and greatly exceeds

   (B) ***

   (C) increase at an alarmingly fast rate, greatly exceeding

   (D) be alarmingly increasing and will greatly exceed

   (E) ***

The correct answer is (C). The original sentence incorrectly uses the adjective *alarming* instead of the adverb *alarmingly* to describe the adjective *fast*. The original sentence also contains an additional, and more conspicuous, flaw. The phrase *and greatly exceeds* improperly suggests that the rate is increasing alarmingly at the present time. However, the sentence as a whole makes clear that this is a future event. Choice (C) corrects both of these problems. Although choice (D) also corrects both problems, it creates a new flaw. The phrase *alarmingly increasing* is an awkward and inappropriate expression of the idea that the sentence attempts to convey.

Error in Choice of Adjective for Comparisons

As you read a GMAT sentence, pay close attention to any adjective ending in *-er*, *-ier*, *-est*, and *-iest*. Adjectives ending in *-er*, *-ier* should be used to compare *two* things, while adjectives ending in *-est* and *-iest* should be used in dealing with three or more things.

Another way of making a comparison is to precede the adjective with a word such as *more*, *less*, *most*, or *least*. But if both methods are used together, the sentence is incorrect.

INCORRECT: Frank is less intelligent than the other four students.

CORRECT: Frank is the *least* intelligent among the *five* students.

CORRECT: Frank is *less* intelligent than *any* of the other four students (The word *any* is singular, so the comparative form is proper.)

INCORRECT: Francis is *more healthier* than Greg.

CORRECT: Francis is *healthier* than Greg.

Q: The more busier the trading floor at the stock exchange, the less opportunities large institutional investors have to influence the direction of price by initiating large leveraged transactions.

   (A) The more busier the trading floor at the stock exchange, the less opportunities

   (B) A busier trading floor at the stock exchange results in less opportunities

   (C) The busier the trading floor at the stock exchange, the fewer opportunities

   (D) ***

   (E) ***

The correct answer is (C). In the original sentence, the phrase *more busier* incorrectly uses both comparative methods. Choice (C) corrects this flaw by using *busier*. The original sentence includes another flaw as well. The phrase *less opportunities* is incorrect; the word *fewer* should be used instead of *less* in referring to countable things. Choice (C) corrects this flaw. Choice (B) does not.

GRAMMATICAL ERRORS INVOLVING PRONOUNS

Pronouns come in two varieties: *personal* and *relative*. Personal pronouns include words such as *they*, *me*, *his*, and *itself*—words that refer to specific people, places, and things. The English language contains only seven relative pronouns: *which*, *who*, *that*, *whose*, *whichever*, *whoever*, and *whomever*.

Error in Choice of Personal Pronoun

Personal pronouns take different forms depending on how they are used in a sentence. You can generally trust your ear when it comes to detecting personal-pronoun errors. In some cases, however, your ear can betray you, so make sure you are "tuned in" to the following uses of pronouns.

INCORRECT: Either *him* or Trevor would be the best spokesman for our group.

INCORRECT: The best spokesperson for our group would be either Trevor or *him*.

CORRECT: Either Trevor or *he would be* the best spokesperson for our group.

CORRECT: The best spokesperson for our group *would be* either *he* or Trevor.

(Any form of the verb *to be* is followed by a subject pronoun, such as *he*.)

INCORRECT: One can't help admiring *them* cooperating with one another.

CORRECT: One can't help admiring *their cooperating* with one another.

(The possessive form is used when the pronoun is part of a "noun clause," such as *their cooperating*.)

INCORRECT: In striving to understand others, we also learn more about *us*.

CORRECT: In striving to understand others, *we* also learn more about *ourselves.*

(A reflexive pronoun is used to refer to the sentence's subject.)

What appears to be a reflexive pronoun may not even be a real word! Here's a list of "non-words," any of which might masquerade as a reflexive pronoun in a GMAT sentence: *ourself, our own selves, theirselves, theirself, themself, their own self,* and *their own selves.*

Q: Those <u>of the legislators opposing the swampland protection bill have only theirselves</u> to blame for the plight of the endangered black thrush bird.

(A)   of the legislators opposing the swampland protection bill have only theirselves

(B)   ***

(C)   legislators, who oppose the swampland protection bill, have only themselves

(D)   legislators opposed to the swampland protection bill have only themselves

(E)   ***

The correct answer is (D). The original sentence suffers from two flaws. First, *theirselves* is a not a word and should be replaced with the reflexive pronoun *themselves.* Second, the phrase *those of the legislators opposing,* while not grammatical incorrect, is wordy and awkward. Choice (D) provides a briefer and clearer alternative phrase, as well as correcting the pronoun error. Choice (C) also corrects the pronoun error. However, choice (C) alters the original sentence's meaning; in choice (C), it is simply *those legislators,* rather than certain legislators among that group, who are to blame.

Error in Choice of Relative Pronoun

Don't worry about what the term "relative pronoun" means. Instead, just remember the following rules about when to use each one.

1. Use *which* to refer to things.
2. Use either *who* or *that* to refer to people.
INCORRECT: Amanda, *which* was the third performer, was the best of the group.
CORRECT: Amanda, *who* was the third performer, was the best of the group.

CORRECT: The first employee *that* fails to meet his or her sales quota will be fired.
CORRECT: The first employee *who* fails to meet his or her sales quota will be fired.
3. Whether you should use *which* or *that* depends on what the sentence is supposed to mean.
ONE MEANING: The third page, *which* had been earmarked, contained several typographical errors.
DIFFERENT MEANING: The third page *that* had been earmarked contained several typographical errors.
(The first sentence merely describes the third page as earmarked. The second sentence also suggests that the page containing the errors was the third earmarked page.)
4. Whether you should use *who* (*whoever*) or *whom* (*whomever*) depends on the grammatical function of the person (or people) being referred to.
INCORRECT: It was the chairman *whom* initiated the bill.
CORRECT: It was the chairman *who* initiated the bill.
INCORRECT: First aid will be available to *whomever* requires it.
CORRECT: First aid will be available to *whoever* requires it.

To make sure that *who* (*whoever*) and *whom* (*whomever*) are being used correctly, substitute a regular pronoun, then rearrange the clause (if necessary) to form a simple sentence. If a subject-case pronoun works, then *who* (*whoever*) is the right choice. On the other hand, if an object-case pronoun works, then *whom* (*whomever*) is the right choice. Here's how it works with the foregoing sentences:

It was the chairman *whom* initiated the bill.
He initiated the bill.
(*He* is a subject-case pronoun, so *whom* should be replaced with *who.*)

First aid will be available to *whomever* requires it.
She requires it.
(*She* is a subject-case pronoun, so *whomever* should be replaced with *whoever.*)

Q: The Civil War's <u>bloodiest battle was initiated on behalf of those, the indentured black slaves, for who life was most precious</u>.

(A) bloodiest battle was initiated on behalf of those, the indentured black slaves, for who life was most precious

(B) indentured black slaves, for whom life was most precious, initiated the war's bloodiest battle

(C) ***

(D) ***

(E) bloodiest battle was initiated on behalf of the indentured black slaves, for whom life was most precious

The correct answer is (E). The original sentence suffers from two flaws. First, the relative pronoun *who* should be replaced with *whom*. (Replace the last clause with: *Life was most precious for them.* The pronoun *them* is an object-case pronoun, so the correct choice is *whom.*) Secondly, the word *those*, probably intended to refer to the slaves, should be omitted because it is unnecessary and because it confuses the meaning of the sentence. The comma following *those* should also be omitted. Choice (E) corrects both flaws. Choice (B) also corrects both flaws, but it radically alters the sentence's meaning, improperly suggesting that the slaves initiated the bloodiest battle (rather than properly communicating that it was on the slaves' behalf that the battle was fought).

Error in Pronoun-Antecedent Agreement

An *antecedent* is simply the noun to which a pronoun refers. In GMAT sentences, make sure that pronouns agree in *number* (singular or plural) with their antecedents.

SINGULAR: Studying other artists actually helps a young *painter* develop *his* or *her* own style.

PLURAL: Studying other artists actually helps young *painters* develop *their* own style.

Singular pronouns are generally used in referring to antecedents such as *each, either, neither,* and *one*.

CORRECT: *Neither* of the two countries imposes an income tax on *its* citizens.

CORRECT: *One* cannot be too kind to *oneself*.

Q: <u>Many powerful leaders throughout history, such as President Nixon during the Watergate debacle, had become victimized by his own paranoia.</u>

(A) Many powerful leaders throughout history, such as President Nixon during the Watergate debacle, had become victimized by his own paranoia.

(B) Many powerful leaders throughout history, such as President Nixon during the Watergate debacle, have become victims of their own paranoia.

(C) Throughout history, many a powerful leader, such as President Nixon during the Watergate debacle, have by his or her own paranoia become a victim.

(D) ***

(E) ***

The correct answer is (B). The original sentence intends to make the point that *many leaders* (plural) *have* (plural verb) become victimized by *their* (plural pronoun) own paranoia. However, by using the singular *had* and *his*, the final clause seems to refer to Nixon instead of to leaders. Choice (B) correctly uses the plurals *have* and *their*. In choice (C), the plural subject leaders has been transformed into a singular subject (*many a powerful leader*). This form is grammatically acceptable. However, the subject's verb, as well as any pronouns that refer to the subject, should now be singular as well. Although the singular *his or her* is correct, the plural verb *have* is incorrect. Choice (C) also separates the words *have* and *become*. These two words are part of the same grammatical unit, which should not be split.

Error in Pronoun Reference

A pronoun (e.g., *she, him, their, its*) is a "shorthand" way of referring to an identifiable noun—person(s), place(s) or thing(s). Nouns to which pronouns refer are called *antecedents*. Make sure every pronoun in a sentence has a clear antecedent!

UNCLEAR: Minutes before Kevin's meeting with Paul, *his* wife called with the bad news. (Whose wife called—Kevin's or Paul's?)

CLEAR: *Kevin's* wife called with the bad news minutes before *his* meeting with Paul.

CLEAR: Minutes before Kevin's meeting with Paul, *Kevin's* wife called with the bad news.

Pronoun reference errors are usually corrected in one of two ways:

1. By placing the noun and pronoun as near as possible to each other, without other nouns coming between them (second sentence above)

2. Replacing the pronoun with its antecedent (third sentence above)

Also, look for the vague use of *it, you, that,* or *one*—without clear reference to a particular antecedent.

VAGUE: When the planets are out of alignment, *it* can be disastrous. (*It* does not refer to any noun)

CLEAR: Disaster can occur when the planets are out of alignment.

Q: Email accounts administered by <u>an employer belong to them, and they can be seized and used</u> as evidence against the employee.

(A) an employer belongs to them, and they can be seized and used

(B) employers belong to them, who can seize and use it

(C) an employer belong to the employer, who can seize and use the accounts

(D) ***

(E) ***

The correct answer is (C). There are two pronoun problems in the original sentence. First, the word *them* is used vaguely, without clear reference to *employers,* which seems to be the intended antecedent. Adding to this confusion is the fact that the pronoun *them* is plural, yet its intended antecedent, *employer,* is singular. Second, the antecedent of *they* is unclear because *they* is separated from its intended antecedent *accounts* by two other nouns (*them* and *employer*). Choice (C) corrects the first problem by replacing the pronoun *them* with its (singular) antecedent *employer.* Choice (C) also corrects the second problem by using *who,* which clearly refers to *employer,* since the two words appear immediately next to each other. Choice (B) is riddled with problems! First, choice (B) does not correct the vague

use of *them* (although the use of the plural *employers* is an improvement). Second, choice (B) leaves it unclear as to which noun *who* refers; presumably, *who* refers to *them,* yet the antecedent of *them* is uncertain. Third, although the pronoun *it* is intended to refer to *accounts,* the reference is unclear because the pronoun and antecedent are separated by other nouns. Finally, the pronoun *it* is singular, yet its antecedent *accounts* is plural. (Both should be either singular or plural.)

GRAMMATICAL ERRORS IN SUBJECT-VERB AGREEMENT

A sentence's subject, which is always a noun, should be consistent—either singular or plural— with the verb that refers to the subject. Problems in subject-verb agreement typically arise in these two scenarios:

- the verb is separated from the subject
- when the subject is either a pronoun or a compound subject

Error in Subject-Verb Agreement (When the Verb Is Separated From Its Subject)

A verb should always "agree" in number—either singular or plural—with its subject. Don't be fooled by any words or phrases that might separate the verb from its subject. In each sentence below, the singular verb *was* agrees with its subject, the singular noun *parade*:

CORRECT: The *parade was* spectacular.

CORRECT: The *parade* of cars *was* spectacular.

CORRECT: The *parade* of cars and horses *was* spectacular.

An intervening clause set off by commas can serve as an especially effective "smokescreen" for a subject-verb agreement error. Pay careful attention to what comes immediately before and after the intervening clause. Reading the sentence without the clause might reveals a subject-verb agreement error.

INCORRECT: John, as well as his sister, *were* absent from school yesterday.

CORRECT: *John,* as well as his sister, *was* absent from school yesterday.

Q: Grade school instruction in ethical and social values, particularly the <u>values of respect and of tolerance, are</u> required for any democracy to thrive.

(A) values of respect and of tolerance, are

(B) value of respect, together with tolerance, is

(C) values of respect and tolerance, is

(D) ***

(E) ***

The correct answer is (C). In the original sentence, the subject of the plural verb *are* is the singular noun *instruction*. The correct answer choice must correct this subject-verb agreement problem. Also, the second *of* in the underlined phrase should be omitted because its use results in an awkward and nonsensical clause, which seems to suggest that *of tolerance* is a value. Both choices (B) and (C) correct the problem by changing *are* to *is* and by dropping the second *of*. However, choice (B) creates two new problems. First, using the word *value* instead of *values* distorts the meaning of the underlined phrase. Respect and tolerance are not referred to in choice (B) as values. However, the original sentence, considered as a whole, clearly intends to refer to respect and tolerance as examples of ethical and social *values*. Secondly, the phrase *together with tolerance* (set off by commas), adds an unnecessary clause and results in a sentence that is wordy and awkward. Choice (C) is more clear and concise.

Error in Subject-Verb Agreement (Pronoun and Compound Subjects)

You can easily determine whether a personal pronoun such as *he*, *they*, or *its* is singular or plural. But other pronouns are not so easily identified as either singular or plural. Here are two lists, along with some sample sentences, to help you keep these pronouns straight in your mind:

Singular pronouns:

anyone, anything, anybody

each

either, neither

every, everyone, everything, everybody

nobody, no one, nothing

what, whatever

who, whom, whoever, whomever

Even when they refer to a "compound" subject joined by *and*, the pronouns listed above remain *singular*.

> **CORRECT:** *Each adult and child* here *speaks* fluent French.
> **CORRECT:** *Every* possible *cause and suspect was* investigated.

Plural pronouns:

both

few

many

several

some

others

It's especially easy to overlook a subject-verb agreement problem in a sentence involving a compound subject (multiple subjects joined by connectors such as the word *and* or the word *or*). If joined by *and*, a compound subject is usually plural (and takes a plural verb). But if joined by *or*, *either...or*, or *neither...nor*, compound subjects are usually singular.

> **PLURAL:** The chorus *and* the introduction *need* improvement.
> **SINGULAR:** *Either* the chorus *or* the introduction *needs* improvement.
> **SINGULAR:** *Neither* the chorus *nor* the introduction *needs* improvement.

Q: Neither his financial patron nor Copernicus <u>himself were expecting the societal backlash resulting from him</u> denouncing the Earth-centered Ptolemaic model of the universe.

(A) himself were expecting the societal backlash resulting from him

(B) ***

(C) himself was expecting the societal backlash resulting from his

(D) were expecting the societal backlash resulting from his

(E) ***

The correct answer is (C). The original sentence contains two grammatical errors. First, the singular verb *was* should be used instead of the plural *were* because *neither...nor* calls for a singular subject and because both parts of the subject (*patron* and *Copernicus*) are singular. Secondly, the phrase *him denouncing* is improper; *denouncing* is a gerund (a verb turned into a noun by adding *-ing*), and gerunds always take possessive pronouns (*his* in this case). Choice (C) corrects both errors without creating any new ones. Choice (D) corrects the first error, but not the second one. Also, notice that choice (D) omits *himself*. In doing so, choice (D) actually obscures the intended meaning of the sentence, which makes it clear, through the use of *himself*, that the word "his"

(appearing twice in the sentence) refers to Copernicus rather than to someone else. So choice (D) actually creates a new problem.

IF YOU HAVE MORE TIME TODAY

To practice the Sentence Correction tips you learned today, log on to the author's GMAT Web site (www.west.net/~stewart/gmat) and attempt a Sentence Correction mini-test. (To find the mini-test click on "Verbal Ability" in the "Test Yourself" area.) Some of the mini-test questions will cover the rules of grammar you reviewed today, while others will cover tomorrow's topics. So this mini-test can serve as both a *review* and a *preview*!

Day 10

Sentence Correction Lesson 2: Grammar Review, Effective Expression

Today's Topics:

1. Problems with the Sentence as a Unit
2. Problems with Tense, Voice, and Mood
3. Problems with Placement of Modifying Phrases
4. Faulty Parallelism
5. Use of Too Many (or Too Few) Words

Today you'll continue to grapple with grammar, broadening your focus to problems involving *phrases* and *entire sentences*. You'll also learn to recognize and remedy *ineffective expression* when you see it on the GMAT.

PROBLEMS WITH THE SENTENCE AS A UNIT

In GMAT Sentence Correction, you might encounter any of the following three problems involving the sentence as a unit:

- Two main clauses are connected improperly.
- The so-called "sentence" is only a fragment of a complete sentence.
- Part of the sentence is out of balance with another part.

Two Main Clauses Connected Improperly

A *main clause* is any clause that can stand alone as a complete sentence. There's nothing wrong with combining two main clauses into one sentence—as long

as the clauses are properly connected. On the GMAT, look for any of these three flaws:

1. No punctuation between main clauses
2. A comma between main clauses but no connecting word (such as *and, or, but, yet, for*)
3. A confusing or inappropriate connecting word

Q: The Aleutian Islands of Alaska include many islands near the mainland, <u>the majority of them are</u> uninhabited by humans.

(A) the majority of them are

(B) ***

(C) yet the majority of them are

(D) ***

(E) so the majority of them are

The correct answer is (C). Notice that choice (C) includes a connecting word (*yet*) that gives the sentence a reasonable meaning—by underscoring the contrast between the mainland (which is populated) and the unpopulated nearby islands. Although choice (E) adds a connecting word (*so*), this word is inappropriate—inferring that the islands are unpopulated *be-*

cause they are near the mainland. The resulting sentence is nonsensical, so choice (E) can't be the best answer choice. (By the way: In the foregoing sentence, notice the appropriate use of *so* as a connector!)

Sentence Fragments (Incomplete Sentences)

Unless a sentence includes both a subject and a predicate, it is incomplete and is known as a *sentence fragment*.

FRAGMENT: Expensive private colleges, generally out of financial reach for most families with college-aged children.
FRAGMENT: Without question, responsibility for building and maintaining safe bridges.

An especially long fragment might escape your detection if you're not paying close attention.

Q: One cannot deny that, even after the initial flurry of the feminist movement subsided, Congresswoman Bella Abzug, undeniably her female constituency's truest voice, <u>as well as its most public advocate</u>.

(A) as well as its most public advocate

(B) who was her constituency's most public advocate

(C) ***

(D) was also its most public advocate

(E) ***

The correct answer is (D). If you use choice (D), the sentence can be distilled down to this: *One cannot deny that Bella Abzug was its [the feminist movement's] most public advocate.* Adding the verb *was* is the key to transforming the original fragment into a complete sentence. Neither choice (A) nor choice (D) provides the verb needed for a complete sentence.

Part of a Sentence
out of Balance with Another Part

An effective sentence gets its point across by placing appropriate emphasis on its different parts. If you're dealing with two equally important ideas, they should be separated as two distinct "main clauses," and they should be similar in length (to suggest equal importance).

UNBALANCED: Julie and Sandy were the first two volunteers for the fund-raising drive, *and* they are twins.
BALANCED: Julie and Sandy, *who* are twins, were the first two volunteers for the fund-raising drive.

COMMINGLED (CONFUSING): Julie and Sandy, *who* are twins, are volunteers.
SEPARATED (BALANCED): Julie and Sandy are twins, *and* they are volunteers.

On the other hand, if you're dealing with only one main idea, be sure that it receives greater emphasis (as a main clause) than the other ideas in the sentence.

EQUAL EMPHASIS (CONFUSING): Jose and Victor were identical twins, *and* they had completely different ambitions.
EMPHASIS ON SECOND CLAUSE (BETTER): *Although* Jose and Victor were identical twins, they had completely different ambitions.

Q: <u>Treating bodily disorders by noninvasive methods is generally painless, and these methods</u> are less likely than those of conventional Western medicine to result in permanent healing.

(A) Treating bodily disorders by noninvasive methods is generally painless, and these methods

(B) Treating bodily disorders by noninvasive methods is generally painless, but they

(C) ***

(D) ***

(E) Although treating bodily disorders by noninvasive methods is generally painless, these methods

The correct answer is (E). Notice that the original sentence contains two main clauses, connected by *and*. Two problems should have occurred to you as you read the sentence: (1) the connector *and* is inappropriate to contrast differing methods of treatment (it fails to get the point across), and (2) the second clause expresses the more important point but does not receive greater emphasis than the first clause. Choice (E) corrects both problems by transforming the first clause into a subordinate one and by eliminating the connecting word *and*. What about choice (B)? Replacing *and* with *but* is not as effective in shifting the emphasis to the second clause as the method used in choice (E). Moreover, by replacing *these methods* with *they*, choice (B) creates a pronoun-reference problem: It is unclear whether *they* refers to *disorders* or to *methods*.

PROBLEMS WITH TENSE, VOICE, AND MOOD

A sentence should be proper and consistent in tense, voice, and mood. In this section, I'll define each of these three concepts and show you common Sentence Correction errors involving each one—and how to fix them.

Error in Verb Tense

Tense refers to how a verb's form indicates the *time frame* (past, present or future) of the sentence's action. An incorrect sentence might needlessly *mix* tenses or *shift* tense from one timeframe to another in a confusing manner.

> **INCORRECT:** If it rains tomorrow, we cancel our plans.
> **CORRECT:** If it rains tomorrow, we *will cancel* our plans.

> **INCORRECT:** By the time Bill arrived, Sal still did not begin to unload the truck.
> **CORRECT:** By the time Bill *had* arrived, Sal still *had not begun* to unload the truck.

Q: Companies that <u>fail in their making cost-of-living adjustments of salaries of workers could not</u> attract or retain competent employees.

   (A) fail in their making cost-of-living adjustments of salaries of workers could not

   (B) ***

   (C) ***

   (D) will fail to adjust worker salaries to reflect cost-of-living changes can neither

   (E) fail to make cost-of-living adjustments in their workers' salaries cannot

The correct answer is (E). The original sentence mixes present tense (*fail*) with past tense (*could not attract*). Also, the phrases *fail in their making* and *of salaries of workers* are awkward and unnecessarily wordy. Choice (E) renders the sentence consistent in tense by replacing *could* with *can*. Choice (E) is also more concise than the original sentence. Choice (D) improperly mixes future tense (*will fail*) with present tense (*can...retain*). Choice (D) also uses *neither* to form the improper correlative pair *neither...or*. (The proper correlative is *neither...nor*.)

Unnecessary Use of the Passive Voice

In a sentence expressed in the *active voice*, the subject "acts upon" an object. Conversely, in a sentence expressed in the passive voice, the subject "is acted upon" by an object. The passive voice can sound a bit awkward, so the active voice is generally preferred.

> **PASSIVE (AWKWARD):** Repetitive tasks are performed tirelessly by computers.
> **ACTIVE (BETTER):** Computers perform repetitive tasks tirelessly.

Mixing the active and passive voices results in an even more awkward sentence.

> **MIXED (AWKWARD):** Although the house was built by Gary, Kevin built the garage.
> **PASSIVE (LESS AWKWARD):** Although the house was built by Gary, the garage was built by Kevin.
> **ACTIVE (PREFERRED):** Although Gary built the house, Kevin built the garage.

Although the active voice is usually less awkward than the passive voice, sometimes the passive voice is appropriate for emphasis or impact.

> **ACTIVE (LESS EFFECTIVE):** Yesterday a car hit me.
> **PASSIVE (MORE EFFECTIVE):** Yesterday, I was hit by a car.

ACTIVE (LESS EFFECTIVE): Only the sun itself *surpasses* the Tetons in beauty.
PASSIVE (MORE EFFECTIVE): Sunrise over the Tetons *is surpassed* in beauty only *by* the sun itself.

Keep in mind that the passive voice is *not* grammatically wrong. So, don't eliminate an answer choice merely because it uses the passive voice. Check for grammatical errors among all five choices. If the one that uses the passive voice is the only one without a grammatical error, then it's the best choice.

Q: It is actually a chemical in the brain that creates the sensation of eating enough, a chemical that is depleted by consuming simple sugars.

(A) It is actually a chemical in the brain that creates the sensation of eating enough, a chemical that is

(B) ***

(C) The sensation of having eaten enough is actually created by a chemical in the brain that is

(D) A chemical actually creates the sensation in the brain of having eaten enough, and this chemical is

(E) ***

The correct answer is (C). The original sentence isn't terrible, but it nevertheless contains two flaws. First, the awkward *eating enough* should be replaced; *having eaten enough* employs the appropriate tense here. Both choices (C) and (D) correct this flaw. Second, notice that *a chemical* appears twice in the sentence. A more effective sentence would avoid repetition. Only choice (C) avoids repeating this phrase by reconstructing the first clause. In doing so, choice (C) admittedly uses the passive voice. Nevertheless, choice (C) is more concise and less awkward overall than the original sentence. One more point about choice (D): it also creates a new problem. It separates *the sensation* from *of having eaten enough*, thereby creating an awkward and confusing clause. The phrase *in the brain* should be moved to either an earlier or later position in the sentence.

Error in Using the Subjunctive Mood

The *subjunctive mood* should be used to express a *wish* or a *contrary-to-fact* condition. These sentences should include words such as *if, had, were,* and *should.*

INCORRECT: I wish it *was* earlier.
CORRECT: I wish it *were* earlier.

INCORRECT: Suppose he speeds up suddenly.
CORRECT: Suppose he *were* to speed up suddenly.

INCORRECT: If the college lowers its tuition, I would probably enroll.
CORRECT: *Should* the college lower its tuition, I *would* probably enroll.
CORRECT: *If* the college *were* to lower its tuition, I *would* probably enroll.

The subjunctive mood can be tricky because it uses its own idiomatic verb forms and because you can't always trust your ear when it comes to catching an error. Just remember: If the sentence uses a regular verb tense (past, present, future, etc.) to express a wish or contrary-to-fact condition, then it is grammatically incorrect, even if the subjunctive verb form is also used.

Q: The Environmental Protection Agency would be overburdened by its detection and enforcement duties if it fully implemented all of its own regulations completely.

(A) if it fully implemented all of its own regulations completely.

(B) if it was to implement all of its own regulations completely.

(C) were it to fully implement all of its own regulations.

(D) ***

(E) ***

The correct answer is (C). The original sentence poses two problems. First, the sentence clearly intends to express a hypothetical or contrary-to-fact situation; yet the underlined phrase does not use the subjunctive *were.* Second, *fully* and *completely* are redundant; one of them should be omitted. Choice (C) corrects both problems without creating a new one. Choice (B) corrects the redundancy problem by deleting *fully*. However, it incorrectly uses *was* instead of the subjunctive *were*.

PROBLEMS WITH PLACEMENT OF MODIFYING PHRASES

A *modifier* is a phrase that describes, restricts, or qualifies another word or phrase. A vague or improperly placed modifier can render a sentence ambiguous, confusing, or awkward (or all three).

Improper Placement of Modifiers

Modifying phrases are typically set off with commas, and many such phrases begin with a relative pronoun (*which, who, that, whose, whom*). Modifiers should generally be placed as close as possible to the word(s) they modify. Positioning a modifier in the wrong place can result in a confusing or even nonsensical sentence.

> **MISPLACED:** His death shocked the entire family, which occurred quite suddenly.
> **BETTER:** His death, which occurred quite suddenly, shocked the entire family.

> **UNCLEAR:** Bill punched Carl while wearing a mouth protector.
> **CLEAR:** While wearing a mouth protector, Bill punched Carl.

Q: Exercising contributes frequently to not only a sense of well being but also to longevity.

  (A) Exercising contributes frequently to not only a sense of well being but also to longevity.

  (B) ***

  (C) Exercising frequently contributes not only to a sense of well being but to longevity.

  (D) ***

  (E) Frequent exercise contributes not only to a sense of well being but also to longevity.

The correct answer is (E). In the original sentence, *frequently* is probably intended to describe (modify) *exercising* (frequent exercise). But separating these words makes it appear as though *frequently* describes *contributing*, which makes no sense in the overall context of the sentence. The original sentence also suffers from so-called "faulty parallelism." The phrase following *not only* should parallel the phrase following *but also*, so that the two phrases can be interchanged and still make sense grammatically. But in the original sentence, the two phrases are not parallel. (You'll explore faulty parallelism in more detail later today.) Choice (E) corrects both problems. In choice (E), it is clear that what is "frequent" is *exercise* (rather than *contributing*). Also, the phrases following each part of the *not only...but also* pair are now parallel. (Notice that each phrase begins with *to*.) Choice (C) fails to clear up the confusion as to whether *frequently* describes *exercising* or *contributes*. Also, choice (C) improperly uses *not only...but* instead of the proper idiom *not only...but also*.

Improper Splitting of a Grammatical Unit

Splitting apart clauses or phrases (by inserting another clause between them) often results in an awkward and confusing sentence.

> **SPLIT:** The government's goal this year *is to provide* for its poorest residents *an economic safety net.*
> **SPLIT:** *The government's goal* is to provide an economic safety net *this year* for its poorest residents.
> **BETTER:** The government's goal this year is to provide an economic safety net for its poorest residents.

Whenever you see a clause set off by commas in the middle of the sentence, check the words immediately before and after the clause. If keeping those words together would sound better to your ear or would more effectively convey the sentence's main point, then the sentence (answer choice) is wrong, and you can safely eliminate it.

Q: Typographer Lucian Bernhard was influenced, perhaps more so than any of his contemporaries, by Toulouse-Lautrec's emphasis on large, unharmonious lettering.

(A) Typographer Lucian Bernhard was influenced, perhaps more so than any of his contemporaries, by Toulouse-Lautrec's emphasis on large, unharmonious lettering.

(B) Perhaps more so than any of his contemporaries, typographer Lucian Bernhard was influenced by Toulouse-Lautrec's emphasis on large, unharmonious lettering.

(C) ***

(D) ***

(E) Typographer Lucian Bernhard was influenced by Toulouse-Lautrec's emphasis on large, unharmonious lettering perhaps more so than any of his contemporaries.

The correct answer is (B). The original sentence awkwardly splits the main clause with an intervening subordinate one (set off by commas). Both choices (B) and (E) keep the main clause intact. However, choice (E) creates a pronoun reference problem. In choice (E), it is unclear as to whom the pronoun *his* refers—Bernhard or Toulouse-Lautrec.

Dangling Modifier Errors

A *dangling modifier* is a modifier that doesn't refer to any particular word(s) in the sentence. The best way to correct a dangling-modifier error is to reconstruct the sentence.

> **DANGLING:** *Set by an arsonist*, firefighters were unable to save the burning building. (This sentence makes no reference to whatever was set by an arsonist.)
> **BETTER:** Firefighters were unable to save the burning building from *the fire set by an arsonist*.

Q: By imposing artificial restrictions in price on oil suppliers, these suppliers will be forced to lower production costs.

(A) By imposing artificial restrictions in price on oil suppliers, these suppliers will be forced

(B) Imposing artificial price restrictions on oil suppliers will force these suppliers

(C) By imposing on oil suppliers artificial price restrictions, these suppliers will be forced

(D) ***

(E) ***

The correct answer is (B). The original sentence includes a dangling modifier. The sentence makes no reference to whomever (or whatever) is imposing the price restrictions. Choice (B) corrects the problem by reconstructing the sentence. Choice (B) also improves on the original sentence by replacing *restrictions in price* with the more concise *price restrictions*. Choice (C) does not correct the dangling modifier problem. Also, the grammatical construction of the first clause in choice (C) is awkward and confusing.

Too Many Subordinate Clauses in a Row

A "subordinate clause" is one that does not stand on its own as a complete sentence. Stringing together two or more subordinate clauses can result in an awkward and confusing sentence.

> **AWKWARD:** Barbara's academic major is history, *which* is a very popular course of study among liberal arts students *who* are also contributing to the popularity of political science as a major.
> **BETTER:** Barbara's academic major is history, which, along with political science, is a very popular course of study among liberal arts students.

Q: By relying unduly on anecdotal evidence, which often conflicts with more reliable data, including data from direct observation and measurement, a scientist risks losing credibility among his or her peers.

(A) By relying unduly on anecdotal evidence, which often conflicts with more reliable data, including data from direct observation and measurement, a scientist risks losing credibility among his or her peers.

(B) ***

(C) ***

(D) A scientist, by relying unduly on anecdotal evidence, which often conflicts with more reliable data, including data from direct observation and measurement, risks losing credibility among his or her peers.

(E) A scientist risks losing credibility among his or her peers by relying unduly on anecdotal evidence, which often conflicts with more reliable data, including data from direct observation and measurement.

The correct answer is (E). The original sentence contains four clauses (separated by commas). The first three are all subordinate clauses. The result is that you are left in suspense as to who unduly relies on anecdotal evidence (first clause) until you reach the last (and main) clause. The solution is to rearrange the sentence to join the first and last clauses, thereby minimizing the string of subordinate clauses and eliminating confusion. Choice (E) provides this solution. Choice (D) solves the problem only partially—by moving only part of the main clause (*the scientist*) to the beginning of the sentence. In fact, in doing so choice (D) creates more confusion.

FAULTY PARALLELISM

When a sentence is intended to equate two or more phrases, grammatically speaking, the sentence should have similarly constructed phrases. Otherwise, the sentence results in what is referred to as *faulty parallelism*. In GMAT Sentence Correction, be on the lookout for faulty parallelism involving:

- Lists, or strings, of items
- So-called "correlatives"

Faulty Parallelism (Lists)

Sentence elements that are grammatically equal—such as a list, or "string," of items—should be constructed similarly. Whenever you see a string of items, look particularly for inconsistent or mixed use of:

- prepositions (such as *in*, *with*, or *on*)
- gerunds (verbs with an *-ing* added to the end)
- infinitives (plural verbs preceded by *to*)
- articles (such as *a* and *the*)

FAULTY: Among *the* mountains, *the* sea, and desert, we humans have yet to fully explore only the sea.
PARALLEL: Among *the* mountains, sea, and desert, we humans have yet to fully explore only the sea.
PARALLEL: Among *the* mountains, *the* sea, and *the* desert, we humans have yet to fully explore only the sea.

FAULTY: Being understaffed, lack of funding, and being outpaced by competitors soon resulted in the fledgling company's going out of business. (Only two of the three listed items begin with the gerund *being*.)
PARALLEL: Understaffed, underfunded, and outpaced by competitors, the fledgling company soon went out of business.

Q: Long before the abolition of slavery, many freed indentured servants were able to acquire property, <u>to interact with people of other races, and maintain</u> their freedom.

(A) to interact with people of other races and maintain

(B) ***

(C) interact with people of other races, and maintain

(D) to interact with people of other races, as well as maintaining

(E) ***

The correct answer is (C). Notice the string of three items in this sentence. In the original version, the second item repeats the preposition to, but the third item does not. Choice (C) corrects this faulty parallelism. Choice (E) improperly mixes the use of a prepositional phrase (beginning with *to*) with a construction that instead uses a gerund (*maintaining*).

Faulty Parallelism (Correlatives)

You just saw how items in a list can suffer from faulty parallelism. Now look at how this problem shows up in what are called *correlatives*. Here are the most commonly used correlatives:

- Either...or...
- Neither...nor...
- Both...and...
- Not only...but also...

Whenever you spot a correlative in a sentence, make sure that the element immediately following the first correlative term is parallel in construction to the element following the second term.

> **FAULTY:** All students wishing to participate should *either* contact us by telephone *or* should send email to us.
> **PARALLEL:** All students wishing to participate should *either* contact us by telephone *or* send email to us.

Q: Species diversity in the Amazon basin results <u>not from climate stability, as once believed, but</u> climate disturbances.

   (A) not from climate stability, as once believed, but

   (B) ***

   (C) not only from climate stability, as once believed, but instead from

   (D) ***

   (E) not from climate stability, as once believed, but rather from

The correct answer is (E). As it stands, the original sentence might carry one of two very different meanings: (1) stability and disturbances *both* contribute to species diversity or (2) disturbances, *but not* stability, contribute to species diversity. The reason for the ambiguity is the use of an improper correlative as well as faulty parallelism (*from* appears only in the first correlative term). The correct answer choice must make the sentence's meaning clear, probably by using one of two correlatives: *not only...but also* or *not...but rather...*Also, the two correlative terms must be parallel. Choice (E) corrects the faulty parallelism (*from* appears in each correlative term) and clears up the sentence's meaning. Although choice (B) corrects the faulty parallelism, it uses the nonsensical (and improper) correlative *not only...but instead*.

USE OF TOO MANY (OR TOO FEW) WORDS

A sentence that is grammatically correct might nevertheless be ineffective because it uses either more or fewer words than needed to convey its intended meaning. In this section, we'll look at four distinct problems:

- *Redundancy* (needlessly conveying the same idea twice in a sentence)
- *Superfluous* words (unnecessary words, which can simply be omitted)
- *Wordiness* and *awkwardness* (where a phrase can be made more simple, clear, and/or concise)
- *Omission* (where a key word is missing, possibly resulting in an illogical sentence)

Redundant Words and Phrases

Look for words and phrases that express the same essential idea twice. This syndrome is known as "redundancy." In many cases, correcting the problem is as simple as omitting one of the redundant phrases. On the GMAT, redundancies are most likely to spring up in sentences having the following themes and keywords:

- Words establishing cause-and-effect (*because, since, if, then, therefore*)
- References to time (*age, years, hours, days*)
- Words used in conjunctions (*both, as well, too, also*)
  REDUNDANT: *The reason that* we stopped for the night was *because* we were sleepy.
  REDUNDANT: *Because* we were sleepy, we *therefore* stopped for the night.
  BETTER: We stopped for the night because we were sleepy.

  REDUNDANT: The German Oktoberfest takes place *each October of every year.*
  BETTER: The German Oktoberfest takes place *every October.*

REDUNDANT: *Both* unemployment *as well as* interest rates can affect stock prices.
BETTER: Unemployment levels and interest rates both can affect stock prices.
BETTER: Unemployment levels as well as interest rates can affect stock prices.

Q: Due to a negligible difference in Phase III results as between patients using the drug and those using a placebo, the Food and Drug Administration refused to approve it on this basis.

(A) Due to a negligible difference in Phase III results as between patients using the drug and those using a placebo, the Food and Drug Administration refused to approve the drug on this basis.

(B) The Food and Drug Administration refused to approve the drug based upon a negligible difference in Phase III results as between patients using it and those using a placebo.

(C) Due to a negligible difference in Phase III results as between patients using the drug and those using a placebo, the Food and Drug Administration refused to approve the drug.

(D) ***

(E) ***

The correct answer is (C). There are three distinct problems with the original version. First, *due to* and *on this basis* serve the same function—to express that the FDA's refusal was based on the Phase III results. (The redundancy is easy to miss since one phrase begins the sentence while the other phrase ends it.) Second, the intended antecedent of *it* is *the drug*, but the intervening noun *placebo* obscures the reference. Third, the sentence is ambiguous. Did the FDA refuse to approve the drug, or did it approve the drug on some basis other than the one mentioned in the sentence? The sentence is ambiguous as to which meaning is intended. Choice (C) corrects all three problems, simply by omitting *on this basis* and by replacing *it* with *the drug*. Choice (B) corrects the first two problems—by omitting *due to* and reconstructing the sentence. But choice (B) fails to clarify the meaning of the sentence.

Superfluous (Unnecessary) Words

You just looked at one variety of unnecessary verbiage: redundancy. Now look at some other kinds of sentences in which certain words can simply be omitted without affecting the meaning or effectiveness of the original sentence. Remember: Briefer is better!

Each sentence in the first group below contains an *ellipsis*: a word or phrase that can be omitted because it is clearly implied. (In the incorrect version, the ellipsis is italicized.)

SUPERFLUOUS: The warmer the weather *is,* the more crowded the beach *is.*
CONCISE: The warmer the weather, the more crowded the beach.

SUPERFLUOUS: He looks exactly like Francis *looks.*
CONCISE: He looks exactly like Francis.

SUPERFLUOUS: That *shirt* is the ugliest *shirt that* I have ever seen.
CONCISE: That is the ugliest shirt I have ever seen.

Each sentence in the next group includes a superfluous preposition. (In the incorrect version, the preposition is italicized.)

SUPERFLUOUS: One prominent futurist predicts a nuclear holocaust by the year *of* 2020.
CONCISE: One prominent futurist predicts a nuclear holocaust by the year 2020.

SUPERFLUOUS: The children couldn't help *from* laughing at the girl with the mismatched shoes.
CONCISE: The children couldn't help laughing at the girl with the mismatched shoes.

SUPERFLUOUS: The waiter brought half *of* a loaf of bread to the table.
CONCISE: The waiter brought half a loaf of bread to the table.

Superfluous words can also appear in a series of parallel clauses. Both versions of the next sentence use proper parallelism, but briefer is better—as long as the meaning of the sentence is clear.

> **SUPERFLUOUS:** My three goals in life are to be healthy, *to be* wealthy, and *to be* wise.
> **CONCISE:** My three goals in life are to be healthy, wealthy, and wise.

Q: Only through a comprehensive, federally funded vaccination program can a new epidemic of tuberculosis be curbed, just like the spread of both cholera <u>as well as the spread of typhoid was curbed</u>.

   (A) as well as the spread of typhoid was curbed

   (B) ***

   (C) ***

   (D) and typhoid

   (E) as well as typhoid was curbed

The correct answer is (D). The original version contains no fewer than three distinct verbiage problems. First, the correlative *both...as well as* is redundant (and improper). Since *both* is not underlined, *as well as* should be replaced with *and*. Second, because the preposition *like* sets up an ellipsis, *were curbed* is implied and can be omitted. Third, the second occurrence of *the spread of* can be omitted because it is implied through a parallel construction. Choice (D) pares down the underlined phrase to its most concise form. Choice (E) fails to correct the redundant correlative *both...as well as*. Choice (E) also fails to omit the unnecessary *was curbed*.

Wordy and Awkward Phrases

Just because a sentence is grammatically acceptable, you shouldn't assume that there is no room for improvement. You've already seen that unnecessary words can sometimes be omitted, thereby improving a GMAT sentence. Now look at some phrases that can be *replaced* with clearer, more concise phrases.

> **WORDY:** There are fewer buffalo on the plains today than *there ever were* before.
> **CONCISE:** There are fewer buffalo on the plains today than *ever* before.

> **WORDY:** Discipline is crucial to *the attainment of* one's objectives.
> **CONCISE:** Discipline is crucial to *attaining* one's objectives.

> **AWKWARD:** Calcification *is when* (or *is where*) calcium deposits form around a bone.
> **CLEARER:** Calcification *occurs when* calcium deposits form around a bone.

> **AWKWARD:** The wind poses a serious threat to the old tree and *so does* the snow.
> **CLEARER:** The wind and snow both pose a serious threat to the old tree.

The wordy and awkward phrases that the GMAT CAT can throw at you are limited in variety only by the collective imagination of the test makers. So, the phrases I've provided here are just a small sampling.

Q: To avoid confusion between oral medications, <u>different pills' coatings should have different colors, and pills should be different in shape and size</u>.

   (A) different pills' coatings should have different colors, and pills should be different in shape and size

   (B) pills should differ in color as well as in shape and size

   (C) ***

   (D) pills should be able to be distinguished by their color, shape, and size

   (E) ***

The correct answer is (B). There are several problems with the original version. The first is that *different pills' coatings* is very awkward. Second, the word *coatings* is probably superfluous here; *color* suffices to make the point. Thirdly, *have different colors* is awkward (*differ in color* would be better). Fourth, the phrase *be different* is ambiguous (different from what?). Finally, a parallel series including color, shape, and size would be more concise and less awkward than the construction used in the original version. Choice (B) corrects all these problems. In choice (D), the phrase *be able to be distinguished* awkwardly mixes the active and passive voices. The phrase *be distinguishable* would be better.

Omission of Necessary Words

On the flip side of redundancy and wordiness is the error of *omission*. The exclusion of a necessary word can obscure or confuse the meaning of the sentence. Check for the omission of key "little" words—prepositions, pronouns, conjunctives, and especially the word *that*.

> **OMISSION:** The newscaster announced the voting results were incorrect. (What did the newscaster announce: the results or the fact that the results were incorrect?)
> **CLEARER:** The newscaster announced *that* the voting results were incorrect.

Look out especially for an omission that results in an illogical comparison, as in the following sentences. It can easily slip by you if you're not careful!

> **ILLOGICAL:** The color of the blouse is different from the skirt.
> (This sentence illogically compares a color with a skirt.)
> **LOGICAL:** The color of the blouse is different from *that* of the skirt.

> **ILLOGICAL:** China's population is larger than that of any country in the world.
> (This sentence suggests illogically that China is not a country.)
> **ILLOGICAL:** China's population is larger than any other country in the world.
> (This sentence suggests illogically that "population" is a country.)
> **LOGICAL:** China's population is larger than *that of* any *other* country in the world.

One little word can make all the difference! Your mind can easily trick you by filling in a key word that is not actually there. The moral here is: read every GMAT sentence slowly and carefully.

Q: Some evolutionary theorists <u>believe the main reason humans began to walk in an upright posture is they</u> needed to reach tree branches to obtain food.

   (A) believe the main reason humans began to walk in an upright posture is they

   (B) believe the main reason humans began to walk in an upright posture is that they

   (C) ***

   (D) ***

   (E) believe that the main reason humans began to walk in an upright posture is that they

The correct answer is (E). The original version commits two omission errors involving the word *that*. Choice (E) corrects these errors. Choice (B) only corrects the second omission.

IF YOU HAVE MORE TIME TODAY

For special insight about making close judgment calls between Sentence Correction answer choices, log on to the author's GMAT Web site (www.west.net/~stewart/gmat) and explore the Q&A entitled "GMAT Sentence Correction—Why Effective Expression Is Not All in the Ear of the Beholder." (You'll find it in the "Q&A Corner" of the Web site.)

Day 11

Sentence Correction Lesson 3: Mini-Test and Review

Today's Topics:

Today you will apply what you learned on Days 9 and 10 to 15 sentence correction problems. After taking this mini-test under timed conditions, review the explanations that follow.

MINI-TEST (SENTENCE CORRECTION)

Number of questions: 15
Suggested time: 20 minutes

Directions (as provided on the test):
In each of the following sentences, some part of the sentence or the entire sentence is underlined. Beneath each sentence you will find five ways of phrasing the underlined part. The first of these repeats the original; the other four are different. If you think the original is the best of these responses, choose the first response; otherwise, choose one of the others. Select the best version.

This is a test of correctness and effectiveness of expression. In choosing answers, follow the requirements of standard written English; that is, pay attention to grammar, choice of words, and sentence construction. Choose the answer that produces the most effective sentence; this answer should be clear and exact, without awkwardness, ambiguity, redundancy, or grammatical error.

1. History shows that while simultaneously attaining global or even regional dominance, a country generally succumbs to erosion of its social infrastructure.

   (A) History shows that while simultaneously attaining
   (B) History would show that while attaining
   (C) History bears out that in the course of attaining
   (D) During the course of history the attainment of
   (E) Throughout history, during any country's attaining

2. According to Newtonian physics, the greater the resistance between two particles, given the so-called "gravitational constant," the less will be the gravitational force between them.

   (A) the greater the distance between two particles, given the so-called "gravitational constant," the less will be the gravitational force between them
   (B) the greater the distance the less the gravitational force between two particles, given the so-called "gravitational constant"

(C) given the so-called "gravitational constant," more distance between two particles will result in a lesser gravitational force between them

(D) the less of a gravitational force between two particles, the more of a distance between them, given the so-called "gravitational constant"

(E) given the so-called "gravitational constant," the greater the distance between two particles, the smaller the gravitational force between them

3. For generations after Napoleon posed for his portrait with hand in vest, men, especially Civil War generals, similarly posed for their portraits.

(A) For generations after Napoleon posed for his portrait with hand in vest, men, especially Civil War generals

(B) Generations of men after Napoleon, who posed for his portrait with hand in vest, especially Civil War generals

(C) After Napoleon posed for his portrait with hand in vest, generations of men, especially Civil War generals

(D) For generations after Napoleon posed for his portrait with hand in vest, Civil War generals especially, and men in general

(E) Generations of men after Napoleon, especially Civil War generals, who posed for his portrait with hand in vest

4. To ensure the integrity of fossil evidence found at climatically unstable archeological sites, the immediate coating of newly exposed fossils with a specially formulated alkaline solution is as crucial, if not more crucial than, the prompt removal of the fossil from the site.

(A) crucial, if not more crucial than,

(B) crucial as, if not more crucial than,

(C) crucial as, if not more than crucial,

(D) crucial, if not more crucial, than

(E) crucial, if not more crucial, as

5. In 19th century Europe, a renewed interest in Middle Eastern architecture was kindled not only by increased trade but also by increased tourism and improved diplomatic relations.

(A) not only by increased trade but also by

(B) by not only increased trade but also by

(C) not only by increased trade but also

(D) not only by increased trade but

(E) by increased trade and also by

6. Upon man-made toxins invading the human body, special enzymes are deployed, rebuilding any DNA strands damaged resulting from it.

(A) Upon man-made toxins invading the human body, special enzymes are deployed, rebuilding any DNA strands damaged resulting from it.

(B) Upon man-made toxins' invasion of the human body, special enzymes are deployed that rebuild any damaged DNA strands resulting from the invasion.

(C) When man-made toxins invade the human body, special enzymes are deployed to rebuild any DNA strands damaged as a result.

(D) Special enzymes are deployed whenever man-made toxins invade the human body, which rebuild any damage that results to DNA strands.

(E) Damage to DNA strands that result when man-made toxins invade the human body are repaired by deployed special enzymes.

7. The California gold rush, the historical development instilling the greatest sense of manifest destiny in the populace, wore not the clothing of political ideology but rather a suit spun of gold and greed.

(A) The California gold rush, the historical development instilling the greatest sense of manifest destiny in the populace, wore not the clothing of political ideology but rather a suit spun of gold and greed.

(B) The historical development which most greatly instilled a sense of manifest destiny in the populace wore not the clothing of political ideology but instead a suit spun of gold and greed; it was the California gold rush.

(C) The historical development most instilling in the populace a sense of manifest destiny was the California gold rush, wearing a suit of greed and gold, not the clothing of political ideology.

(D) It was the California gold rush, not the clothing of political ideology, but rather a suit of gold and greed, that most greatly instilled in the populace a sense of manifest destiny.

(E) The greatest sense of manifest destiny in the populace was instilled by the California gold rush, which historical development wore a suit of gold and greed rather than the clothing of political ideology.

8. The government's means of disposal of war surplus following World War II met with vociferous objections by industrialists, prominent advisors, and many others.

(A) of disposal of

(B) in disposing

(C) to dispose

(D) used in disposing

(E) of disposing

9. Too many naive consumers hasty and happily provide credit information to unscrupulous "merchants," who provide nothing in exchange but a credit fraud nightmare.

(A) hasty and happily provide

(B) hastily and happily provide

(C) hasty and happy providing

(D) hastily and happily providing

(E) providing hastily and happily

10. Despite sophisticated computer models for assessing risk, such a model is nevertheless limited in their ability to define what risk is.

(A) Despite sophisticated computer models for assessing risk, such a model is nevertheless

(B) Sophisticated computer models, which assess risk, are nevertheless

(C) Despite their sophistication, computer models for assessing risk are

(D) Assessment of risk can be achieved with computer models; but their sophistication is

(E) Assessing risk with sophisticated computer models is limited because such models are

11. That which is self-evident cannot be disputed, and that in itself is self-evident.

(A) That which is self-evident cannot be disputed, and that in

(B) That that is self-evident cannot be disputed, of which

(C) It is self-evident that which cannot be disputed, and this fact

(D) The self-evident cannot be disputed, and this fact

(E) That which is self-evident cannot be disputed, which

12. If the corporate bureaucracy persists in its discriminatory hiring and job advancement practices, its chief executives will expose themselves to class-action litigation by the groups prejudiced thereby.

(A) its chief executives will expose themselves

(B) its chief executives would expose themselves

(C) their chief executives will expose themselves

(D) its chief executives themselves would become exposed

(E) the chief executives will, by themselves, be exposed

13. Of approximately one thousand chemicals in coffee, less than thirty have been tested, most of which produce cancer in laboratory rats.

(A) less than thirty have been tested, most of which produce cancer in laboratory rats

(B) most of which produce cancer in laboratory rats, fewer than thirty have been tested

(C) fewer than thirty have been tested, and most of these produce cancer in laboratory rats

(D) less than thirty of which have been tested, most of them produce cancer in laboratory rats

(E) most of the less than thirty tested produced cancer in laboratory rats

14. <u>The volatility of the "fabulous fifteen" stock index, less than eighty percent of broader stock indices.</u>

    (A) The volatility of the "fabulous fifteen" stock index, less than eighty percent of broader stock indices.

    (B) The "fabulous fifteen" stock index is less than eighty percent as volatile as broader stock indices.

    (C) The "fabulous fifteen" stock index is less than eighty percent as volatile as that of broader stock indices.

    (D) Volatility is less than eighty percent for the "fabulous fifteen" stock index compared to broader stock indices.

    (E) The volatility of the "fabulous fifteen" stock index is less than eighty percent of broader stock indices.

15. The media often hasten to malign celebrities who have come into sudden and unexpected prominence, whether <u>they be actors, musicians, or some other high-profile vocation</u>.

    (A) they be actors, musicians, or some other high-profile vocation

    (B) their vocation be acting, music, or some other high-profile vocation

    (C) they are actors, or musicians, or some other high profile vocation

    (D) their vocation is that of actor, musician, or otherwise a high-profile one

    (E) they are actors, are musicians, or in some other high-profile vocation

Quick Answer Guide

Mini-Test: Sentence Correction

1.	C	9.	B
2.	E	10.	C
3.	C	11.	D
4.	B	12.	A
5.	A	13.	C
6.	C	14.	B
7.	A	15.	B
8.	E		

EXPLANATIONS

1. The correct answer is (C). (moderate).

Choice (A) is confusing in its intended meaning; the use of the word "simultaneously" suggests that two or more items are attained. If the sentence had continued with the phrase "global and regional dominance," the use of the word "simultaneously" would have made more sense.

Choice (B) confuses the perspective (tense) of the sentence with the use of the word "would." The present tense is preferable here to convey the sentence's intended meaning.

Choice (C) excludes the confusing word "simultaneously" to clarify the sentence's meaning.

Choice (D) creates a nonsensical sentence by failing to set up a subordinate modifying clause before "a country."

Choice (E) includes the awkward phrase "during any country's attaining." Also, the use of "a country" twice is unnecessarily wordy and redundant.

2. The correct answer is (E). (moderate).

Choice (A) creates confusion by separating the two parallel clauses "the greater . . . " and "the less . . . ."

Also, "will be" is unnecessary and undermines the parallel structure of the two clauses.

Choice (B) improperly omits "between two particles" immediately following "distance," thereby creating confusion as to what the word "distance" refers to.

Choice (C) creates a faulty parallel between the two main clauses; "a lesser" should be replaced with "less" to parallel "more" in the preceding clause.

Choice (D) includes two related idiomatic problems: "the less of a" and "the more of a" are both idiomatically improper. Both phrases should exclude the word "of."

Choice (E) remedies both problems with the original sentence. The words "smaller" and "lesser" are properly used interchangeably here, because both refer to amount rather than quantity.

3. The correct answer is (C). (easier).

The original sentence, while not grammatically incorrect *per se*, awkwardly sets off "men" by itself with commas, improperly suggesting that "men" is one item in a series of items.

Choice (B) misplaces the modifying clause "especially Civil War generals"; this clause should appear closer to its antecedent ("men").

Choice (C) remedies the original sentence's problem, clarifying the sentence's meaning by positioning "generations" immediately before "men."

Choice (D) includes the awkwardly constructed phrase "Civil War generals especially, and men in general." Not only is the phrase clumsy and unnecessarily wordy, the word "general" carries a different meaning the second time that the sentence uses it, creating further confusion.

Choice (E) misplaces the modifier "especially Civil War generals," suggesting that Napoleon was a Civil War general, as well as presenting an apparent pronoun disagreement between "generals" and "his."

4. The correct answer is (B). (moderate).

The original sentence A presents an incomplete form of the idiomatic comparative phrase " . . . as [adjective] as . . . ." Removing the second comparison (set off by commas) reveals the omission of "as" ("is as crucial . . . *as*").

Choice (B) completes the form of the idiomatic phrase by including the word "as."

Choice (C) presents an incomplete form, omitting "crucial" in the second comparison.

Choice (D) improperly uses "than" instead of "as" in the first comparison ("as crucial . . . than"). At the same time, the second comparison is incomplete; the comparative clause set off by commas must embrace "than."

Choice (E) corrects only the first of the two problems with choice (D), as well as creating a new problem: The word "as" should precede (not follow) the parenthetical comparison.

5. The correct answer is (A). (moderate).

The original sentence properly uses the modifying pair "not only . . . but also." The two modifying phrases ("not only by increased" and "but also by increased") are grammatically parallel.

Choice (B) suffers from faulty parallelism. The second use of "by" is redundant.

Choice (C) also suffers from faulty parallelism: The word "by" is improperly omitted after "but also."

Choice (D) improperly uses the modifying pair "not only . . . but" instead of the idiomatically proper "not only . . . but also."

Choice (E) is awkwardly phrased; it should exclude "also."

6. The correct answer is (C). (moderate).

The original sentence is faulty in two respects. The noun clause (preceding the first comma) is awkward. Also, it is unclear what "it" refers to in the modifying prepositional phrase "from it."

Choice (B) improperly uses "that" instead of "which." Also, it is unclear what "resulting" refers to here—DNA strands or damage to the DNA strands.

Choice (C) improves on the awkward use of a noun clause in the first part of the original sentence. The infinitive "to rebuild" and the phrase "as a result" clarify the meaning of the second part of the sentence. In spite of its use of the passive voice ("enzymes are deployed"), choice (C) is the best response.

Choice (D) separates the relative pronoun "which" from its intended antecedent "enzymes."

Choice (E) improperly uses the plural "are repaired" and "result" in reference to the singular "damage." Also, the phrase "deployed special enzymes" awkwardly strings together a verb (used as an adjective) and another adjective.

7. The correct answer is (A). (challenging).

The original sentence is the best choice; it contains no errors in grammar, diction, or usage.

Choice (B) improperly uses "which" instead of "that." Also, "but rather" is idiomatically preferable to "but instead" in this sentence. Finally, this sentence's overall construction, especially considering the final clause, is somewhat awkward.

Choice (C) includes the awkward phrase "most instilling." Also, placing the phrase "in the populace" between the verb "instilling" and the direct object "a sense . . . " confuses the sentence's meaning.

Choice (D) is awkwardly constructed. The modifying phrase "a suit of gold and greed" should appear immediately after the subject to which it refers—the California gold rush.

Choice (E) uses the awkward passive construction ("was instilled by") instead of the preferred active construction ("gold rush instilled").

8. The correct answer is (E). (moderate).

Choice (A) uses "of" twice; the result is wordy and arguably idiomatically improper.

Choices (B) and (C) are idiomatically improper; a person is said to dispose *of* something.

Choice (D) is redundant in its use of the word "used"; The word "means" adequately conveys the meaning.

Choice (E) is idiomatically proper.

9. The correct answer is (B). (easier).

The original sentence improperly uses the adjective "hasty" instead of the adverb "hastily" to modify the verb "provide."

Choice (B) remedies the problem in the original sentence.

Choice (C) fails to correct the error in the original sentence and commits a similar error in its use of "happy" instead of "happily." Choice (C) also creates two successive modifying phrases ("providing . . . " and "who . . . ") but no predicate; the result is a long sentence fragment.

Choice (D) also creates a long but incomplete sentence.

Choice (E) creates confusion by separating the verb "providing" from its object "credit information." Also, like choices (C) and (D), choice (E) establishes a long but incomplete sentence.

10. The correct answer is (C). (moderate).

The original sentence is faulty in two respects. First, the singular "model" disagrees with the plural "their" (which logically refers to "models"). Second, the first clause is inconsistent in grammatical construction with the second clause, making for an awkward and confusing sentence.

Choice (B) improperly uses the modifying phrase "which assess risk" to describe computer models in general, thereby distorting the sentence's probable meaning.

Choice (C) remedies both problems in the original sentence. The plural "models" agrees with the pronoun "their," and the construction of the first clause is grammatically consistent with that of the second clause.

Choice (D) improperly modifies "sophistication" with the possessive pronoun "their." It is unclear whether "their ability" refers to "computer models" or "sophistication."

Choice (E) improperly uses the phrase "is limited" to describe "assessing risk." The computer models' ability, not assessing risk, is limited.

11. The correct answer is (D). (challenging).

Choice (A) contains a vague pronoun reference. It is unclear what the second "that" refers to.

Choice (B) improperly uses "That that" instead of the idiomatically proper "That which" in the main clause that begins the sentence. Also, the phrase "of which" leaves it unclear as to what "itself" refers.

Choice (C) reverses the subject and predicate of the main clause, resulting in a confusing and awkward sentence.

Choice (D) restates the idea of the first clause of the original sentence more succinctly and clearly, as well as making it clear by the use of "and this fact" that the idea in the latter part of the sentence refers to the earlier statement itself.

Choice (E) creates a vague and ambiguous modifying clause (following the comma). It is unclear what the relative pronoun "which" refers to.

12. The correct answer is (A). (easier).

The original sentence correctly uses the singular pronoun "its" in referring to the singular "bureaucracy." Also, choice (A) is consistent in its future tense and perspective.

Choice (B) confuses the sentence's time perspective (tense). The use of "would" calls for the use of the subjunctive in the beginning of the sentence: "should the corporate bureaucracy persist . . . ."

Choice (C) improperly uses the plural pronoun "their" in referring to the singular "bureaucracy."

Choice (D) confuses the sentence's tense in the same manner as choice (B). Also, the placement of "themselves" obscures the sentence's meaning.

Choice (E) uses an ambiguous syntax that suggests (perhaps improperly) that *only* chief executives will be exposed to class-action litigation.

13. The correct answer is (C). (moderate).

The original sentence improperly uses "less" instead of "fewer" in reference to a numerical quantity (the number of chemicals tested). Also, the modifier "most of which" is separated from its antecedent ("thirty"), resulting in confusion as to whether "most of which" refers to the thirty chemicals tested or the tests themselves.

Choice (B) confuses the meaning of the sentence by placing "most of which" immediately after "one thousand chemicals in coffee." This construction improperly suggests that one thousand chemicals produce cancer in laboratory rats.

Choice (C) remedies both problems in the original sentence.

Choice (D) improperly uses "less" instead of "fewer." Also, it is unclear whether "most of them" refers to "one thousand chemicals" or to "less than thirty"; the construction is ambiguous and confusing.

Choice (E) improperly uses "less" instead of "fewer." Also, the phrase "most of the less than" is awkward and confusing.

14. The correct answer is (B). (easier).

The original sentence is not a complete sentence.

Choice (B) completes the sentence without committing any errors in grammar or diction.

Choice (C) improperly uses "that of," which in this construction refers to nothing (it is a dangling modifier).

Choice (D) is nonsensical; the basis for comparison as well as what is being compared is ambiguous.

Choice (E) improperly (and nonsensically) suggests that volatility is less than eighty percent of "broader stock indices" (instead of "the volatility of broader stock indices").

15. The correct answer is (B). (moderate).

The original sentence suffers from faulty parallelism. Each of the three items in the underlined clause should be similar in grammatical construction. Although "actors" and "musicians" both describe the celebrities themselves, "some other high-profile vocation" does not.

Choice (B) establishes a consistent (parallel) grammatical construction among the three items in the series. In choice (B), each of the three items refers clearly to a vocation.

Choice (C) fails to establish parallel grammatical construction among the three items in the series.

Choice (D) also fails to establish parallel grammatical construction; "otherwise a high profile one" refers to a vocation, not a person.

Choice (E) creates a new faulty parallel structure by including "are" in only two of the three items in the series.

Day 12

Critical Reasoning Lesson 1:
Overview, Strategies, and Common Question Types

Today's Topics:

1. Critical Reasoning—at a Glance

2. Anatomy of a Critical Reasoning Question

3. The Terminology of GMAT Critical Reasoning

4. General Strategies for Critical Reasoning

5. Reasoning Flaws in Critical-Reasoning Passages

6. Unstated-Assumption Questions

7. Weakening-Evidence Questions

8. Supporting-Evidence Questions

Today you'll familiarize yourself with the format of Critical Reasoning questions, learn general strategies for tackling them, and learn how to handle the three most common types.

CRITICAL REASONING—AT A GLANCE

HOW MANY: 14–15 questions
WHERE: In the Verbal Ability section, interspersed with Reading Comprehension and Sentence Correction questions.
BASIC FORMAT: A paragraph-length passage followed by a question about the passage and five answer choices
SKILLS TESTED: Your ability to follow an argument's line of reasoning, to recognize reasoning flaws, and to assess the effect of additional evidence on arguments. More specifically, each Critical Reasoning question is designed to gauge one of seven distinct abilities:

1. To identify an argument's unstated assumptions

2. To recognize how an argument can be weakened

3. To recognize how an argument can be strengthened

4. To draw an inference from a series of stated premises

5. To recognize the main point, or final conclusion, of an argument

6. To make valid deductions based on a series of premises or a premise and conclusion

7. To recognize patterns of reasoning (especially flawed reasoning)

On the GMAT, expect to encounter at least *three* questions covering each of abilities 1–4 and *one* question covering each of the remaining three. (You'll explore each ability as a distinct question type later today and tomorrow in the sequence listed above.)

Directions:

Here are the directions that will appear on your computer screen immediately before the test presents your first Critical Reasoning question (to proceed to the first Critical Reasoning question you'll click on the DISMISS DIRECTIONS button):

> For this question, select the best of the answer choices given.
> To review these directions for subsequent questions of this type, click on HELP.

ANATOMY OF A CRITICAL REASONING QUESTION

Each Critical Reasoning question will consist of three elements:

1. A brief passage (usually one paragraph in length), which usually provides all or a portion of an argument (I'll define "argument" just ahead)
2. A question or other prompt based on the passage
3. Five answer choices, which are alternative responses to the question or prompt

Here's a typical example of a Critical Reasoning question. This question is average in length (the total amount of reading involved) as well as difficulty level (we'll analyze this question a bit later today):

Q: Worldwide retail sales of home entertainment systems, which include a television and an audio system, increased twenty-five percent this year over last year. At the same time, worldwide retail sales of new automobiles declined by about the same percent. These statistics show that consumers can no longer afford to purchase both types of products during the same year.

Which of the following, if true, would cast most serious doubt on the conclusion drawn above?

(A) Fewer advertisements for new cars appeared on television during the most recent year than during the previous year.

(B) Consumers are spending more money on home entertainment systems than on new cars.

(C) People who own home entertainment systems do not drive their automobiles as often as other people.

(D) Prices of home entertainment systems and new cars were higher during the most recent year than during the previous year.

(E) The reliability of automobiles this year improved significantly over last year.

THE TERMINOLOGY OF GMAT CRITICAL REASONING

For GMAT Critical Reasoning, you won't need to know the technical terminology of formal logic, except for a few basic terms with which you're probably already familiar. Here are the terms you should know, along with their definitions:

ARGUMENT: The process of reasoning—from premises to conclusion.

PREMISE: A proposition helping to support the argument's conclusion; premises form the basis on which reasoning proceeds; premises are often signaled with words and phrases such as "since," "because," and "given that."

ASSUMPTION: Something taken for granted to be true in the argument; strictly speaking, assumptions are actually unstated, assumed premises.

CONCLUSION: A proposition derived by deduction or inference from the premises of an argument. Conclusions are typically signaled by words and phrases such as "as a result," "consequently," "therefore," and "it follows that."

INFERENCE: The process of deriving from assumed premises either the strict logical conclusion or a conclusion that is to some degree probable.

DEDUCTION: The process of reasoning in which the conclusion follows necessarily from the stated premises. Deduction is a specific kind of inference.

GENERAL STRATEGIES FOR CRITICAL REASONING

Here are some basic strategies you should follow for any type of Critical Reasoning question:

1. Always read the question stem (the question or prompt but NOT the answer choices) first—before reading the passage. It will contain useful clues about what to look for and think about as you read the passage. (Reading answer choices before reading the passage is wasted time, because you'll invariably need to read them again.)

2. As you read the passage, assume that all premises—statements asserted as factual—are indeed factual. Critical Reasoning questions are not designed to test your real-world knowledge of passage topics. Although Critical Reasoning premises often resemble real-world facts, whether they are factual is beside the point.

3. Most passages will contain a conclusion. The conclusion might appear at the beginning, in the middle, or at the end of the passage. If a passage confuses you, look for the conclusion, then try to follow the argument's line of reasoning from premises to conclusion.

4. Read every answer choice before confirming your response. Remember: the test directions ask you to select the best response, and the qualitative difference between the best and second-best choices can be subtle. Unless you carefully consider all five answer choices, you might select the second-best response without even reading the best one.

5. For most test takers, Critical Reasoning questions require more thought than Sentence Correction and Reading Comprehension questions (the other types of Verbal Ability questions). Moreover, for all but the easiest Critical Reasoning questions, you'll probably need to read the passage and answer choices twice before deciding on an answer. Thus, plan to devote a bit more time on Critical Reasoning questions (at least two minutes per question, on average) than on other Verbal Ability questions.

6. When in doubt, go with your initial hunch about whether an answer choice is viable or not. It's remarkably easy to over-analyze any Critical Reasoning question to the point that you second-guess your own judgment. Although you should carefully consider all five answer choices, don't violate your instincts.

REASONING FLAWS IN CRITICAL-REASONING PASSAGES

During the rest of today's lesson, you'll learn how to handle the following three question types (which together account for about nine of the 14–15 Critical Reasoning questions you'll encounter on the GMAT):

- Unstated-assumption questions
- Weakening-evidence questions
- Supporting-evidence questions

These three question types have a lot in common. In each type, the passage provides an argument—premise(s) and conclusion—whose reasoning is flawed in some respect. Although your specific task is different for each type, for all types, you'll need to recognize the flaw to respond intelligently to the question. Moreover, regardless of the question type, the sorts of flaws you'll encounter are the same for each type.

These three question types also have a lot in common with the GMAT Analysis-of-Argument section (the essay section you learned about on Day 4). In fact, Critical Reasoning and Analysis-of-Argument passages involve the same reasoning flaws! Here's a list of those flaws (from Day 4):

- Drawing a weak analogy between two things
- Confusing a cause-and-effect relationship with a mere correlation or temporal sequence
- Assuming that characteristics of a group apply to every member of the group
- Assuming that a certain condition is necessary and/or sufficient for a certain outcome
- Relying on potentially unrepresentative statistical results
- Assuming that all things remain unchanged over time

- Making a recommendation (or prediction) based on narrow either-or reasoning

At this point, I suggest you go back to Day 4, pages 33–37, and review these reasoning errors and the examples given for each one. Then proceed through the rest of today's lesson, during which you'll learn how to tackle unstated-assumption, weakening-evidence, and supporting-evidence questions.

UNSTATED-ASSUMPTION QUESTIONS

In this type of question the passage will contain a series of premises and a conclusion. However, in order for the argument's conclusion to be probable, at least one additional premise must be *assumed*. In other words, the argument will rely on at least one *unstated assumption*. Your task is to identify which of the five answer choices indicates such an assumption. Think of the structure of the argument this way:

> *Argument:* stated premise(s) + assumption -> inference (conclusion)

You know you're dealing with an unstated-assumption question when the question stem looks something like one of the following (a question stem might refer to specific passage information as well):

> "The argument in the passage depends on which of the following assumptions?"

> "Which of the following is an assumption that enables the conclusion above to be properly drawn?"

> "The conclusion drawn in the first sentence logically depends on which of the following assumptions?"

How to Identify Unstated Assumptions

To identify unstated assumptions in arguments, always ask yourself this question:

> "In addition to the stated premises, what *must* be assumed as factual to justify the argument's logical leap from premises to conclusion—for the conclusion to be probable?"

Try asking and answering this question for Arguments 1 and 2 below. For each argument, try to think of at least one or two assumptions, then jot them down on paper. (NOTE: On the GMAT premises and conclusions are not labeled as they are here.)

Argument 1:

Premise: More new Jupiter Motors automobiles were sold this year than any other brand.

Premise: Jupiter Motors automobiles have the lowest sticker prices, which are the manufacturers' suggested retail prices, of any new automobiles on the market.

Conclusion: Consumers rank low purchase price as the most important factor when purchasing new automobiles.

Argument 2:

Premise: Three years ago a business tax credit for research and development was enacted into law for the purpose of stimulating these business activities.

Premise: Overall business profits have risen steadily since the enactment of this law.

Conclusion: The tax credit has failed to achieve its objective of stimulating research and development.

Now read the following assumptions. Think about each assumption until you understand the necessary link it provides in the argument's chain of reasoning—from premises to conclusion. Without the assumption the argument falls apart, doesn't it?

Assumption (Argument 1): Comparative sticker prices coincide with comparative prices consumers actually pay for new automobiles.

Assumption (Argument 2): New investment in research and development does not generally enhance business profits within a brief (three-year) period.

Did you identify these necessary assumptions, or did you instead jot down various propositions that merely lend additional support to the argument, such as the ones below? Any of these propositions, if factual, *might* lend support to the argument, rendering its conclusion more probable. Yet the argument would not fall apart without them, would it?

Additional supporting evidence (Argument 1):

- The supply of new automobiles other than Jupiter Motors automobiles is sufficient to meet demand for them.

- Jupiter Motors salespeople are no more adept at salesmanship than salespeople who sell other automobiles.

- Warranties, service contracts, and other purchase incentives besides sticker price are no more attractive for Jupiter Motors automobiles than those for other brands.

- Jupiter Motors automobiles provide no advantage over other brands with respect to features other than price—such as safety, functionality, and appearance.

Additional supporting evidence (Argument 2):

- The tax credit is small compared to the costs of new research and development.

- The general economic climate for business has remained at least as healthy as it was three years ago.

- Taxes on businesses have otherwise either remained at current levels or declined during the same time period.

- Major corporate research initiatives begun prior to the enactment of the law began to enhance profits during the last three years.

Be sure you understand the qualitative difference between *necessary* assumptions and merely *helpful* additional evidence. Why? *In any GMAT unstated-assumption question, the best answer choice will provide a necessary assumption.*

A Typical Unstated-Assumption Question

Now that you know how to identify and distinguish between necessary assumptions and other supporting evidence, attempt the following GMAT-style unstated-assumption question. (This one is a bit easier than average.) As you tackle the question, follow these steps:

1. Identify the argument's conclusion and premises.

2. Try to identify at least one necessary assumption, and jot it down—before reading the answer choices.

3. Scan the answer choices for that assumption—or one similar to it.

4. Earmark other choices you think provide supporting evidence.

5. For each remaining answer choice, ask yourself why it is not a viable choice.

Then read my analysis of the question and of each answer choice.

Q: For several consecutive years, poultry prices at each of three statewide grocery-store chains have exceeded the national average by about fifty percent. In fact, the per-pound difference in poultry prices among these three chain stores never amounted to more than a few pennies, while among grocery stores in other states the prices varied by nearly a dollar over the same period. This evidence demonstrates that the three chains conspired to not compete among themselves for consumers' poultry business and to fix their poultry prices at mutually agreed-upon levels.

The claim that the three grocery-store chains conspired to fix poultry prices rests on which of the following assumptions for the time period referred to above?

(A) No other grocery store charged higher prices for poultry than the three chains.

(B) Average poultry prices in the state where the three chains operate exceeded the national average.

(C) The price that grocery stores paid for poultry did not vary significantly from state to state.

(D) Consumers in the state where the three chains operate generally prefer poultry over other meats even if poultry is more expensive than other meats.

(E) Other grocery stores operating in the same state as the three chains also sell poultry to consumers.

Analysis:

The argument relies on the assumption that all other possible factors in the price grocery stores charge for poultry were essentially the same in the state where the three chains operate as in other states. One such factor is wholesale price (the price grocery stores pay suppliers for poultry). A higher wholesale price generally leads to higher prices for consumers. Choice (C) expressly eliminates this factor. Admittedly, an "ideal" answer choice would provide a more sweeping statement—that all factors possibly affecting poultry price were the same from state to state. Nevertheless, choice (C) is the only answer choice that serves to affirm the assumption; thus, choice (C) is the best choice.

Choice (A) admittedly provides *some support* for the argument. Higher poultry prices at another store would weaken the argument that the three chains conspired to fix prices; thus given the inverse—that no other store charges higher poultry prices—the argument's conclusion becomes more probable. However, choice (A) is not a necessary assumption. Even if a certain grocery store charged higher prices for poultry during the period, this fact would probably not be statistically significant in light of the much lower national average—especially if that store were located in another state and therefore did not compete with the three chains.

Choice (B) actually serves to *weaken* the argument. Given choice (B), the greater the number of other grocery stores in the same state the more likely that these other stores also charged high prices for poultry. This fact would in turn help refute the claim that the three chains were motivated by any concern other than to compete effectively against other stores in the state.

Choice (D) is *not relevant* to the argument, which is concerned with poultry prices charged by the three chains compared to poultry prices in other states, *not* compared to prices of other meats.

Choice (E) actually serves to *weaken* the argument. The more competitors, the less likely these three chains together hold a statewide poultry monopoly. (Monopolists are more likely to charge whatever price they wish for their products.)

Tips for Tackling Unstated-Assumption Questions

1. Draft your own "best" answer choice as your read the passage—by filling in the missing logical link between the argument's premises and its conclusion. If you know what to look for among the five answer choices, you're more likely to find it and less likely to fall prey to the test maker's wrong-answer ploys.

2. Don't spend too much time brainstorming; if the missing link (a necessary assumption) doesn't occur to you within 10 or 15 seconds, go ahead and read the answer choices.

3. If a necessary assumption occurred to you as you read the passage, scan the answer choices quickly for it (or a statement similar to it). If you spot it, immediately select it (click on the button to the left of it) as your tentative response.

4. If more than one answer choice seems viable to you, for each choice ask yourself whether the proposition provides a link in the argument's chain of reasoning. If it doesn't, eliminate that answer choice even if it lends support to the argument.

5. Look out for the following types of wrong answers (in addition to those that provide supporting but unessential additional evidence):

   • Additional information that serves to weaken the argument

   • Information that might either strengthen or weaken the argument, depending on additional, unknown facts

   • Superfluous information, which is not directly relevant to the argument

WEAKENING-EVIDENCE QUESTIONS

In this type of question, the passage will look just like a passage for an unstated-assumption question; the passage will contain a series of premises, along with a conclusion whose probability depends on one or more assumptions. Here's the basic structure again:

> *Argument:* stated premise(s) + assumption(s) -> inference (conclusion)

In a weakening-evidence question, however, your task is to identify which of the five answer choices *most seriously weakens* the argument. You know you're dealing with a weakening-evidence question when the question stem looks similar to one of the following (a question stem might refer to specific passage information as well):

> "Which of the following, if true, would most weaken the argument above?"

> "The argument in the passage would be most seriously weakened if it were true that"

> "Which of the following, if true, is most damaging to the conclusion above?"

> "Which of the following statements, if true, provides the best evidence that the reasoning in the argument above is flawed?"

> "Each of the following, if true, raises a consideration against the conclusion above, EXCEPT:"

> *(Your task here is to identify the only answer choice that does NOT weaken the argument.)*

How to Weaken an Argument

To understand how an argument by inference can be weakened, consider Argument 1 on page 106. Here it is again:

Argument 1

Premise: More new Jupiter Motors automobiles were sold this year than any other brand.

Premise: Jupiter Motors automobiles have the lowest sticker prices, which are the manufacturers' suggested retail prices, of any new automobiles on the market.

Conclusion: Consumers rank low purchase price as the most important factor when purchasing new automobiles.

There are many ways to weaken an argument like the one above. One way is to essentially point out as a matter-of-fact that the conclusion is false, or that a stated premise needed for the conclusion to be probable is false. However, in a GMAT weakening-evidence question, you're unlikely to find either method among the five choices—because both are a bit too obvious. Instead, the test makers prefer the following two methods:

1. Directly refute a necessary assumption—in other words, provide evidence that the assumption is false as a matter of fact.

   Example: New automobiles with comparatively high sticker prices are often sold to consumers for less than automobiles with lower sticker prices.

2. Refute other possible supporting evidence—evidence that does not pertain directly to a necessary assumption but that, if true, would nevertheless increase the conclusion's probability.

   Example A: Production at the plants of Jupiter Motors' main competitor has been hampered by numerous labor strikes during the last three years.

   Example B: Warranties and other non-price purchase incentives vary widely among retailers of new automobiles.

Here's what you need to know about these two methods when analyzing a GMAT weakening-evidence question:

- A method-1 answer choice is always better than a method-2 choice—because the former is a *direct* attack on a *necessary* assumption.

- If no method-1 proposition appears among the answer choices, then the best choice will be the best among the method-2 propositions listed. (*Example A* above would be a better choice than *Example B*. Why? *Example B* leaves open the possibility that non-price incentives at Jupiter retailers are *less* attractive than at other retailers—which would actually *strengthen* the argument.)

A Typical Weakening-Evidence Question

Now that you know how to weaken an argument and distinguish between propositions that merely weaken and those that completely undermine the argument, take another look at the GMAT-style question you encountered near the beginning of today's lesson. (This question is average in difficulty level.) This time around, as you tackle the question:

1. Identify the argument's conclusion and premises.

2. Try to identify at least one necessary assumption, and jot it down—before reading the answer choices.

3. Scan the answer choices for a proposition that directly refutes, or contradicts, that assumption.

4. Earmark other choices you think serve to weaken the argument—then rank them in quality (degree of damage to the conclusion).

5. For each remaining answer choice, ask yourself why it is not a viable choice.

Then read my analysis of the question and of each answer choice.

Q: Worldwide retail sales of home entertainment systems, which include a television and an audio system, increased twenty-five percent this year over last year. At the same time worldwide retail sales of new automobiles declined by about the same percent. These statistics show that consumers can no longer afford to purchase both types of products during the same year.

Which of the following, if true, would cast most serious doubt on the conclusion drawn above?

(A) Fewer advertisements for new cars appeared on television during the most recent year than during the previous year.

(B) Consumers are spending more money on home entertainment systems than on new cars.

(C) People who own home entertainment systems do not drive their automobiles as often as other people.

(D) Prices of home entertainment systems and new cars were higher during the most recent year than during the previous year.

(E) The reliability of automobiles this year improved significantly over last year.

Analysis:

The argument relies on the assumption that all other possible factors influencing consumers' buying decisions respecting the two products remained unchanged from last year to this year. An ideal "best" answer would directly refute or provide strong evidence against this assumption. Choice (E) accomplishes this better than any other choice—by providing an alternative explanation for the fact that consumers are buying fewer new cars *and* more entertainment centers. Specifically, if a car is more reliable it is less likely to be replaced by a new one. By the same token, if people keep their cars longer and do not need to spend much money to repair them, then people can better afford to purchase other consumer items such as entertainment centers.

Choice (A) might explain why sales of new cars have declined. However, choice (A) does not explain increased sales of home entertainment centers.

Choice (B) reinforces the argument's premise, thereby *strengthening* the argument.

Choice (C) is irrelevant to the argument. Choice (C) provides a reason why people with home entertainment systems might replace their cars less often. However, even if this were the case it would have no bearing on whether these people can afford both items.

Choice (D) does not explain why consumers have chosen one type of product over another.

Tips for Tackling Weakening-Evidence Questions

1. As you read the passage, try to identify at least one necessary assumption. There are two general types of assumptions that are especially common in weakening-evidence arguments:

   • The assumption that *all other factors are equal*—if the argument seeks to explain certain differences between two phenomena

- The assumption that *all other relevant conditions remain unchanged over time*—if the argument seeks to explain or predict some sort of change from one point in time (or period of time) to another

2. Scan the answer choices for a proposition that directly refutes an unstated assumption. If you spot one, immediately select it (click on the button to the left of it) as your tentative response.

3. In all likelihood, more than one answer choice will serve to weaken the argument. Always select a choice that directly addresses, and attacks, a necessary assumption over any other choice that weakens the argument.

4. Before confirming your response, ask yourself whether the proposition you selected serves to destroy a logical link needed for a convincing argument; if it doesn't, look around for a better answer choice.

5. If no answer choice refutes a necessary assumption, you'll need to weigh the comparative quality of all answer choices that serve to weaken the argument.

6. Look out for the following types of wrong answers:

   - A statement that affirms a necessary assumption—in other words, that accomplishes just the opposite of what the question asks for

   - A statement that serves to strengthen (rather than weaken) the argument in some other way

   - A statement that could either strengthen or weaken the argument, depending on additional unknown facts

   - A statement that contains superfluous information, which is not directly relevant to the argument

---

SUPPORTING-EVIDENCE QUESTIONS

For a supporting-evidence question, your task is to identify which of five propositions provides *the most support* for the argument—just the opposite as for a weakening-evidence question. You know you're dealing with a supporting-evidence question when the question stem looks similar to one of the following (a question stem might refer to specific passage information as well):

> "Which of the following, if true, most strongly supports the author's argument?"

> "Which of the following statements, if true, would most strengthen the argument above?"

> "Which of the following, if true, provides the best indication that the conclusion in the argument above was logically well supported?"

> "Which of the following best completes the passage below?"
>
> *(At the end of the passage you'll see a blank line signifying a missing statement.)*

How to Strengthen an Argument

To understand how an argument by inference can be supported, or strengthened, consider Argument 2 on page 106. Here it is again:

Argument 2:

Premise: Three years ago a business tax credit for research and development was enacted into law for the purpose of stimulating these business activities.

Premise: Overall business profits have risen steadily since the enactment of this law.

Conclusion: The tax credit has failed to achieve its objective of stimulating research and development.

There are *two* methods of strengthening an argument like the one (the first is more effective):

1. Provide a necessary assumption (assert it is factual) or provide strong evidence that it is factual.

   Example: Investing in research and development does not generally enhance profitability until several years after the investment.

2. Provide evidence that adds weight or credibility to the argument, but that does not affirm a necessary assumption.

Example A: Costs of certain raw materials used in many areas of research and development have increased since the law was enacted.

Example B: Many large corporations curtailed significant research and development shortly before the law was enacted.

Here's what you need to know about these two methods for analyzing a GMAT supporting-evidence question:

- A proposition that affirms a necessary assumption (method 1) provides better support for an argument than one that does not.

- If no method-1 proposition appears among the answer choices, then the best choice will be the strongest method-2 proposition listed. (*Example A* above would be a better choice than *Example B*. Why? The degree of support *Example B* lends to the argument depends entirely on our assumption that new research and development cannot enhance profits within three years; *Example A* lends support to the argument irrespective of this assumption.)

A Typical Supporting-Evidence Question

Now that you know how to strengthen an argument and distinguish among propositions of varying degrees of support, attempt the following GMAT-style supporting-evidence question. (This one is a bit more difficult than average.) As you tackle the question:

1. Identify the argument's conclusion and premises.

2. Try to identify at least one necessary assumption, and jot it down—before reading the answer choices.

3. Scan the answer choices for a proposition that essentially provides that assumption.

4. Earmark other choices you think serve to strengthen the argument—then rank them in quality (degree of support).

5. For each remaining answer choice, ask yourself why it is not a viable choice.

Then read my analysis of the question and of each answer choice.

Q: PharmaCorp, which manufactures the drug Aidistan, claims that Aidistan is more effective than the drug Betatol in treating Puma Syndrome. To support its claim PharmaCorp cites the fact that one of every two victims of Puma Syndrome is treated successfully with Aidistan alone, as opposed to one out of every three treated with Betatol alone. However, PharmaCorp's claim cannot be taken seriously, in light of the fact that the presence of Gregg's Syndrome has been known to render Puma Syndrome more resistant to any treatment.

Which of the following, if true, would most support the allegation that PharmaCorp's claim cannot be taken seriously?

(A) Among people who suffer from both Puma Syndrome and Gregg's Syndrome, fewer are treated with Aidistan than with Betatol.

(B) Among people who suffer from both Puma Syndrome and Gregg's Syndrome, fewer are treated with Betatol than with Aidistan.

(C) Gregg's Syndrome reduces Aidistan's effectiveness in treating Puma Syndrome more than Betatol's effectiveness in treating the same syndrome.

(D) Betatol is less effective than Aidistan in treating Gregg's Syndrome.

(E) Neither Aidistan nor Betatol is effective in treating Gregg's Syndrome.

Analysis:
This augment relies on the assumption that Gregg's Syndrome is more prevalent among Puma Syndrome victims who take Betatol than among those who take Aidistan. Choice (A) essentially affirms this assumption, although it expresses it in a somewhat different way. Given that Gregg's Syndrome renders any Puma Syndrome treatment less effective, if victims who have both syndromes are treated with Betatol while victims who have only Puma Syndrome are treated with Aidistan, then Aidistan

will appear to be more effective, although the absence of Gregg's Syndrome might in fact be the key factor that explains the differing results.

Choice (B) would actually support PharmaCorp's claim that Aidistan is more effective than Betatol—by the same reasoning as above.

Choice (C) provides no useful information, as it stands. Without additional information—about the number of people suffering from both syndromes who are treated with Aidistan compared to the number treated with Betatol—it is impossible to assess the effect of choice (C) on the argument.

Choice (D) actually supports PharmaCorp's claim that Aidistan is more effective than Betatol. Given that Betatol is less effective in treating Gregg's Syndrome, the result is that Aidistan renders Puma Syndrome less resistant to treatment. (In other words, Aidistan is more effective in treating Puma Syndrome.)

Choice (E) provides no useful information to compare the effectiveness of Aidistan with that of Betatol in treating Puma Syndrome.

Tips for Tackling Supporting-Evidence Questions

1. As you read the passage, try to identify a necessary assumption. There are two general types of assumptions that are especially common in supporting-evidence questions:

   - The assumption that *all other factors are equal*— if the argument seeks to explain certain differences between two phenomena

   - The assumption that *all other relevant conditions remain unchanged over time*—if the argument seeks to explain or predict some sort of change from one point in time (or period of time) to another

2. Scan the answer choices for a proposition that provides that assumption. If you spot it, immediately select it (click on the button to the left of it) as your tentative response.

3. In all likelihood, more than one answer choice will serve to strengthen the argument. Always

select a choice that directly affirms a necessary assumption over any other choice.

4. If no answer choice affirms a necessary assumption, you'll need to weigh the comparative quality of all answer choices that serve to strengthen the argument.

5. Look out for the following types of wrong answers:

   - A statement that weakens rather than strengthens the argument

   - A statement that could either strengthen or weaken the argument, depending on additional unknown facts.

   - A statement that contains superfluous information, which is not directly relevant to the argument.

IF YOU HAVE MORE TIME TODAY

For additional insight about the three question types covered in today's lesson, check out the author's online Q&A entitled "Unstated Assumptions: The Inner Sanctum of GMAT Critical Reasoning." You can link to it from the "Q&A Corner" of the author's GMAT Web site (www.west.net/~stewart/gmat).

Day 13

Critical Reasoning Lesson 2: Additional Question Types

Today's Topics:

1. Probable-Inference Questions

2. Main-Point Questions

3. Necessary-Inference Questions

4. Parallel-Argument Questions

Today you'll learn how to handle four additional types of Critical Reasoning questions.

PROBABLE-INFERENCE QUESTIONS

For a GMAT probable-inference question, the passage will simply provide a series of premises—various information that you are to accept as factual. Your task is to identify among the five answer choices the statement that provides the most reliable—or probable—conclusion from the passage information. Expect to encounter at least two, and probably three, questions of this type on the GMAT. You know you're dealing with a probable-inference question when the question stem looks similar to one of the following:

"Which of the following statements draws the most reliable conclusion from the information above?"

"Which of the following conclusions about…is best supported by the passage?"

"Which of the following can most properly be inferred from the information in the passage above?"

"Which of the following, if true, best explains the fact that…?"

"Each of the following, if true, could explain [one of the premises] EXCEPT:"

Notice that each of these question stems (except the last one) contains the word "most" or "best." These are important words. For a probable-inference question, even the best answer choice will *not necessarily* follow from the premises; yet, it will be *more probable* than any other answer choice. (For the last question stem above, the best answer choice will be *less probable* than any of the others.)

NOTE: Arguments in which conclusions are necessarily either true or false involve *deductive* reasoning. GMAT deductive-reasoning questions are a distinct animal, which you'll learn about later today.

How to Identify Probable Inferences

How do you recognize a probable, or reliable, inference among five answer choices and distinguish it from less reliable ones? The best way to answer this question is by example. Consider the following two GMAT-style passages. After reading each one, ask yourself, "Given this information, what else is probably true?" Try to think of at least one answer—then jot it down as if you were drafting your own best answer choice for a GMAT inference question. (Expect an easier time with passage 1 than 2.)

> **Passage 1:**
>
> Many sociologists argue that science-fiction television programs play a crucial role in fostering the belief that intelligent aliens have visited Earth. However, in countries where relatively few people have access to television, belief that intelligent aliens have visited Earth is at least as prevalent as in other countries.

> **Passage 2:**
>
> To subsidize the profits of domestic farms that grow a certain crop, country X imposes a tariff on exports of the crop. As a result, foreign food-product manufacturers that must use the crop in their products find it more difficult to compete with country X businesses that must use the same crop in their products.

Next, for each passage, read the following conclusions (inferences). Think about each one until you understand that the one listed as a possible best answer choice *makes sense*; that it is *reasonably inferable* from the passage; that it is *probable to some degree*. Then compare it to the ones listed as typical wrong-answer choices. Notice that each of these unreliable inferences depends on additional, unsubstantiated assumptions and is therefore far less probable.

Conclusions (Inferences) from Passage 1

Reliable inference (potential "best" answer choice):

Science-fiction television programs are not the only factor in determining whether a person believes intelligent aliens have visited Earth.

Unreliable inferences (typical wrong-answer choices):

- Science-fiction television programs do not affect whether people believe that intelligent aliens have visited Earth.
- People who do not watch television are more likely to believe that intelligent aliens have visited Earth than people who do.
- Science-fiction television programming is not realistic enough to persuade people that intelligent aliens have visited Earth.

Conclusions (Inferences) from Passage 2

Reliable inference (potential "best" answer choice):

Importing the crop from country X is less costly for foreign businesses than if these businesses obtain the crop from another source.

Unreliable inferences (typical wrong-answer choices):

- The farms of country X are the only sources of the crop.
- Other countries that produce the crop also impose export tariffs on the crop.
- The total demand for the crop produced in Country X declined as a result of the export tariff.

Compare the reliable inferences to the unreliable ones listed above. Notice that the unreliable ones either depend on additional assumptions that find no support in the passage and/or go too far—beyond the reliable inference to one that amounts to a sweeping, all-encompassing conclusion.

A Typical Probable-Inference Question

Now that you know how to identify and distinguish between reliable and unreliable inferences, attempt the following GMAT-style probable-inference question, which is a bit more difficult than average. As you tackle the question, follow these steps:

1. Try to answer the question "What else is probably true" after reading the passage—but before reading the answer choices. If you think of an answer, jot it down.

2. Scan the answer choices for your answer—or one similar to it.

3. For each statement you eliminated, be sure you can think of an additional assumption needed for the statement to make sense as a conclusion.

Then read my analysis of the question and of each answer choice.

Q: During each of the last five years, both the demand for beverage containers and the quantity of beverage containers recycled to produce new beverage containers have increased steadily. At the same time, the number of freshly cut trees used to produce beverage containers has declined each year.

If the statements above are all true, they provide most support for which of the following conclusions about the last five years?

(A) The number of new beverage containers not made of recycled materials has decreased.

(B) More beverage containers have been recycled for producing new beverage containers than have not been recycled for this purpose.

(C) Recycled beverage containers have been used only for making new beverage containers.

(D) The number of beverage containers made of tree materials has decreased.

(E) The number of used beverage containers not being recycled has decreased.

Analysis:
The fact that the number of recycled beverage containers has been increasing while the number of new trees used to make beverage containers has been declining lends considerable support to choice (A). Moreover, choice (A) allows for the possibility that some beverage containers are made of recycled materials other than tree materials. Admittedly, demand for beverage containers in general has increased recently, reducing the likelihood that choice (A) is true. On balance, however, choice (A) is more strongly supported than any of the other answer choices.

Choice (B) is not inferable from the statements, which provide information about *changes* in numbers from one year to the next, not *total* numbers. The passage provides no information that would permit a comparison between the total numbers of recycled beverage containers and non-recycled beverage containers.

Choice (C) is not inferable. The passage provides no information permitting the sweeping inference that the increasing demand for beverage containers has been so great as to necessitate the use *all* recycled beverage containers to meet this increased demand.

Choice (D) is not inferable. Although the decrease in the number of freshly cut trees each year tends to show that choice (D) might be true, the increase in demand for beverage containers and in the number of recycled beverage containers tend to show just the opposite. In any event, choice (D) also requires more information (additional assumptions) about the *percentage* of beverage containers, both new and recycled, made of tree products.

Choice (E) is not inferable. Just because the number of beverage containers being recycled has increased each year, it is unfair to conclude that the number of beverage containers *not* being recycled has been decreasing. In fact, given the increased demand for beverage containers in general, it is just as likely that consumers are recycling more beverage containers *and* discarding more beverage containers.

Tips for Tackling Probable-Inference Questions

1. All statements in the passage are premises; thus, you should assume they are all factual (even if in real life they seem somewhat dubious).

2. Try to pre-phrase the best answer, then scan the five choices for it. But after 10 or 15 seconds of brainstorming, if you haven't conjured up a good conclusion for the passage, go ahead and read the answer choices.

3. If an answer choice makes sense as a conclusion only if additional facts are assumed, you can safely eliminate it.

4. If an answer choice draws a sweeping conclusion (an all-encompassing generalization), you can probably eliminate it as the best answer choice. When in doubt, choose a narrower conclusion over a broader one.

MAIN-POINT QUESTIONS

In this type of question, the passage will provide an argument in which the conclusion is *implicit* in the passage's information *as a whole*. Your task is to identify which statement among five choices expresses that implicit conclusion—or main point. You know you're dealing with a main-point question when the question stem looks similar to one of the following:

"In the passage the author argues that"

"Which of the following best expresses the main point of the passage above?"

These questions are inherently a bit easier than average, so expect to see a main-point question on your GMAT only if the testing system is moving you down the difficulty ladder (in other words, only if you've been responding incorrectly to Critical Reasoning questions of average difficulty). In any event, don't expect to encounter more than one main-point question on your GMAT.

How to Identify an Argument's Main Point

A main-point question is similar to a probable-inference question in that the best answer choice will express a conclusion of the argument. However, to respond to a main-point question, no logical inference is required; in other words, the best answer will require no step in reasoning beyond what the passage already provides. To identify the argument's main point, ask yourself:

"What's the main thrust of this argument?"

"What point is the passage's author trying to make here?"

Try asking and answering these questions for the following GMAT-style passage (Passage 1). Jot down a brief sentence that you think expresses the argument's main point without drawing any inferences from the passage information.

Passage 1:

In order to save money, many manufacturers of chemical products decide to emit harmful chemicals into the environment instead of disposing of them safely. However, these emissions invariably cause health problems for people who live near the source of the emissions. Eventually, manufacturers engaging in these activities are compelled by our court system to compensate their victims for these health problems.

Now read the following statement, which would be the best answer choice for a main-point question. Is the statement you jotted down similar to this one?

Main Point (Passage 1):

Emitting harmful chemicals in order to reduce costs will result in an increase in a manufacturer's other expenses.

Compare this statement with the following two. Notice that, unlike the statement above, each of the following provides information not already implicit in the passage and that the probability of each one depends on certain assumptions. Both statements would be typical wrong-answer choices for a main-point question involving Passage 1.

Inferences (Passage 1):

- These manufacturers will eventually discontinue emitting harmful chemicals into the environment.
- These manufacturers will not save money by emitting harmful chemicals into the environment.

A GMAT main-point question might also require that you distinguish between an *intermediate* conclusion and a *final* conclusion. For example, notice in Passage 2, on the following page, that the intermediate conclusion is merely a stepping stone toward the passage's final conclusion, or main point. Thus, an answer choice that expresses an argument's intermediate conclusion would not be the best choice for a main-point question.

Passage 2:

Some animal-rights activists argue that the media's inaccurate portrayal of bats as dangerous animals threatens the survival of this species, in light of the fact that many animals perceived as threatening to human safety have been hunted by humans to extinction. However, these activists overlook the fact that the global population of bats is actually increasing.

Intermediate Conclusion (passage 2):

It is less likely that an animal will be hunted to extinction if its population is increasing than otherwise.

Final Conclusion or Main Point (passage 2):

The increase in the bat population suggests that the activists' concern that bats might become extinct might be unwarranted.

The following statements would also be wrong-answers to a main-point question involving Passage 2 because they involve inferences, which depend on additional unstated premises.

Inferences (Passage 2):

- People's perceptions of bats are not affected by how the media portray them.
- Animals that are not in fact dangerous are not likely to be hunted to extinction by humans.

A Typical Main-Point Question

Now that you know how to recognize an argument's main point and distinguish it from an intermediate conclusion and from inferences, which require additional premises, attempt the following GMAT-style main-point question, which would be rated average in difficulty level for this question type. As you tackle the question, follow these steps:

1. After reading the passage, but before reading the answer choices, ask yourself: "What's the main thrust of this argument?" Jot down a statement you think expresses the main idea.

2. Scan the answer choices for your statement—or one similar to it.

3. Earmark each answer choice you think requires an inference, or logical step.

Then read my analysis of the question and of each answer choice.

Q: *City Official:* I cannot deny that sodium monofluoride, which is used in all major brands of toothpaste to help prevent tooth decay, has been shown to be more toxic than lead. Those who oppose our plan to treat the public water supply with sodium monofluoride cite warnings on the back of toothpaste tubes advising the user to contact a poison control center if the user swallows more toothpaste than needed for brushing. But these same opponents ignore the fact that, even though nobody reads these warnings, virtually no cases of toothpaste poisoning have ever been reported.

Which of the following best expresses the city official's main point in the argument above?

(A) Sodium monofluoride warnings on toothpaste tubes should be more conspicuous to toothpaste users.

(B) Fluoride in toothpaste is not as toxic as warnings on toothpaste tubes would lead users to believe.

(C) Neither fluoridated water nor fluoridated toothpaste contains lead.

(D) Suppliers of public water treated with sodium monofluoride should not be required to warn their customers about its toxicity.

(E) Fluoridated water is not as toxic as opponents of water treated with sodium monofluoride might claim.

Analysis:

The argument as a whole can be characterized as an attempt to rebut an argument against treating water with sodium monofluoride. To rebut the argument, the city official provides evidence tending to show that sodium monofluoride is not as harmful as some might believe. Choice (E) accurately expresses the main point that the city official is attempting to make. Choice (E) is the best response.

Choice (A) is tangential to the city official's main concern, which is to refute an argument against public water fluoridation.

Choice (B) is the city official's intermediate conclusion. But the official's ultimate point is that fluoridated *water*, not toothpaste, is less toxic than some might claim.

Choice (C) is likely to be true, based on the information in the first sentence. However, choice (C) is not relevant to the city official's main concern for refuting an argument against public water fluoridation.

Choice (D) goes beyond the main point that the city official seeks to make, which is that the city should be allowed to treat its water supply with sodium monofluoride because it is not as harmful as some might claim. Choice (D) assumes this point, then goes further by arguing that the city need not warn its customers about the hazards of treating water with sodium monofluoride.

Tips for Tackling Main-Idea Questions

1. Don't overlook the obvious. Main-idea questions are not like inference questions. No reasoning is required; the passage's main idea will be implicit in the passage itself.

2. No single sentence in the passage will adequately express its main idea. Instead, the main idea will encompass all of the passage's premises.

3. Look out for the following types of wrong answers:

   - A statement that provides an intermediate conclusion

   - A statement that requires an inference, based on assumptions

   - A statement that merely reiterates, or paraphrases, part of the passage

NECESSARY-INFERENCE QUESTIONS

This type of GMAT question involves *deductive* reasoning, in which an argument's conclusion is *necessarily* inferable (or not inferable) from its premises—in other words, necessarily true (or false). Expect to encounter at least one necessary-inference question on your GMAT.

GMAT necessary-inference questions come in two varieties. In one type, the passage provides a series of premises, and your task is to determine which of the five answer choices must be true (or false) based on the premises. You know you're dealing with this type when the question stem looks similar to one of the following:

"If the statements above are true, which of the following statements can logically be derived from them?"

"Which of the following must be true on the basis of the statements above?"

"Which of the following can be correctly inferred from the statements above?"

"If the statements above are true, any of the following statements might also be true EXCEPT:"

In the second type of necessary-inference question, the passage provides one or more premises along with a conclusion, and your task is to determine what additional premise is necessary for the conclusion to be necessarily inferable (true). You know you're dealing with this type when the question stem looks similar to one of the following:

"The passage's conclusion is true only if which of the following statements is also true?"

"The conclusion of the argument above cannot be true unless which of the following is true?"

"Any of the following, if introduced into the argument as an additional premise, makes the argument above logically correct EXCEPT:"

Notice the absence of words like "best," "most," and "least" in both groups of questions above. That's because deductive reasoning does not involve a conclusion's probability but rather its certainty—whether it is true or false, valid or invalid, correct or incorrect, inferable or not inferable—based on the premises. So, the mode of reasoning for necessary-inference questions is entirely different than for the question types we've covered up to this point. If you're ready to shift to this other mode, read on.

Forms and Fallacies of Deductive Reasoning

To master GMAT necessary-inference questions, you need to recognize certain basic argument forms and fallacies. (A "fallacy" is simply an argument by deduction whose conclusion is incorrect—or whose *inference is invalid*.) The following series of forms are the ones you're most likely to encounter on the GMAT. The best way to identify a form is to first use symbols in premises and conclusions, then analyze an example that matches the form.

Based on the following premise, there is only one valid inference. Notice that the valid inference switches A with B, and negates both.

Argument 1

Premise: If A, then B.

Valid inference: If not B, then not A.

Invalid inference: If B, then A.

Invalid inference: If not A, then not B.

Example (Argument 1)

Premise: If I strike the window with a hammer, the window will break.

Valid inference: If the window is not broken, then I have not struck it with a hammer.

Invalid inference: If the window is broken, I have struck it with a hammer.

Invalid inference: If I do not strike the window with a hammer, the window will not break.

(Both invalid inferences overlook that the window might be broken for any number of reasons besides my having struck it with a hammer.)

The following argument form and accompanying fallacies are logically identical to the ones above.

Argument 2

Premise: All A are B.

Valid inference: All non-B's are non-A's. (No non-B is an A.)

Invalid inference: All B are A.

Invalid inference: No non-A's are B's.

Example (Argument 2)

Premise: All red gremlins are spotted.

Valid inference: No gremlin that is not spotted is red.

Invalid inference: All spotted gremlins are red.

Invalid inference: No gremlins that are not red are spotted.

(Both invalid inferences overlook that a spotted gremlin might be a color other than red.)

This next form involves two premises and a third symbol, C, which allows inferences (and inviting fallacies) in addition to the ones covered in arguments 1 and 2 above.

Argument 3

Premise: If A, then B.

Premise: If B, then C.

Valid inference: If A, then C.

Valid inference: If not C, then not A.

Invalid inference: If not A, then not C.

Invalid inference: If C, then A.

Example (Argument 3)

Premise: If I strike the window with a hammer, the window will break.

Premise: If the window is broken, the cold outside air will blow into the house.

Valid inference: If I strike the window with a hammer, then the cold outside air will blow into the house.

Valid inference: If the cold outside air has not blown into the house, then I have not struck the window with a hammer.

Invalid inference: If I do not strike the window with a hammer, the window will not break.

Invalid inference: If cold outside air has blown into the house, I have struck the window with a hammer.

The following argument is logically identical to argument 3 above.

Argument 4

Premise: All A are B.

Premise: All B are C.

Valid inference: All A are C.

Valid inference: No non-C is an A.

Invalid inference: No non-A is a C.

Invalid inference: All C are A.

Example (Argument 4)

Premise: All red gremlins are spotted.

Premise: All spotted gremlins are female.

(*Assumption:* A gremlin must be either male or female, but not both.)

Valid inference: All red gremlins are female.

Valid inference: No male gremlin is red.

Invalid inference: No gremlin that is not red is female.

Invalid inference: All female gremlins are red.

In arguments 1–4, each statement is essentially an all-or-none assertion (signaled by words such as "all" and "no"). In this next series of arguments, the word "some" is introduced into a premise. For each form, try conjuring up your own example (perhaps involving red, spotted, and female gremlins).

Argument 5

Premise: Some A are B.

Valid inference: Some B are A.

Invalid inference: Some A are not B.

Invalid inference: Some B are not A.

(In formal logic, the word "some" means at least one and possibly as many as all; thus, the premise

allows for the possibility that all A are B and that all B are A.)

Argument 6

Premise: Some A are B.

Premise: Some B are C.

Valid inference: Some B are A.

Valid inference: Some C are B.

Invalid inference: Some A are C.

Invalid inference: Some C are A.

(If a B is an A, it is not necessarily a C as well; in other words, the set of B's that are also A's does not necessarily overlap the set of B's that are also C's.)

Argument 7

Premise: Some A are B.

Premise: All B are C.

Valid inference: Some B are A.

Valid inference: Some A are C.

Valid inference: Some C are A.

Invalid inference: All C are B.

Invalid inference: All C are A.

The following two arguments involve "either-or" forms:

Argument 8

Premise: Either A or B, but not both.

Valid inference: If A, then not B.

Valid inference: If B, then not A.

Valid inference: If not B, then A.

Valid inference: If not A, then B.

Argument 9

Premise: Either A or B, but not both.

Premise: Either B or C, but not both.

Valid inference: If B, then not C (and not A).

Valid inference: If A, then C (but not B).

Valid inference: If C, then A (but not B).

A Typical Necessary-Inference Question

Now that you know how to recognize various forms of deductive reasoning and distinguish between valid and invalid inferences, attempt the following GMAT-style question, which is a bit more difficult than average for this question type. As you tackle the question, follow these steps:

1. Try to reduce the passage to simple statements using symbols (letters). Jot down the premise and conclusion using those symbols.

2. Before reading the answer choices, try to determine the missing premise for yourself.

3. Scan the answer choices for your answer.

4. For each answer choice you eliminated, try to determine what valid conclusion (if any) would be inferable by adding the premise provided in the answer choice.

Then read my analysis of the question and of each answer choice.

Q: In the country of Xania, periods of political instability are always accompanied by a volatile Xania stock market and by volatility of Xania's currency compared to currencies of other countries. At the present time, Xania's currency is experiencing volatility. Hence, the Xania stock market must also be experiencing volatility.

Which of the following allows the conclusion above to be properly drawn?

(A) Whenever Xania is politically stable, the Xania currency is stable as well.

(B) Whenever the Xania currency is stable, Xania is politically stable as well.

(C) Whenever the Xania stock market is unstable, Xania is politically unstable as well.

(D) Whenever the Xania stock market is unstable, the Xania currency is unstable as well.

(E) Whenever the Xania stock market is stable, the Xania currency is stable as well.

Analysis:
The argument boils down to the following:

Premise #1: If there is political instability, then the stock market is volatile (unstable).

Premise #2: If there is political instability, then the currency is volatile (unstable).

Premise #3: The currency is volatile (unstable).

Conclusion: The stock market is volatile (unstable).

To reveal the structure of the argument, let's reduce it to symbols:

Premise #1: If A, then B.

Premise #2: If A, then C.

Premise #3: C.

Conclusion: B.

The conclusion above requires the following additional premise:

Premise #4: If the currency is volatile (unstable), then there is political instability.

Premise #4: If C, then A.

Only choice (A) provides this essential premise. Note that premise #4 above is essentially the same proposition as choice (A). In other words, the following two propositions are logically identical:

Premise #4: If C, then A.

Answer choice (A): If not A, then not C.

Choice (B) merely reiterates premise #2. In other words, the following two statements are essentially the same:

If X, then Y.

If not Y, then not X.

Choice (C) commits the following fallacy:

Premise: If X, then Y.

Conclusion: If Y, then X.

Choice (D) would lead to the conclusion that if the stock market is volatile (unstable), then the currency is volatile (unstable). In other words, choice (D) commits the same fallacy as choice (C):

Premise: If X, then Y.

Conclusion: If Y, then X.

Choice (E) merely reiterates the argument's conclusion. In other words, the following two statements are essentially the same:

If X, then Y.

If not Y, then not X.

Tips for Tackling Necessary-Inference Questions

1. If the question asks for a missing premise, identify the premise(s) and conclusion in the passage.

2. If you're having trouble following the logic, reduce each part of the passage to simple statements using letters as symbols. Write down the form of the argument on paper.

3. Pre-phrase the answer to the question by determining the additional premise needed for the conclusion to be valid (or the conclusion that necessarily follows from the stated premises). Express your answer using symbols.

4. If you're having trouble making sense of a particular statement in the passage, try to rephrase it so its logical meaning is clearer. Eliminating double negatives can be particularly helpful.

   Confusing: Only gremlins that are spotted are red.
   Clear: All red gremlins are spotted.

   Confusing: If a gremlin is not spotted, then it cannot be red.
   Confusing: A gremlin is spotted only if it is red.
   Clear: If a gremlin is red, then it must be spotted.

5. Look out for the following types of wrong answers:

   • A statement that results in one of the logical fallacies identified in this lesson

   • A statement that merely reiterates a stated premise (or stated conclusion), expressing it in a slightly different way

PARALLEL-ARGUMENT QUESTIONS

In this type of question, the passage and the five answer choices each provide an argument (one or more premises and a conclusion). Your task is to determine which of the five choices provides the argument most similar *in its pattern of reasoning* to the pattern in the passage. Don't expect to encounter more than one question of this type on your GMAT.

You know you're dealing with a parallel-argument question when the question stem looks similar to one of the following (notice that the first two are essentially the same, but the third one suggests a slightly different task):

> "Which of the following is most like the argument above in its logical structure?"

> "Which of the following illustrates a pattern of reasoning most similar to the pattern of reasoning in the argument above?"

> "The flawed reasoning in the argument above is most similar to the reasoning in which of the following arguments?"

Parallel-argument questions almost always involve *deductive* reasoning. To handle these questions, you apply the forms and fallacies you just learned to the unique parallel-argument format.

A Typical Parallel-Argument Question

Attempt the following GMAT-style parallel-argument question, which is average in difficulty. As you tackle the question, follow these steps:

1. Try to reduce the passage to simple statements using symbols (letters). Jot down the premise and conclusion using those symbols.

2. Perform the same task (step 1) for each answer choice in turn.

3. Compare the structure of each answer choice to the structure of the original passage.

Then read my analysis of the question and of each answer choice.

Q: Very few software engineers have left MicroFirm Corporation to seek employment elsewhere. Thus, unless CompTech Corporation increases the salaries of its software engineers to the same level as those of MicroFirm, these CompTech employees are likely to leave CompTech for another employer.

The flawed reasoning of the argument above is most similar to the reasoning in which of the following arguments?

(A) Robert does not gamble, and he has never been penniless. Therefore, if Gina refrains from gambling she will also avoid being penniless.

(B) If Dan throws a baseball directly at the window, the windowpane will surely break. The windowpane is not broken, so Dan has not thrown a baseball directly at it.

(C) If a piano sits in a humid room, the piano will need tuning within a week. This piano needs tuning. Therefore, it must have sat in a humid room for at least a week.

(D) Diligent practice results in perfection. Thus, one must practice diligently in order to achieve perfection.

(E) More expensive cars are stolen than inexpensive cars. Accordingly, owners of expensive cars should carry auto theft insurance, whereas owners of inexpensive cars should not.

Analysis:
The original argument's line of reasoning is essentially as follows:

Premise: The well-paid engineers at MicroFirm do not quit their jobs.

Conclusion: If CompTech engineers are not well paid, they will quit their jobs.

To reveal the argument's structure, let's express it using letters as symbols:

Premise: All A's are B's.

Conclusion: If not A, then not B.

The reasoning is flawed because it fails to account for other possible reasons why MicroFirm engineers have not left their jobs. (Some B's might not be A's.)

Choice (D) is the only answer choice that demonstrates the same essential pattern of flawed reasoning. To recognize the similarity, we can rephrase the argument's sentence structure to match the essence of the original argument:

Premise: All people who practice diligently, choice (A), achieve perfection, choice (B).

Conclusion: If one does not practice diligently (not choice (A)) one cannot achieve perfection (not choice (B)).

Choice (A) reasons essentially as follows: One certain A is B. Therefore, if A then B. (This reasoning is flawed, but in a different respect than the reasoning in the original argument.)

Choice (B) reasons essentially as follows: If A, then B. Not B. Therefore, not A. This reasoning is sound (not flawed).

Choice (C) reasons essentially as follows: If A, then B. Therefore, if B, then A. (This reasoning is flawed, but in a different respect than the reasoning in the original argument.)

Choice (E) is not a deductive, and cannot readily be expressed symbolically. Without additional evidence, it is impossible to determine the strength of the argument.

Tips for Tackling Parallel-Argument Questions

1. Before reading the answer choices, reduce the original passage to its basic structure. Express the argument in general terms—perhaps using letters as symbols—that incorporate the argument's logic but not its subject matter.

2. Don't equate logical structure with sequence. The passage might provide the conclusion first, while the best answer choice provides its conclusion last (or vice-versa). In other words, try to identify parallel *logic*—not parallel *sequence*.

3. Don't equate logical structure with subject matter. Be suspicious of any answer choice involving a topic that is similar to the topic of the passage. Although that answer choice *might* be the best one, more than likely it is not.

IF YOU HAVE MORE TIME TODAY

To practice the skills you learned today and yesterday, log on to the author's GMAT Web site (www.west.net/~stewart/gmat) and attempt a Critical Reasoning mini-test. (To find the mini-test click on "Verbal Ability" in the "Test Yourself" area.). Each of the seven question types is represented in the mini-test.

Day 14

Critical Reasoning Lesson 3: Mini-Test and Review

Today's Topic

Today you apply what you learned on Days 12 and 13 to a series of 14 Critical Reasoning questions. After taking this mini-test under timed conditions, review the explanations that follow.

MINI-TEST (CRITICAL REASONING)

Number of Questions: 14
Suggested time: 28 minutes
Directions (as provided on the test): For each question select the best of the answer choices given.

1. A reliable survey indicates that college graduates change employers four times on average during the first ten years after college graduation. Therefore, in order to avoid employee turnover, business administrators in charge of hiring new employees should favor job applicants who obtained college degrees at least ten years earlier over other job applicants.

   The advice about how to avoid employee turnover rests on which of the following assumptions?

   (A) Employee turnover among businesses that hire employees without college degrees is greater than turnover among businesses that hire only employees with college degrees.

   (B) Job changes within the same company are less common than job changes from one employer to another.

   (C) Employees who graduated from college at least ten years ago change employers less frequently on average than other employees.

   (D) Most employees who leave their jobs do so upon either request or demand of their employers rather than by their own initiative.

   (E) The survey excluded college graduates who interrupted their vocational careers to pursue advanced academic degrees.

2. This county's current dumping ordinance, which requires that all refuse be hauled at least ten miles outside the city limits for dumping, should be repealed in the interest of public health. The purpose of the ordinance in the first place was to prevent the spread of Smith's Disease, which has been found to be most prevalent in regions near outdoor dumps. But the county funds used to maintain the roads to the dumping sites have been diverted from a proposed countywide education program for Smith's Disease awareness, which would have been more effective than the dumping ordinance in preventing the disease.

Which of the following, if true, would best support the assertion that the dumping ordinance should be repealed?

(A) The geographic area within the city limits is more heavily populated than the area outside the city limits.

(B) Treating Smith's Disease is more expensive on average than preventing it in the first place.

(C) The roads to the dumping sites are of no practical use other than for transport between the city limits and the dumping sites.

(D) The proposed education program would have been available to all county residents.

(E) The most effective means of preventing Smith's disease is an expensive vaccine that is not readily available.

3. Topical application of oil from the bark of aoli trees, which are quite rare and grow only in certain regions of South America, has been shown to be the only effective means of treating certain skin disorders. At the current rate of harvesting bark for aoli oil, however, aoli trees will become extinct within fifty years. Clearly, measures must be taken soon to reduce the demand for aoli oil; otherwise, fifty years from now, it will no longer be possible to treat these skin disorders effectively.

Which of the following, if true, would most seriously weaken the argument above?

(A) One of the skin disorders for which aoli oil is an effective treatment is caused by exposure to chemicals used in a manufacturing process that is quickly becoming obsolete.

(B) The bark of newly planted aoli trees can be harvested for oil within twenty years after the new trees are planted.

(C) The cause of skin disorders treatable with aoli oil is also the cause of certain other health problems that are treated effectively by ingesting aoli oil.

(D) In South America, aoli tree bark is widely used in making a variety of decorative craft items and utensils.

(E) Only people who live in the regions of South America where aoli trees are found suffer from skin disorders treatable with aoli oil.

4. *Gwen:* As we both know, the most popular restaurants among college students here in Collegetown are the ones that provide delivery service. So, local economic conditions, which rely on the student population, would improve if expensive Collegetown restaurants were replaced by less expensive ones that also provide delivery service.

Jose: I disagree. After all, many expensive Collegetown restaurants also provide delivery service.

Which of the following best expresses the point of disagreement between Gwen and Jose?

(A) Whether inexpensive restaurants are more popular among Collegetown students than expensive restaurants

(B) Whether Collegetown should reduce the number of restaurants providing delivery service

(C) Whether inexpensive restaurants in Collegetown should provide delivery service

(D) Whether Collegetown students prefer delivery meal service over sit-down meal service

(E) Whether inexpensive restaurants are popular among Collegetown students

5. State X requires employers to pay hourly-wage employees 50 percent more than their regular wage for every work hour in excess of 8 on any workday. State Y requires employers to pay these employees the same overtime rate, but only for work hours in excess of 40 during any given week. Most hourly-wage employees prefer to work in state Y over state X.

Based only on the statements above, which of the following best explains why most hourly-wage employees prefer to work in state Y over state X?

(A) Most hourly-wage employees prefer to work for employers that do not provide overtime work.

(B) Most hourly-wage employees work at least five days per week.

(C) Most hourly-wage employees prefer to work for employers that provide overtime work.

(D) Overtime work hours for most hourly-wage employees exceed regular work hours by at least 50 percent.

(E) Most hourly-wage employees work less than forty hours per week.

6. Only one pie can win first place at the annual pie-baking contest held at the county fair. Pies will be judged for flavor, freshness of ingredients, proper "doneness," and distinctness among the pies entered in the contest. The contest rules provide that only fruit-filled pies may be entered.

Which of the following would best support a prediction that the winning pie at the pie-baking contest will be a cherry pie?

(A) More cherry pies than any other type of pie have been entered in the contest.

(B) Achieving proper doneness is more difficult with fresh cherries than with other pie ingredients.

(C) Fresh fruits are not available to any of the pie-baking contestants.

(D) Judges prefer the flavor of cherry pies over the flavors of other pies.

(E) Baking fresh cherries to their proper doneness results in over-baking the pie's crust.

7. Our nation's public policy dictates that our lands be put to their most economically productive uses. Although farm subsidies help farmers avoid bankruptcy during years in which they lose their crops due to natural disasters, in the long term, subsidies provide a disincentive for farmers to farm productively. Therefore, farms will be less productive economically over time as a result of the current subsidy system than they would be without any subsidy system at all.

Which one of the following best expresses the main point of the argument above?

(A) Farm subsidies result in less than optimal farm productivity.

(B) Our nation's public policy should be modified to accommodate farm subsidies.

(C) Farmers should strive to make more productive use of their farmland.

(D) Farm productivity is more important than whether farmers operate their farms profitably.

(E) The current farm subsidy system amounts to a violation of our nation's public policy.

8. Some people with a Bachelor's degree are eligible for the internship program with the district attorney's office. If a person meets the eligibility requirements for the program, that person is likely to gain admission to the local law school if he or she applies, whether or not that person actually participates in the internship program. However, no person without a Bachelor's degree is eligible to participate in the internship program.

If the statements above are all true, which of the following is properly inferred from them?

(A) All people with a Bachelor's degree who apply for admission to the local law school are likely to gain admission.

(B) Some people likely to gain admission to the local law school would not have been eligible for the internship program.

(C) Some people with a Bachelor's degree are likely to gain admission to the local law school if they apply.

(D) All people eligible for the internship program hold Bachelor degrees.

(E) Without a Bachelor's degree, a person cannot gain admission to the local law school.

9. A child's conception of whether certain behavior is right or wrong, referred to as "behavioral predisposition," is fully developed by the age of 10. During a person's teenage years, other teenagers with whom the person associates regularly have a significant influence on whether the person later acts in accordance with his or her predisposition.

In other words, teenagers tend to mimic their peers' behavior. It is interesting to note that the vast majority of adult criminals also committed crimes as teenagers and associated primarily with other teenagers who later became adult criminals.

Which of the following conclusions can most properly be drawn from the information above?

(A) A child's conception of whether certain behavior is right or wrong can change during the child's teenage years.

(B) Until a child becomes a teenager, it is impossible to predict whether the child will eventually become an adult criminal.

(C) Law-abiding adults are unlikely to have developed a predisposition for adult criminal behavior.

(D) An adult criminal is likely to have been predisposed as a child to criminal behavior.

(E) Preteen children who are not predisposed to criminal behavior are unlikely to become adult criminals.

10. Driving excessively fast has been demonstrated to decrease the number of miles one can drive per gallon of fuel. Gary has recently been experiencing a decrease in mileage per gallon of fuel while driving his car. This clearly proves that Gary has been driving excessively fast lately.

Which of the following statements, if true, would most seriously weaken the conclusion about Gary's driving?

(A) Recently, Gary's speedometer has been indicating the speed of his car as lower than the car's actual speed.

(B) Recently Gary has been driving more miles per day on average than before he began experiencing a decrease in fuel mileage.

(C) Other tests have shown that a car's speed affects fuel mileage more than any other single factor.

(D) Before Gary began driving excessively fast, his speedometer overrepresented his car's actual speed.

(E) Recently, the tires on Gary's car have been losing air pressure, and low tire air pressure is known to lower fuel mileage.

11. According to the school's principal, no teacher who refuses to participate in the afternoon conference was allowed to attend the buffet dinner immediately after the conference. Sanjay, who is one of the school's teachers, is not the sort of person to refuse a buffet dinner; yet I'm certain Sanjay was not at the dinner. I can only conclude that Sanjay refused to participate in the conference.

Which of the following demonstrates a pattern of reasoning most like the flawed reasoning in the argument above?

(A) All attentive students are rewarded with high grades in school. Alan is not attentive as a student. Therefore, he will not be rewarded with high grades in school.

(B) Every person seated in the front row can hear the coach's instructions to his players. Ursula can hear the coach's instructions. Therefore, Ursula must be seated in the front row.

(C) Anyone who claims to have been abducted by aliens is either not being truthful or is mistaken about whether he or she has been abducted by aliens. Sandy is always truthful. Therefore, she has not been abducted by aliens.

(D) Every legislator is in favor of the bill. Martha is not in favor of the bill. Therefore, she must not be a legislator.

(E) This sculpture is either priceless or a worthless fake. This sculpture is not a worthless fake. Therefore, it is priceless.

12. Since the release of MicroTeam Corporation's newest version of its ActiveWeb software, more copies of this new version have been sold than any software product that competes with ActiveWeb. Therefore, MicroTeam Corporation's marketing campaign to promote the new version of ActiveWeb was highly effective.

Which of the following, if true, provides the best indication that the conclusion in the argument above is logically well supported?

(A) The number of potential purchasers of ActiveWeb and of products that compete with it has increased since the release of the new version of ActiveWeb.

(B) The number of products competing with ActiveWeb has diminished since the release of the new version of ActiveWeb.

(C) The new version of ActiveWeb corrected every known operational problem with previous versions.

(D) More copies of the new version of ActiveWeb have been sold than of any earlier version of ActiveWeb.

(E) Shortly after the release of the new version of ActiveWeb, a popular and influential magazine recommended a competing product over the new version of ActiveWeb.

13. Because people are living longer, they are developing more new types of ailments. Pharmaceutical companies are responding by developing new prescription drugs that prevent these new ailments. But elderly people of modest financial means must essentially choose among ailments because our federal health-insurance program for the elderly does not cover prescription drugs. Thus, to promote health among our elderly citizens, the federal government should force pharmaceutical companies to lower their prices for these new drugs.

Each of the following, if true, weakens the conclusion above EXCEPT:

(A) If forced to reduce their prices for the new drugs, pharmaceutical companies could not afford to develop drugs for the prevention of more new ailments.

(B) The new drugs prevent not only new types of ailments but also ailments already common among elderly people.

(C) Other new drugs are available to treat, but not prevent, the same new ailments.

(D) None of the new drugs has been shown to prolong an elderly person's life.

(E) The federal health insurance program for the elderly covers all medical expenses of the elderly other than prescription drugs.

14. Everybody agrees that a decline in the quality of television programming invariably results in a decrease in television viewership. Members of the Television Writers Union are threatening to go on strike this season in order to compel the television studios to meet certain demands. Clearly, the movie studios whose movies are shown in theaters should hope that the television writers will indeed decide to go on strike.

Each of the following must be assumed to be true in order for the conclusion above to be properly drawn EXCEPT:

(A) Television writers are not the same writers who write screenplays for movies shown in movie theaters.

(B) An increase in movie theater attendance will result in increased profits for movie theaters.

(C) A television writers' strike would result in a decline in the quality of television programming.

(D) Movie studio profits are directly correlated to the profits of the movie theaters themselves.

(E) When people watch less television, their movie theater attendance increases.

Quick Answer Guide

1.	C	8.	C
2.	C	9.	D
3.	B	10.	E
4.	A	11.	B
5.	B	12.	E
6.	D	13.	D
7.	E	14.	A

EXPLANATIONS

1. The correct answer is (C). Assumption (easier).

The argument fails to explicitly provide that employees who are at least ten years out of college change employers less frequently on average than other employees. This premise is essential to the argument's conclusion, and choice (C) supplies this additional premise.

Choice (A) is relevant to the argument, since the argument's conclusion appears to recommend college graduates of at least ten years over *all* other job applicants (including college graduates as well as candidates *without college degrees*). However, choice (A) compares the job attrition rate among applicants without college degrees to the rate among all college graduates. The argument's conclusion recommends one group of college graduates over another. Since choice (A) does not distinguish between these two groups, it fails to provide a necessary assumption.

Choice (B) is irrelevant to the argument, which seeks only to make a recommendation for reducing employee turnover and not for minimizing the frequency of job changes within a company.

Choice (D) is irrelevant as it stands. The argument provides no information about whether employees who graduated college at least ten years ago are more or less likely than other employees to

leave their jobs at the request or demand of their employers, as opposed to leaving by their own initiative.

Choice (E) is irrelevant to the argument, which seeks only to recommend one group of college graduates over other job applicants. Admittedly, whether recent college graduates are more or less likely than other college graduates to resign their jobs in order to pursue advanced degrees would be significant in determining how to minimize employee turnover. However, the survey involved only the former group, not the latter group. Thus, choice (E) would be relevant to the argument only under the additional assumption provided by choice (C).

2. The correct answer is (C). Supporting-evidence (challenging).

The argument relies on the unstated assumption that the funds used to maintain the roads would be available for the education program should the ordinance be repealed. Choice (C) provides evidence that this assumption is a reasonable one; if the roads are of no other practical use, then there would be no need to continue to spend county funds to maintain them.

Choice (A) actually tends to *weaken* the argument. Choice (A) provides some evidence that trash is being hauled away from where most of the people are—evidence that the ordinance makes sense and should not be repealed.

Choice (B) is irrelevant to the argument, which is concerned only with preventing Smith's disease, and not with its treatment.

Choice (D) does admittedly lend some measure of support to the argument. Common sense tells us that the education program would be effective only if the group or individual whom it is designed to benefit actually benefit from it. However, we are not informed whether the entire population is, in fact, susceptible to Smith's Disease. Without this additional information, it is impossible to assess the degree to which choice (D) strengthens the argument.

Choice (E) actually *weakens* the argument. If no other practical means of preventing Smith's Disease are available, this fact would provide strong support for the argument that the dumping ordinance should remain in effect.

3. The correct answer is (B). Weakening-evidence (challenging).

The argument assumes that the proposed course of action—reducing demand for aoli tree bark—is necessary to prevent total depletion of aoli tree bark within fifty years. However, the argument ignores the possibility of increasing supply as an alternative means of achieving this goal. Choice (B) provides this alternative.

Choice (A) actually *strengthens* the argument. The fact that a certain activity resulting in the use of aoli oil is becoming obsolete suggests a decline in demand for the oil in the future and thus, less urgency in taking steps to save aoli trees from extinction.

Choice (C) tends to *strengthen* the argument by providing evidence of an additional use for aoli bark. The more potential uses, the more likely that the rate of use will increase and hence that the bark will be depleted within fifty years.

Choice (D) tends to *strengthen* the argument for the same reason as choice (C).

Choice (E) is irrelevant to the argument, which turns on the *rate of use* of aoli oil, not where the users of the oil reside.

4. The correct answer is (A). Assumption (moderate).

Gwen's argument relies on the assumption that expensive restaurants are not as popular among the college students as inexpensive restaurants. Jose provides one reason why expensive restaurants are *not necessarily* less popular among the college students, suggesting that the disagreement is about whether expensive restaurants are in fact less popular among the college students than inexpensive restaurants.

Choice (B) is irrelevant to the argument, in which Jose and Gwen disagree about whether the number of expensive restaurants should be reduced, not whether the number of restaurants providing delivery service should be reduced.

Choice (C) is irrelevant to the argument in which Jose and Gwen disagree about whether the number of expensive restaurants should be reduced, not whether inexpensive restaurants should provide delivery service.

Choice (D) is not a point of disagreement between Jose and Gwen. On the contrary, the premise of Gwen's argument (first sentence) strongly suggests that Jose and Gwen agree on this point.

Choice (E) misses the key point of disagreement: whether inexpensive restaurants are *relatively* popular *compared to* expensive restaurants among Collegetown students.

5. The correct answer is (B). Probable-inference (moderate).

If an hourly-wage employee works less than five days per week, the employee would need to work more than 8 hours per day *on average* to qualify for overtime pay in state Y. On the other hand, the same employee would need to work more than 8 hours per day *only on one day* to qualify for overtime pay in state X. Thus, employees working less than five days per week would prefer to work in state X. Given that most employees prefer to work in state Y, it is reasonable to conclude that most employees work at least five days per week.

Choices (A) and (C) are not inferable. Each of these two choices assumes that employers in one state provide overtime work while employers in the other state do not. However, the passage provides no information that might help affirm this assumption.

Choice (D) confuses the use of the percentage cited in the argument.

Choice (E) is not inferable. In fact, the *reverse* of choice (E) is readily inferable from the facts; that is, most employees probably work *more* than 40 hours per week if they prefer to work in state Y over state X.

6. The correct answer is (D). Supporting-evidence (easier).

One of the judging criteria is flavor. If the judges prefer the flavor of cherry pies over other flavors, this fact would increase the likelihood that a cherry pie will win the contest. Admittedly, flavor is only one judging criterion. Nevertheless, choice (D) is the best of the five answer choices.

Choice (A) does not firmly support any conclusion. On the one hand, the more cherry pies entered in the contest, the more statistically likely the winner will be a cherry pie. On the other hand, one of the judging criterion is distinctness, and the more cherry pies entered, the less distinctive any cherry pie is likely to be.

Choice (B) tends to support the opposite conclusion. If a fresh cherry pie is difficult to bake to proper doneness, then a fresh cherry pie is less likely to win the contest. Moreover, since freshness is also a judging criterion, a canned cherry pie is less likely to win, and therefore any cherry pie is less likely to win. Also, whether a pie is difficult to bake properly is not one of the judging criteria; in this respect, then, choice (C) is irrelevant.

Choice (C) does not support any conclusion about the likelihood that a cherry pie will win. On the contrary, choice (D) provides evidence that none of the pies entered in the contest hold an advantage over any other with respect to one particular judging criterion.

Choice (E) does not strongly support the conclusion. While a cherry pie that is fresh and is baked to the cherries' proper doneness is more likely to win as a result, a pie whose crust is over-baked (not baked to proper doneness) is less likely to win as a result.

7. The correct answer is (E). Main-point (easier).

The best expression of the argument's conclusion must embrace every relevant component of the passage, including the first sentence. Accordingly, the argument boils down to the following:

Premise: Public policy requires the most productive use of land.
Premise: Farm subsidies discourage farm productivity.
Intermediate conclusion: Farms are less productive with subsidies than without them.
Final conclusion (implied): Farm subsidies violate public policy.
Choice (E) expresses the final conclusion.

Choice (A) expresses only the argument's intermediate conclusion and therefore is not the best answer.

Choice (B) runs contrary to the passage, which suggests that the current farm subsidy system should be changed (or even abolished) in order to conform to public policy, not the other way around.

Choice (C) is supported by the passage but is off focus in terms of the argument's final conclusion.

Choice (D) is supported by the passage but is not the argument's final conclusion.

8. The correct answer is (C). Necessary-inference (moderate).

According to the argument, *any* person eligible for the internship program is likely to gain admission to the local law school if he or she applies, and *some* people eligible for the program hold Bachelor degrees. It follows logically that *some* people with a Bachelor's degree are likely to gain admission to law school if they apply. To follow these logical steps, it helps to express the premises and conclusion symbolically, as follows (E = eligible for the program), A = likely to gain admission to law school, B = Bachelor's degree):

Premise: All E are A.
Premise: Some E are B.
Conclusion: Some B are A.
None of the other choices provides a valid conclusion.

9. The correct answer is (D). Probable-inference (challenging).

Based on the last sentence of the passage, we can conclude that juvenile criminals associate primarily with other juvenile criminals, and that adult criminals constitute the same group of people who were juvenile criminals. For choice (D) to *not* be readily inferable would require that most adult criminals associate primarily with law abiding peers as teenagers. But this contradicts what we know about adult criminals, based on the passage information. Thus, choice (D) is strongly inferable.

Choice (A) is not readily inferable. In fact, choice (A) is explicitly contradicted by one of the argument's stated premises (the first sentence).

Choice (B) is not readily inferable. Before we can determine whether the prediction to which choice (B) refers is "impossible," we would need to compare the significance of behavioral predisposition to the influence of a person's teenage peers. But the passage does not provide sufficient information for this comparison. (The passage indicates merely that the latter factor is "significant.")

Choice (C) is not readily inferable. The passage information leaves open the possibility that many, or perhaps even most, law-abiding adults *did* develop a predisposition for criminal behavior, but were influenced by their teenage peers to act contrary to that predisposition. Admittedly, this possibility runs contrary to the passage information as a whole. Nevertheless, unlike choice (D), choice (C) does not find *explicit* support in the passage; thus choice (D) is a better answer choice than choice (C).

Choice (E) is not readily inferable. The passage information leaves open the possibility that most preteen children who are not predisposed to criminal behavior are later influenced by their teenage peers to act contrary to that predisposition and eventually become adult criminals.

10. The correct answer is (E). Weakening-evidence (easier).

The argument relies on the unstated assumption that no factor other than Gary's driving speed might be responsible for the recent decrease in his fuel mileage; in other words, no other circumstances that might affect fuel mileage have changed recently. One effective way to weaken the argument would be to refute this assumption. Choice (E) accomplishes this by providing a convincing alternative explanation for the decrease.

Choice (A) is irrelevant to the argument; whether or not Gary knows how fast he is driving bears no relation to his car's actual fuel mileage, which is based on the number of miles driven and the amount of fuel consumed.

Choice (B) is irrelevant as it stands. Admittedly, the number of miles Gary travels *might* affect Gary's fuel mileage under some circumstances—for example, if additional wear and tear on the engine from additional or more frequent driving causes lower fuel mileage. Yet without clear evidence to this effect, it is impossible to assess the extent to which choice (B) would weaken the argument.

Choice (C) actually *strengthens* the argument, by providing additional evidence that Gary's driving speed is indeed the cause of the decrease in his fuel mileage.

Choice (D) is irrelevant for the same reason as choice (A): whether or not Gary knows how fast he is driving bears no relation to his car's actual fuel mileage.

11. The correct answer is (B). Parallel-argument (moderate).

The original argument boils down to the following:

> *Premise:* If a teacher refuses to attend the conference, then the teacher will not attend the buffet.
> *Premise:* Sanjay did not attend the buffet.
> *Conclusion:* Sanjay refused to attend the conference.

To reveal the argument's structure (and its flawed reasoning), express the argument using symbols:

> *Premise:* If A, then B.
> *Premise:* X is B.
> *Conclusion:* X is A.

This reasoning is fallacious, and choice (B) demonstrates the same basic pattern:

> *Premise:* If a person is seated in the front row, then the person can hear the coach. (If A, then B.)

Premise: Ursula can hear the coach. (X is B.)
Conclusion: Ursula is seated in the front row. (X is A.)

12. The correct answer is (E). Supporting-evidence (challenging).

The argument asserts, essentially, that it was the marketing campaign, and not some other factor, that was responsible for the high number of sales of the new version of ActiveWeb compared to competing products. One way to support the argument is to rule out one or more other factors that might have been responsible instead for this phenomenon. By implication, choice (E) provides just this sort of evidence. While *favorable* third-party reviews of ActiveWeb would serve to weaken the claim that the marketing campaign was the cause of the sales results, *unfavorable* reviews would accomplish just the opposite.

Choice (A) is irrelevant to the argument, which seeks to explain the success of the new version of ActiveWeb vis-à-vis competing products; the mere fact that the total market size has increased accomplishes nothing toward explaining this *comparative* success.

Choice (B) has little effect on the argument, at least without additional information. On the one hand, *if* the decrease in the number of competitors was the direct result of MicroTeam's marketing efforts, then choice (B) would serve to *strengthen* the argument. On the one hand, by providing an alternative explanation for the sales comparison indicated in the argument's first sentence, choice (B) tends to *weaken* the argument.

Choice (C) *weakens* the argument, by providing an alternative explanation for the sales comparison indicated in the argument's first sentence. Specifically, choice (C) provides evidence that it is the product itself and not the marketing campaign that is responsible for the product's comparative success in the marketplace.

Choice (D) is not directly relevant to the argument. Admittedly, the fact that more copies of the new version of ActiveWeb have been sold than any previous version *might* be explained by a suc-

cessful marketing campaign. However, this fact could just as easily be explained by other factors.

13. The correct answer is (D). Weakening-evidence (moderate).

Choice (D) actually *strengthens* the argument, insofar as by prolonging life the new drugs would make it possible for the elderly to develop even more new ailments. (The argument does *not* equate health with prolonged life.)

Choice (A) weakens the argument, by providing evidence that elderly people might be *more* likely to develop new ailments—and thus suffer from poor health—if the government limits the price of the new drugs.

Choice (B) serves to weaken the argument. If a prescribed dosage of a new drug treats or prevents multiple ailments just as effectively as it treats one new ailment, then the total amount elderly people pay for all drugs will be less than it would be otherwise—and accordingly elderly people can better afford the new drugs.

Choice (C) weakens the argument by providing an alternative to the expensive new drugs that prevent the new ailments. (Just as preventing the new ailments would promote heath, so would treating them.)

Choice (E) weakens the argument. Given choice (E), health expenses incurred by elderly people are not as great as they would be otherwise, and so the new drugs are more affordable than they would be otherwise. Accordingly, government limits on prices are less likely to be necessary than they would be otherwise.

14. The correct answer is (A). Assumption (moderate).

Choice (A) is irrelevant to the argument without certain additional assumptions. Even if the same writers who write for television also write for movies, the passage provides no information about whether these writers would also strike against movie studios. Even if they would, we are not informed how the impending strike might affect the quality of new movie screenplays, if at all, and how this outcome might in turn affect movie-theater attendance and profits, if at all.

Choice (B) is a necessary assumption. Unless we can assume that an increase in movie theater attendance will result in increased profits for the theaters and, in turn, for the movie studios, then a writers' strike will not necessarily have any impact on the movie studios. (Without this assumption, it is possible, for example, that the price of tickets might decrease so that an increase in movie attendance would not result in an increase in profits.)

Choice (C) is a necessary assumption. Unless the quality of television programming declines as a result of a writers' strike, it is impossible to conclude with any certainty whether movie theater attendance, and therefore movie studio profits, will increase.

Choice (D) is a necessary assumption that goes hand-in-hand with answer choice (B). Unless we can assume that movie studios will also profit from the profits of movie theaters, then a writers' strike will not necessarily have any impact on the movie studios.

Choice (E) is a necessary assumption. Unless people attend movie theaters more often as a result of watching less television, it is impossible to conclude with any certainty that movie theater profits, and therefore movie studio profits, will increase.

Day 15

Quantitative Ability Lesson 4: Algebra—Basic Concepts

Today's Topics:

1. Basic terminology
2. Manipulating algebraic expressions
3. Solving linear equations
4. Solving quadratic equations
5. Solving algebraic inequalities
6. Equations that can't be solved
7. Algebra exercises

Today's lesson covers the "building blocks" that you need to handle GMAT algebra problems. After reviewing the rules for combining and simplifying algebraic expressions, you learn how to solve both linear and factorable quadratic equations.

BASIC TERMINOLOGY

Algebra involves the use of *variables* (such as x or a) in mathematical expressions to represent unknown values. An *algebraic expression* is any mathematical expression that includes one or more variables. Here is an example of an algebraic expression with two variables (a and b):

$a - 2b + 5$

Every algebraic expression includes either one *term* or a series of two or more terms separated by + or − signs. The preceding expression includes three terms: a, $2b$, and 5. a and $2b$ are called *variable terms* (because their values can vary); 5 is called a *constant term* (because its value does not vary). In the second term, 2 is called the *coefficient* of b. 5 is the coefficient of the constant third term. Algebraic expressions

with more than one term are usually called *polynomials*. *Binomials* and *trinomials* are polynomials with two and three terms, respectively:

$7x + 15yz$ (binomial)

$-\dfrac{2}{3}p - 9q + 17$ (trinomial)

Algebraic expressions without exponents (variables raised to a power) are called *linear* algebraic expressions. Those with variables raised to the second power are called *quadratic* expressions:

$2x + 3y$ (linear)
$2x^2 + 3y$ (quadratic)
$2x^2 + 3y^2$ (quadratic)

MANIPULATING ALGEBRAIC EXPRESSIONS

Many GMAT Quantitative questions require you to manipulate algebraic expressions—that is, to restate them in some other form. Keep in mind that all the rules for arithmetical operations and for exponents and roots (see Day 7) apply to algebraic terms and expressions. In manipulating algebraic expressions, you might possibly do the following:

- Simplify a particular term by combining or canceling:

$$4x^2 \cdot 2x^3 = 8x^5$$

$$(x^2)^3 = x^6$$

$$\frac{a^4b^3}{a^2bc} = \frac{a^2b^2}{c}$$

$$\frac{b^2}{ab^3} = \frac{1}{ab^2}$$

$$\frac{\sqrt{16x^3y^2}}{\sqrt{4x^2y^2}} = \frac{4xy\sqrt{x}}{2xy} = 2\sqrt{x}$$

- Combine two (or more) terms having the same variable and same exponent:

$$a + a = 2a$$

$$\frac{1}{3}y - 6y = -\frac{17}{3}y$$

$$2\sqrt{x^2 + y} + \sqrt{x^2 + y} = 3\sqrt{x^2 + y}$$

You cannot, however, combine these expressions:

$a^2 + a$ (the exponents are different)

$2a + 2b$ (the variables are different)

- Factor out numbers and variables common to all terms:

$$2x + 4xy + 10x^2y^2 = 2x(1 + 2y + 5xy^2)$$

(each term includes the coefficient 2 and the variable x)

- Distribute a term among two or more other terms (the reverse of factoring out numbers and variables common to all terms):

$$-3b(-8x - bx + 3) = 24bx + 3b^2x - 9b$$

($-3b$ is distributed among three other terms)

SOLVING LINEAR EQUATIONS

Algebraic expressions are usually used in algebra to form equations. An equation sets two expressions equal to each other. An equation whose variables are in the first power only and whose graph is a straight line is a *linear equation*. For example,

$$11s - \frac{12}{11}t = 75$$

Solving Linear Equations in One Variable

To solve a linear equation (that is, to find the value of the variable that satisfies the equation), isolate the variable on one side of the equation. To accomplish this, perform the same operation on both sides of the equation, as the following paragraphs describe.

Add or subtract the same term from both sides of the equation. Doing so does not change the equality; it merely restates the equation in a different form.

$$2x - 6 = x - 9$$

First, place x-terms on the same side by subtracting x from both sides:

$$2x - 6 - x = x - 9 - x$$

$$x - 6 = -9$$

Next, isolate x by adding 6 to both sides:

$$x - 6 + 6 = -9 + 6$$

$$x = -3$$

Multiply or divide both sides of the equation by the same non-zero term. Doing so does not change the equality; it merely restates the equation in a different form. Here's an example:

$$-12 = \frac{11}{x}$$

Multiply both sides by x:

$$(-12)(x) = \frac{11}{x}(x)$$

Isolate x by dividing both sides by -12:

$$\frac{-12x}{-12} = \frac{11}{-12}$$

$$x = -\frac{11}{12}$$

Here's another example:

$$15x + \frac{1}{3} = 3$$

Isolate the x-term on one side:

$$15x = 2\frac{2}{3} \text{ or } \frac{8}{3}$$

$$\frac{15x}{15} = \frac{\frac{8}{3}}{15}$$

Multiply $\frac{8}{3}$ by reciprocal of 15:

$$x = \left(\frac{8}{3}\right)\left(\frac{1}{15}\right) = \frac{8}{45}$$

Where the original equation involves fractions, use *cross-multiplication* to eliminate the fractions. Multiply the numerator from one side of the equation times the denominator from the other side. (In effect, cross-multiplication is a shortcut method of multiplying both sides of the equation by both denominators.) Set the product equal to the product of the other numerator and denominator:

$$\frac{7a}{8} \quad \frac{a+1}{3}$$

$(3)(7a) = 8(a + 1)$	(result of cross-multiplication)
$21a = 8a + 8$	(distributing 8 to both a and 1)
$21a - 8a = 8a + 8 - 8a$	(isolating a-terms on one side)
$13a = 8$	
$\frac{13a}{13} = \frac{8}{13}$	(isolating a by dividing both sides by 13)
$a = \frac{8}{13}$	

Square both sides of the equation to eliminate radical signs. Where the variable is indicated under a radical sign (square root), remove the radical sign by squaring both sides of the equation. (Use a similar technique for cube or other roots.)

$$2 = \frac{11}{3}\sqrt{2x}$$

$$\frac{6}{11} = \sqrt{2x}$$

Square both sides and solve for x:

$$\frac{36}{121} = 2x$$

$$\frac{18}{121} = x$$

In some instances, however, squaring both sides of what appears to be a linear equation might reveal that the equation is nonlinear. The following example is a quadratic equation that has two possible values (or roots):

$$6x = \sqrt{3x}$$
$$36x^2 = 3x$$
$$36x^2 - 3x = 0$$
$$x(36x - 3) = 0$$
$$x = 0 \text{ or } 36x - 3 = 0$$
$$x = 0, \frac{1}{12}$$

You'll examine quadratic equations in more detail a bit later.

Linear Equations in More Than One Variable

A single linear equation with more than one variable cannot be solved. That is to say, you cannot determine the value of any variable. Consider the following equation:

$$4x - 9 = \frac{3}{2}y$$

Because this equation includes more than one variable, it is impossible to determine the value of either x or y. You *can*, however, express either x or y in terms of the other variable. Referring to the preceding equation, you can solve for x in terms of y:

$$4x = \frac{3}{2}y + 9$$

$$x = \frac{3}{8}y + \frac{9}{4}$$

You can also solve for y in terms of x:

$$\frac{4x-9}{\frac{3}{2}} = y$$

$$\frac{8}{3}x - 6 = y$$

Solving a System of Two Linear Equations in Two Variables

A *system of equations* involves two or more equations with one or more common variables. Here is a system of two equations with two variables:

$$\frac{2}{5}x + y = 3y - 10$$

$$y = 10 - x$$

Solving (determining a number value) for either of two variables requires at least *two distinct* equations (that is, two equations and two unknowns).

The substitution method. One way to solve for the two variables is to express one of them in terms of the other using one of the equations, and then *substitute* that value in the other equation. Consider again the following system of equations:

Equation 1: $\frac{2}{5}x + y = 3y - 10$

Equation 2: $y = 10 - x$

The value of y in equation 2 can be substituted for y in Equation 1 (first combine the two y-terms in equation 1) to solve for x:

$$\frac{2}{5}x = 2y - 10$$

$$\frac{2}{5}x = 2(10 - x) - 10$$

$$\frac{2}{5}x = 20 - 2x - 10$$

$$\frac{2}{5}x = 10 - 2x$$

$$\frac{2}{5}x + 2x = 10$$

$$\frac{12}{5}x = 10$$

$$x = \frac{50}{12} \text{ or } \frac{25}{6}$$

You can then substitute this x-value for x in either Equation 1 or 2 to determine the value of y. Using Equation 2:

$$y = 10 - \frac{25}{6}$$

$$y = \frac{60}{6} - \frac{25}{6}$$

$$y = \frac{35}{6}$$

The addition-subtraction method. Another way to solve for x and y is to make the coefficients of one of the variables the same (disregarding the sign) in both equations and either add the equations or subtract one equation from the other. Here's an example:

$$3x + 4y = -8$$

$$x - 2y = \frac{1}{2}$$

In the second equation, multiply both sides by 2 (to make the y-coefficients the same) to solve for x by adding the equations:

$$3x + 4y = -8$$
$$\underline{2x - 4y = 1}$$
$$5x + 0 = -7$$

$$x = -\frac{7}{5}$$

Similarly, to solve for y, multiply both sides of the second equation by 3 (to make the x-coefficients the same), then subtract the second equation from the first:

$$3x + 4y = -8$$

$$3x - 6y = \frac{3}{2}$$

$$\overline{}$$

$$0 + 10y = -9\frac{1}{2}$$

$$10y = -\frac{19}{2}$$

$$y = -\frac{19}{20}$$

You can also combine the addition-subtraction and substitution methods. Simply solve for one variable using the former method, then substitute the value of that variable in either equation to determine the other variable's value.

SOLVING QUADRATIC EQUATIONS

A *quadratic equation* is an equation that you can express in the general form $ax^2 + bx + c = 0$, where a, b, and c are real numbers and $a \neq 0$. Note that the b-term and c-term are not essential—that is, b and/or c can equal zero. (A quadratic equation has *at most* two real-number solutions, but might have only one or no real-number solutions.)

You can solve any quadratic equation by using the following formula:

$$x = \frac{-b \pm \sqrt{b^2 - 4ac}}{2a}$$

However, the GMAT does not require that you apply this formula. GMAT problems involving quadratic expressions are almost always *factorable,* and thus you can simplify and solve them without resorting to the preceding formula, as discussed in the following sections.

Factoring Quadratic Expressions

Solving quadratic equations on the GMAT usually calls for the following three-step process:

1. Put the equation into the *standard form* $(ax^2 + bx + c = 0)$.

2. Factor the terms of the left side of the equation into two linear expressions (roots) whose product is zero.

3. Independently set each linear expression (root) equal to zero and solve for the variable in each.

You will find that equations in which the coefficient of either the b-term or c-term is zero are easier to factor, whereas equations with coefficients other than 0 and 1 are usually more difficult to factor. To illustrate this process, consider the following three quadratic equations in turn:

Equation 3: $3x^2 = 10x$ (easier)

Equation 4: $-3y = 4 - y^2$ (tougher)

Equation 5: $-7z = 15 - 2z^2$ (toughest)

Equation 3. In Equation 3 (which does not include a c-term), it is easy to recognize that you can factor out an a-term as one of the two roots:

$3x^2 = 10x$		[the original equation]
$3x^2 - 10x (+ 0) = 0$		[general form $(ax^2 + bx + c = 0)$]
$x(3x - 10) = 0$		the two roots are x and $(3x - 10)$]
$x = 0, 3x - 10 = 0$		[each root is set equal to zero]
$x = 0, \dfrac{10}{3}$		[two possible values of x (two roots)]

Equation 4 and the FOIL method. Solving more complex quadratic equations is a bit trickier. For example, in Equation 4, after putting the equation into the general form, you can see that there are no common variables or coefficients that you can factor out of all three terms:

$-3y = 4 - y^2$		[the original equation]
$y^2 - 3y - 4 = 0$		[general form $(ax^2 + bx + c = 0)$]

Instead, you must factor the quadratic expression into two linear *binomial* expressions, using the FOIL (First-Outer-Inner-Last) method. Under the

FOIL method, the sum of the following four terms is equivalent to the original (nonfactored) quadratic expression:

- F, the product of the *first* terms of the two binomials
- O, the product of the *outer* terms of the two binomials
- I, the product of the *inner* terms of the two binomials
- L, the product of the *last (second)* terms of the two binomials

  Note the following relationships:

- F is the ax^2 term (the first term) of the quadratic expression.
- O + I is the bx term (the second term) of the quadratic expression.
- L is the c term (the third term) of the quadratic expression.

Applying the FOIL method to Equation 4, you can first set up the following equation with two binomial factors:

$$(y + ?) \, (y + ?) = 0$$

To determine the missing values of the two second terms, find two numbers for which the product is c (in this case, -4) and the sum of which is b (in this case, -3). Those two numbers are -4 and 1:

$$(y - 4) \, (y + 1) = 0$$
$$y - 4 = 0, \, y + 1 = 0$$
$$y = 4, -1$$

To check your work, reverse the process, using the FOIL method to multiply the two binomials together:

$$y^2 \text{ (first)} + y \text{ (outer)} - 4y \text{ (inner)} - 4 \text{ (last)} = 0$$
$$y^2 \, (+ y - 4y \,) - 4 = 0$$
$$y^2 - 3y - 4 = 0$$

Equation 5 and the FOIL method. In Equation 5, z^2 has a coefficient of 2. This complicates the process of factoring into two binomials. A bit of trial and

error might be required to determine all coefficients in both binomials. Restate the equation in the general form and set up two binomial roots:

$$-7z = 15 - 2z^2$$
$$2z^2 - 7z - 15 = 0$$
$$(2z + ?)(z + ?) = 0$$

One of the two missing constants must be negative, because their product (the "L" term under the FOIL method) is -15. The possible integral pairs for these constants are $(1, -15)$, $(-1, 15)$, $(3, -5)$, and $(-3, 5)$. Substituting each value pair for the two ?s in Equation 5 reveals that 3 and -5 are the missing constants (remember to take into account that the first x-term includes a coefficient of 2):

$$(2z + 3)(z - 5) = 0$$

Check your work by reversing the process:

$$2z^2 \, (- 10z + 3z) - 15 = \quad 0 \qquad \text{[FOIL]}$$
$$2z^2 - 7z - 15 = \quad 0$$

Now, solve for z:

$$(2z + 3)(z - 5) = \quad 0$$
$$2z + 3 = 0, \, x - 5 = \quad 0$$
$$z = -\frac{3}{2}, 5$$

Nonlinear Expressions in Two Variables

On the GMAT, if you encounter nonlinear expressions in two variables, you probably won't have to determine numerical values for the variables. Instead, your task will be to factor and simplify the expression. Three related nonlinear expressions that appear over and over again on the GMAT are worth noting (use the FOIL method to verify these equations):

Sum of two variables, squared: $\quad (x+y)^2 = x^2 + 2xy + y^2$

Difference of two variables, squared: $\quad (x-y)^2 = x^2 - 2xy + y^2$

Difference of two squares: $\quad x^2 - y^2 = (x+y)(x-y)$

Memorize each of these three expressions in both factored and nonfactored forms. When you see either form on the exam, in all likelihood the problem will require you to convert it to the other form.

EQUATIONS THAT CAN'T BE SOLVED

Never assume that one equation with one variable is solvable. Similarly, never assume that a system of two equations with two variables is solvable. The test makers love to use the Data Sufficiency format to find out if you know an unsolvable equation when you see one. You'll need to be on the lookout for three different types:

1. Identities

2. Quadratic equations in disguise

3. Equivalent equations

Identities

Beware of equations that you can reduce to 0 = 0. You cannot solve any such equation. Here's an example:

$$3x - 3 - 4x = x - 7 - 2x + 4$$
$$-x - 3 = -x - 3$$
$$0 = 0$$

All terms on both sides of the equation cancel out. Thus, x might be any real number.

Quadratic Equations in Disguise

Some equations that appear linear (variables include no exponents) may actually be quadratic. For the GMAT, here are the two situations you need to be on the lookout for:

1. The same variable inside a radical also appears outside:

$$\sqrt{x} = 5x$$
$$\left(\sqrt{x}\right)^2 = \left(5x\right)^2$$
$$x = 25x^2$$
$$25x^2 - x = 0$$

2. The same variable that appears in the denominator of a fraction also appear elsewhere in the equation:

$$\frac{2}{x} = 3 - x$$
$$2 = x(3 - x)$$
$$2 = 3x - x^2$$
$$x^2 - 3x + 2 = 0$$

As you can see, in both scenarios you're dealing with a quadratic (nonlinear) equation, and x has more than one possible value.

Equivalent Equations

In some cases, what appears to be a system of two equations with two variables is actually one equation expressed in two different ways. Consider the following system:

$$a + b = 30$$
$$2b = 60 - 2a$$

At first glance, these two equations appear to provide a system of two linear equations with two unknowns. Not so! You can easily manipulate the second equation so that it is identical to the first:

$$2b = 60 - 2a$$
$$2b = 2(30 - a)$$
$$b = 30 - a$$
$$a + b = 30$$

So, you're really dealing with one equation, even considering both equations together. Thus, you can't determine the value of either variable.

SOLVING ALGEBRAIC INEQUALITIES

You solve algebraic inequalities in the same manner as you solve equations. Isolate the variable on one side of the equation, factoring and canceling wherever possible. However, one important rule distinguishes inequalities from equations: Whenever you *multiply or divide by a negative number*, you must *reverse* the order of the inequality—that is, the inequality symbol. (This rule does not apply, however, to other operations.)

$$12 - 4x < 8$$

Subtract 12 from each side; inequality unchanged:

$-4x < -4$

Divide both sides by –4; reverse inequality:

$x > 1$

PUTTING IT ALL TOGETHER

On the GMAT, whenever you encounter a complex and intimidating algebraic expression or equation, always ask yourself the following questions about each expression contained in the problem:

- Do the terms include common variables or coefficients that I can factor out?

- Can I combine common variables and coefficients within a term?

- Do any of the variables include exponents? If so, can a quadratic expression be isolated and factored into two binomials?

IF YOU HAVE MORE TIME TODAY

Before you move ahead to tomorrow's advanced algebra lesson, apply the basic algebraic concepts covered today by attempting the following 10 questions (answers and explanations immediately follow).

Algebra Exercises

1. If $\dfrac{2y}{9} = \dfrac{y-1}{3}$, then $y =$

(A) $\dfrac{1}{3}$ (B) $\dfrac{4}{9}$ (C) $\dfrac{9}{15}$ (D) $\dfrac{9}{4}$ (E) 3

2. If $x + y = a$, and $x - y = b$, then $x =$

(A) $a + b$ (B) $a - b$ (C) $\dfrac{1}{2}(a + b)$ (D) $\dfrac{1}{2}ab$

(E) $\dfrac{1}{2}(a - b)$

3. If $x^2 - 4x = 21$, then $x =$

(A) 7 or 3 (B) –7 or –3 (C) –7 or 3 (D) 7 or –3
(E) 7 only

4. If $\sqrt{4x+4} - 4 = 8$, then $x =$

(A) 15 (B) 35 (C) 39 (D) 47 (E) 51

5. Which of the following is a factor of $x^2 - x - 20$?

(A) $x - 4$ (B) $x - 10$ (C) $x + 4$ (D) $x - 2$ (E) $x + 5$

6. If $x + y = 16$, and if $x^2 - y^2 = 48$, then $x - y$ equals

(A) 3 (B) 4 (C) 6 (D) 32 (E) 36

7. If $\dfrac{\frac{3x-1}{3}}{x} = 10$, then $x =$

(A) –9 or $-\dfrac{3}{10}$ (B) $\dfrac{3}{5}$ or –2 (C) 9 or $-\dfrac{10}{3}$

(D) $\dfrac{10}{3}$ or –3 (E) 10 or –3

8. If $-2x > -5$, then

(A) $x > \dfrac{5}{2}$ (B) $x < \dfrac{5}{2}$ (C) $x > -\dfrac{2}{5}$ (D) $x < \dfrac{2}{5}$

(E) $x > -\dfrac{5}{2}$

9. If $3x + 2y = 5a + b$ and $4x - 3y = a + 7b$, then $x =$

(A) $a + b$ (B) $a - b$ (C) $2a + b$
(D) $4a - 6b$ (E) $17a + 17b$

10. If $x + y = 8$, $x + z = 7$, and $y + z = 6$, what is the value of x?

(A) 3 (B) 3.5 (C) 4 (D) 4.5 (E) 5

Answers and Explanations

1. The correct answer is (E).

$$9(y - 1) = 2y(3)$$
$$9y - 9 = 6y$$
$$3y = 9$$
$$y = 3$$

2. The correct answer is (C). Add the two equations:

$$x + y = a$$
$$x - y = b$$
$$2x = a + b$$

$$x = \frac{1}{2}(a + b)$$

3. The correct answer is (D).

$$x^2 - 4x - 21 = 0$$
$$(x - 7)(x + 3) = 0$$
$$x - 7 = 0, x + 3 = 0$$
$$x = 7, -3$$

4. The correct answer is (B).

$$2\sqrt{x+1} = 12$$
$$\sqrt{x+1} = 6$$
$$x + 1 = 36$$
$$x = 35$$

5. The correct answer is (C).

$$x^2 - x - 20 =$$
$$x^2 - 5x + 4x - 20 =$$
$$(x - 5)(x + 4)$$

6. The correct answer is (A).

$$x^2 - y^2 = (x + y)(x - y) = 48$$

Substituting 16 for $x + y$:

$$16(x - y) = 48$$
$$x - y = 3$$

7. The correct answer is (D). Invert the denominator fraction and multiply it by the numerator. Set the quadratic expression equal to 0, then find the two root values of x:

$$\frac{3x^2 - x}{3} = 10$$
$$3x^2 - x = 30$$
$$3x^2 - x - 30 = 0$$
$$(3x - 10)(x + 3) = 0$$
$$3x - 10 = 0, x + 3 = 0$$

$$x = \frac{10}{3}, -3$$

8. The correct answer is (B). Multiply both sides of the equation by −1 and reverse the order of the inequality:

$$2x < 5$$

$$x < \frac{5}{2}$$

9. The correct answer is (A). Multiply the first equation by 3, the second by 2, then add the following:

$$9x + 6y = 15a + 3b$$
$$8x - 6y = 2a + 14b$$
$$17x + 0y = 17a + 17b$$
$$x = a + b$$

10. The correct answer is (D). This problem involves a system of three equations with three variables. The following solution employs both the substitution and addition-subtraction methods.

Express x in terms of y: $x = 8 - y$. Substitute this expression for x in the second equation: $(8 - y) + z = 7$ or $-y + z = -1$. Add this equation to the third equation in the system.

$$-y + z = -1$$
$$y + z = 6$$
$$2z = 5$$
$$z = 2.5$$

Substitute z's value for z in the second equation to find the value of x:

$$x + 2.5 = 7$$
$$x = 4.5$$

Day 16

Quantitative Ability Lesson 5: Algebra Story Problems

Today's Topics:

1. Work problems
2. Motion problems
3. Mixture problems
4. Age problems

5. Overlapping set problems
6. Weighted average problems
7. Currency problems
8. Investment problems

Today you'll learn how to handle the various types of quantitative story problems appearing commonly on the GMAT and that involve setting up and solving algebraic equations.

WORK PROBLEMS

Work problems involve one or more "workers" (people or machines) accomplishing a task or job. In work problems, there is an inverse relationship between the number of workers and the time that it takes to complete the job—in other words, the more workers, the quicker the job gets done. A GMAT work problem might specify the rates at which certain workers work alone and ask you to determine the rate at which they work together, or vice versa. Here is the basic formula for solving a work problem:

$$\frac{1}{x}+\frac{1}{y}=\frac{1}{A}$$

In this formula, x and y represent the time needed for each of two workers—x and y—to complete the job alone, and a represents the time it takes for both x and y to complete the job working aggregately (together). The reasoning is that in one unit of time (that is, one hour) x performs $\frac{1}{x}$ of the job, y performs $\frac{1}{y}$ of the job, and x and y perform $\frac{1}{A}$ of the job.

NOTE: In the real world, if two workers can perform a given task in the same amount of time working alone, they might not be capable of performing that same task in half that time working together. However, in GMAT work problems, you can assume that there is no individual efficiency gained or lost by two or more workers working together.

Now look at two work problems, one requiring you to determine the aggregate rate of the workers (working together), the other requiring you to determine an individual worker's rate (working alone).

Example 16-1: Individual rates given

One printing press can print a daily news-paper in 12 hours, while another press can print it in 18 hours. How long will the job take if both presses work simultaneously?

The rate of the faster press is $\frac{1}{12}$ (it can print $\frac{1}{12}$ of the paper in one hour), and the rate of the slower press is $\frac{1}{18}$:

$$\frac{1}{12} + \frac{1}{18} = \frac{1}{A}$$

$$\frac{3}{36} + \frac{2}{36} = \frac{1}{A}$$

$$\frac{5}{36} = \frac{1}{A}$$

$$5A = 36$$

$$A = \frac{36}{5}$$

It takes both presses $\frac{36}{5}$ hours, or 7 hours and 12 minutes, to print the daily paper working together.

Example 16-2: Aggregate rate given

Petra and Belinda can make a particular quilt in two days when working together. If Petra requires six days to make the quilt alone, how many days does Belinda need to make the quilt alone?

Petra can complete one-sixth of the quilt in one day. The aggregate rate of Belinda and Petra working together is $\frac{1}{2}$ (together they can complete one half of the quilt in one day):

$$\frac{1}{6} + \frac{1}{b} = \frac{1}{2}$$

$$\frac{b+6}{6b} = \frac{1}{2}$$

$$2(b + 6) = 6b$$

$$2b + 12 = 6b$$

$$4b = 12$$

$$b = 3$$

It takes Belinda three days working alone to make the quilt.

In some cases, a second worker might slow or impede the other worker's progress, contributing a negative rate of work. Nevertheless, your approach should be basically the same, as in Example 16-3.

Example 16-3: Negative rate of work

A certain tank holds a maximum of 450 cubic meters of water. If a hose can fill the tank at a rate of 5 cubic meters per minute, but the tank has a hole through which a constant $\frac{1}{2}$ cubic meters of water escapes each minute, how long does it take to fill the tank to its maximum capacity?

In this problem, the hole is the "second worker" but is acting counterproductively, so that you must subtract its rate from the hose's rate to determine the aggregate rate of the hose and the hole. The hose alone takes 90 minutes to fill the tank. The hole alone empties a full tank in 900 minutes. Thus, the hose and the hole, "working" together, fill the tank as follows:

$$\frac{1}{90} - \frac{1}{900} = \frac{1}{A}$$

$$\frac{10}{900} - \frac{1}{900} = \frac{1}{A}$$

$$\frac{9}{900} = \frac{1}{A}$$

$$9A = 900$$

$$A = 100$$

It takes 100 minutes to fill the tank to its maximum capacity.

MOTION PROBLEMS

Motion problems involve the linear movement of persons or objects over time. Fundamental to all GMAT motion problems is the following simple and familiar formula:

distance = rate × time

You can also express this formula as follows:
$$d = (r)(t)$$

Some GMAT motion problems track two objects (or persons) that move either in the same direction or in opposite directions. Others involve one moving object (or person), tracking two parts or "legs" of a trip (for example, away and back during a round trip). In any case, one of the three variables—distance, rate, or time—is *constant* (that is, the same for both moving objects or both legs of a trip). This feature enables you to set up an equation and to solve for the missing value. Don't confuse *motion* problems with *work* problems. Although both involve rate, work problems do not involve movement over a distance but rather rate of work and results of production.

Nearly every GMAT motion problem falls into one of three categories:

- Two objects moving in opposite directions

- Two objects moving in the same direction

- One object making a round trip

(A fourth type of motion problem involves perpendicular (right-angle) motion—for example, where one object moves in a northerly direction while another moves in an easterly direction. However, this type is really just as much a geometry as an algebra problem, because you determine the distance between the two objects by applying the Pythagorean Theorem to determine the length of a hypotenuse. See Day 21.)

Now take a look at one example of each of the three types of motion problems.

Example 16-4: Motion in opposite directions (time constant)

A passenger train and a freight train leave at 10:30 a.m. from stations that are 405 miles apart. The trains travel toward each other, with the rate of the passenger train 45 miles per hour (mph) faster than that of the freight train. If they pass each other at 1:30 p.m., how fast is the passenger train traveling?

Notice in this problem that each train traveled exactly three hours—in other words, time is the constant in this problem. Let x equal the rate (speed) of the freight train. You can express the rate of the passenger train as $x + 45$. Substitute these values for time and rate into the motion formula for each train:

Passenger: $(x + 45)(3) = 3x + 135$

Freight: $(x)(3) = 3x$ (rate × time = distance)

The total distance that the two trains cover is given as 405 miles. Express this algebraically and solve for x:

$$(3x + 135) + (3x) = 405$$
$$6x = 270$$
$$x = 45$$

Accordingly, the rate of the passenger train was 45 + 45, or 90 mph.

Example 16-5: Motion in same direction (distance constant)

Janice left her home at 11 a.m., traveling along Route 1 at 30 mph. At 1 p.m., her brother Richard left home and started after her on the same road at 45 mph. At what time did Richard catch up to Janice?

Notice that the distance that Janice covered is equal to that of Richard—that is, distance is constant. Letting x equal Janice's time, you can express Richard's time as $x - 2$. Substitute these values for time and the values for rate given in the problem into the motion formula for Richard and Janice:

Janice: $(30)(x) = 30x$

Richard: $(45)(x - 2) = 45x - 90$

Because the distance is constant, Janice's distance as expressed algebraically can be equated with Richard's distance, and you can determine the value of x as follows:

$$30x = 45x - 90$$
$$15x = 90$$
$$x = 6$$

Janice had traveled 6 hours when Richard caught up with her. Because Janice left at 11:00 a.m., Richard caught up with her at 5:00 p.m.

Example 16-6: Motion involving a round trip (distance constant)

How far can Scott drive into the country if he drives out at 40 mph, returns over the same road at 30 mph, and spends 8 hours away from home including a one-hour stop for lunch?

Scott's actual driving time is 7 hours, which you must divide into two parts: his time spent driving into the country and his time spent returning. Letting the first part equal x, the return time is what remains of the 7 hours, or $7 - x$. Substitute these expressions into the motion formula for each of the two parts of Scott's journey:

Going: $(40)(x) = 40x$

Returning: $(30)(7 - x) = 210 - 30x$

Because the journey is round trip, the distance going equals the distance returning. Accordingly, you can determine the value of x algebraically:

$40x = 210 - 30x$

$70x = 210$

$x = 3$

If Scott traveled 40 mph for 3 hours, he traveled 120 miles.

MIXTURE PROBLEMS

In mixture problems, you combine substances with different characteristics, resulting in a particular mixture or proportion. There are really two types of mixture problems:

- *Wet mixture problems* involve liquids, gases, or granules, which are measured and mixed by volume or weight, not by number (quantity).

- *Dry mixture problems* involve a number of discreet objects, such as coins, cookies, or marbles, that are measured and mixed by number (quantity) as well as by relative weight, size, value, and so on.

Your approach toward wet and dry mixture problems should be similar. Take a look at an example of each type:

Example 16-7: Wet mixture

How many quarts of pure alcohol must you add to 15 quarts of a solution that is 40% alcohol to strengthen it to a solution that is 50% alcohol?

The original amount of alcohol is 40% of 15. Letting x equal the number of quarts of alcohol that you

must add to achieve a 50% alcohol solution, $.4(15) + x$ equals the amount of alcohol in the solution after adding more alcohol. You can express this amount as 50% of $(15 + x)$. Thus, you can express the mixture algebraically as follows:

$(.4)(15) + x = (.5)(15 + x)$

$6 + x = 7.5 + .5x$

$.5x = 1.5$

$x = 3$

You must add three quarts of alcohol to achieve a 50% alcohol solution.

If you have difficulty expressing mixture problems algebraically, use a table such as the following to indicate amounts and percentages, letting x equal the amount or percentage that you are asked to solve for:

	# of quarts	$\times$ % alcohol	$=$ amount of alcohol
original	15	40%	6
added	x	100%	x
new	$15 + x$	50%	$.5(15 + x)$

Example 16-8: Dry mixture

How many pounds of nuts selling for 70 cents per pound must you mix with 30 pounds of nuts selling at 90 cents per pound to make a mixture that sells for 85 cents per pound?

The cost (in cents) of the nuts selling for 70 cents per pound can be expressed as $70x$, letting x equal the number that you are asked to determine. You then add this cost to the cost of the more expensive nuts $(30 \times 90 = 2,700)$ to obtain the total cost of the mixture, which you can express as $85(x + 30)$. You can state this algebraically and solve for x as follows:

$70x + 2700 = 85(x + 30)$

$70x + 2700 = 85x + 2550$

$150 = 15x$

$x = 10$

You must add 10 pounds of 70-cent-per-pound nuts to make a mixture that sells for 85 cents per pound.

As with wet mixture problems, if you have trouble formulating an algebraic equation needed to solve the problem, indicate the quantities and values in a table such as the one shown in the below figure letting x equal the value that you are asked to determine.

	# of pounds	× price per pound	= total value
less expensive	x	70	$70x$
more expensive	30	90	2,700
mixture	$x + 30$	85	$85(x + 30)$

AGE PROBLEMS

Age problems ask you to compare ages of two or more people at different points in time. In solving age problems, you might have to represent a person's age at the present time, several years from now, or several years ago. Any age problem allows you to set up an equation to relate the ages of two or more people, as in the following examples:

- If X is 10 years younger than Y at the present time, you can express the relationship between X's age and Y's age as $x = y - 10$ (or $x + 10 = y$).

- Five years ago, if A was twice as old as B, you can express the relationship between their ages as $2(a - 5) = b - 5$, where a and b are the present ages of A and B, respectively.

Example 16-9

Eva is 24 years older than her son Frank. In eight years, Eva will be twice as old as Frank will be then. How old is Eva now?

Letting x equal Frank's present age, you can express Frank's age eight years from now as $x + 8$. Similarly, you can express Eva's present age as $(x + 24)$, and her age eight years from now as $(x + 32)$. Set up the following equation relating Eva's age and Frank's age eight years from now:

$$x + 32 = 2(x + 8)$$
$$x + 32 = 2x + 16$$
$$16 = x$$

Frank's present age is 16, and Eva's present age is 40.

OVERLAPPING SET PROBLEMS

Overlapping set problems involve distinct sets that share some number of members. Do not confuse these problems with the set problems that you examined on day 7, which involve combinations of set members. GMAT overlapping set problems come in one of two varieties: single overlap and double overlap (the latter type is more complex). Now look at an example of each.

Example 16-10: Single overlap

Each of the 24 people auditioning for a community-theater production is either an actor, a musician, or both. If 10 of the people auditioning are actors and 19 of the people auditioning are musicians, how many of the people auditioning are musicians but not actors?

This problem presents three mutually exclusive sets: actors who are not musicians, musicians who are not actors, and actors who are also musicians. The total number of people among these three sets is 24. You can represent this scenario with the following algebraic equation (n = number of actors/musicians), solving for $19 - n$ to respond to the question:

$$(10 - n) + n + (19 - n) = 24$$
$$29 - n = 24$$
$$n = 5$$
$$19 - n = 14$$

There are 14 musicians auditioning who are not actors. With problems such as this one, it might be helpful to use a Venn diagram in which overlapping circles represent the set of musicians and the set of actors, as shown in the next figure.

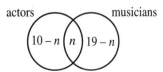

You can, of course, approach this problem less formally as well. The number of actors plus the number of musicians equals 29 (10 + 19 = 29); however, only

24 people are auditioning. Thus, 5 of the 24 are actor-musicians, so 14 of the 19 musicians must not be actors.

Example 16-11: Double overlap

Adrian owns 48 neckties, each of which is either 100% silk or 100% polyester. Forty percent of his ties are striped, and 13 of his ties are silk. How many ties does Adrian own that are polyester but are not striped?

This double overlap problem involves four distinct sets: striped silk ties, striped polyester ties, nonstriped silk ties, and nonstriped polyester ties. The number of ties among these four discreet sets totals 48. Although you can approach this problem formally, the best way to handle it is to set up a table representing the four sets, filling in the information given in the problem as shown in the figure (the value required to answer the question is indicated by the question mark).

	silk	polyester	
striped			40%
non-striped		?	60%
	13	35	

Given that 13 ties are silk (see the left column), 35 ties must be polyester (see the right column). Also, given that 40% of the ties are striped (see the top row), 60% must be nonstriped (see the bottom row). Thus, 60% of 35 ties, or 19 ties, are polyester and nonstriped.

WEIGHTED AVERAGE PROBLEMS

On Day 7, you examined the concept of simple average (arithmetic mean). Recall the formula for determining the average (A) of a series of terms (numbers), where n equals the number of terms (numbers) in the series:

$$A = \frac{a+b+c...}{n}$$

Thus, the arithmetic mean of –2, 7, 22, and 19 is 11.5:

$$A = \frac{-2+7+22+19}{4} = \frac{46}{4} = 11.5$$

When some numbers among the terms to be averaged are given greater "weight" than others, however, the foregoing formula is inadequate. In such problems, you must adjust the various terms to reflect differing weights. As a simple illustration, suppose that a student receives grades of 80 and 90 on two exams, but the former grade receives three times the weight of the latter exam. The student's weighted-average grade is not 85 but rather some number closer to 80 than 90. One way to approach this problem is to think of the first grade (80) as three scores of 80, which added to the score of 90 and divided by 4 (not 2) results in the weighted average:

$$WA = \frac{80+80+80+90}{4} = \frac{330}{4} = 82.5$$

You can also approach this problem more intuitively (less formally). You are looking for a number between 80 and 90 (a range of 10). The simple average would obviously lie midway between the two. Given that the score of 80 receives three times the weight of the score of 90, the weighted average is three times closer to 80 than to 90, or three-fourths of the way from 90 to 80. Dividing the range into four segments, it is clear that the weighted average is 82.5. Similarly, if 80 received twice the weight of 90, the weighted average is 83 $\frac{1}{3}$, and if 80 received four times the weight of 90, the weighted average is 82. Apply both the formal algebraic and less formal approaches to the following examples:

Example 16-13: Weighted average is given

Mike's average monthly salary for the first four months that he worked was $3,000. What must his average monthly salary be for each of the next eight months, so that his average monthly salary for the year is $3,500?

In this relatively easy example, the $3,000 salary receives a weight of 4, while the unknown salary receives a weight of 8. You can approach this problem in a strict algebraic manner as follows:

$$3,500 = \frac{4(3,000)+8x}{12}$$

$$(12)(3,500) = 12,000 + 8x$$
$$30,000 = 8x$$
$$x = 3,750$$

Mike's salary for each of the next eight months must be $3,750 for Mike to earn an average of $3,500 a month during the entire 12 months. You can also approach this problem more intuitively. One-third of the monthly salary payments are "underweighted" (less than the desired $3,500 average) by $500. Thus, to achieve the desired average with 12 salary payments, you must overweight the remaining two-thirds of the payments (exceeding $3,500) by half that amount—that is, by $250.

Example 16-14: Terms to be averaged are given

Cynthia drove for seven hours at an average rate of 50 mph and for one hour at an average rate of 60 mph. What was her average rate for the entire trip?

As in the exam-grade illustration earlier, think of Cynthia's average rate as the average of eight equally-weighted one-hour trips. Seven of those trips receive a weight of 50, and one of the trips receives a weight of 60. You can express this algebraically as follows:

$$AR = \frac{7(50)+60}{8} = \frac{350+60}{8} = \frac{410}{8} = 51.25$$

Cynthia's average rate during the entire trip was 51.25 mph. Of course, you can approach this problem more intuitively. The single faster hour of the eight-hour trip boosts what would otherwise have been a 50-mph average rate up one-eighth of the way to 60—that is, up by 1.25 to 51.25.

CURRENCY PROBLEMS

Currency problems are a bit like weighted-average problems, because each item (bill or coin) in a problem is weighted according to its monetary value. Unlike weighted average problems, however, the "average" value of all the bills or coins is not at issue. In solving currency problems, remember the following:

- You must formulate algebraic expressions involving both *number* of items (bills or coins) and *value* of items.

- You should convert the value of all moneys to a common unit (that is, cents or dollars) before formulating an equation. If converting to cents, for example, you must multiply the number of nickels by 5, dimes by 10, and so forth.

Example 16-15

Jim has $2.05 in dimes and quarters. If he has four fewer dimes than quarters, how much money does he have in dimes?

Letting x equal the number of dimes, $x + 4$ represents the number of quarters. The total value of the dimes (in cents) is $10x$, and the total value of the quarters (in cents) is $25(x + 4)$ or $25x + 100$. Given that Jim has $2.05, the following equation emerges:

$$10x + 25x + 100 = 205$$
$$35x = 105$$
$$x = 3$$

Jim has three dimes, so he has 30 cents in dimes.

INVESTMENT PROBLEMS

GMAT investment problems usually involve interest and require more than simply calculating interest earned on a given principal amount at a given rate. They usually call for you to set up and solve an algebraic equation. In solving GMAT investment problems, remember the following:

- It's best simply to eliminate percentage signs (or multiply terms by 100 to eliminate decimals).

- Don't try to solve these problems intuitively; they are generally too complex.

Example 16-16

Dr. Kramer plans to invest $20,000 in an account paying 6% interest annually. How many additional dollars must she invest at the same time at

3% so that her total annual income during the first year is 4% of her entire investment?

Letting x equal the amount invested at 3%, you can express Dr. Kramer's total investment as $20,000 + x$. The interest on $20,000 plus the interest on the additional investment equals the total interest from both investments. You can state this algebraically as follows:

$$.06(20,000) + .03x = .04(20,000 + x)$$

Multiplying all terms by 100 to eliminate decimals, solve for x:

$$6(20,000) + 3x = 4(20,000 + x)$$
$$120,000 + 3x = 80,000 + 4x$$
$$40,000 = x$$

She must invest $40,000 at 3% for her total annual income to be 4% of her total investment ($60,000).

IF YOU HAVE MORE TIME TODAY

To put into practice what you've learned in today's and yesterday's lessons, log on to the author's GMAT Web site (www.west.net/~stewart/gmat) and attempt an Algebra mini-test, which includes story problems as well as other questions, in both formats: Problem Solving and Data Sufficiency. (To find the mini-test click on "Quantitative Ability" in the "Test Yourself" area.)

Day 17

Quantitative Ability Lesson 6: Mini-Test and Review (Algebra)

Today's Topics:

Today you apply what you learned from the previous two days to a 20-question mini-test, which includes Problem Solving questions as well as Data Sufficiency questions.

MINI-TEST (ALGEBRA)

Number of questions: 20
Suggested time: 40 minutes

Directions: Attempt the following 20 Quantitative questions under simulated exam conditions. After completing the mini-test, review the explanations that follow. Preceding the explanation for each question, the question type and difficulty level are indicated.

1. ABC Company pays an average of $140 per vehicle each month in outdoor parking fees for three of its eight vehicles. The company pays garage parking fees for the remaining five vehicles. If ABC pays an average of $240 per vehicle overall each month for parking, how much does ABC pay per month in garage parking fees for its vehicles?
   - (A) $300
   - (B) $420
   - (C) $912
   - (D) $1,420
   - (E) $1,500

2. If $\frac{9b^3 - 15b^2 - 6b}{18b^2 + 6b} = 13b - 17$, then $b =$
   - (A) $\frac{-14}{5}$
   - (B) $\frac{5}{16}$
   - (C) $\frac{32}{25}$
   - (D) 3
   - (E) $\frac{7}{2}$

3. Each computer in a computer lab is equipped with either a modem, a sound card, or both. What percentage of the computers are equipped with modems but not sound cards?
   - (1) Twenty percent of the computers are equipped with both modems and sound cards.
   - (2) Twenty-five percent of the computers are equipped with sound cards but not with modems.

   - (A) Statement 1 ALONE is sufficient, but statement 2 alone is not sufficient to answer the question asked.

(B) Statement 2 ALONE is sufficient, but statement 1 alone is not sufficient to answer the question asked.

(C) BOTH statements 1 and 2 TOGETHER are sufficient to answer the question asked; but NEITHER statement ALONE is sufficient.

(D) EACH statement ALONE is sufficient to answer the question asked.

(E) Statements 1 and 2 TOGETHER are NOT sufficient to answer the question asked, and additional data specific to the problem are needed.

4. An investor wants to sell some of the stock that he owns in MicroTron and Dynaco Corporations. He can sell MicroTron stock for $36 per share, and he can sell Dynaco stock for $52 per share. If he sells 300 shares altogether at an average price per share of $40, how many shares of Dynaco stock has he sold?

(A) 52

(B) 75

(C) 92

(D) 136

(E) 184

5. Dan drove home from college at an average rate of 60 miles per hour. On his trip back to college, his rate was 10 miles per hour slower and the trip took him one hour longer than the drive home. How far is Dan's home from the college?

(A) 65 miles

(B) 100 miles

(C) 200 miles

(D) 280 miles

(E) 300 miles

6. The denominator of a certain fraction is twice as large as the numerator. If you add 4 to both the numerator and denominator, the value of the new fraction is $\frac{5}{8}$. What is the denominator of the original fraction?

(A) 3

(B) 6

(C) 9

(D) 12

(E) 13

7. How long would it take five typists to type 30 pages if all five typists type at the same speed?

(1) One typist can type four pages in 30 minutes.

(2) Three typists can type eight pages in 20 minutes.

(A) Statement 1 ALONE is sufficient, but statement 2 alone is not sufficient to answer the question asked.

(B) Statement 2 ALONE is sufficient, but statement 1 alone is not sufficient to answer the question asked.

(C) BOTH statements 1 and 2 TOGETHER are sufficient to answer the question asked; but NEITHER statement ALONE is sufficient.

(D) EACH statement ALONE is sufficient to answer the question asked.

(E) Statements 1 and 2 TOGETHER are NOT sufficient to answer the question asked, and additional data specific to the problem are needed.

8. If x is a nonzero integer, what is the value of x?

(1) $-4x - 7 > -14$

(2) $5x + 3 > -2(x + 1)$

(A) Statement 1 ALONE is sufficient, but statement 2 alone is not sufficient to answer the question asked.

(B) Statement 2 ALONE is sufficient, but statement 1 alone is not sufficient to answer the question asked.

(C) BOTH statements 1 and 2 TOGETHER are sufficient to answer the question asked; but NEITHER statement ALONE is sufficient.

(D) EACH statement ALONE is sufficient to answer the question asked.

(E) Statements 1 and 2 TOGETHER are NOT sufficient to answer the question asked, and additional data specific to the problem are needed.

9. If a portion of $10,000 is invested at 6% and the remaining portion is invested at 5%, and if x represents the amount invested at 6%, what is the annual income in dollars from the 5% investment?

(A) $5(x - 10,000)$

(B) $.05(x + 10,000)$

(C) $.05(10,000 - x)$

(D) $5(10,000 - x)$

(E) $.05(x - 10,000)$

10. Jill is now 20 years old and her brother Gary is now 14 years old. How many years ago was Jill three times as old as Gary was at that time?

(A) 3

(B) 8

(C) 9

(D) 11

(E) 13

11. If $|a| > |b|$ and if a and b are both integers, is $\sqrt{a^2 - b^2}$ an integer?

(1) $a^2 + 1 = \dfrac{a^2}{b^2}$

(2) $a - b$ is an odd integer.

(A) Statement 1 ALONE is sufficient, but statement 2 alone is not sufficient to answer the question asked.

(B) Statement 2 ALONE is sufficient, but statement 1 alone is not sufficient to answer the question asked.

(C) BOTH statements 1 and 2 TOGETHER are sufficient to answer the question asked; but NEITHER statement ALONE is sufficient.

(D) EACH statement ALONE is sufficient to answer the question asked.

(E) Statements 1 and 2 TOGETHER are NOT sufficient to answer the question asked, and additional data specific to the problem are needed.

12. In a group of m workers, if b workers earn D dollars per week and the rest earn half that amount each, which of the following represents the total number of dollars paid to the entire group of workers in a week?

(A) $bD + b - m$

(B) $bD + \dfrac{1}{2}mD$

(C) $\dfrac{3}{2}bD + mD$

(D) $\dfrac{3}{2}D(b + m)$

(E) $\dfrac{1}{2}D(b + m)$

13. Lisa has 45 coins, which are worth a total of $3.50. If the coins are all nickels and dimes, how many more dimes than nickels does she have?

(A) 5

(B) 10

(C) 15

(D) 20

(E) 25

14. If a train travels $r + 2$ miles in h hours, which of the following represents the number of miles the train travels in one hour and 30 minutes?

(A) $\dfrac{3r+6}{2h}$

(B) $\dfrac{3r}{h+2}$

(C) $\dfrac{\frac{r+2}{h+3}}{2}$

(D) $\dfrac{r}{h+6}$

(E) $2h + 6r$

15. How many ounces of soy sauce must you add to 18 ounces of a peanut sauce and soy sauce mixture consisting of 32% peanut sauce to create a mixture that is 12% peanut sauce?

(A) $38\dfrac{2}{5}$

(B) 30

(C) $26\dfrac{2}{3}$

(D) $24\dfrac{3}{4}$

(E) 21

16. What is the numerical value of the second term in the following sequence: $x, x + 1, x + 3, x + 6, x + 10, x + 15 \ldots$?

    (1) The sum of the first and second terms is one-half the sum of the third and fourth terms.

    (2) The sum of the sixth and seventh terms is 43.

    (A) Statement 1 ALONE is sufficient, but statement 2 alone is not sufficient to answer the question asked.

    (B) Statement 2 ALONE is sufficient, but statement 1 alone is not sufficient to answer the question asked.

    (C) BOTH statements 1 and 2 TOGETHER are sufficient to answer the question asked; but NEITHER statement ALONE is sufficient.

    (D) EACH statement ALONE is sufficient to answer the question asked.

    (E) Statements 1 and 2 TOGETHER are NOT sufficient to answer the question asked, and additional data specific to the problem are needed.

17. Among all sales staff at Listco Corporation, college graduates and those without college degrees are equally represented. Each sales staff member is either a level 1 or level 2 employee. How many sales staff members without college degrees are level 2 employees?

    (1) Level 1 college graduates account for 15% of Listco's sales staff.

    (2) Listco employs 72 level 1 employees, 30 of whom are college graduates.

    (A) Statement 1 ALONE is sufficient, but statement 2 alone is not sufficient to answer the question asked.

    (B) Statement 2 ALONE is sufficient, but statement 1 alone is not sufficient to answer the question asked.

    (C) BOTH statements 1 and 2 TOGETHER are sufficient to answer the question asked; but NEITHER statement ALONE is sufficient.

    (D) EACH statement ALONE is sufficient to answer the question asked.

    (E) Statements 1 and 2 TOGETHER are NOT sufficient to answer the question asked, and additional data specific to the problem are needed.

18. Two buses are 515 miles apart. At 9:30 a.m., they start traveling toward each other at rates of 48 and 55 miles per hour. At what time will they pass each other?

    (A) 1:30 p.m.

    (B) 2:00 p.m.

    (C) 2:30 p.m.

    (D) 3:00 p.m.

    (E) 3:30 p.m.

19. During the first three weeks of his 10-week diet program, Bob lost an average of five pounds per week. During the final seven weeks of the program, he lost an average of two pounds per week. How much weight had Bob lost after the seventh week of the diet program?

    (1) Bob lost an average of one pound per week during the fifth and sixth weeks of the program.

    (2) Bob lost the same amount of weight during the first three weeks of the program as during the last three weeks of the program.

    (A) Statement 1 ALONE is sufficient, but statement 2 alone is not sufficient to answer the question asked.

    (B) Statement 2 ALONE is sufficient, but statement 1 alone is not sufficient to answer the question asked.

    (C) BOTH statements 1 and 2 TOGETHER are sufficient to answer the question asked; but NEITHER statement ALONE is sufficient.

    (D) EACH statement ALONE is sufficient to answer the question asked.

    (E) Statements 1 and 2 TOGETHER are NOT sufficient to answer the question asked, and additional data specific to the problem are needed.

20. Two water hoses feed a 40-gallon tank. If one of the hoses dispenses water at the rate of 2 gallons per minute, and the other hose dispenses water at the rate of 5 gallons per minute, how many minutes does it take to fill the 40-gallon tank, if the tank is empty initially?

    (A) $2\frac{5}{8}$

    (B) $5\frac{5}{7}$

    (C) 7

    (D) $8\frac{4}{9}$

    (E) 28

Quick Answer Guide

Mini-Test: Algebra

1.	E	11.	A
2.	C	12.	E
3.	C	13.	A
4.	B	14.	A
5.	E	15.	B
6.	D	16.	D
7.	D	17.	C
8.	C	18.	C
9.	C	19.	B
10.	D	20.	B

EXPLANATIONS

1. The correct answer is (E). Weighted average (easier).

The total parking fee that ABC pays each month is $1,920 ($240 × 8). Of that amount, $420 is paid for outdoor parking for three cars. The difference ($1,920 – $420 = $1,500) is the total garage parking fee that the company pays for the other five cars.

2. The correct answer is (C). Factorable quadratic equations (moderate).

Here are the steps required to solve for b:

$$\frac{3b(3b^2 - 5b - 2)}{6b(3b+1)} = 13b - 17$$

$$\frac{3b(3b+1)(b-2)}{6b(3b+1)} = 13b - 17$$

$$\frac{b-2}{2} = 13b - 17$$

$$b - 2 = 26b - 34$$

$$25b = 32$$

$$b = \frac{32}{25}$$

3. The correct answer is (C). Overlapping sets, single overlap (easier).

Neither statement 1 nor 2 alone suffices to answer the question. You still do not know what portion of the remaining computers are equipped only with modems. However, both statements together establish that 55% (100–20–25) are equipped only with modems.

4. The correct answer is (B). Dry mixture (challenging).

The value of Dynaco shares sold plus the value of MicroTron shares sold must be equal to the value of all shares sold (that is, the "mixture"). Letting x represent the number of shares of Dynaco sold, you can represent the number of shares of MicroTron sold by $300 - x$. The figure on the following page represents all values algebraically.

	# of shares	X price per share	= total value
Dynaco	x	52	$52x$
MicroTron	$300-x$	36	$36(300-x)$
mixture	300	40	12,000

Set up an equation in which the value of Dynaco shares sold plus the value of MicroTron shares sold equals the total value of all shares sold, and solve for x:

$$\$52(x) + \$36(300 - x) = \$40(300)$$
$$52x + 10,800 - 36x = 12,000$$
$$16x = 1,200$$
$$x = 75$$

The investor has sold 75 shares of Dynaco stock. Checking your work:

$$\$52(75) + \$36(300 - 75) = \$12,000$$
$$\$3,900 + \$36(225) = \$12,000$$
$$\$3,900 + \$8,100 = \$12,000$$

5. The correct answer is (E). Motion, round trip (challenging).

You can express the distance both in terms of Dan's driving time going home and going back to college. Letting x equal the time (in hours) it took Dan to drive home, you can express the distance between his home and his workplace both as $60x$ and as 50 $(x + 1)$. Equate the two distances (because distance is constant) and solve for x as follows:

$$60x = 50(x + 1)$$
$$60x = 50x + 50$$
$$10x = 50$$
$$x = 5$$

It took Dan five hours at 60 miles per hour to drive from college to home, so the distance is 300 miles.

6. The correct answer is (D). Linear equations, one variable (moderate).

Represent the original fraction by $\frac{x}{2x}$, and add 4 to both the numerator and denominator:

$$\frac{x+4}{2x+4} = \frac{5}{8}$$
$$8x + 32 = 10x + 20 \text{ (cross-multiplication)}$$
$$12 = 2x$$
$$x = 6$$

The original denominator is $2x$, or 12.

7. The correct answer is (D). Work problem (easier).

To answer the question, you must determine the speed (or rate) at which a typist types, in terms of pages per unit of time. Each of the two statements provides that information. Although it is not necessary to work any further (the correct response is D), you can set up a general equation to express the time required by a typist to type one page:

$$\frac{(\# \text{ of typists})(\text{time})}{\# \text{ of pages}} = \text{time per page}$$

Based on the values provided in either statement 1 or 2, the typing rate of a single typist is $7\frac{1}{2}$ minutes per page:

$$\frac{(1 \text{ typist})(30 \text{ minutes})}{4 \text{ pages}} = 7\frac{1}{2} = \frac{(3 \text{ typist})(20 \text{ minutes})}{8 \text{ pages}}$$

Accordingly, five typists could type 30 pages in 45 minutes:

$$\frac{(5 \text{ typists})(45 \text{ minutes})}{30 \text{ pages}} = 7\frac{1}{2}$$

8. The correct answer is (C). Solving algebraic inequalities (moderate).

You can solve for x in statement 1:

$$14x - 7 > x - 14$$
$$-5x - 7 > -14$$
$$-5x > -7$$
$$-x > -\frac{7}{5}$$
$$x < \frac{7}{5}$$

You can solve for x in statement 2:

$$5x + 3 > -2(x + 1)$$
$$5x + 3 > -2x - 2$$
$$7x + 3 > -5$$
$$x > -\frac{5}{7}$$

Neither statement 1 nor 2 alone suffices to determine the value of x. However, considering both statements together, $-\frac{5}{7} < x < \frac{7}{5}$. Only two integral x-values—0 and 1—fall within this range. Given that x is a nonzero integer, $x = 1$. Both statements 1 and 2 together suffice to determine the value of x, which is 1.

9. The correct answer is (C). Investment (moderate).

The amount invested at 5% is $10,000 - x$ dollars. Thus, the income from that amount is $.05(10,000 - x)$ dollars.

10. The correct answer is (D). Age (easier).

Jill's age x years ago can be stated algebraically as $20 - x$. At that time, Gary's age was $14 - x$. The following equation emerges:

$$20 - x = 3(14 - x)$$
$$20 - x = 42 - 3x$$
$$2x = 22$$
$$x = 11$$

Jill was three times as old as Gary 11 years ago. (Jill was 9 and Gary was 3.)

11. The correct answer is (A). Equations with radicals (challenging).

Manipulate the equation in statement 1 to isolate a term that bears a clear relationship to $\sqrt{a^2 - b^2}$:

$$a^2 + 1 = \frac{a^2}{b^2}$$
$$b^2(a^2 + 1) = a^2$$
$$b^2 a^2 + b^2 = a^2$$
$$b^2 a^2 = a^2 - b^2$$
$$(ab)^2 = a^2 - b^2$$
$$ab = \sqrt{a^2 - b^2}$$

Given that a and b are both integers, ab must be an integer. Accordingly, $\sqrt{a^2 - b^2}$ must be an integer, and statement 1 suffices alone to answer the question. Turning to statement 2, given that $a - b$ is an integer, whether $\sqrt{a^2 - b^2}$ is also an integer depends on the values of a and b. For example; if $a = 5$ and $b = 4$, $5 - 4 = 1$ (an odd integer), and $\sqrt{5^2 - 4^2} = \sqrt{9} = 3$ (an integer). However if $a = 5$ and $b = 2$, $5 - 2 = 3$ (an integer), but $\sqrt{5^2 - 2^2} = \sqrt{21}$ (not an integer). Thus, statement 2 alone is insufficient to answer the question.

12. The correct answer is (E). Weighted average (moderate).

The money earned by b workers at D dollars per week is bD dollars. The number of workers remaining is $(m - b)$, and because they earn $\frac{1}{2}D$ dollars per week, the money they earn is $\frac{1}{2}D(m - b) = \frac{1}{2}mD - \frac{1}{2}bD$. Thus, the total amount earned is $bD + \frac{1}{2}mD - \frac{1}{2}bd = \frac{1}{2}bd + \frac{1}{2}mD = \frac{1}{2}D(b + m)$.

13. The correct answer is (A). Currency (moderate).

Let x equal the number of nickels:

$$45 - x = \text{the number of dimes}$$
$$5x = \text{the value of all nickels (in cents)}$$
$$450 - 10x = \text{the value of all dimes (in cents)}$$

Given a total value of 350 cents:

$$5x + 450 - 10x = 350$$
$$-5x = -100$$
$$x = 20$$

Lisa has 20 nickels and 25 dimes; thus, she has five more dimes than nickels.

14. The correct answer is (A). Motion (moderate).

Given that the train travels $r + 2$ miles in h hours, you can express its rate in miles per hour as $\frac{r+2}{h}$. In

$1\frac{1}{2}$ hours, the train would travel $\frac{3}{2}$ this distance, or $\left(\frac{3}{2}\right)\left(\frac{r+2}{h}\right) = \frac{3r+6}{2h}$.

15. The correct answer is (B). Wet mixture (challenging).

Letting x equal the number of ounces of soy sauce added to the mixture, $18 + x$ equals the total amount of the mixture after you add the soy sauce. You can represent all values algebraically as shown in the figure on page 149.

	# of ounces	$\times$ % peanut sauce	= amount of peanut sauce
original	18	32	5.76
added	x	0	0
new	$x + 18$	12	$12x + 216$

The amount of peanut sauce (5.76 ounces) must equal 12% of the new total amount of the mixture, which is $18 + x$. You can express this as an algebraic equation and solve for x:

$$5.76 = .12(x + 18)$$
$$576 = 12(x + 18)$$
$$576 = 12x + 216$$
$$360 = 12x$$
$$x = 30$$

You must add 30 ounces of soy sauce to achieve a mixture that includes 12% peanut sauce.

16. The correct answer is (D). Linear equations, one variable (easier).

Statement 1 establishes a linear equation with one variable: $x + (x + 1) = \frac{1}{2} [(x + 3) + (x + 6)]$. You can determine the second term by solving for x, and statement 1 suffices to answer the question. [The second term is 4.5 ($x = 3.5$); however, you need not determine these values.] Statement 2 also establishes a linear equation with one variable: $(x + 15) + (x + 21) = 43$. The seventh term is $(x + 21)$ because each successive term in the sequence adds to x a

number that is one greater than the number that the previous term added to x. Statement 2 alone suffices to answer the question. (Again, $x = 3.5$ and the second term is 4.5, although you need not determine either value.)

17. The correct answer is (C). Overlapping sets, double overlap (moderate).

You can organize the information in this problem as shown in the following figure.

	Level 1	Level 2	
cg			50%
non-cg			50%

Statement 1 provides no information about the number of sales staff members. Thus, you can easily eliminate answers A and D. Statement 2, although providing the number of level 1 sales employees of each type, is insufficient alone to determine the numbers of the level 2 employees. However, statements 1 and 2 together suffice to answer the question. You can fill in the table as follows:

	Level 1	Level 2	
cg	30(15%)	70(35%)	50%
non-cg	42(21%)	58(29%)	50%
	72(36%)	128(64%)	

18. The correct answer is (C). Motion, opposite directions (moderate).

The total distance is equal to the distance that one bus traveled plus the distance that the other bus traveled (to the point where they pass each other). Letting x equal the number of hours traveled, you can express the distances that the two buses travel in that time as $48x$ and $55x$. Equate the sum of these distances with the total distance and solve for x:

$$48x + 55x = 515$$
$$103x = 515$$
$$x = 5$$

The buses will pass each other five hours after 9:30 a.m.—at 2:30 p.m.

19. The correct answer is (B). Weighted average (challenging).

Statement 1 alone is insufficient to answer the question, because you cannot determine Bob's weight loss during the fourth through seventh weeks. Statement 2 alone, however, suffices to answer the question. Given that Bob lost an average of 5 pounds per week during the first three weeks, his total weight loss during that period was 15 pounds. With statement 2, his total weight loss during all but the fourth through seventh weeks was 30 pounds. Given that he lost 29 pounds altogether during the week $[(3 \times 5) + (7 \times 2)]$, he must have gained 1 pound during the fourth through seventh week. Accordingly, he had lost 14 pounds $(-15 + 1)$ after the first seven weeks.

20. The correct answer is (B). Work problem (moderate).

The first hose can perform $\frac{1}{20}$ of the job in one minute. The second hose can perform $\frac{1}{8}$ of the job in one minute. You can add the two rates together to obtain the aggregate rate per minute:

$$\frac{1}{20} + \frac{1}{8} = \frac{1}{A}$$

$$\frac{2}{40} + \frac{5}{40} = \frac{1}{A}$$

$$\frac{7}{40} = \frac{1}{A}$$

$$7A = 40$$

$$A = 5\frac{5}{7}$$

It takes $5\frac{5}{7}$ minutes for both hoses together to fill the tank.

Day 18:

Reading Comprehension Lesson 1: Format, Strategies, and Reading Techniques

Today's Topics:

1. GMAT Reading Comprehension—At a Glance
2. What Reading Comprehension Sets Look Like
3. Key Features of Reading Comprehension Sets
4. Approaching a Reading Comprehension Set—a 7-Step Strategy
5. Analysis of Sample Question Set
6. Tips to Help You Read More Effectively

Today you'll familiarize yourself with the format of Reading Comprehension question sets and learn basic strategies for reading the passages quickly and effectively.

GMAT READING COMPREHENSION— AT A GLANCE

WHERE: In the GMAT Verbal section, mixed in with Sentence Correction and Critical Reasoning questions

HOW MANY: 12 questions, based on 4 passages (3 questions per passage)

FORMAT: 3 short passages (150–200 words) with 3 questions each, and 1 longer passage (275–325 words) with 3 questions

SUGGESTED TIME: 5–6 minutes per question set (20–24 minutes altogether)

GROUND RULES:

- Consider each question independently of all others.

- Answer each question based *only* on what is stated or implied in the passage; don't bring your outside knowledge of the subject matter (if any) to bear in answering the questions.

WHAT'S COVERED: You'll be tested on the following reading skills:

- Recognizing the main point or primary purpose of the passage

- Recalling information explicitly stated in the passage

- Making inferences from specific information stated in the passage

- Recognizing the purpose of specific passage information

- Recognize the author's tone or attitude as revealed in the language of the passage

- Applying and extrapolating from the ideas presented in the passage

DIRECTIONS: Here are the directions for GMAT Reading Comprehension. You'll encounter these directions just before your first set of Reading Comprehension questions:

The questions in this group are based on the content of a passage. After reading the passage, choose the best answer to each question. Answer all questions on the basis of what is *stated* or *implied* in the passage.

To review these directions for subsequent questions of this type, click on HELP.

WHAT READING COMPREHENSION SETS LOOK LIKE

Each Reading Comprehension set includes a passage and three questions pertaining to the passage. The GMAT presents the questions one at a time; you must confirm your response to each one in turn before the test presents the next one.

Here's a typical Reading Comprehension set. The difficulty level of the passage itself is moderate, while the difficulty level of the three questions varies. Take about 5 minutes to read the passage and attempt the questions. (I'll discuss the passage and analyze the question just ahead.)

The encounter that a portrait records is most tangibly the sitting itself, which may be brief or extended, collegial or confrontational. Cartier-Bresson has expressed his passion for portrait pho-
(5) tography by characterizing it as "a duel without rules, a delicate rape." Such metaphors contrast quite sharply with Richard Avedon's conception of a sitting. While Cartier-Bresson reveals himself as an interloper and opportunist, Avedon con-
(10) fesses—perhaps uncomfortably—to a role as diagnostician and (by implication) psychic healer: not as someone who necessarily transforms his subjects, but as someone who reveals their essential nature. Both photographers, however, agree
(15) that the fundamental dynamic in this process lies squarely in the hands of the artist.

A quite-different paradigm has its roots not in confrontation or consultation but in active collaboration between the artist and sitter. This very dif-
(20) ferent kind of relationship was formulated most

vividly by William Hazlitt in his essay entitled "On Sitting for One's Picture" (1823). To Hazlitt, the "bond of connection" between painter and sitter is most like the relationship between two lovers.
(25) Hazlitt fleshes out his thesis by recalling the career of Sir Joshua Reynolds. According to Hazlitt, Reynold's sitters were meant to enjoy an atmosphere that was both comfortable for them and conducive to the enterprise of the portrait painter,
(30) who was simultaneously their host and their contractual employee.

1. The author of the passage quotes Cartier-Bresson (lines 5–6) in order to

   (A) refute Avedon's conception of a portrait sitting

   (B) provide one perspective of the portraiture encounter

   (C) support the claim that portrait sittings are, more often than not, confrontational encounters

   (D) show that a portraiture encounter can be either brief or extended

   (E) distinguish a sitting for a photographic portrait from a sitting for a painted portrait

2. Which of the following characterizations of the portraiture experience as viewed by Avedon is most readily inferable from the passage?

   (A) a collaboration

   (B) a mutual accommodation

   (C) a confrontation

   (D) an uncomfortable encounter

   (E) a consultation

3. Which of the following best expresses the passage's main idea?

   (A) The success of a portrait depends largely on the relationship between artist and subject.

   (B) Portraits, more than most other art forms, provide insight into the artist's social relationships.

   (C) The social aspect of portraiture sitting plays an important part in the sitting's outcome.

(D) Photographers and painters differ in their views regarding their role in portrait photography.

(E) The paintings of Reynolds provide a record of his success in achieving a social bond with his subjects.

KEY FEATURES OF READING COMPREHENSION SETS

- **Every fifth line of the passage will be numbered.** Passage lines are always numbered as shown in the preceding passage because questions occasionally refer to portions of the passage by line number.

- **The passages are condensed from larger works in the humanities, social sciences, and physical sciences.** Specific sources include professional journals, dissertations, and periodicals of intellectual interest. The test makers edit the source material in order to pack it with test-worthy material.

- **Passages appear on the left side of the computer screen, and questions appear (one at a time) on the right side.** You'll have to scroll vertically to read each entire passage, even the short ones—as in the simulated "screen shot" on page 13 (Day 2).

- **Reading Comprehension questions are designed to test a lot more than just your short-term memory and your knack for finding information quickly.** Although your ability to recall what you've read is part of what's being tested, all but the easiest questions also gauge your ability to assimilate, interpret, and apply the ideas presented.

- **Some questions require that you focus on an isolated sentence or two; others require that you assimilate information from various parts of the passage.** Understandably, questions that cover disparate parts of passage tend to be tougher than the ones that you can answer just be reading a particular sentence or two.

- **Questions about information appearing early in the passage tend to come before other questions.** But this isn't a hard-and-fast rule; so don't assume you can simply scroll down the passage to answer each question in turn.

- **Tougher questions include not only a "best" response but also a tempting second-best response.** Recognizing the difference in quality between the two most viable responses is the key to answering the questions correctly.

- **Reading Comprehension questions are not designed to test your vocabulary.** Sure, you'll find the occasional erudite word (such as "interloper" and "paradigm" in the passage you just read). But the test makers don't intentionally load the passages with tough vocabulary. Also, if a reading passage introduces a technical term, don't worry—the passage will supply all you need to know about the term to respond to the questions.

- **Prior knowledge of a passage's subject matter is not important. All questions are answerable based solely on the passage's information.** The exam includes passages from a variety of disciplines, so it is unlikely that any particular test taker knows enough about two or more of the areas included on the test to hold a significant advantage over other test takers.

APPROACHING A READING COMPREHENSION SET— A 7-STEP STRATEGY

Here's a 7-step plan for handling any GMAT Reading Comprehension set.

1. **Read the first question (including the answer choices), before you begin reading the passage.** Try to anticipate what the passage is about and the sort of information you should be on the lookout for in order to answer the first question.

2. **Begin reading the passage, actively thinking about a possible thesis (main idea) and how the author attempts to support that thesis.** Also, begin your reading with an eye for information useful in answering the first question.

3. **When you think you've learned enough to take a stab at the first question, go ahead and choose a tentative answer.** You probably won't have to read very far to at least take a reasoned guess at the first question. But don't confirm you're response yet!

4. **Read the remainder of the passage, formulating an outline as you go.** As you read, try to: (1) separate main ideas from supporting ideas and examples; (2) determine the basic structure of the passage (e.g., chronology of events, classification of ideas or things, comparison between two or more ideas, events, or things); and (3) determine the author's attitude or opinion about the subject. Make notes on your scratch paper as needed to see the "flow" of the passage and to keep the passage's details straight in your mind. Make outlines and summaries as brief as possible. Don't write complete sentences, just jot down key words.

5. **Sum up the passage; formulate a brief thesis (main idea) statement.** Take a few seconds to review your outline, then in your own words express the author's main point—in one sentence. Jot it down on your scratch paper. Your thesis statement should reflect the author's attitude (e.g., critical, supportive, neutral) toward the ideas presented in the passage.

6. **Confirm your response to the first question.** Eliminate any answer choice that is inconsistent with your thesis statement. Tomorrow you'll learn how to resolve close judgment calls between answer choices.

7. **Move on to the remaining question(s), considering all of the answer choices for each question.** Tomorrow you'll learn some tips to help you tackle different question types and to zero in on the best answer choices.

ANALYSIS OF SAMPLE QUESTION SET

Let's tackle the sample passage and questions you encountered earlier, applying the 7-step approach you just learned.

1. The first question tells you a lot about what you might expect in the passage. In all likelihood, the passage will be primarily about the portraiture experience, and the author will probably provide different viewpoints and insights on this experience, from the perspective of particular artists.

2. The first four sentences (lines 1–14) reinforce your initial prediction about the passage's content. Based on these initial lines, it appears that the author will indeed be comparing and contrasting different views of the portraiture experience. At this point, you don't know whether the passage will involve the views of any artist other than Cartier-Bresson and Richard Avedon, nor do you know whether the author has any opinion on the subject. But you should be on the lookout for answers to these unknowns during step 4.

3. Consider question 1 based on what you've read so far. The author points out in lines 4–14 that Cartier-Bresson's conception is quite different from that of Avedon. Choices (A), (B) and (C) all appear to be viable choices, at least based on lines 4–14. But whether the author's purpose here is to *refute* Avedon's view (choice (A)), *support* Cartier-Bresson's view (choice (C)), or simply *provide* one of at least two perspectives without taking sides (choice (B)) remains to be seen. You'll have to read on to find out. In any event, you can probably eliminate choices (D) and (E), since neither one seems relevant to the Cartier-Bresson quotation. Don't confirm a response yet; go on to step 4.

4. Your goal in step 4 is to formulate a mental outline of the passage as your read from start to finish. You might want to jot down some key word and phrases to help you see how the ideas flow and to keep the four individuals discussed in the passage straight in your mind. Here's my outline of the passage:

PARAGRAPH 1
Contrast:
- CB: confrontation (rape)
- Avedon: diagnosis (consultation)
- BUT agree artist is key

PARAGRAPH 2
3rd view: Hazlitt (writer)
- collaboration (like lovers)
- e.g. Reynolds

5. Now let's sum up the passage based on the outline you formulated in step 4. It's a good idea to jot it down. Notice that the thesis is neutral; the author does not side with any viewpoint presented in the passage.

> THESIS: Portraiture is a social experience, but artists disagree about their role in it.

6. Having read the entire passage, return to the question. Nowhere in the passage does the author attempt to either refute or support any of the viewpoints presented. So, you can eliminate choices (A) and (C). Accordingly, choice (B) is the best response to the question. Notice also that choice (B) is consistent with our thesis statement. Regardless of the particular question, you can eliminate any answer choice that is inconsistent with your thesis statement.

7. Move ahead to questions 2 and 3. In the following analysis, notice the qualitative difference (from best to worst) among the answer choices. Also, note how I've labeled (described) what's wrong with each wrong-answer choice; you'll learn more about these and other wrong-answer ploys tomorrow.

Question 2:
The best response is choice (E). In the first sentence of the second paragraph, the author distinguishes a "quite-different paradigm" (that is, the case of Reynolds) from the conceptions of Cartier-Bresson and Avedon in that the Reynolds paradigm "has its roots not in confrontation or consultation but in active collaboration between artist and sitter." The third sentence of the passage makes clear that Cartier-Bresson conceives the encounter as "confrontational"; thus, you can *reasonably infer* that the author characterizes an Avedon sitting as a "consultation."

Choice (B) is also a good response but nevertheless not as good as choice (E). Although the term "mutual accommodation," which does not appear in the passage, is not altogether inconsistent with Avedon's view, the term suggests a relationship in which both artist and painter allow for the other's needs or desires. Such a description is closer to Hazlitt's analogy of two lovers than to Avedon's view of the artist as diagnostician and psychic healer.

Choice (A) also has merit, yet it is not as good a response as either choice (B) or choice (E). Admittedly, the idea of "a collaboration" is not in strong opposition to the idea of "a consultation." However, the author explicitly ascribes this characterization to the Reynolds paradigm, not to Avedon's view. Thus, choice (A) *confuses the passage's information*.

Choices (C) and (D) are the qualitatively worst responses among the five. Choice (C) *confuses the passage's information*. The quotation in the first paragraph makes it clear that Cartier-Bresson (not Avedon) conceives the encounter as "confrontational." Choice (D) also *confuses the passage's information*. According to the passage, Avedon confesses "uncomfortably" to his role as diagnostician and psychic healer. It does not necessarily follow, however, that Avedon finds his encounters with his sitters to be uncomfortable.

Question 3:
The best response is choice (C). Although this passage doesn't seem to convey a strong central idea or thesis, the author seems to be most concerned with emphasizing that a portrait sitting is a social encounter, not just an artistic exercise, and that artists consider their relationship with their sitters to be somehow significant. For this reason, choice (C) is a good statement of the author's main point.

Choice (A) also has merit. In fact, but for choice (C), choice (A) would be the best response because it embraces the passage as a whole and properly focuses on the author's primary concern with exploring the relationship between the artist and the sitter. However, the passage does not discuss how or whether this relationship results in a "successful" portrait; thus, choice (A) *distorts the passage's information*.

Choice (D) has merit in that the author does claim that the Reynolds paradigm (described in the second paragraph) is "quite different" from the two paradigms that the first paragraph discusses. The latter does indeed involve a painter (Reynolds), whereas the other two paradigms involve photographers (Cartier-Bresson and Avedon). However, the author does not generalize from this fact that a portrait artist's approach or view depends on whether the artist is a painter or a photographer. Thus, choice (D) is a bit *off focus* as well as calling for an *unwarranted generalization*.

Choices (B) and (E) are qualitatively the worst responses among the five choices. Choice (B) *distorts* the information in the passage and departs from the topic at hand. Although the passage does support the notion that a portrait might reveal something about the relationship between the artist and the sitter, the author neither states nor implies that a portrait reveals anything about the artist's other relationships. Moreover, nowhere in the passage does the author compare portraiture with other art forms.

Choice (E) is *too narrow* and refers to information *not mentioned* in the passage. The passage is not just about Reynolds but about the portraiture encounter in general. Also, the author does not comment on Reynold's "success" or about how his relationship with his sitters might have contributed to his success.

TIPS TO HELP YOU READ MORE EFFECTIVELY

Here are six suggestions for improving your reading efficiency and comprehension as you read GMAT passages. (Tomorrow I'll provide suggestions for tackling the questions themselves.)

1. Read actively, not passively, with pencil in hand. Pause after each logical "block" (perhaps after each paragraph) to think briefly about what basic points the author makes in the block, how these points are connected to earlier ones, and where the discussion is likely to go from here. Jot down a brief outline as you go.

2. Don't get bogged down in details as you read the passage, especially the long passage. Gloss over the details (lists, statistics and other numbers, dates, titles, and so forth). Just take note of where the details were, so you can find them quickly if you need them to answer a particular question.

3. Read the entire passage before confirming your response to any question. Even if a question seems clearly to involve only a portion of the passage, it is always possible that relevant information will appear elsewhere as well.

4. Pay attention to the overall structure, or "flow," of the passage. The passage might be organized as a chronology of events, a critique of a theory, a comparison of two or more things, or a classification system. Understanding how the passage "flows" will help you to locate details more quickly and to zero in on the best answers to the questions.

5. Summarize the passage after reading it. Take a few seconds to recap the main thrust of the passage. Chances are, you'll be able to respond correctly to at least one of the questions based solely on the passage main idea, or thesis.

6. Don't do more vertical scrolling than necessary. You'll need to scroll to read the entire passage. But try to minimize scrolling by developing a good outline, so you won't have to reread the passage to search for information needed to respond to a question. Besides, scrolling and rereading use up valuable time and adds to eyestrain and fatigue.

IF YOU HAVE MORE TIME TODAY

Here are two suggestions for supplementing today's lesson:

1. For additional advice on scoring your best on GMAT Reading Comprehension, log on to the author's GMAT Web site (www.west.net/~stewart/gmat) and explore the Q&A entitled "GMAT Reading Comprehension — Strategies for Score Optimization." (You'll find it in the "Q&A Corner" of the Web site.)

2. To practice the 7-step approach and other strategies you learned today, try your hand at the following Reading Comprehension question set, then read the analysis that follows.

Questions 1–3 refer to the following passage:

For absolute dating of archeological artifacts, the radiocarbon method emerged during the latter half of the twentieth century as the most reliable and precise method. The results of obsidian
(5) (volcanic glass) dating, a method based on the belief that newly exposed obsidian surfaces absorb moisture from the surrounding atmosphere at a constant rate, proved uneven. It was initially thought that the thickness of the hydration layer
(10) would provide a means of calculating the time elapsed since the fresh surface was made. But this method failed to account for the chemical variability in the physical and chemical mechanism of obsidian hydration. Moreover, each geographic
(15) source presented unique chemical characteristics, necessitating a trace element analysis for each such source.

Yet despite its limitations, obsidian dating helped archeologists identify the sources of many
(20) obsidian artifacts, and to identify in turn ancient exchange networks for the flow of goods. Nor were ceramic studies and fluoride analysis supplanted entirely by the radiocarbon method, which in use allows for field labeling and laboratory errors, as
(25) well as sample contamination. In addition, in the 1970s, dendrochronological (tree-ring) studies on the bristlecone pine showed that deviation from radiocarbon values increases as one moves back in time. Eventually calibration curves were devel-
(30) oped to account for this phenomenon; but in the archeological literature we still find dual references to radiocarbon and sidereal, or calendar, time.

1. Based on the information in the passage, which of the following is LEAST likely to have been a means of dating archeological artifacts?

(A) ceramics studies

(B) radiocarbon dating

(C) dendrochronological studies

(D) fluoride analysis

(E) obsidian hydration-layer analysis

2. In the passage, the author mentions all of the following as problems with radiocarbon dating EXCEPT:

(A) disparities with the calendar dating system

(B) deterioration of samples

(C) identification errors by archeological field workers

(D) contamination of artifacts

(E) mistakes by laboratory workers

3. With which of the following statements would the passage's author most likely agree?

(A) The greater the time that has elapsed since exposure of obsidian surface to moisture, the less reliable the results of obsidian dating.

(B) The hydration layer accumulating through obsidian moisture absorption varies in thickness depending on the amount of surface area exposed to moisture.

(C) An obsidian artifact can be reliably dated using the obsidian method only if certain environmental conditions where the artifact was found are considered.

(D) The results of obsidian dating are as reliable and precise as those of fluoride analysis only if trace element analysis is performed for the geographic source of the obsidian.

(E) The unpredictability of the obsidian hydration process renders the obsidian dating method problematic as a means of determining historical trade routes.

Answers and Analysis

1. **The correct answer is (C).** As the passage indicates, dendrochronological studies involve analyzing tree rings. Although the wood from trees might have been used for creating items that are now considered archeological artifacts, the author does not indicate explicitly that tree rings are studied for the purpose of dating such artifacts. Choice (A) is mentioned along with fluoride analysis as not "supplanted entirely" by the radiocarbon dating method. It is reasonably inferable based on this context that ceramic studies are another means of dating artifacts. Choice (B) is referred to explicitly in both paragraphs as a method of dating artifacts. Choice (D) is mentioned along with ceramic studies as not "supplanted entirely" by the radiocarbon dating method. It is reasonably inferable based on this context that fluoride analysis is another means of dating artifacts. Choice (E) is referred to in the first paragraph as a method of dating volcanic glass. Then, in the first sentence of the second paragraph the author indicates that many archeological artifacts were made of obsidian.

2. **The correct answer is (B).** In the second paragraph, the author mentions choices (A), (C), (D), and (E) as problems with radiocarbon dating. Nowhere in the passage, however, does the author mention any problem involving sample deterioration.

3. **The correct answer is (C).** In mentioning that a trace element analysis is needed for the geographic source of an obsidian artifact, the author strongly infers that an accounting for specific conditions of the geographic area is needed in order to determine the age of the obsidian artifact by measuring its hydration layer. Choice (A) is unsupported in the passage, and confuses the discussion of obsidian dating (in the first paragraph) with the calibration problem involving carbon dating (in the second paragraph). Choice (D) is unsupported in the passage, in which the author makes no attempt to compare the reliability of fluoride analysis with that of obsidian dating. Choice (E) exaggerates the limits of the obsidian dating method—especially considering that in the second paragraph's first sentence the author explicitly states that the obsidian dating method has been useful for the purpose mentioned in choice (E).

Day 19

Reading Comprehension Lesson 2: Question Types

Today's Topics:

1. A Sample Question Set

2. Question Types and Wrong-answer Ploys

3. Recognizing the Main Idea or Primary Purpose

4. Recalling Explicit Information

5. Inferring from or Interpreting Specific Information

6. Recognizing the Function of Specific Information

7. Extrapolating from or Applying Passage Ideas

8. The GMAT's Favorite Wrong-answer Ploys

9. Tips for Tackling GMAT's Reading Comprehension Questions

Today you'll examine and learn to handle the various question types that appear in Reading Comprehension sets, focusing particularly on common wrong-answer "ploys."

A SAMPLE QUESTION SET

Before examining question types and wrong-answer ploys, take 5–6 minutes to read the following passage and to respond to the three accompanying questions. These questions help illustrate the materials that follow.

The decline of the Iroquois Indian nations began during the American Revolution of 1776. Disagreement as to whether they should become involved in the war began to divide the Iroquois.
(5) Because of the success of the revolutionaries and the encroachment upon Iroquois lands that followed, many Iroquois resettled in Canada, while those who remained behind lost the respect they had enjoyed among other Indian nations. The in-
(10) troduction of distilled spirits resulted in widespread alcoholism, leading in turn to the rapid decline of both the culture and population. The influence of the Quakers impeded, yet in another sense contributed, to this decline. By establishing
(15) schools for the Iroquois and by introducing them to modern technology for agriculture and husbandry, the Quakers instilled in the Iroquois some hope for the future yet undermined the Iroquois' sense of national identity.

(20) Ironically, it was Handsome Lake who can be credited with reviving the Iroquois culture. Lake, the alcoholic half-brother of Seneca Cornplanter, perhaps the most outspoken proponent among the Iroquois for assimilation of white customs
(25) and institutions, was a former member of the Great Council of Iroquois nations. Inspired by a near-death vision in 1799, Lake established a new religion among the Iroquois which tied the more useful aspects of Christianity to traditional Indian beliefs and customs.

1. The passage mentions all the following events as contributing to the decline of the Iroquois culture EXCEPT:

   (A) new educational opportunities for the Iroquois people

   (B) divisive power struggles among the leaders of the Iroquois nations

   (C) introduction of new farming technologies

   (D) territorial threats against the Iroquois nations

   (E) discord among the nations regarding their role in the American Revolution

2. Among the following reasons, it is most likely that the author considers Handsome Lake's leading a revival of the Iroquois culture to be "ironic" because

   (A) he was a former member of the Great Council

   (B) he was not a full-blooded relative of Seneca Cornplanter

   (C) he was related by blood to a chief proponent of assimilation

   (D) Seneca Cornplanter was Lake's alcoholic half-brother

   (E) his religious beliefs conflicted with traditional Iroquois beliefs

3. Assuming that the reasons asserted in the passage for the decline of the Iroquois culture are historically representative of the decline of cultural minorities, which of the following developments would most likely contribute to the demise of a modern-day ethnic minority?

   (A) a bilingual education program in which children who are members of the minority group learn to read and write in both their traditional language and the language prevalent in the present culture

   (B) a tax credit for residential-property owners who lease their property to members of the minority group

   (C) increased efforts by local government to eradicate the availability of illegal drugs

   (D) a government-sponsored program to assist minority-owned businesses in using computer technology to improve efficiency

   (E) the declaration of a national holiday commemorating a past war in which the minority group played an active role

---

QUESTION TYPES AND WRONG-ANSWER PLOYS

The Iroquois question set includes examples of three of the five types of questions that you'll encounter in GMAT Reading Comprehension sets, distinguished by the skill that is being tested:

1. Recognizing the passage's main idea or primary purpose

2. Recalling explicit information in the passage

3. Inferring from or interpreting specific passage information

4. Recognizing the function or purpose of specific information in the passage

5. Extrapolating from or applying passage ideas (this type appears less frequently than the others)

The wrong-answer choices in the Iroquois question set illustrate many of the test maker's favorite wrong-answer types, which include answer choices that do the following:

• Distort, understate, or overstate the ideas presented in the passage

• Are mentioned in the passage but do not respond to the question at hand

• Call for speculation or unsupported inference

• Are contrary to or contradicted by the passage or are stated "backward" (a backward answer might confuse cause with effect or author argument with author disagreement)

• Confuse one opinion or position with another

• Are too narrow or specific

- Are too broad, general, or vague
- Bring in extrinsic information that the passage does not include

Now take a closer look at each of the five question types, focusing on the proper approach and wrong-answer ploys commonly used with each type. As you do so, you'll revisit the three questions accompanying the Iroquois passage as well as the three questions accompanying the portraiture passage in Day 18.

QUESTION TYPE 1: RECOGNIZING THE MAIN IDEA OR PRIMARY PURPOSE

Some questions test whether you recognize the author's main point or overall concern or purpose. These questions require you to discern between the forest and the trees—that is, to distinguish broader and larger ideas and points from supporting evidence and details. Here's how to approach these questions:

- After reading the entire passage, formulate your own thesis statement and a statement of the author's purpose—*before* considering the answer choices. By knowing what sort of response to look for, you will be far less tempted by the other (wrong) responses. Ask yourself two questions:

  1. Toward what point is the author's effort primarily directed?
  2. What does the author spend most of his or her time discussing? (This question might sound simplistic, but it helps to keep your thinking straight for this type of question.)

- Every passage has a "main idea" (thesis) and primary purpose. You *might* find a particular sentence or two, perhaps at the beginning or end of the passage, that sums up the passage. However, don't expect every passage to be so helpful; many passages do not include *explicit* thesis statements or primary-purpose statements.

- There should be a consistency between the passage's main idea and the author's primary purpose. If both question types appear in the question set, your responses to these two questions should be consistent with each other.

- As you read the passage, pay particular attention to all words and phrases that indicate or suggest the author's *attitude* (tone, opinion, perspective, and so on). The best response must reflect or at least show consistency with the author's attitude.

Look for These Wrong Answer Ploys

- **The response that is *too narrow* in scope.** The response focuses on one element of the passage, ignoring other important elements. If the passage discusses a particular topic in only one of three or four paragraphs, you can pretty safely conclude that the author's primary concern is not with that specific topic. Be particularly suspicious of a response that refers to a single *specific person, event, idea,* or *work* (such as a book or composition). For example:

  If the passage is concerned with comparing two phenomena, a response that ignores this concern and focuses on only one of the two phenomena is too narrow to be a viable best response.

  If the author uses specific examples to support an argument, a response that ignores the author's larger point and focuses on one of the examples is too narrow to be a viable best response.

  If the author describes two existing theories and goes on to propose and describe a new and better theory, the author's primary purpose is not to examine, describe, or criticize current theories; the best response would go further and include the author's concern with proposing a new theory.

- **The response that is *too broad* in scope.** The response encompasses the author's main concern or idea but extends that concern or idea beyond the author's intended scope. For example, the response's scope might extend beyond the topic, geographic region, or time frame that the passage discusses.

- **The response that *distorts* the author's position.** For example, if the author's ultimate concern is to argue for a particular position or to propose a new and better explanation for some phenomenon, any response that ignores the author's opinion and instead implies objectivity on the author's part is not a viable best response.

An Example from Yesterday's Question Set

Referring to Day 18's portraiture passage, consider this question:

1. Which of the following best expresses the passage's main idea?

   (A) The success of a portrait depends largely on the relationship between artist and subject.
   (This response distorts the passage's information.)

   (B) Portraits, more than most other art forms, provide insight into the artist's social relationships.
   (This response distorts the passage's information.)

   (C) The social aspect of portraiture sitting plays an important part in the outcome of the sitting.
   (This is the correct response.)

   (D) Photographers and painters differ in their views regarding their role in portrait photography.
   (This response distorts the passage's information.)

   (E) The paintings of Reynolds provide a record of his success in achieving a social bond with his subjects.
   (This response is too narrow.)

(For a more detailed analysis of this question, see Day 18.)

QUESTION TYPE 2: RECALLING EXPLICIT INFORMATION

Some questions are designed to measure your ability to assimilate details—more specifically, your ability to process detailed information accurately as well as your efficiency in looking up information. The question might either ask which choice (among the five) *is* mentioned or which choice (among the five) is *not* mentioned. Here's how to approach these questions:

- Effective notes or a mini-outline will help you locate the relevant information quickly. Wherever some sort of list is included in the passage—a list of characteristics, a list of examples, or some other list—take note of it. You can be sure that there will be an explicit detail question that focuses on that list.

- Do not insist that answer choices repeat word-for-word what the passage states. Answer choices are usually not expressed exactly as they are in the passage, but instead paraphrase the language used in the passage.

- Do not rely on your memory for details to answer these questions. Always go to the relevant portion of the passage, and read around (from the preceding sentence to the following sentence) the particular excerpt referred to in the question stem.

Look for These Wrong-Answer Ploys

- **The response that confuses the information in the passage by referring to unrelated details.** These questions are quite specific in the information to which they refer. For example, consider question 1 from the Iroquois question set:

  The passage mentions all the following events as contributing to the decline of the Iroquois culture EXCEPT:

  An answer choice that is mentioned in the passage but is nevertheless not mentioned specifically as a contributing factor to the decline of the Iroquois culture would be incorrect. Accordingly, look out for answer choices that involve unrelated details.

- **The response that is not mentioned in the passage.** One or more answer choices might provide information completely unsupported by or not mentioned anywhere in the passage. These wrong answers can be quite tempting; your natural reaction is that the information appeared somewhere in the passage, but you missed it. Well, probably not! Don't fall for this ploy.

- **The response that contradicts the information in the passage.** The response might at first glance appear to be a viable response, but it actually contradicts what the passage states. This ploy will trap you if you fail to read each answer choice carefully.

An Example from Today's Question Set

1. The passage mentions all the following events as contributing to the decline of the Iroquois culture EXCEPT:

   (A) new educational opportunities for the Iroquois people
   (The passage explicitly mentions this.)

   (B) divisive power struggles among the leaders of the Iroquois nations
   (This is the correct response.)

   (C) introduction of new farming technologies
   (The passage explicitly mentions this.)

   (D) territorial threats against the Iroquois nations
   (The passage explicitly mentions this.)

   (E) discord among the nations regarding their role in the American Revolution
   (The passage explicitly mentions this.)

   Choice (B) is the best response. Nowhere in the passage does the author mention any power struggles among the leaders of the Iroquois nations. Although the first paragraph does refer to a dispute among the Iroquois leaders, the dispute involved the role that the Iroquois should play in the American Revolution. Thus, choice (B) confuses the information in the passage by referring to unrelated details. The passage explicitly refers to the events mentioned in choices (A), (C), (D), and (E) as factors contributing to the decline of the Iroquois culture.

QUESTION TYPE 3: INFERRING FROM OR INTERPRETING SPECIFIC INFORMATION

Some questions require you to draw simple inferences or to recognize somewhat broader points by interpreting specific passage information. Here's how to approach these questions:

- Don't overlook the obvious! Questions calling for inference require you to make only very "tight" inferences; in other words, the passage will suggest the inference so strongly that no other interpretation is really reasonable. Do not fight the passage by looking for a more subtle or deeper interpretation.

- An author inference usually requires that you piece together (logically speaking) no more than two consecutive sentences. To analyze the question, locate the relevant line or lines in the passage, read around those lines—the sentence preceding and the sentence following. The inference should be clear enough to you.

- The question stem might refer to specific lines or a specific paragraph in the passage. In any event, you will discover that, based on the information in the question stem, you can locate the relevant portion of the passage within 5 to 10 seconds (which is quite helpful if you are short of time).

Look for These Wrong-Answer Ploys

- **The unwarranted or unsupported inference or interpretation.** This response will leap to a conclusion not supported by the part of the passage that makes the inference. Such a response might bring in material that is outside of the passage or might exaggerate or distort the author's relatively narrow inference.

- **The response that is either backward or runs contrary to the passage.** You might be surprised how easily you can turn around certain facts or, perhaps confusing cause with effect, confuse author agreement with author disagreement. The test maker knows this and typically includes an answer choice that is contradicted by, runs contrary to, or states backward some information in the passage.

- **The response that confuses one thing with another.** The response might mention details that the passage mentions elsewhere but that do not respond to the question at hand.

• **The response that distorts the meaning of the information in the passage.** This response might either twist or exaggerate the author's intended meaning.

An Example from Yesterday's Question Set

3. Which of the following best characterizes the portraiture experience as viewed by Avedon?

(A) a collaboration
(This answer confuses information from the passage.)

(B) a mutual accommodation
(This response distorts information from the passage.)

(C) a confrontation
(This response confuses information from the passage.)

(D) an uncomfortable encounter
(This response distorts information from the passage.)

(E) a consultation
(This is the correct answer.)

(For a more detailed analysis of this question, see Day 18.)

An Example from Today's Question Set

2. Among the following reasons, it is most likely that the author considers Handsome Lake's leading a revival of the Iroquois culture to be "ironic" because

(A) he was a former member of the Great Council
(This response confuses details from the passage.)

(B) he was not a full-blooded relative of Seneca Cornplanter
(This response confuses details from the passage.)

(C) he was related by blood to a chief proponent of assimilation
(This is the correct answer.)

(D) Seneca Cornplanter was Lake's alcoholic half-brother
(This response states information from the passage backward.)

(E) his religious beliefs conflicted with traditional Iroquois beliefs
(This response is contrary to the passage's information.)

Choice (C) is the best response. The passage states that Cornplanter was an outspoken proponent of assimilation and that Handsome Lake was related to Cornplanter as a half-brother. The fact that Lake was responsible for the Iroquois reasserting their national identity is ironic, then, in light of Lake's blood relationship to Cornplanter.

Choices (A) and (B) are both accurate statements, based on the information in the passage. However, they confuse passage information by referring to unrelated details, thereby failing to respond to the question. Choice D gets the information in the passage backward; it was Lake, not Cornplanter, who was alcoholic.

Choice (E) runs contrary to the information in the passage and is unresponsive to the question. Lake emphasized the similarities between Christianity and his brand of Iroquois religion; the passage does not deal with the differences between Christianity and the Iroquois' traditional beliefs. Moreover, even if the passage did support choice E, it is not the irony to which the author refers.

QUESTION TYPE 4: RECOGNIZING THE FUNCTION OR PURPOSE OF SPECIFIC INFORMATION

Some questions are designed to determine whether, in immersing yourself in the details, you lost sight of the author's reason for including the details. To avoid falling into this trap, be sure to interact with the passage at all times, asking yourself what role or function specific information plays in the context in which the passage mentions it. Here's how to approach these questions:

• Maintain an active mind set as you read. When you come across detailed information in the passage, ask yourself what role these details play in the discussion. Is the author trying to support his or her point with several specific examples? Is the author observing similarities and differences between two things? As you read, remember that it is more important for you to understand *why* the author mentions details than to remember the details themselves (you can always look them up later).

- Some inference is required. You will not find an explicit answer to this question in the passage. In other words, the author is not going to state outright that the reason that he or she is mentioning a particular detail is to support a particular assertion. Instead, you must infer the author's purpose in mentioning the detail.

- As with inference questions, these questions call for you to make only very "tight" inferences; in other words, the passage will suggest the author's purpose so strongly that no other interpretation is really reasonable.

Look for These Wrong-Answer Ploys

- **The response that is unsupported.** This response infers a purpose that the passage's information does not support, possibly by bringing in extrinsic material from outside the passage.

- **The response that exaggerates or distorts the author's purpose.** As noted earlier, you must make only narrow or tight inferences when inferring the author's purpose in mentioning details. A wrong answer might distort or exaggerate the author's relatively narrow inference.

- **The response that confuses the information in the passage.** Such a response restates a point made elsewhere in the passage. This response will tempt you if you recall reading the statement and are confident that the statement is true or accurately states the author's position. Don't let such responses fool you. By focusing your attention on only the relevant portion of the passage, you can be confident that this response, while possibly an accurate statement, is a wrong answer.

- **The response that confuses the author's position with that of another, possibly contradicting the information in the passage.** The author might men-

tion certain details to support his or her argument against a position or theory. Be sure not to confuse the author's argument with opposing views.

An Example from Yesterday's Question Set

2. The author quotes Cartier-Bresson in order to

(A) refute Avedon's conception of a portrait sitting
(This response exaggerates the passage's information.)

(B) provide one perspective of the portraiture encounter
(This is the correct response.)

(C) support the claim that portrait sittings are, more often than not, confrontational encounters
(This response distorts the passage's information.)

(D) show that a portraiture encounter may be either brief or extended
(This response confuses the passage's information.)

(E) distinguish a sitting for a photographic portrait from a sitting for a painted portrait
(The passage does not support this response.)

(For a more detailed analysis of this question, see Day 18.)

QUESTION TYPE 5: EXTRAPOLATING FROM OR APPLYING PASSAGE IDEAS

These questions are not nearly as common as the other types. Such questions ask you either to apply passage information to new situations or to speculate as to how the passage would continue. The approach here is similar to that of handling inference and interpretation questions.

Common Wrong-Answer Ploys

- **The response that the ideas referred to in the question stem do not support.** Such a response might require an unwarranted inference, or might depart from the topic or be irrelevant to the ideas presented in the passage.

- **The response that runs contrary to the ideas to which the question stem refers.** This answer choice can fool you, because it might include all the right words and phrases. However, the answer turns around the idea presented in the passage, possibly by including or excluding a key word.

- **The response that covers old ground when the question asks for a logical continuation of the passage.** The author's discussion is unlikely to reverse its "flow" and rehash material already treated in the earlier parts of the passage. However, don't rule out this possibility. For example, the author might continue by examining in more detail one of two or three points made in the passage. If this is the case, the final sentences probably will provide a clue that this is the next area of discussion.

An Example from Today's Question Set

3. Assuming that the reasons that the passage asserts for the decline of the Iroquois culture are historically representative of the decline of cultural minorities, which of the following developments would most likely contribute to the demise of a modern-day ethnic minority?

    (A) a bilingual education program in which children who are members of the minority group learn to read and write in both their traditional language and the language prevalent in the present culture
    (The passage does not fully support this response.)

    (B) a tax credit for residential-property owners who lease their property to members of the minority group
    (This response is too general and the passage does not support it.)

    (C) increased efforts by local government to eradicate the availability of illegal drugs
    (This response is contrary to the passage's information.)

    (D) a government-sponsored program to assist minority-owned businesses in using computer technology to improve efficiency
    (This is the correct response.)

    (E) the declaration of a national holiday commemorating a past war in which the minority group played an active role
    (The passage's information does not support this response; in fact, this response contradicts the passage's information.)

Choice (D) is the best response. According to the passage, the Quakers' introduction of new technology to the Iroquois was partly responsible for the decline of the Iroquois culture in that it contributed to the tribe's loss of national identity. Choice (D) presents a similar situation.

Choice (A) is probably the second-best response. Insofar as the children referred to in choice (A) learn the language of the prevailing culture, assimilation and a resulting loss of ethnic identity might tend to occur. However, this sense of identity might be reinforced by their learning to read and write in their traditional language as well. Therefore, choice (A) is not as likely to lead to the demise of the minority group as choice (D), at least based on the Iroquois' experience as discussed in the passage.

Choice (B) is too vague, and the passage does not support it. Whether a government incentive to provide housing for members of the minority group actually undermines the group's sense of ethnic identity would probably depend on whether the incentives result in integration or segregation. Moreover, because the passage does not address whether the Iroquois became geographically integrated (assimilated), it does not support choice (B).

Choice (C) runs contrary to the result called for in the question. The scenario posed in choice (C) would actually contribute to the minority group's retaining its ethnic identity, at least based on the information in the passage. According to the passage, the introduction of spirits to the Iroquois population led to rampant alcoholism, which in turn contributed to the culture's decline. Similarly, widespread drug abuse might have a similar effect today. Accordingly, any effort to curb such abuse—as response choice (C) suggests—would tend to impede a decline rather than contribute to it.

Choice (E), like choice (C), runs contrary to the result of that called for in the question. Also, the passage does not support choice (E). Any ceremony or holiday calling attention to the ethnic population as a distinct group and helping to bring the population together as a group under a shared experience would tend to reinforce a sense of identity. Moreover, the passage does not refer to any developments during the time of the Iroquois decline that might be similar in any way to choice (E); accordingly, the passage does not support choice (E).

THE GMAT'S FAVORITE WRONG-ANSWER PLOYS

Keep a mental list of the wrong-answer types or ploys. When you have trouble narrowing down the answer choices to the best response, review this list in your mind, and the remaining wrong answers should reveal themselves. Here is a checklist, in order of frequency of use on the GMAT:

- **The response distorts the information in the passage.** It might understate, overstate, or twist the passage's information or the author's point in presenting that information.

- **The response uses information from the passage but does not respond to the question.** Such a response might include information found in the passage but not respond appropriately to the question posed.

- **The response relies on speculation or an unsupported inference.** It calls for some measure of speculation in that the statement is not readily inferable from the information given.

- **The response is contrary to the passage or stated backward.** Such a response contradicts the passage's information or gets information backward.

- **The response confuses one opinion or position with another.** Such a response incorrectly represents the position or opinion of one person or group as that of another.

- **The response is too narrow (specific).** It focuses on particular information in the passage that is too specific or narrowly focused in terms of the question posed.

- **The response is too broad (general).** It embraces information or ideas that are too general or widely focused in terms of the question posed.

- **The response relies on information that the passage does not mention.** Such a response brings in extrinsic information not found anywhere in the passage.

TIPS FOR TACKLING READING COMPREHENSION QUESTIONS

Don't Second-Guess the Test Maker

The directions for the GMAT Reading Comprehension sets instruct you to choose the "best" response among the five choices. Isn't this awfully subjective? True, there is an element of subjective judgment involved in reading comprehension. However, these questions are tested and revised several times before they appear as scored questions on an actual GMAT. *Do not second-guess the test maker's judgment or command of standard written English.* If you think that there are two or more viable "best" responses, *you* have either misread or misinterpreted the passage, the question, or the answer choices.

Read Every Answer Choice in Its Entirety

You're looking for the "best" response. Often, more than one answer choice is viable. Don't hastily select or eliminate answer choices without reading them all. *GMAT test takers miss more questions for this reason than for any other!*

Don't Over-Analyze Questions or Second-Guess Yourself

If you believe that you understood the passage fairly well but a particular answer choice seems confusing or a bit nonsensical, do not assume that it's your fault. Many wrong-answer choices simply don't make much sense. If an answer choice strikes you this way, don't examine it further; eliminate it. Similarly, if you've considered all five choices, and one response strikes you as the best one, *more often than not, your initial response will be the correct one.*

Don't Overlook the Obvious

If a particular response seems obviously correct or incorrect, don't assume that you are missing something. You might simply be up against a relatively easy question.

Eliminate Responses
That Run Contrary to the Thesis

Regardless of the type of question that you're dealing with, keep in mind the overall thesis, main idea, or point that the author is making in the passage as a whole. You can eliminate any answer choice to any question that runs contrary to or is inconsistent with that thesis. You might be surprised how many questions you can answer correctly using only this technique.

Keep in Mind Common Wrong-Answer Ploys to Avoid Falling into the Test Maker's Traps

Be assured: The test makers will try again and again to bait you with their favorite wrong-answer ploys. Learn to recognize these ploys, and keep them in mind as you take tomorrow's mini-test as well as the Verbal Section of the practice test later in this book.

IF YOU HAVE MORE TIME TODAY

To put into practice what you learned today and yesterday, log on to the author's GMAT Web site (www.west.net/~stewart/gmat) and attempt a Reading Comprehension mini-test. (To find the mini-test click on "Verbal Ability" in the "Test Yourself" area.)

Day 20

Reading Comprehension Lesson 3: Mini-Test and Review

Today's Topics:

Today you will apply what you learned on Days 18 and 19 to three Reading Comprehension passages. After taking this mini-test under timed conditions, review the explanations that follow. Preceding the explanation for each question, the question type and difficulty level are indicated.

MINI-TEST (READING COMPREHENSION)

Number of questions: 9
Suggested time: 18 minutes

> **Directions (as indicated on the test):** "Each passage is followed by a group of questions based on its content. After reading the passage, choose the best answer to each question and fill in the corresponding oval. Answer all questions on the basis of what is stated or implied in the passage."

Questions 1–3 are based on the following passage:

Dorothea Lange was perhaps the most notable of the photographers commissioned during the 1930s by the Farm Security Administration (FSA), part of a federal plan to revitalize the nation's
(5) economy and to communicate its human and social dimensions. The value of Lange's photographs as documents for social history is enhanced by her technical and artistic mastery of the medium. Her well-composed, sharp-focus images reveal a wealth
(10) of information about her subjects and show historical evidence that would scarcely be known but for her camera. Her finest images, while according with conditions of poverty that prompted political response, portray people who appear indomitable,
(15) unvanquished by their reverses. "Migrant Mother," for example, portrays a sense of the innocent victim, of perseverance, of destitution as a temporary aberration calling for compassion, solutions, and politics to alter life for the better. The power of that photo-
(20) graph, which became the symbol of the photographic file of the FSA, endures today.

The documentary book was a natural genre for Lange and her husband Paul Taylor, whose narrative accompanied Lange's FSA photographs. In *An*
(25) *American Exodus*, produced by Lange and Taylor, a sense of the despair of Lange's subjects is heightened by the captioned quotations of the migrants. Taken from 1935 to 1940, the *Exodus* pictures became the accepted vision of the migration of Dust Bowl farm
(30) workers into California.

1. According to the passage, the photograph entitled "Migrant Mother"
   - (A) appeared in the documentary book *An American Exodus*
   - (B) was accompanied by a caption written by Lange's husband
   - (C) was taken by Lange in 1935
   - (D) portrays the mother of a Dust Bowl farm worker
   - (E) is considered by the author to be one of Lange's best photographs

2. The passage provides information for responding to all the following questions EXCEPT:
   - (A) What was the FSA's purpose in compiling the photographic file to which Lange contributed?
   - (B) How did the FSA react to the photographs taken by Lange under its commission?
   - (C) In what areas of the United States did Lange take the photographs that appear in *An American Exodus*?
   - (D) Why did Lange agree to work for the FSA?
   - (E) What qualities make Lange's photographs noteworthy?

3. Among the following characterizations, the passage is best viewed as
   - (A) a survey of the great photographers of the Depression era
   - (B) an examination of the photographic techniques of Dorothea Lange
   - (C) an argument for the power of pictures to enact social change
   - (D) a discussion of the goals and programs of the FSA's photographic department
   - (E) an explanation of Lange's interest in documenting the plight of Depression victims

Questions 4–6 are based on the following passage:

Those who criticize the United States government today for not providing health care to all citizens equate health-care provision with medical insurance coverage. By this standard, 17th and 18th
(5) Century America lacked any significant conception of public health law. However, despite the general paucity of bureaucratic organization in preindustrial America, the vast extent of health regulation and provision stands out as remarkable.
(10)   Of course, the public role in the protection and regulation of 18th Century health was carried out in ways quite different from those today. Organizations responsible for health regulation were less stable than modern bureaucracies, tending to appear
(15) in crises and wither away in periods of calm. The focus was on epidemics that were seen as unnatural and warranting a response, not to the many endemic and chronic conditions that were accepted as part and parcel of daily life. Additionally, religious
(20) influence was significant, especially in the 17th Century. Finally, in an era that lacked sharp demarcations between private and governmental bodies, many public responsibilities were carried out by what we would now consider private associations.
(25) Nevertheless, the extent of public health regulation long before the dawn of the welfare state is remarkable and suggests that the founding generation's assumptions about the relationship between government and health were more complex than is com-
(30) monly assumed.

4. Which of the following statements about the United States government's role in the provision of health care finds the least support in the passage?
   - (A) The government today addresses health concerns that formerly were not considered serious enough to warrant government involvement.
   - (B) What were once public health-care functions are now served by the private sector.
   - (C) Philosophical considerations play a less significant role today in the formulation of public health-care policies than in previous centuries.
   - (D) Public health care today is guided largely by secular rather than religious values.
   - (E) Modern public health-care agencies are typically established not as temporary measures but as permanent establishments.

5. Which of the following best expresses the author's point of contention with "those who criticize the

United States government for not providing health care to all citizens" (lines 1–3)?

(A) Their standard for measuring such provision is too narrow.

(B) They underestimate the role that insurance plays in the provision of health care today.

(C) They fail to recognize that government plays a more significant role today in health care than in previous eras.

(D) They misunderstand the intent of the founding generation with respect to the proper role of the government in the area of health care.

(E) They lack any significant conception of public health law.

6. Which of the following best expresses the passage's main point?

(A) The government's role in health care has not expanded over time to the extent that many critics have asserted.

(B) The government should limit its involvement in health care to epidemiological problems.

(C) Health problems plaguing preindustrial America resulted largely from inadequate public health care.

(D) History suggests that the United States government has properly played a significant role in provision of health care.

(E) Private insurance is an inadequate solution to the problem of health care.

Questions 7–9 are based on the following passage:

Radiative forcings are changes imposed on the planetary energy balance; radiative feedbacks are changes induced by climate change. Forcings can arise from natural or anthropogenic causes. For (5) example, the concentration of sulfate aerosols in the atmosphere can be altered by volcanic action or by the burning of fossil fuels. The distinction between forcings and feedbacks is sometimes arbitrary; however, forcings are quantities normally specified (10) in global climate model simulations, whereas feedbacks are calculated quantities. Examples of radiative forcings are greenhouse gases (such as carbon dioxide and ozone), aerosols in the troposphere, and surface reflectivity. Radiative feedbacks include

(15) clouds, water vapor in the troposphere, and sea-ice cover.

The effects of forcings and feedbacks on climate are complex and uncertain. For example, clouds trap outgoing radiation, and thus provide a warming (20) influence. However, they also reflect incoming solar radiation, and thus provide a cooling influence. Current measurements indicate that the net effect of clouds is to cool the Earth. However, scientists are unsure whether the balance will shift in the future as (25) the atmosphere and cloud formation are altered by the accumulation of greenhouse gases. Similarly, the vertical distribution of ozone affects both the amount of radiation reaching the Earth's surface and of reradiated radiation that is trapped by the greenhouse (30) effect. These two mechanisms affect the Earth's temperature in opposite directions.

7. It can be inferred from the information in the passage that "burning of fossil fuels" (line 7)

(A) is an anthropogenic cause of radiative forcings

(B) results in both radiative forcings and radiative feedbacks

(C) does not affect atmospheric forcings or feedbacks

(D) is a significant type of radiative forcing

(E) is an anthropogenic cause of radiative feedbacks

8. According to the passage, radiative forcings and radiative feedbacks can usually be distinguished in which of the following ways?

(A) whether the radiative change is global or more localized

(B) the precision with which the amounts of radiative change can be determined

(C) the altitude at which the radiative change occurs

(D) whether the amount of radiative change is specified or calculated

(E) whether the radiative change is directed toward or away from the Earth

9. The author discusses the effect of clouds on atmospheric temperature probably to show that

   (A) radiative feedbacks can be more difficult to isolate and predict than radiative forcings

   (B) the climatic impact of some radiative feedbacks is uncertain

   (C) some radiative feedbacks cannot be determined solely by global climate model simulations

   (D) the distinction between radiative feedbacks and radiative forcings is somewhat arbitrary

   (E) the effects of radiative forcings on planetary energy balance are both complex and uncertain

Quick Answer Guide

Mini-Test: Reading Comprehension

1.	E	6.	D
2.	D	7.	A
3.	C	8.	D
4.	C	9.	B
5.	A		

EXPLANATIONS

1. The correct answer is (E). Explicit detail (moderate).

The author cites "Migrant Mother" as an example of "her finest images"—that is, as an example of her best photographs.

Choice (A) calls for speculation. The photograph might have appeared in Lange's book; however, the passage does not explicitly say so.

Choice (B) calls for speculation. Lange's husband wrote narrative captions for the photographs appearing in *Exodus*. However, the passage does not indicate that "Migrant Mother" was accompanied by a caption or even that the photograph appeared in the book.

Choice (C) provides information not mentioned in the passage. Although it is reasonable to assume that Lange took the photograph during the 1930s, the passage neither states nor implies what year she took the photo.

Choice (D) calls for speculation. According to the passage, the photographs appearing in *Exodus* "became the accepted vision of the migration of Dust Bowl farm workers to California." However, the author does not indicate either that "Migrant Mother" appeared in the book or that the woman portrayed in the photograph was indeed the mother of a Dust Bowl farm worker.

2. The correct answer is (D). Explicit detail (moderate).

The passage provides absolutely no information about Lange's motives or reasons for accepting her FSA commission.

The passage's first sentence answers choice (A) implicitly: " . . . the FSA, part of a federal plan to revitalize the economy and to communicate its human and social dimensions." Thus, the photographic file was compiled in furtherance of that purpose.

The first paragraph's last sentence answers choice (B) implicitly. The FSA thought highly enough of one of Lange's photographs to use it as a symbol for its photographic file.

The second paragraph answers choice (C) implicitly. According to the passage, the *Exodus* pictures recorded the migration of Dust Bowl farm workers into California. Thus, some (and probably all or nearly all) of these photographs were taken in the Dust Bowl region of the U.S. or in California.

The passage answers choice (E) in the first paragraph, where the author mentions Lange's "well-composed, sharp-focus" images.

3. The correct answer is (C). Primary purpose (moderate).

Admittedly, choice (C) is not an ideal characterization of the passage, which seems more concerned with Lange's work than with making a broader argument about the power of pictures. Nevertheless, the author does allude to Lange's ability to convey a need for social change through her photographs. Accordingly, the passage can be characterized as presenting one example (Lange) to support the broader point suggested by choice (C).

Choice (A) is far too broad. Lange is the only photographer that the passage discusses.

Choice (B) is too narrow. Although the author mentions some of Lange's techniques (for example, her "well-composed, sharp-focus images"), the author does not examine them in any detail.

Choice (D) distorts the passage and is too broad. First, the passage does not indicate that a distinct photographic department within the FSA existed; in this sense, choice (D) distorts the passage's information. Second, although the first sentence alludes to the FSA's overall purpose, the passage offers no further discussion of the agency's goals or program, other than the discussion of Lange's involvement in compiling its photographic file; in this sense, choice (D) is far too broad.

Choice (E) distorts the passage. The author does not discuss Lange's motive or reasons for photographing Depression victims other than that the FSA commissioned her to do so.

4. The correct answer is (C). Explicit detail (challenging).

The passage does not support choice (C); nowhere does the author suggest that the government policies today regarding health care are guided less by philosophical considerations than in previous eras. The term "philosophical" should not be equated with the term "religious" (otherwise, choices (C) and (D) would be essentially the same responses).

Choice (A) is the second-best response. Support for choice (A) is less explicit than for any other incorrect answer choice. Nevertheless, choice (A) finds support from the author's point that the government did not formerly address many nonepidemic diseases because they were considered part and parcel of daily life. You can reasonably infer from this excerpt that epidemic diseases were considered a greater threat (that is, more serious), thereby warranting government's attention.

Choice (B) restates the author's assertion that "many public responsibilities were carried out by what we would now consider private associations."

Choice (D) is readily inferable. The author asserts that the public role in health care is carried out in different ways today than it was in prior centuries. The author then points out that "religious influence was significant, especially in the 17th Century." It is reasonably inferable, then, that religion does not play a significant role today in public health-care decisions.

Choice (E) restates the author's point that government health-care organizations in previous eras were less stable than modern bureaucracies.

5. The correct answer is (A). Interpretation (moderate).

According to the author, the critics equate the degree (extent) of health-care provision with insurance coverage. The author contends that by this standard of measurement, public health care during the 18th Century was practically nonexistent. In fact, however, the government played a significant role in health care during that century in ways other than providing insurance to its citizens. Thus, the critics' standard for measuring the extent of the government's role in health care is far too narrow in that it ignores all the other possible ways in which government can play a role in health care.

The passage does not support choice (B). Nowhere does the author state or imply that insurance plays a larger role in health care than the critics contend. Also, choice (B) makes no distinction between private and public insurance.

Choice (C) is not well supported. Based on the information in the second paragraph, it appears that the United States government has played a significant role in health care throughout history; the author does not contend that the government's role in health care is greater today than in previous eras (implicitly, some of the evidence in the second paragraph supports this contention, whereas other evidence undermines it). Moreover, even if the passage strongly supported choice (C), the statement is nevertheless not the author's point of contention with the critics.

Choice (D) is unsupported and does not respond to the question. The author makes no attempt to evaluate the critics' understanding of the founding generation's intent. Even if the passage supported choice (D), it is nevertheless not the author's point of contention with the critics.

Choice (E) confuses the details in the second paragraph. It was America that, by the critics' standards, "lacked any significant conception of public health law." Choice (E) asserts, however, that the critics were the ones who lacked such conception.

6. The correct answer is (D). Interpretation (moderate).

In the passage, the author rebuts the critics' argument that government is not providing health care to all citizens and implies, at the close of the passage, that the founding generation probably intended that government play a significant ("complex") role in health care.

Choice (A) is unsupported and runs contrary to the passage. The passage's evidence is conflicting as to whether the government's role has in fact expanded over time, and the author does not really address this issue. Also, according to the passage, the critics assert that the government plays too small a role in health care; thus, choice (A) actually tends to run contrary to the critics' contention.

The passage does not support choice (B), which calls for an unwarranted inference. Although acknowledging that the government in fact has expanded its health concerns from epidemics to chronic and endemic disorders, the author does not take a position on whether such expansion is desirable or proper.

Choice (C) is wholly unsupported. The author makes no attempt in the passage to identify the health problems of preindustrial America or their causes.

Choice (E) distorts the main idea. Although choice (E) is consistent with the author's implicit argument that the government should play a significant role in health care, it fails to express the broader point that the author seeks to make.

7. The correct answer is (A). Inference (easier).

The author states in the first paragraph that "forcings can arise from natural or anthropogenic causes." In the following sentence, the author describes two specific causes of forcings, presumably to illustrate the point of the previous sentence. By considering both sentences together, you can reasonably infer that the first example (volcanic activity) is a natural cause, whereas the second (the burning of fossil fuels) is an anthropogenic cause.

The passage only partly supports choice (B). Although you can infer that the burning of fossil fuels causes radiative forcings, the author neither states nor suggests that this activity also causes radiative feedbacks.

Choice (C) contradicts the information in this part of the passage. The passage states explicitly that the concentration of sulfate aerosols is affected ("can be altered") by burning of fossil fuels. Thus, although burning of fossil fuels might not affect radiative feedbacks, you can infer that such activity does affect radiative forcings.

Choice (D) is nonsensical. The burning of fossil fuels is a cause, not a type, of radiative forcing.

Choice (E) confuses forcings with feedbacks.

8. The correct answer is (D). Explicit detail (moderate).

According to the passage, radiative "forcings are quantities normally specified in global climate model situations, whereas feedbacks are calculated quantities."

Choice (A) is wholly unsupported by the passage. The author never discusses the geographic extent of radiative changes in any context.

The passage does not support choice (B). The fact that feedbacks are "calculated quantities" whereas forcings are "specified" quantities does not in itself suggest that one can be more precisely determined than the other.

Choices (C) and (E) confuse the information in the passage in a similar way. The second paragraph discusses altitude as a factor influencing the relative effects on ozone changes (a radiative forcing) of radiation directed toward Earth and radiation directed away from Earth. This area of discussion involves forcings only, not feedbacks.

9. The correct answer is (B). Purpose of detail (moderate).

Choice (B) restates the author's point in the first sentence of the second paragraph. Immediately thereafter, the author discusses clouds as an example of this point—it is difficult to predict the impact of greenhouse gases on clouds and thus on temperature.

The passage does not support choice (A). In the second paragraph, the author discusses two particular examples of radiative changes: one involving radiative forcings and the other involving radiative feedbacks. The author's purpose in discussing these two phenomena is to illustrate the author's previous point that "the effects of some forcings and feedbacks on climate are complex and uncertain." However, the author makes no attempt to compare the relative complexity or uncertainty of these two effects.

Choice (C) confuses the information in the passage and is somewhat nonsensical. The global climate model simulations specifies (do not determine) forcings (not feedbacks). Moreover, choice (C) is wholly unsupported by the information in the second paragraph; nowhere does the author discuss or mention global climate simulations in relation to the effects of clouds on atmospheric temperatures.

The passage supports choice (D), but that answer does not respond to the question. In the first paragraph, the author attempts to distinguish between forcings and feedbacks and does indeed mention that the distinction can be somewhat arbitrary. However, this point is completely unrelated to the discussion in the second paragraph.

Choice (E) is the second-best response. The passage's first sentence defines radiative forcings as "changes imposed on the planetary energy balance." Choice (E) is indeed one of the author's points in the second paragraph. However, choice (E) does not respond to the question, which deals with feedbacks rather than forcings.

Day 21

Quantitative Ability Lesson 7:
Basic Geometry

Today's Topics:

1. Lines and Angles
2. Triangles
3. Quadrilaterals
4. Geometry Exercises

Today you learn how to handle GMAT geometry problems involving intersecting lines, triangles, and quadrilaterals. Then you test your competency with the concepts covered by attempting the exercises at the end of the lesson.

LINES AND ANGLES

Lines and line segments are the basic building blocks of all GMAT geometry problems. In fact, some GMAT geometry problems involve nothing more than intersecting lines (and the angles created thereby). Two types are most common on the GMAT:

- Problems involving *wheel spokes*
- Problems involving *parallel lines* and *transversals*

Before examining these two problems types, review some basic terminology and some fundamental rules. Referring to the next figure, the following symbols are used on the GMAT to denote lines, line segments, and angles that result from intersecting lines:

- l_1 identifies line *AC*, and l_2 identifies line *BD*. On the GMAT, lines and line segments are always assumed to be straight.

- *AB* and $\overline{AB}$ are used interchangeably to identify line segment *AB*; you can also use them to denote the *length* of line segment *AB*.

- Point *E* is the *vertex* of any of the angles formed by the intersection of l_1 and l_2.

- ∠*AED* denotes the angle having point *E* as its vertex and $\overrightarrow{EA}$ and $\overrightarrow{ED}$ as the two *rays* leading away from the vertex and forming the angle. The size of ∠*AED* is x°—that is, ∠*AED* has a degree measure of *x*.

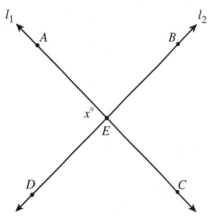

- *Opposite* angles are the same size, or *congruent* (≅), or equal in degree measure. In the figure on page 193, the following are true:

  $\angle AED \cong \angle BEC$

  $\angle AEB \cong \angle DEC$

- *Supplementary* angles form a straight line when added together; their degree measures total 180. In fact, a straight line is actually a 180° angle. In the figure on page 193, the following are true:

  $\angle AED + \angle AEB = 180°$ (a straight line)

  $\angle AEB + \angle BEC = 180°$ (a straight line)

  $\angle BEC + \angle CED = 180°$ (a straight line)

  $\angle CED + \angle AED = 180°$ (a straight line)

Wheel Spokes

Building on the foregoing rules, the sum of all angles where two or more lines intersect at the same point is 360° (regardless of how many angles are involved). Thus, in the figure on page 193, the following is true:

$\angle AEB + \angle BEC + \angle CED + \angle AED = 360°$

A *right angle* is an angle measuring 90°. The intersection of two *perpendicular* lines results by definition in a right angle. If you know that one angle formed by two intersecting lines is a right (90°) angle, then you know that the two lines are perpendicular and that all four angles formed by the intersection are right angles, as shown below.

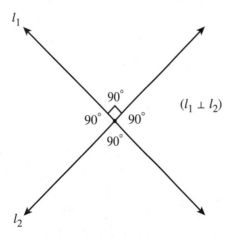

$(l_1 \perp l_2)$

Combining all the foregoing rules, the following relationships among the angles in the diagram below emerge (the last two are less obvious and therefore more "testworthy" for the GMAT):

- $y + v = 180$ (y and v form a straight line; they are supplementary)

- $x + w = 180$ (x and w form a straight line; they are supplementary)

- $v + z + w = 180$ (v, z, and w form a straight line; they are supplementary)

- $x + y - z = 180$ ($x + y$ exceed 180 by the amount of their overlap, which equals z, the angle opposite to the overlapping angle)

- $x + y + v + w = 360$ (the sum of all angles, excluding z, is 360°; z is excluded because it is already accounted for by the overlap of x and y)

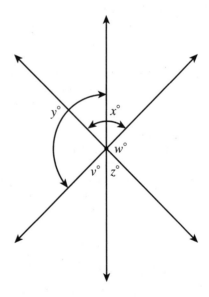

Parallel Lines and Transversals

Parallel lines are lines that never intersect, even continuing infinitely in both directions. A GMAT problem would denote two parallel lines, 1 and 2, as follows:

$l_1 \parallel l_2$

GMAT problems involving parallel lines also involve at least one *transversal,* which is a line that intersects each of two (or more) parallel lines. In the figure below, $l_1 \parallel l_2$, and l_3 *transverses* (is a transversal of) l_1 and l_2.

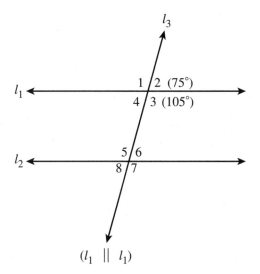

$(l_1 \parallel l_1)$

In the figure above, because $l_1 \parallel l_2$, the upper "cluster" of angles (created by the intersection of l_1 and l_3) looks identical to, or "mirrors," the lower "cluster" (created by the intersection of l_2 and l_3). For example, $\angle 1$ is congruent (equal in size or degree measure) to $\angle 5$ ($\angle 1$ and $\angle 5$ are said to be *corresponding* angles). Because opposite angles are congruent, the following relationships among the eight angles in the foregoing diagram emerge:

- All the *odd*-numbered angles are congruent (equal in size) to one another.

- All the *even*-numbered angles are congruent (equal in size) to one another.

Moreover, if you know the size of just one of the eight angles, you can determine the size of all eight angles. For example, if $\angle 2$ measures 75°, then angles 4, 6, and 8 also measure 75° each, whereas angles 1, 3, 5, and 7 each measure 105° (75° + 105° = 180° which forms a straight line). If you add a second

transversal paralleling the first one, the resulting four-sided figure is a *parallelogram*—a quadrilateral with two pairs of parallel sides. Applying the transversal analysis to parallelogram *ABCD* shown below, the following are evident:

- $\angle 1 \cong \angle 4$

- $\angle 2 \cong \angle 3$

- $\angle 1 + \angle 2 = 180°, \angle 1 + \angle 3 = 180°$

- $\angle 2 + \angle 4 = 180°, \angle 3 + \angle 4 = 180°$

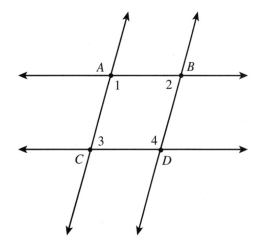

In fact, all four "clusters" of angles (defined by vertices *A*, *B*, *C*, and *D*) mirror one another in their corresponding angle measures. If you know the size of just one angle, you can determine the size of all 16 angles!

TRIANGLES

The *triangle* (defined as a three-sided polygon) is the GMAT's favorite geometric figure. Triangle problems appear in a variety of scenarios—by themselves in a pure mathematical setting, as word problems, and in "hybrid" geometry problems involving triangular components of quadrilaterals and circles. To score high on the GMAT, you must know all the following properties and rules involving triangles.

Properties of All Triangles

Referring to the triangle shown on page 180, the following properties apply to *all* triangles.

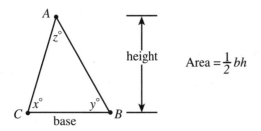

$$\text{Area} = \frac{1}{2}bh$$

Length of the sides. Each side is shorter than the sum of the lengths of the other two sides:

$AC < AB + BC$

$BC < AB + AC$

$AB < BC + AC$

Angle measures. The sum of the three angles = 180°:

$x + y + z = 180$

$180 - x = y + z$

$180 - y = x + z$

$180 - z = x + y$

Accordingly, the sum of the measures of any two (of the three) angles must be less than 180°:

$x + y < 180$ $(x < 180 - y, y < 180 - x)$

$x + z < 180$ $(x < 180 - z, z < 180 - x)$

$y + z < 180$ $(y < 180 - z, z < 180 - y)$

Angles and opposite sides. The relative angle sizes correspond to the relative lengths of the sides opposite those angles. In other words, the smaller the angle, the smaller the side opposite the angle, and vice versa. In the triangle above, for example:

If $x > y > z$, then $AB > AC > BC$

Accordingly, if two angles are equal in size, the sides opposite those angles are of equal length (and vice versa).

Caution: Do not take this rule too far. The sizes of angle measures do *not* correspond precisely to lengths of opposite sides! For example, if a certain triangle has angle measures of 30°, 60°,

and 90°, the ratio of the angles is 1:2:3. However, this does *not* mean that the ratio of the opposite sides is also 1:2:3 (it is *not*, as you will soon learn!).

Area. The area of any triangle is equal to one-half the product of its base and its height (altitude)—that is, $A_t = \frac{1}{2}(b)(h)$. You can use any side as the base to calculate area.

Right Triangles and the Pythagorean Theorem

In a *right triangle,* one angle measures 90° and, of course, each of the other two angles measures less than 90°. The two sides forming the 90° angle are commonly referred to as the triangle's *legs* (*a* and *b* in the figure below), whereas the third (and longest side) is referred to as the *hypotenuse* (*c* in the figure below).

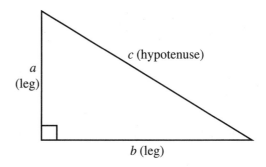

The *Pythagorean Theorem* expresses the relationship among the sides of any right triangle (*a* and *b* are the two legs, and *c* is the hypotenuse):

$$a^2 + b^2 = c^2 \quad or \quad \sqrt{a} + \sqrt{b} = \sqrt{c}$$

The Pythagorean Theorem is the single most useful formula in GMAT geometry problems. With any right triangle, if you know the length of two sides, you can determine the length of the third side with the Theorem. *Remember:* The Pythagorean Theorem applies only to *right* triangles, not to any others.

Pythagorean side triplets. These are sets of numbers that satisfy the Pythagorean Theorem. In each of the following triplets, the first two numbers represent the relative lengths of the two legs, whereas the third—and largest—number represents the relative length of the hypotenuse:

Ratio	Theorem
• 1:1:$\sqrt{2}$	$1^2 + 1^2 = \left(\sqrt{2}\right)^2$
• 1:$\sqrt{3}$:2	$1^2 + \left(\sqrt{3}\right)^2 = 2^2$
• 3:4:5	$3^2 + 4^2 = 5^2$
• 5:12:13	$5^2 + 12^2 = 13^2$
• 8:15:17	$8^2 + 15^2 = 17^2$
• 7:24:25	$7^2 + 24^2 = 25^2$

Each of the preceding triplets is expressed as a *ratio* because it represents the relative proportion of the triangle's sides. All right triangles with sides having the same ratio or proportion have the same shape (they are *similar* to one another). For example, a right triangle with sides 5, 12, and 13 units long is smaller but exactly the same shape (proportion) as one with sides 15, 36, and 39 units long. Learn to recognize given numbers (lengths of triangle sides) as multiples of Pythagorean triplets to save valuable time in solving GMAT right-triangle problems.

Now look at some examples. All three squares in the figure below include two 1:1:$\sqrt{2}$ triangles.

 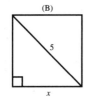 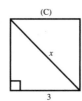

(A) indicates the basic triplet. In (B), the hypotenuse is given as 5. To calculate either leg's length, divide 5 by $\sqrt{2}$, *or* multiply 5 by $\frac{\sqrt{2}}{2}$: $x = \frac{5\sqrt{2}}{2}$. In (C), the leg's length is given as 3. To calculate the hypotenuse, multiply 3 by $\sqrt{2}$: $x = 3\sqrt{2}$.

In the next figure, all three triangles are 1:$\sqrt{3}$:2 triangles.

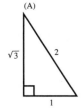 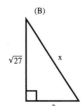 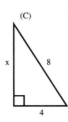

(A) indicates the basic triplet. In (B), the length of the legs are given as 3 and $\sqrt{27}$ (or 3$\sqrt{3}$), and the ratio of 3$\sqrt{3}$ to 3 is $\sqrt{3}$:1. Thus, this is a 1:$\sqrt{3}$:2 triangle. Calculate the hypotenuse from either leg:

• $x = 3 \times 2 = 6$

• $x = 3\sqrt{3} \times \dfrac{2}{\sqrt{3}} = 6$

In (C), the lengths of the hypotenuse and of one leg are given as 8 and 4. This ratio is 2:1. Thus, this is a 1:$\sqrt{3}$:2 triangle. Calculate the length of leg x from either the other leg or the hypotenuse:

• $x = (4)\left(\sqrt{3}\right) = 4\left(\sqrt{3}\right)$

• $x = (8)\left(\dfrac{\sqrt{3}}{2}\right) = 4\sqrt{3}$

In the figure below, all three triangles are 3:4:5 triangles.

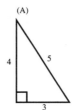 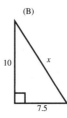 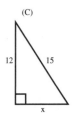

(A) indicates the basic triplet. (B) gives the length of the legs. The ratio of 10 to 7.5 is 4:3. Thus, this is a 3:4:5 triangle. Calculate the hypotenuse from either leg:

• $x = (7.5)\left(\dfrac{5}{3}\right) = 12.5$

• $x = (10)\left(\dfrac{5}{4}\right) = 12.5$

(C) gives the length of the hypotenuse and of one leg as 15 and 12. This ratio is 5:4. Thus, this is a 3:4:5 triangle. Calculate the length of leg x from either the other leg or the hypotenuse:

• $x = (15)\left(\dfrac{3}{5}\right) = 9$

• $x = (12)\left(\dfrac{3}{4}\right) = 9$

Pythagorean angle triplets. In two (and only two) of the unique triangles identified in the preceding section as Pythagorean triplets, *all degree measures are integers:*

- The corresponding angles opposite the sides of a $1:1:\sqrt{2}$ triangle are 45°, 45°, and 90°.

- The corresponding angles opposite the sides of a $1:\sqrt{3}:2$ triangle are 30°, 60°, and 90°.

The figure below shows these angle triplets and their corresponding side triplets.

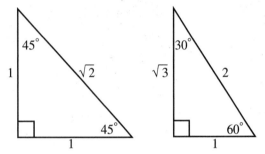

Thus, to determine *all* angle measures and lengths of *all* sides of a triangle quickly, all you need to know is the following:

- that the triangle is a right triangle
- that one of the angles is either 30°, 45°, or 60°
- the length of any one of the three sides

Isosceles Triangles

An isosceles triangle is one in which two sides are equal in length and, accordingly, two angles are equal in size. In any isosceles triangle, an *altitude* line from the angle formed by the congruent sides always bisects the opposite side. Thus, if you know the lengths of the sides, you can easily determine the triangle's area by applying the Pythagorean Theorem. Consider, for example, isosceles triangle *ABC* in the figure below.

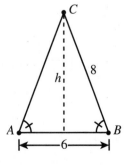
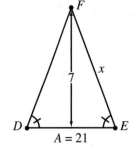

You can determine the height by applying the Pythagorean Theorem:

$$3^2 + h^2 = 8^2$$
$$h^2 = 64 - 9 = 55$$
$$h = \sqrt{55}$$

Thus, the area of triangle $ABC = \frac{1}{2}(6)(\sqrt{55}) = 3\sqrt{55}$. If you knew h but not the length of CB or AC, you could determine these lengths. The altitude line (h) bisects the base AB, creating two "mirror-image" right triangles, each with legs of length 3 and $\sqrt{55}$. Apply the Pythagorean Theorem:

$$x^2 = 3^2 + (\sqrt{55})^2$$
$$x^2 = 9 + 55 = 64$$
$$x = 8$$

In isosceles triangle *DEF*, the area is given as 21, and the height is 7. To find x, first determine b:

$$A = \frac{1}{2}(b)(h)$$
$$21 = \frac{1}{2}(b)(7)$$
$$b = 6$$

Now use $\frac{1}{2}b$ as a leg of a right triangle, and apply the Pythagorean Theorem to find x.

$$x^2 = 3^2 + 7^2$$
$$x^2 = 9 + 49 = 58$$
$$x = \sqrt{58}$$

Equilateral Triangles

An equilateral triangle is a special triangle in which all three sides are the same length and, accordingly, all three angles are the same size (60°). Any line bisecting one of the 60° angles will divide an equilateral triangle into two right triangles with angle measures of 30°, 60°, and 90°—that is, two $1:\sqrt{3}:2$ triangles.

The area of an equilateral triangle $= \frac{s^2}{4}\sqrt{3}$, where s is the length of a side. In the lefthand figure below, if $s = 6$, the area of the triangle $= 9\sqrt{3}$.

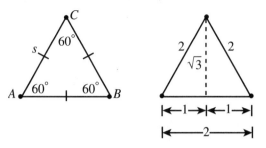

To confirm this formula, bisect the triangle into two 30-60-90 ($1:\sqrt{3}:2$) triangles (as in the righthand figure above). The area of this equilateral triangle is $\frac{1}{2}(2)(\sqrt{3})$ or $\sqrt{3}$. The area of each smaller right triangle is $\frac{\sqrt{3}}{2}$.

On the GMAT, you are most likely to encounter equilateral triangles in problems involving *circles* (one of tomorrow's lesson topics).

QUADRILATERALS

A quadrilateral is a four-sided figure. The specific types of quadrilaterals that appear most frequently on the GMAT include the following:

- A *square*, which is a special type of rectangle

- A *rectangle*, which is a special type of parallelogram

- A *parallelogram*, which is a special type of quadrilateral

Although the following two types of quadrilaterals appear less frequently on the GMAT, you should also be familiar with them:

- *Rhombus*

- *Trapezoid*

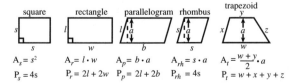

Each of these five types of quadrilaterals has its own properties (characteristics) that should be second nature to you as you approach the GMAT. The following are the two most important properties:

- *Area* (the surface covered by the figure on a plane)

- *Perimeter* (the total length of all sides)

The figure that follows indicates the area (A) and perimeter (P) formulas for each of these five quadrilaterals. Memorize these formulas!

The Properties of a Square

This next figure shows a square. All squares have the following properties:

- All four sides are equal in length.

- All four angles are right angles (90°).

- The perimeter = 4s.

- The area = s^2.

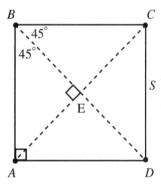

Diagonals are line segments connecting opposite corners of a quadrilateral. When you add diagonals to a square, the following are true:

- The area of the square = $\frac{(AC)^2}{2}$ or $\frac{(BD)^2}{2}$ (diagonal squared, divided by 2; this formula applies only to squares, not to other quadrilaterals!).

- The diagonals are equal in length ($AC = BD$).

- The diagonals are perpendicular; their intersection creates four right angles.

- The diagonals *bisect* each 90° angle of the square; that is, they split each angle into two equal (45°) angles.

- You create four distinct *congruent* (the same shape and size) triangles, each having an area of one-half that of the square: *ABD, ACD, ABC,* and *BCD.*

- You create four distinct congruent triangles, each having an area of one-fourth that of the square: *ABE, BCE, CDE,* and *ADE.*

- All eight triangles created are *right isosceles* triangles (with angle measures of 45°, 45°, and 90°).

The Properties of a Rectangle

This next figure shows a rectangle. All rectangles have the following properties:

- The opposite sides are equal in length.

- All four angles are right angles (90°).

- The perimeter = $2l + 2w$.

- The area = $l \times w$.

- The maximum area of a rectangle with a given perimeter is a square.

- Conversely, the minimum perimeter of a rectangle with a given area is a square.

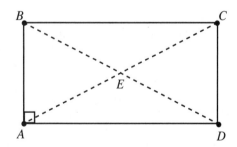

When you add diagonals to a rectangle, the following are true:

- The diagonals are equal in length ($AC = BD$).

- The diagonals are *not* perpendicular (unless the rectangle is a square).

- The diagonals do *not* bisect each 90° angle of the rectangle (unless the rectangle is a square).

- $AE = BE = CE = DE.$

- You create four distinct congruent triangles, each having an area of one-half that of the rectangle: *ABD, ACD, ABC,* and *BCD.*

- *ABE* is congruent to *CDE*; both triangles are isosceles (but they are right triangles *only* if the rectangle is a square).

- *BEC* is congruent to *AED*; both triangles are isosceles (but they are right triangles *only* if the rectangle is a square).

The Properties of a Parallelogram

The next figure shows a parallelogram. All parallelograms have the following properties:

- Opposite sides are parallel.

- Opposite sides are equal in length.

- Opposite angles are the same size (equal in degree measure).

- All four angles are equal in size *only* if the parallelogram is a rectangle—that is, if the angles are right angles.

- The perimeter = $2l + 2w$.

- The area = base (b) × altitude (a).

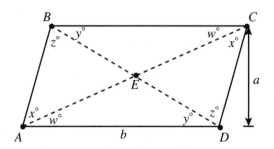

When you add diagonals to a parallelogram, the following are true:

- The diagonals (*AC* and *BD*) are *not* equal in length (unless the figure is a rectangle).

- The diagonals are *not* perpendicular (unless the figure is a square or rhombus).

- The diagonals do *not* bisect each angle of the parallelogram (unless it is a square or rhombus).

- The diagonals bisect each other ($BE = ED$, $CE = AE$).

- You create two pairs of congruent triangles, each having an area of one-half that of the parallelogram: ABD is congruent to BCD, and ACD is congruent to ABC.

- The triangle ABE is congruent to CED (they are mirror-imaged horizontally *and* vertically); the triangles are isosceles only if the quadrilateral is a rectangle.

- The triangle BEC is congruent to AED (they are mirror-imaged horizontally *and* vertically); the triangles are isosceles only if the quadrilateral is a rectangle.

The Properties of a Rhombus

The next figure shows a rhombus. All rhombuses have the following properties:

- All sides are equal in length.

- Opposite sides are parallel.

- No angles are right angles (angle measures $\neq 90°$).

- The perimeter = $4s$.

- The area = side (s) × altitude (a).

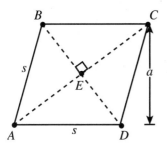

If you add diagonals (AC and BD) to a rhombus, the following are true:

- The area = $\frac{AC \times BD}{2}$ (one-half the product of the diagonals; this formula applies to a rhombus and a square, but not to any other quadrilaterals!).

- The diagonals bisect each other ($BE = ED$, $AE = EC$).

- The intersection of diagonals creates four right angles (diagonals are perpendicular).

- The diagonals are *not* equal in length ($AC \neq BD$).

- The diagonals bisect each angle of the rhombus.

- You create two pairs of congruent isosceles triangles, each triangle having an area of one-half that of the rhombus, (triangle ABD is congruent to BCD, and triangle ACD is congruent to ABC); none of these four triangles are right triangles.

- Triangle ABE is congruent to CED; both are right triangles (but not isosceles).

- Triangle BEC is congruent to AED; both are right triangles (but not isosceles).

The Properties of a Trapezoid

This next figure shows a trapezoid. All trapezoids have the following properties:

- Only one pair of opposite sides are parallel ($BC \parallel AD$).

- The perimeter = $AB + BC + CD + AD$.

- The area = $\frac{BC + AD}{2}$ × altitude (a) (one-half the sum of the two parallel sides multiplied by the altitude).

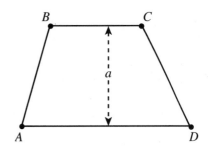

No predictable patterns emerge from the addition of two diagonals to a trapezoid.

IF YOU HAVE MORE TIME TODAY

Before you move ahead to tomorrow's advanced geometry lesson, make sure that you understand the basic geometry concepts covered today by attempting the following 10 questions. Answers and explanations immediately follow.

Geometry Exercises

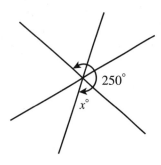

1. In the above figure, $x =$

   (A) 50 (B) 55 (C) 60 (D) 70 (E) 80

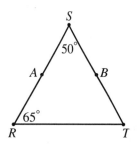

2. In triangle RST above, if A is the midpoint of RS, and if B is the midpoint of ST, then

   (A) $SA > ST$ (B) $BT > BS$ (C) $BT = SA$

   (D) $SR > ST$ (E) $RT > ST$

3. What is the perimeter of an equilateral triangle whose area is $16\sqrt{3}$?

   (A) 16 (B) 24 (C) $24\sqrt{3}$ (D) 48 (E) $48\sqrt{3}$

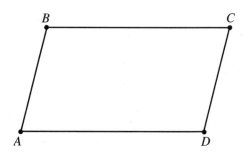

4. In parallelogram $ABCD$ above, $\angle A$ measures $60°$. The sum of the degree measures $\angle B$ and $\angle D$ is

   (A) $60°$ (B) $120°$ (C) $180°$ (D) $210°$ (E) $240°$

5. If you double both a rectangle's length and width, you increase the area by what percent?

   (A) 50 (B) 100 (C) 200 (D) 300 (E) 400

6. What is the perimeter of a square whose diagonal is 8?

   (A) 16 (B) $16\sqrt{2}$ (C) 32 (D) $32\sqrt{2}$ (E) $32\sqrt{3}$

7. A rectangular door measures $5'$ by $6'8"$. What is the distance from one corner of the door to the diagonally opposite corner?

   (A) $8'4"$ (B) $8'10"$ (C) $9'$ (D) $9'4"$ (E) $9'6"$

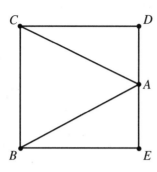

8. Isosceles triangle *ABC* is inscribed in square *BCDE* as shown above. If the area of *BCDE* is 4, what is the perimeter of *ABC*?

(A) $2 + \sqrt{5}$ (B) $2 + \sqrt{10}$ (C) 8
(D) $2 + 2\sqrt{5}$ (E) 12

9. In a parallelogram with an area of 15, the base is represented by $x + 7$ and the altitude is $x - 7$. What is the length of the parallelogram's base?

(A) 1 (B) 5 (C) 8 (D) 15 (E) 34

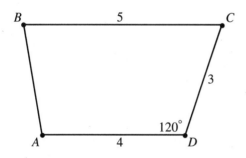

10. What is the area of trapezoid *ABCD* in the above figure?

(A) $5\sqrt{2}$ (B) $\dfrac{9\sqrt{3}}{(2)}$ (C) $\dfrac{27\sqrt{3}}{(4)}$ (D) $13\dfrac{1}{2}$ (E) 16

Answers And Explanations

1. The correct answer is (D).

Referring to the figure below, the total degree measure of all angles is 360. Given that all angles but a and b total 250, $a + b = 110$. $a + b + x = 180$ (they form a straight line). Thus, $x = 70$.

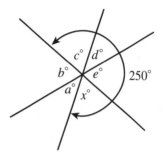

2. The correct answer is (C).

$\angle T = 65°$, so triangle *RST* is isosceles, and $RS = ST$. $BT = \frac{1}{2}ST$, and $SA = \frac{1}{2}SR$. Thus, $BT = SA$.

3. The correct answer is (B).

The area of an equilateral triangle $= \dfrac{s^2}{4}\sqrt{3}$. Therefore, $\dfrac{s^2}{4} = 16$. $s^2 = 64$, and $s = 8$. The perimeter is $8 + 8 + 8 = 24$.

4. The correct answer is (D).

Given that $\angle A = 60°$, angle $B = 120°$, because the angle measures must total 180. $\angle B = \angle D$. Thus, their sum is 240°.

5. The correct answer is (D).

If the dimensions are doubled, the area is multiplied by 2^2, or 4. The new area is four times as great as the original area—that is, it has been increased by 300%.

6. The correct answer is (B).

The diagonal of a square is the hypotenuse of a $1:1:\sqrt{2}$ isosceles right triangle, where the two legs are sides of the square. Thus, given that the hypotenuse is 8, each side is $\dfrac{8}{\sqrt{2}}$, and the perimeter of the square is $4 \times \dfrac{8}{\sqrt{2}} = \dfrac{32}{\sqrt{2}} = 16\sqrt{2}$.

7. The correct answer is (B).

The width of the door is 60" (5'), and its length is 80" (6'8"). This is a 6:8:10 triangle (conforming to the 3:4:5 Pythagorean triplet), with a diagonal of 100", or 8'4".

8. The correct answer is (D).

Each side of the square = 2. If $BE = 2$, $EA = 1$, then by the Pythagorean Theorem, BA and AC each equals $\sqrt{5}$. Thus, the perimeter of triangle $ABC = 2 + 2\sqrt{5}$.

9. The correct answer is (D).

The area of a parallelogram = $(b)(h)$:

$$(x + 7)(x - 7) = 15$$
$$x^2 - 49 = 15$$
$$x^2 = 64$$
$$x = 8$$
$$\text{base} = x + 7 = 15$$

10. The correct answer is (C).

The area of a trapezoid is one-half the product of the sum of the two parallel sides ($BC + AD$) and the trapezoid's height. To determine the trapezoid's height, form a right triangle, as shown in the figure below. This right triangle conforms to the 30-60-90 Pythagorean angle triplet. Thus, the ratio of the three sides is $1 : \sqrt{3} : 2$. The hypotenuse is given as 3, so the height is $3\frac{\sqrt{3}}{2}$. The area of the trapezoid =

$$\frac{1}{2}(4 + 5) \cdot \frac{3\sqrt{3}}{2} = \frac{9}{2} \cdot \frac{3\sqrt{3}}{2} = \frac{27\sqrt{3}}{4}.$$

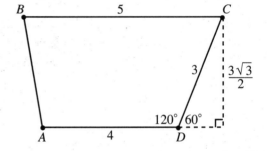

Day 22

Quantitative Ability Lesson 8: Advanced Geometry, Data Interpretation

Today's Topics:

1. Polygons
2. Circles
3. Rectangular Solids
4. Cylinders
5. Pyramids
6. Coordinate Geometry
7. Data Interpretation

Today you complete your review of geometry by examining polygons, circles, geometric solids, and coordinate geometry. You also learn some tips for handling GMAT data interpretation (charts and graphs) problems.

POLYGONS

Yesterday, you focused on three-sided polygons (triangles) and four-sided polygons (quadrilaterals). Now let's look at polygons having more than four sides. For the GMAT, remember these two rules about sides and angles of polygons:

1. If all angles of a polygon are congruent (the same size), then all sides are congruent (equal in length).

2. If all sides of a polygon are congruent (the same size), then all angles are congruent (equal in length).

You can use the following formula to determine the sum of all interior angles of *any* polygon in which all interior angles are smaller than 180° (n = number of sides):

$(n - 2)(180°) =$ sum of interior angles

You can find the average size of the angles by dividing the sum by the number of sides. Let's apply the formula to polygons with three to eight sides:

No. of sides (polygon type)	Sum of angles	Average angle size
3 (triangle)	$(3 - 2)(180°) = 180°$	$180° \div 3 = 60°$
4 (quadrilateral)	$(4 - 2)(180°) = (2)180° = 360°$	$360° \div 4 = 90°$
5 (pentagon)	$(5 - 2)(180°) = (3)180° = 540°$	$540° \div 5 = 108°$
6 (hexagon)	$(6 - 2)(180°) = (4)180° = 720°$	$720° \div 6 = 120°$
7 (heptagon)	$(7 - 2)(180°) = (5)180° = 900°$	$900° \div 7 \cong 129°$
8 (octagon)	$(8 - 2)(180°) = (6)180° = 1,080°$	$1080° \div 8 = 135°$

Memorize the angle sizes of regular polygons from 3 to 8 sides, and you'll save number-crunching time on a GMAT polygon problem.

CIRCLES

A *circle* is the set of all points that lie equidistant from the same point (the circle's *center*) on a plane. For the GMAT, you should know the following terms involving circles:

RADIUS: the distance from a circle's center to any point on the circle

DIAMETER: the greatest distance from one point to another on the circle

CHORD: a line segment connecting two points on the circle

CIRCUMFERENCE: the distance around the circle (its "perimeter")

ARC: a segment of a circle's circumference (an arc can be defined either as a length or as a degree measure)

Properties of a Circle

Every circle has six properties that you should know for the GMAT:

1. Every point on a circle's circumference is equidistant from the circle's center.

2. The total number of degrees of all angles formed from the circle's center is 360.

3. Diameter is twice the radius

4. Circumference = $2\pi r$, or πd

5. Area = πr^2, or $\dfrac{\pi d^2}{4}$

6. The longest possible chord of a circle passes through its center and is the circle's diameter.

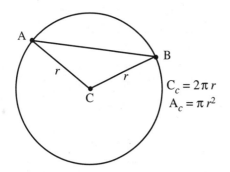

$$C_c = 2\pi r$$
$$A_c = \pi r^2$$

With the area and circumference formulas, you can determine a circle's area, circumference, diameter, and radius, as long as you know just one of these four values. Here are two examples:

If a circle's radius is 4:   Diameter = $2r = (2)(4) = 8$

Circumference = $2\pi r =$
$2\pi(4) = 8\pi$
Area = $\pi r^2 = \pi(4)^2 = 16\pi$

If a circle's area is 9:   To determine the radius:

$$9 = \pi r^2$$
$$r^2 = \frac{9}{\pi}$$

$$r = 3\sqrt{\pi}$$
Diameter = $2r = \dfrac{6}{\sqrt{p}}$

Circumference = $2\pi r =$

$$2\pi\left(\frac{3}{\sqrt{\pi}}\right) = 6\sqrt{\pi}$$

NOTE: The value of π is approximately 3.14, or $\dfrac{22}{7}$. On the GMAT, you probably won't have to work with a value for π any more precise than "a little over 3." In fact, in most circle problems, the solution is expressed in terms of π rather than numerically.

Hybrid Problems (Circles and Other Geometric Figures)

GMAT circle problems typically involve other geometric figures as well. Most common are "hybrid" problems involving circles and triangles. Any triangle with one vertex at the circle's center and the other two vertices on the circle must be isosceles, because the sides forming the vertex at the circle's center are each equal to the circle's radius. If the angle at the circle's center is 90°, the length of the triangle's hypotenuse (chord) must be $r\sqrt{2}$, because the ratio of the triangle's sides is $1:1:\sqrt{2}$ [see triangle *ABC* in figure (A) at top of next page]. If the angle at the circle's center is 60°, the length of the triangle's hypotenuse (chord) must be *r*, because the triangle is equilateral [see triangle *CDE* in figure (A) below]:

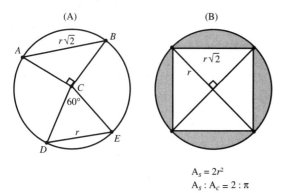

(A) (B)

$A_s = 2r^2$
$A_s : A_c = 2 : \pi$

Assuming the two circles are the same size, the length of chord *AB* in figure (A) is equal to the length of each side of the *inscribed* square in figure, (B). Accordingly, the area of a square inscribed in a circle is $(\sqrt{2}\,r)^2$ or $2r^2$. The ratio of the inscribed square's area to the circle's area is $2:\pi$. The *difference* between the two areas—that is, the total shaded area in the above figure (B)—is $\pi r^2 - 2r^2$. [Accordingly, the area of each crescent-shaped shaded area is $\frac{1}{4}(\pi r^2 - 2r^2)$.]

Distinguish the circle/inscribed-square relationship in the preceeding figure from the square/inscribed-circle relationship illustrated in the next figure. Each side of the square is $2r$. Thus, the square's area is $(2r)^2$, or $4r^2$. The ratio of the square's area to that of the inscribed circle is $\frac{4}{\pi}:1$. The *difference* between the two areas—that is, the total shaded area in the below figure—is $4r^2 - \pi r^2$, or $r^2(4 - \pi)$. (Accordingly, the area of each separate, smaller shaded area is one-fourth that difference.)

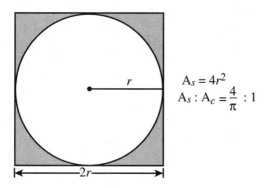

$A_s = 4r^2$
$A_s : A_c = \frac{4}{\pi} : 1$

Concentric Circles

A GMAT circle problem might involve *concentric circles*, which are two or more circles with the same center but unequal radii (creating a "bulls-eye" effect). The relationship between the areas of concentric circles depends, of course, on the relative lengths of their radii. The corresponding relationship is exponential, not linear. For example, if the larger circle's radius is *twice* that of the smaller circle's radius, as in figure (A) below, the ratio of the circles' areas is 1:4 $[(\pi r^2 : \pi(2r)^2)]$. If the larger circle's radius is *three* times the length of that of the smaller circle, as in figure (B) below, the ratio is 1:9 $[(\pi r^2 : \pi(3r)^2)]$. A 1:4 ratio between radii results in a 1:16 area ratio (and so forth).

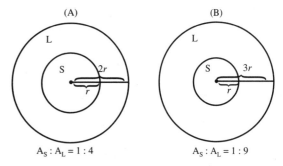

(A) (B)

$A_S : A_L = 1 : 4$ $A_S : A_L = 1 : 9$

Arcs

An *arc* is a segment of a circle's circumference. You can express an arc's size in terms of its degree measure, its length, or both. The length of an arc (as a fraction of the circle's circumference) is directly proportional to the degree measure of the arc (as a fraction of the circle's total degree measure of 360°). Accordingly, an arc of 60° would have a length of $\frac{60}{360}$, or $\frac{1}{6}$ the circle's circumference. Given $C = 2\pi r$, that arc is $\frac{1}{6}(2\pi r)$, or $\frac{\pi r}{3}$ (as illustrated by minor arc *AB* in the figure at the top of page 208).

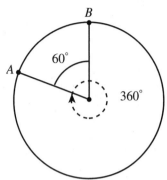

Similarly, the length of a 100° arc is $\frac{100}{360}$ or $\frac{5}{18}$ the circle's circumference ($2\pi r$), or $\frac{5\pi r}{9}$.

RECTANGULAR SOLIDS

A *rectangular solid* is formed by six rectangular surfaces, or *faces*, connecting at right angles at eight corners (see the next figure). The volume of any rectangular solid is the product of its three dimensions: width × length × height.

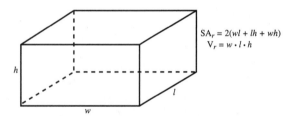

$$SA_r = 2(wl + lh + wh)$$
$$V_r = w \cdot l \cdot h$$

In any rectangular solid, the three pairs of opposing faces are each identical; they have the same dimensions and area. Accordingly, the surface area (SA) of any rectangular solid is $2(lw + lh + wh)$.

A *cube* is a rectangular solid in which all six faces (surfaces) are square. Because all six faces of a cube are identical in dimension and area, given a length s of one of a cube's edges, its surface area is six times the square of s:

$$SA_c = 6s^2$$

Given a *length s* of one of a cube's edges, the *volume* of the cube is s cubed. Conversely, given the volume V of a cube, the length of one edge s is the cube root of V:

$$V = s^3$$
$$s = \sqrt[3]{V}$$

Given the area A of any face of a cube, you can determine the cube's *volume* by cubing the square root of A. Conversely, given the volume V of a cube, you can determine the area of any face by squaring the cube root of V:

$$V_c = \left(\sqrt{A}\right)^3$$
$$A_f = \left(\sqrt[3]{V_c}\right)^2$$

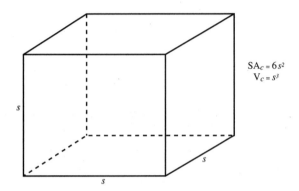

$$SA_c = 6s^2$$
$$V_c = s^3$$

CYLINDERS

This next figure is a right circular cylinder. You can determine a cylinder's *surface area* by adding together three areas: the circular base, the circular top, and the rectangular surface around the cylinder's vertical face. The area of the vertical face is the product of the circular base's circumference (that is, the rectangle's width) and the cylinder's height. Thus, given a radius r and height h of a cylinder, the following is true:

Surface Area $(SA) = 2\pi r^2 + (2\pi r)(h)$

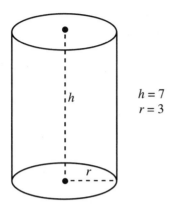

$h = 7$
$r = 3$

Accordingly, the surface area of the cylinder in the figure above is $18\pi + 42\pi$, or 60π.

Given a cylinder's radius and height, you can determine its *volume* by multiplying the area of its circular base by its height:

$V_c = \pi r^2 \times h$

Accordingly, the volume of the cylinder in the figure above is $(9\pi)(7)$, or 63π.

PYRAMIDS

GMAT problems involving pyramids usually involve the *altitude* and/or *surface area* of pyramids with square bases. The altitude of a four-sided pyramid is the pyramid's height—a line segment running from the pyramid's apex down to the center of the square base (*PQ* in the next figure). Given the altitude and the dimensions of the square base, you can determine the area of each triangular face by applying the Pythagorean Theorem. For example, if the altitude $PQ = 6$, and the area of the square base is 36, you can determine the length of *PX* as follows:

Each side of square *ABCD* is $\sqrt{36}$, or 6; thus, $QX = 3$

$6^2 + 3^2 = (PX)^2$

$36 + 9 = (PX)^2$

$PX = 3\sqrt{5}$

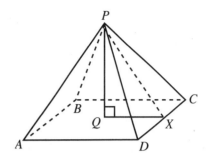

PX ($3\sqrt{5}$) is the (sloping) height of each of the pyramid's triangular faces. The base of each triangle is 6 (because the area of the square base is 36). Thus, the area of triangle *PCD* = $(\frac{1}{2})(6)(3\sqrt{5})$, or $9\sqrt{5}$. Accordingly, the total surface area of all four triangular sides is four times this amount, or $36\sqrt{5}$.

COORDINATE GEOMETRY

On the GMAT, you are likely to encounter one or two *coordinate geometry* questions, which involve the rectangular *coordinate plane* defined by two axes—a horizontal *x-axis* and a vertical *y-axis.* You can define any point on the coordinate plane by using two coordinates: an *x-coordinate* and a *y-coordinate.* A point's *x*-coordinate is its horizontal position on the plane, and its *y*-coordinate is its vertical position on the plane. You denote the coordinates of a point with (x,y), where x is the point's *x*-coordinate and y is the point's *y*-coordinate.

Coordinate Signs and the Four Quadrants

The center of the coordinate plane—the intersection of the x and y axes—is called the *origin.* The coordinates of the origin are $(0,0)$. Any point along the *x*-axis has a *y*-coordinate of 0 $(x,0)$, and any point along the *y*-axis has an *x*-coordinate of 0 $(0,y)$. The coordinate signs (positive or negative) of points lying in the four quadrants I–IV in this next figure are as follows:

- Quadrant I $(+,+)$

- Quadrant II $(-,+)$

- Quadrant III $(-,-)$

- Quadrant IV $(+,-)$

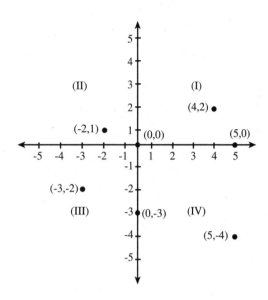

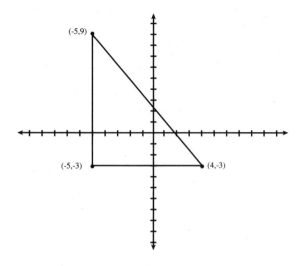

GMAT Coordinate Plane Problems

Most GMAT coordinate geometry problems involve either triangles, circles, or both. In triangle problems, your task is usually to determine the length of a sloping line segment (by forming a right triangle and applying the Pythagorean Theorem). Consider the following question:

> On the *xy*-coordinate plane, what is the length of a line segment with the end points (–5,9) and (4,–3)?

To answer this question, on the coordinate plane construct a right triangle with the line segment as the hypotenuse (see the next figure). The length of the horizontal leg is 9 (the horizontal distance from – 5 to 4), and the length of the vertical leg is 12 (the vertical distance from –3 to 9). Conforming to the 3:4:5 Pythagorean triplet, 9 and 12 are multiples of 3 and 4. Thus, without calculating the length of the line segment using the Theorem, you can quickly determine that the length is 15 (the Pythagorean triplet 3:4:5 is equivalent to 9:12:15).

In circle problems, your task is usually to determine the circumference or area of a circle lying on the plane. Consider the following question:

> On the coordinate plane, what is the area of a circle whose center is located at (2,–1), if the point (–3,3) lies on the circle's perimeter?

To answer this question, construct a right triangle with the circle's radius as the hypotenuse (see the figure below). The length of the triangle's horizontal leg is 5 (the horizontal distance from –3 to 2), and the length of its vertical leg is 4 (the vertical distance from –1 to 3). *Be careful:* These numbers do *not* conform to the Pythagorean triplet 3:4:5, because 4 and 5 are the lengths of the two *legs* here! Instead, you must calculate the length of the hypotenuse (the circle's radius) by applying the Pythagorean Theorem:

$$4^2 + 5^2 = r^2$$
$$16 + 25 = r^2$$
$$41 = r^2$$
$$r = \sqrt{41}$$

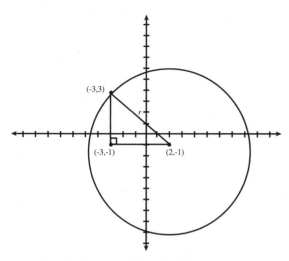

Accordingly, the area of the circle is 41π.

Defining a Line on the Plane Algebraically

You can define any line on the coordinate plane with the following algebraic equation:

$$y = mx + b$$

Any (x,y) pair defining a point on the line can substitute for the variables x and y in this equation. The constant b represents the line's *y-intercept* (the point on the y-axis where the line crosses that axis). The constant m represents the line's *slope*. The slope is best thought of as a fraction in which the numerator indicates the vertical change from one point to another on the line (moving left to right) corresponding to a given horizontal change, which the fraction's denominator indicates. The common term used for this fraction is "rise-over-run." Keep in mind the following characteristics of certain slopes (m-values):

- A line sloping *upward* from left to right has a positive slope (m).

- A line sloping *downward* from left to right has a negative slope (m).

- A *horizontal* line has a slope of zero ($m = 0$, and $mx = 0$).

- A *vertical* line has an undefined slope (the m-term in the equation is ignored).

- A line with a slope of 1 (–1) slopes upward (downward) from left to right at a 45° angle in relation to the x-axis.

- A line with a fractional slope between 0 and 1 (–1) slopes upward (downward) from left to right but at *less* than a 45° angle in relation to the x-axis.

- A line with a slope greater than 1 (less than –1) slopes upward (downward) from left to right at *more* than a 45° angle in relation to the x-axis.

Now consider the following question:

Two points, defined by the (x,y) pairs $(-\frac{3}{2},0)$ and $(0,–2)$, lie along the same line on the xy-coordinate plane. Which of the following points also lies on that line: $(3,–3)$, $(–5,5)$, $(–6,6)$?

To answer this question, first determine the slope of the line:

$$\text{slope} = \frac{-2(\textbf{rise})}{\frac{3}{2}(\textbf{run})} = -\frac{4}{3}$$

You already know that the y-intercept is 2. Thus the equation that defines the line is: $y = -\frac{4}{3}x - 2$. Among the three coordinate pairs, only $(–6,6)$ provides (x,y) values that satisfy this equation.

DATA INTERPRETATION

Data Interpretation questions require you to analyze information presented graphically in statistical graphs, charts, and tables. These questions test your ability to calculate percentages, ratios, and fractions based on the numbers you glean from the graphical data. Expect to encounter 2–4 Data Interpretation questions on your GMAT.

What Data Interpretation Questions Look Like

Data Interpretation questions usually appear in the Problem Solving format. These questions sometimes appear in sets of two, each set pertaining to the same graphical data. Expect to encounter any of the following four types of graphical presentations:

1. Bar graphs

2. Pie charts

3. Line charts

4. Tables

Let's take a look at two Data Interpretation questions. Question 1 involves a bar graph and is easier than average. Question 2 involves two related pie charts and is more difficult than average. Take 1–2 minutes to tackle each question (I'll analyze both questions just ahead):

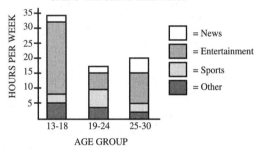

AVERAGE NUMBER OF HOURS PER WEEK
SPENT WATCHING TELEVISION

1. According to the chart above, the two age groups other than the group that spent the greatest number of hours per week watching sports on television accounted for approximately what percent of the total hours spent watching television among all three age groups?

(A) 27

(B) 36

(C) 60

(D) 74

(E) 85

INCOME AND EXPENSES–DIVISIONS A, B, C, AND D OF XYZ COMPANY (YEAR X)

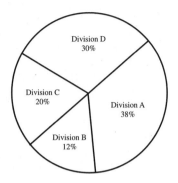

INCOME
(Total Income = $1,560,000)

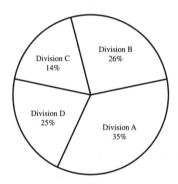

EXPENSES
(Total Expenses = $495,000)

2. Based on the charts above, with respect to the division whose income exceeded its expenses by the greatest percent among the four divisions, by approximately what amount did the division's income exceed its own expenses?

(A) $69,000

(B) $90,000

(C) $150,000

(D) $185,000

(E) $235,000

Key Features of Data Interpretation Questions

Most Data Interpretation questions are long and wordy. Data Interpretation questions are notoriously difficult to understand. Get used to it; that's the way the test makers design them. You'll probably find that you have more trouble interpreting the questions than the figures.

You might need to scroll (vertically) to see the entire display. Graphical presentations usually appear at the top of the screen (above the question) rather than to one side of the question. Some vertical scrolling may be necessary to view the entire presentation, including the information above and below the chart, graph, or table.

Bar graphs and line charts are drawn to scale. *Bar graphs* and *line charts* need to be accurate in scale; otherwise, it would be impossible to interpret them. In contrast, *pie charts* will not necessarily be drawn to scale. In *tables,* visual scale is irrelevant. (You'll see a line graph and a table during tomorrow's mini-test.) **Important assumptions will be provided.** Any additional information that you might need to know to interpret the figures will be indicated above and below the figures. (Be sure to read this information.)

Nearly all questions ask for an approximation. You'll see some form of the word *approximate* in nearly all Data Interpretation questions. This is because the test makers are trying to gauge your ability to interpret graphical data, not your ability to crunch numbers to the "nth" decimal place.

Many of the numbers used are *almost* **round.** This feature relates to the previous one. The GMAT rewards test takers who recognize that rounding off numbers (to an appropriate extent) will suffice to get to the right answer, so they pack Data Interpretation figures with numbers that are close to "easy" ones. (The numbers in the pie charts on page 212 serve as good examples. $1,560,000 is close to $1,500,000 million and $495,000 is close to $500,000.)

Figures are not drawn to deceive you or to test your eyesight. In bar graphs and line charts, you won't be asked to split hairs to determine values. These figures are designed with a comfortable margin for error in visual acuity. Just don't round up or down too far.

Analysis of Sample Questions

Question 1:

The correct answer is (D). The group that spent the most time per week watching sports on television was the group of 19–24 year olds (who spent an average of approximately 6 hours per week watching sports programming). The average hours for all three groups totals approximately 74 (33 + 19 + 22). Of that total, the two groups other than the 19–24 age group accounted for 55 hours, or about 74% ($\frac{55}{74}$) of the total hours for all three age groups.

Question 2:

The correct answer is (E). First size up the two charts, and read the information above and below them. Notice that we're only dealing with one company during one year here. Notice also that dollar totals are provided but that the pie segments are all expressed only as percentages. That's a clue that your main task in this question will be to calculate dollar amounts for various pie segments.

Now consider the question. First, you need to compare profitability—in dollar amount—among the four divisions. You can rule out Division B, since its expenses exceeded its income. That leaves Divisions A, C, and D. Be careful: Question 2 does not ask you to compare the percentages appearing in the two charts, but rather to calculate dollar amounts. For Divisions A, C, and D, compare two dollar figures in terms of percent:

Division A: 38% of total income and 35% of total expenses

Division C: 20% of total income and 14% of total expenses

Division D: 30% of total income and 25% of total expenses

Division C's income was a bit more than $300,000 (20% of $1,500,000). Division C's expenses were approximately $75,000 (15% of $500,000). Perform similar calculations for Divisions A and D, and you'll discover that Division C was the most profitable one in percentage terms. Division C's income exceeds its expense by a bit more than $225,000. Choice (E), $235,000, is the only one close to our approximation. (It's a bit greater than our approximation, but this fact makes sense because we rounded C's income *down*.)

Tips for Tackling Data Interpretation Questions

Look at the "big picture" first. Before plunging into the question, read all the information above and below the figure. Look particularly for

- Totals (dollar figures or other numbers)
- Whether you'll need to add zeros to the numbers (to express thousands or millions)
- How two or more figures are labeled
- Whether graphical data are expressed in numbers or percentages

Pay particular attention to what the question asks for. Most data interpretation questions involve raw data as well as *proportion*—in terms of either percent, fraction, or ratio (usually percent). Always ask yourself whether the solution is

- A raw number or a proportional number
- A comparison between two raw numbers (or proportional numbers)
- An increase or a decrease

You can be sure that the test makers will "bait" you with appropriate incorrect answer choices!

Be sure you're getting the right data from the right part of a chart. This point of advice may seem obvious; nevertheless, reading the wrong data is probably the leading cause of incorrect responses to Data Interpretation questions! To ensure that you don't commit this careless error, point your finger to the proper line, column, or bar on the screen; *put your finger right on it*, and don't move it until you're sure you've got the right data.

Save time and avoid computation errors by rounding off. By now, you're well aware that most Data Interpretation questions call for approximation. Avoid committing careless computational errors and doing more work than needed.

Be careful not to distort numbers by rounding off inappropriately. When you round those numbers, up or down to the nearest appropriate unit or half-unit probably suffices to get to the correct answer. But don't get too rough in your approximations. Also, be sure to round off numerators and denominators of fractions in the same direction (either both up or both down), unless you're confident that a rougher approximation will suffice.

Handle lengthy, confusing questions one part at a time. Data Interpretation questions are often wordy and confusing. Don't panic. Keep in mind that lengthy questions almost always call for two discreet tasks. For the first task, read just the first part of the question. When you're done, go back to the question and read the next part.

Don't split hairs in reading line charts and bar graphs. These are the two types of figures that are drawn to scale. If a certain point on a chart appears to be about 40 percent of the way from one hash mark to the next, don't hesitate to round up to the halfway point. (The number 5 is usually easier to work with than 4 or 6.)

Formulate a clear idea as to the overall size of number the question is calling for. The test makers pack Data Interpretation questions with "sucker bait" answer choices for test takers who make common computational errors. The best way to keep yourself from falling into their trap is to ask yourself what sort of ballpark number you're looking for in a correct answer. You might ask yourself:

- Is it a double-digit number?
- Is it a percentage that is obviously greater than 50 percent?
- Is it a large raw number in the thousands?

By keeping the big picture in mind, you're more likely to catch an error in your calculations before its too late.

IF YOU HAVE MORE TIME TODAY

To apply what you learned today and yesterday to GMAT-style questions, log on to the author's GMAT Web site (www.west.net/~stewart/gmat) and attempt a Geometry mini-test and a Data Interpretation mini-test. (To find these two mini-tests click on "Quantitative Ability" in the "Test Yourself" area.)

Day 23

Quantitative Ability Lesson 9:
Mini-Test and Review
(Advanced Geometry, Data Interpretation)

Today's Topics:

Today you will apply what you learned on Days 21 and 22 to a 20-question mini-test, which includes both Problem Solving and Data Sufficiency questions.

MINI-TEST
(GEOMETRY, DATA INTERPRETATION)

Number of questions: 20
Suggested time: 40 minutes

Directions: Solve the following 20 Quantitative questions under simulated exam conditions. The official Quantitative directions can be found on pages 43 and 47 of "Day 6." After completing the mini-test, review the explanations that follow. Preceding the explanation for each question, the question type and difficulty level are indicated.

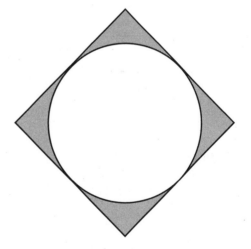

1. If the area of the circle above is 64π, what is the perimeter of the square?

    (A) 16
    (B) 32
    (C) 64
    (D) 32π
    (E) 64π

HARVESTED CROP REVENUES (YEAR X)
(Percent of total revenue among four counties)

	non - subsidized farms	subsidized farms
Willot County	7%	
Tilson County		12%
Stanton County		
Osher County	8%	
(Total Percentages)	30%	

2. Based on the table above, if the total harvested crop revenues for Willot and Tilson counties combined equaled those for Stanton and Osher counties combined, then Stanton County's subsidized farm revenues accounted for what percentage of the total harvested crop revenues for all four counties?

(1) During year X, Osher County's total harvested crop revenues totaled twice those of Tilson county.

(2) During year X, Tilson County's farms contributed 18% of all harvested crop revenues for the four counties.

(A) Statement 1 ALONE is sufficient, but statement 2 alone is not sufficient to answer the question asked.

(B) Statement 2 ALONE is sufficient, but statement 1 alone is not sufficient to answer the question asked.

(C) BOTH statements 1 and 2 TOGETHER are sufficient to answer the question asked; but NEITHER statement ALONE is sufficient.

(D) EACH statement ALONE is sufficient to answer the question asked.

(E) Statements 1 and 2 TOGETHER are NOT sufficient to answer the question asked, and additional data specific to the problem are needed.

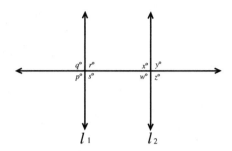

3. In the figure above, is l_1 parallel to l_2?

(1) $q + y = s + w$

(2) $p + x = 180$

(A) Statement 1 ALONE is sufficient, but statement 2 alone is not sufficient to answer the question asked.

(B) Statement 2 ALONE is sufficient, but statement 1 alone is not sufficient to answer the question asked.

(C) BOTH statements 1 and 2 TOGETHER are sufficient to answer the question asked; but NEITHER statement ALONE is sufficient.

(D) EACH statement ALONE is sufficient to answer the question asked.

(E) Statements 1 and 2 TOGETHER are NOT sufficient to answer the question asked, and additional data specific to the problem are needed.

4. On the xy-coordinate plane, what is the area of a right triangle, one side of which is defined by the points (2,3) and (–4,0)?

(1) The triangle's sides cross the y-axis at exactly two points altogether.

(2) The y-coordinate of the third vertex of the triangle is zero.

(A) Statement 1 ALONE is sufficient, but statement 2 alone is not sufficient to answer the question asked.

(B) Statement 2 ALONE is sufficient, but statement 1 alone is not sufficient to answer the question asked.

(C) BOTH statements 1 and 2 TOGETHER are sufficient to answer the question asked; but NEITHER statement ALONE is sufficient.

(D) EACH statement ALONE is sufficient to answer the question asked.

(E) Statements 1 and 2 TOGETHER are NOT sufficient to answer the question asked, and additional data specific to the problem are needed.

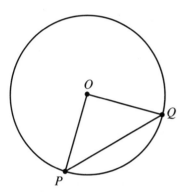

5. In the figure above, if point O lies at the center of the circle, what is the area of triangle OPQ ?

(1) The radius of the circle is 3.

(2) $PO = PQ$

(A) Statement 1 ALONE is sufficient, but statement 2 alone is not sufficient to answer the question asked.

(B) Statement 2 ALONE is sufficient, but statement 1 alone is not sufficient to answer the question asked.

(C) BOTH statements 1 and 2 TOGETHER are sufficient to answer the question asked; but NEITHER statement ALONE is sufficient.

(D) EACH statement ALONE is sufficient to answer the question asked.

(E) Statements 1 and 2 TOGETHER are NOT sufficient to answer the question asked, and additional data specific to the problem are needed.

6. A certain cylindrical pail has a diameter of 14 inches and a height of 10 inches. Approximately how many gallons will the pail hold, if there are 231 cubic inches to a gallon?

(A) 4.8

(B) 5.1

(C) 6.7

(D) $14\frac{2}{3}$

(E) 44

7. In triangle ABC, $AB = BC$. If the size of $\angle B$ is $x°$, which of the following represents the degree measure of $\angle A$?

(A) x

(B) $180 - x$

(C) $180 - \dfrac{x}{2}$

(D) $90 - \dfrac{x}{2}$

(E) $90 - x$

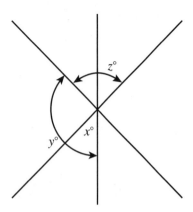

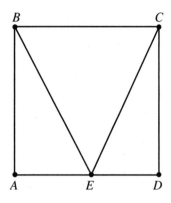

8. In the figure above, what is the value of *x*?

(1) *y* = 130

(2) *z* = 100

(A) Statement 1 ALONE is sufficient, but statement 2 alone is not sufficient to answer the question asked.

(B) Statement 2 ALONE is sufficient, but statement 1 alone is not sufficient to answer the question asked.

(C) BOTH statements 1 and 2 TOGETHER are sufficient to answer the question asked; but NEITHER statement ALONE is sufficient.

(D) EACH statement ALONE is sufficient to answer the question asked.

(E) Statements 1 and 2 TOGETHER are NOT sufficient to answer the question asked, and additional data specific to the problem are needed.

9. If a circle whose radius is *x* has an area of 4, what is the area of a circle whose radius is 3*x*?

(A) $\sqrt{13}$

(B) $4\sqrt{13}$

(C) 12

(D) 36

(E) 144

10. In rectangle *ABCD* above, if *AE* = *ED*, is rectangle *ABCD* a square?

(1) The length of *AE* multiplied by $\sqrt{5}$ is equal to the length of *BE*.

(2) The area of triangle *BCE* is exactly half that of rectangle *ABCD*.

(A) Statement 1 ALONE is sufficient, but statement 2 alone is not sufficient to answer the question asked.

(B) Statement 2 ALONE is sufficient, but statement 1 alone is not sufficient to answer the question asked.

(C) BOTH statements 1 and 2 TOGETHER are sufficient to answer the question asked; but NEITHER statement ALONE is sufficient.

(D) EACH statement ALONE is sufficient to answer the question asked.

(E) Statements 1 and 2 TOGETHER are NOT sufficient to answer the question asked, and additional data specific to the problem are needed.

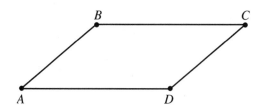

11. In parallelogram *ABCD* above, ∠*B* is five times the size of ∠*C*. What is the degree measure of ∠*B* ?

(A) 30

(B) 60

(C) 100

(D) 120

(E) 150

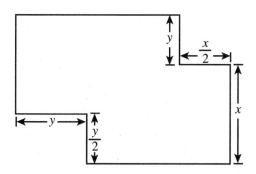

12. A carpet in the shape of a rectangle must be trimmed into the shape shown above. What is the possible area of the carpet before it is trimmed?

(1) $y = 4$

(2) $x = 5$

(A) Statement 1 ALONE is sufficient, but statement 2 alone is not sufficient to answer the question asked.

(B) Statement 2 ALONE is sufficient, but statement 1 alone is not sufficient to answer the question asked.

(C) BOTH statements 1 and 2 TOGETHER are sufficient to answer the question asked; but NEITHER statement ALONE is sufficient.

(D) EACH statement ALONE is sufficient to answer the question asked.

(E) Statements 1 and 2 TOGETHER are NOT sufficient to answer the question asked, and additional data specific to the problem are needed.

13. If the volume of one cube is eight times greater than that of another, what is the ratio of the surface area of the larger cube to that of the smaller cube?

(A) $\sqrt{2}:1$

(B) $2\sqrt{2}:1$

(C) 2:1

(D) 4:1

(E) 8:1

PRICE OF COMMON STOCK OF
XYZ CORP. AND ABC CORP.
(YEAR X)

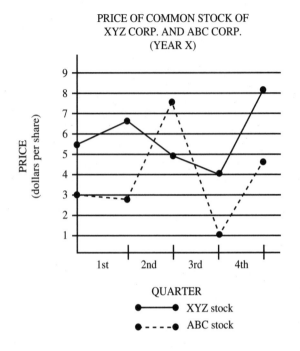

QUARTER

●———● XYZ stock
●- - - -● ABC stock

14. Based on the chart above, at the time during year X when the difference between the price of ABC common stock and the price of XYZ common stock was at its greatest, the price of ABC common stock was approximately what percent of the price of XYZ common stock and ABC common stock combined?

(A) 16%

(B) 31%

(C) 36%

(D) 42%

(E) 103%

15. Eight square window panes of equal size are to be pieced together to form a rectangular French door. What is the perimeter of the door, excluding framing between and around the panes?

(1) Each pane is one square foot in area.

(2) The area of the door, excluding framing between and around the panes, is eight square feet.

(A) Statement 1 ALONE is sufficient, but statement 2 alone is not sufficient to answer the question asked.

(B) Statement 2 ALONE is sufficient, but statement 1 alone is not sufficient to answer the question asked.

(C) BOTH statements 1 and 2 TOGETHER are sufficient to answer the question asked; but NEITHER statement ALONE is sufficient.

(D) EACH statement ALONE is sufficient to answer the question asked.

(E) Statements 1 and 2 TOGETHER are NOT sufficient to answer the question asked, and additional data specific to the problem are needed.

16. The length of an arc of a certain circle is one-fifth the circumference of the circle. If the length of the arc is 2π, what is the radius of the circle?

(A) 1

(B) 2

(C) $\sqrt{10}$

(D) 5

(E) 10

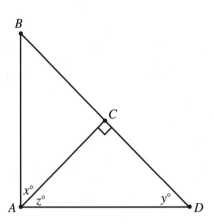

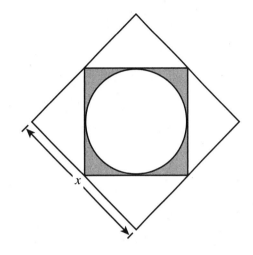

17. In the figure above, if $x + z = 90$, does $x = y$?

   (1) Two sides of triangle ACD are equal in length.

   (2) Two sides of triangle ABC are equal in length.

   (A) Statement 1 ALONE is sufficient, but statement 2 alone is not sufficient to answer the question asked.

   (B) Statement 2 ALONE is sufficient, but statement 1 alone is not sufficient to answer the question asked.

   (C) BOTH statements 1 and 2 TOGETHER are sufficient to answer the question asked; but NEITHER statement ALONE is sufficient.

   (D) EACH statement ALONE is sufficient to answer the question asked.

   (E) Statements 1 and 2 TOGETHER are NOT sufficient to answer the question asked, and additional data specific to the problem are needed.

18. What is the area of the shaded region in the figure above, which contains one circle and two squares?

   (A) $\dfrac{\pi x}{2} - 4$

   (B) $x^2 - 2\pi$

   (C) $\dfrac{x(2 - \pi x)}{4}$

   (D) $\dfrac{7x^2}{4}$

   (E) $\dfrac{x^2(4 - \pi)}{8}$

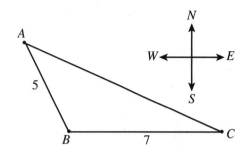

20. On the xy-coordinate plane, two points P and Q, defined by the (x,y) coordinates $(-1,0)$ and $(3,3)$, respectively, are connected to form a chord of a circle that also lies on the plane. If the area of the circle is $\frac{25}{4}\pi$, what are the coordinates of the circle's center?

(A) $\left(\frac{1}{2},\frac{1}{2}\right)$

(B) $\left(1,1\frac{1}{2}\right)$

(C) $(0,1)$

(D) $\left(\frac{1}{2},1\right)$

(E) $\left(-1\frac{1}{2},\frac{1}{2}\right)$

19. Once a month, a crop duster sprays a triangular area defined by three farm houses—A, B, and C—as indicated in the figure above. Farmhouse B lies due west of farmhouse C. Given the compass directions and distances (in miles) indicated in the figure, what is the total area that the crop duster sprays?

(1) Farmhouse C is located 4 miles further south than farmhouse A.

(2) Farmhouse C is located 10 miles further east than farmhouse A.

(A) Statement 1 ALONE is sufficient, but statement 2 alone is not sufficient to answer the question asked.

(B) Statement 2 ALONE is sufficient, but statement 1 alone is not sufficient to answer the question asked.

(C) BOTH statements 1 and 2 TOGETHER are sufficient to answer the question asked; but NEITHER statement ALONE is sufficient.

(D) EACH statement ALONE is sufficient to answer the question asked.

(E) Statements 1 and 2 TOGETHER are NOT sufficient to answer the question asked, and additional data specific to the problem are needed.

Quick Answer Guide

Mini-Test: Geometry

1. C	6. C	11. E	16. D
2. C	7. D	12. E	17. D
3. B	8. C	13. D	18. E
4. B	9. D	14. B	19. D
5. C	10. A	15. E	20. B

EXPLANATIONS

1. The correct answer is (C). Area of circle/ perimeter of square (easier).

The area of the circle = $64\pi = r^2\pi$. Thus, the radius of the circle = 8. The side of the square is twice the circle's radius, or 16. Therefore, the perimeter of the square is $4 \times 16 = 64$.

2. The correct answer is (C). Data interpretation (challenging).

Statement 1 establishes the total contributions of Willot and Tilson counties relative to those of Stanton and Osher counties, but the statement provides no additional information about Stanton County's specific percentage contribution. Statement 1 alone is therefore insufficient to answer the question. Based on statement 2 alone, Tilson County's nonsubsidized farms must have accounted for 6% of all revenues (18%–12%). Accordingly, Stanton County's nonsubsidized farms must have accounted for 9% of all revenues (the percentages in the leftmost column must total 30). However, this information is insufficient to determine Stanton County's subsidized farm contribution. With both statements

1 and 2 together, Osher County's revenues must total 36% (because statement 2 stipulates that Osher County contributed twice the revenues of Tilson County, which you now know contributed 18% of all revenues). At this point, you have partially completed the table:

	non - subsidized farms	subsidized farms		
Willot County	7%			⎫
Tilson County	(6%)	12%	(18%)	⎬ 50%
Stanton County	(9%)			⎫
Osher County	8%	(28%)	(36%)	⎬ 50%
(Total Percentages)	30%	(70%)		

It is now evident that Stanton County's subsidized farms contributed 6% of the total revenues (Stanton and Osher county revenues must account for 50% of the total). Thus, statements 1 and 2 together suffice to answer the question.

3. The correct answer is (B). Parallel lines (easier).

Opposite angles are always congruent. Thus, $q = s$ and $y = w$. Accordingly, $q + y$ must equal $s + w$ in any event, and statement 1 alone does not suffice to answer the question. Given statement 2 alone, p and x are supplementary, and p must equal y as well as w (because $y + x = 180$ and $w + x = 180$). Thus, all corresponding angles are the same, and the two lines are parallel.

4. The correct answer is (B). Coordinate geometry (challenging).

Statement 1 alone allows for more than one possible area:

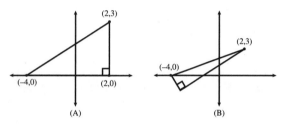

(A)   (B)

Statement 2 alone, however, allows for only one possible area (and shape and position) of the triangle: figure (A) above. Thus, statement 2 alone suffices to answer the question.

5. The correct answer is (C). Equilateral triangles (moderate).

Statement 1 provides no information about the area of triangle OPQ relative to the area of the circle. Thus, that statement alone is insufficient to answer the question. The information in statement 2 establishes that triangle OPQ is an equilateral triangle (all three sides are equal in length, and all three angles are 60°). However, no specific values are provided to determine the area. Thus, statement 2 alone is insufficient to answer the question. Adding that the radius of the circle is 3, however, enables you to compute the area of the equilateral triangle. The base is 3 and the height is $1.5\sqrt{3}$ (an equilateral triangle consists of two $1:\sqrt{3}:2$ right triangles). Thus, statements 1 and 2 together suffice to answer the question. (The area of triangle OPQ is $2.25\sqrt{3}$.)

6. The correct answer is (C). Cylinders (easier).

The volume of the cylindrical pail is equal to the area of its circular base multiplied by its height:

$$V = \pi r^2 h = \left(\frac{22}{7}\right)(49)(10) = 1{,}540 \text{ cubic inches}$$

The gallon capacity of the pail = $\frac{1{,}540}{231}$, or about 6.7.

7. The correct answer is (D). Isosceles triangles (moderate).

The triangle is isosceles, so $\angle A = \angle C$. Letting a, c, and x represent the degree measures of $\angle A$, $\angle C$, and $\angle B$, respectively, solve for a:

$$a + c + x = 180$$
$$2a + x = 180 \; [a = c]$$
$$2a + x = 180$$
$$2a = 180 - x$$
$$a = \frac{180}{2} - \frac{x}{2}$$
$$a = 90 - \frac{x}{2}$$

8. The correct answer is (C). Lines and angles (moderate).

It is obvious that neither statement 1 nor 2 alone provides sufficient information to determine the angle measure of x. Thus, you can easily eliminate A, B, and D. Next, consider statements 1 and 2 together. Notice that $\angle y$ and $\angle z$ together form a degree measure that exceeds 180° (a straight line) by $x°$. Thus, $y + z - x = 180$. Statements 1 and 2 provide the values of y and z and thus suffice to answer the question ($x = 50$).

9. The correct answer is (D). Area of a circle (easier).

The area of a circle is πr^2. The area of a circle with a radius of x is πx^2, which is given as 4. The area of a circle with radius $3x$ is $\pi(3x)^2 = 9\pi x^2 = (9)(4) = 36$.

10. The correct answer is (A). Rectangles/ right triangles (challenging).

Given $(AE)(\sqrt{5}) = BE$ (statement 1), AB must be exactly twice the length of AE. Why? Because triangle ABE is a right triangle, the Pythagorean Theorem establishes that $(AE)^2 + (AB)^2 = (BE)^2$, or $1^2 + 2^2 = \sqrt{5}$. Given that $AE = ED$, $AB = AD$, and the rectangle is indeed a square. Statement 1 alone suffices to answer the question. Considering statement 2, a bit of visualization reveals that the area of triangle BCE is always exactly half that of rectangle $ABCD$, regardless of the rectangle's dimensions. Thus, statement 2 alone is insufficient to answer the question.

11. The correct answer is (E). Parallelograms (easier).

The sum of the angles in a parallelogram is $360°$. Angles B and C account for half, or $180°$. Letting x equal the degree measure of angle C, angle $B = 5x$.

$$5x + x = 180$$
$$6x = 180$$
$$x = 30$$
$$\angle B = 5x = (5)(30) = 150$$

12. The correct answer is (E). Rectangles: area (easier).

You can determine the height of the rectangular carpet with the information provided by statements 1 and 2 together (height = $x + y = 9$). However, even considering both statements 1 and 2, you cannot determine the width of the rectangle carpet, and accordingly, you cannot determine its area (minimum or otherwise).

13. The correct answer is (D). Rectangular solids: cubes (challenging).

The ratio of the two volumes is 8:1; thus, the linear ratio of the cubes' edges is the cube root of this ratio: $\sqrt[3]{8} : \sqrt[3]{1}$, or 2:1. The area ratio is the square of the linear ratio, or 4:1.

14. The correct answer is (B). Data interpretation (easier).

The price difference was at its maximum at the end of the 1st quarter, when the price of ABC stock was about $28 and the price of XYZ stock was about $66. The total price of both was about $94. $28 is $\left(\frac{28}{94}\right)$ or about 31% of $94.

15. The correct answer is (E). Rectangles: area and perimeter (moderate).

You could piece together the panes into either a single column (or row) of eight panes or into two adjacent columns (or rows) of four panes each. Assuming that each pane measures one foot per side, in the first case, the door's perimeter would be 18. In the second case, the door's perimeter would be 12. Thus, statement 1 alone is insufficient to answer the question. Statement 2 alone is insufficient for the same reason. Both statements together still fail to provide sufficient information to determine the shape (or perimeter) of the door.

16. The correct answer is (D). Circles: arcs (moderate).

The circumference is five times the length of the arc:
$$5(2\pi) = 10\pi = \pi d$$
$$d = 10, \text{ and } r = 5$$

17. The correct answer is (D). Isosceles triangles (easier).

Considering statement 1 alone, given that triangle ACD is a right isosceles triangle, the two angles other than the $90°$ angle must each measure $45°$. Because $\angle BAD$ measures $90°$, $x = 45$, and $x = y$. You can apply the same analysis to statement 2, and either statement suffices to answer the question.

18. The correct answer is (E). Circles/ squares/right triangles (challenging).

To determine the area of the shaded region, subtract the area of the circle from the area of the smaller of the two squares. First, determine the area of the smaller square. Each of the four outside triangles is a $1:1:\sqrt{2}$ right triangle, with a side of the smaller square as the hypotenuse. Each leg of these triangles is $\frac{x}{2}$ in length; thus, each side of the smaller square is $\frac{x\sqrt{2}}{2}$ in length. Accordingly, the area of the smaller square is $\left(\frac{x\sqrt{2}}{2}\right)^2$, or $\frac{x^2}{2}$. Next, determine the area of the circle. Its diameter is $\frac{x\sqrt{2}}{2}$ (the length of each side of the smaller square). Thus, its radius is half that amount, or $\frac{x\sqrt{2}}{4}$. The circle's area $= \pi\left(\frac{x\sqrt{2}}{4}\right)^2 = \pi\left(\frac{2x^2}{16}\right) = \frac{\pi x^2}{8}$. Subtract this area from the square's area: $\frac{x^2}{2} - \frac{\pi x^2}{8} = \frac{4x^2 - \pi x^2}{8} = \frac{x^2(4-\pi)}{8}$.

19. The correct answer is (D). Right triangles (easier).

The area of any triangle equals $\frac{1}{2}$(base)(height). Using seven miles as the base of the triangle in this problem, the triangle's height is the north-south (vertical) distance from A to an imaginary line extending westerly from B. Statement 1 explicitly provides the triangle's height. Statement 2 also provides sufficient information to determine this height. As indicated in this next figure, the triangle's height is four miles ($3^2 + 4^2 = 5^2$, per the Pythagorean Theorem). Accordingly, either statement alone suffices to determine the triangle's area.

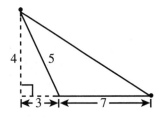

(The area $= \frac{1}{2}(7)(4) = 14$.)

20. The correct answer is (B). Coordinate geometry (challenging).

Given that the area of the circle is $\frac{25\pi}{4}$, you can determine the circle's radius and diameter:

$$A = \pi r^2$$

$$\frac{25\pi}{4} = \pi r^2$$

$$\frac{25}{4} = r^2$$

$$r = \frac{5}{2}$$

$$d = 5$$

On the coordinate plane, the distance between the points whose coordinates are $(-1,0)$ and $(3,3)$ is 5 (the chord forms the hypotenuse of a 3:4:5 right triangle, as illustrated in the figure below). Because these two points are five units apart, chord PQ must be the circle's diameter. The circle's center lies on chord PQ midway between P and Q. The x-coordinate of the center is midway between the x-coordinates of P and Q (-1 and 3), whereas the y-coordinate is midway between the y-coordinates of P and Q (0 and 3). Thus, the center of the circle is the point $(1, 1\frac{1}{2})$.

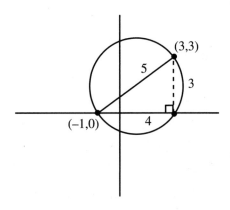

Day 24

Analytical Writing Assessment (AWA) Practice Test

Today's Topics:

Today you'll take an Analytical Writing Assessment practice test, applying what you learned on Days 3, 4, and 5. Allow yourself exactly 30 minutes to complete each of the two essays — 60 minutes altogether.

SECTION 1:
ANALYSIS OF AN ISSUE

Number of questions: 1
Time limit: 30 Minutes

> **Directions:** Using a word processor, compose a response to the following topic and question. Do not use any spell-checking or grammar-checking functions.

"Technological advances that improve our efficiency have ironically resulted in less leisure time, and a pace of life that seems more hurried and frantic than ever."

In your view, how accurate is the statement above? Use relevant reasons and/or examples to support you viewpoint.

SECTION 2:
ANALYSIS OF AN ARGUMENT

Number of questions: 1
Time Limit: 30 Minutes

> **Directions:** Using a word processor, compose an essay for the following argument and directive. Do not use any spell-checking or grammar-checking functions.

The following appeared as part of an article in a popular magazine among college students:

> More than ninety percent of Urbanville University's undergraduate students are employed full-time within six months after they graduate. However, less than half of the University's graduate students find employment in their area of specialization within six months after receiving their graduate-level degrees. The lesson for college students everywhere is clear:

You'll be better off in your career without pursuing an advanced degree after college graduation.

Discuss how well reasoned you find this argument. In your discussion, be sure to analyze the line of reasoning and the use of evidence in the argument. For example, you may need to consider what questionable assumptions underlie the thinking and what alternative explanations or counterexamples might weaken the conclusion. You can also discuss what sort of evidence would strengthen or refute the argument, what changes in the argument would make it more logically sound, and what, if anything, would help you better evaluate its conclusion.

Day 25

Practice Test, Review of Sections 1 and 2: Analytical Writing Assessment

Today's Topics:

Today you'll evaluate the Analytical Writing Assessment practice test (Sections 1 and 2) you took on Day 24. You'll also read a sample response to each question—to further evaluate your analytical writing ability.

SECTION 1 (ANALYSIS OF AN ISSUE)

Evaluate your Issue-Analysis essay on a scale of 1 to 6 (6 being the highest score) according to the following five criteria:

1. Does your essay develop a position on the issue through the use of incisive reasons and persuasive examples?

2. Are your essay's ideas conveyed clearly and articulately?

3. Does your essay maintain proper focus on the issue, and is it well organized?

4. Does your essay demonstrate proficiency, fluency, and maturity in its use of sentence structure, vocabulary, and idiom?

5. Does your essay demonstrate command of the elements of Standard Written English, including grammar, word usage, spelling, and punctuation?

Following is my response to this Issue-Analysis question. As you read it, keep in mind:

- The response meets all the criteria for a top score of 6.

- The response is brief enough (460 words) to compose and type in 30 minutes. Nevertheless, a top-scoring Issue-Analysis essay need be as lengthy as mine.

- There is no "correct" answer, so don't worry if your position on the issue differed from mine. What's important is how effectively you present and support your position.

- I didn't compose this response under time pressure, so don't worry if your essay isn't as finely tuned as mine. You can attain a top score of 6 with a less polished essay.

Sample response

I agree with the speaker that leisure time is declining as a result of efficiencies which technology has brought about. However, whether the irony to which the speaker refers is real or imagined depends on what one considers to be the chief aim of technology.

Few would disagree that technology has enhanced the speed and efficiency with which we travel, prepare our food, plan and coordinate projects, and communicate with one another. And the empirical evidence that as a society we are more pressed for time than ever before is convincing indeed. In 1960, the average U.S. family included only one breadwinner, who worked just over 40 hours per week. Since then, the average workweek has increased steadily to nearly 60 hours today. In fact, in most families there are now two breadwinners who, for lack of leisure time, must delegate food preparation to fast-food workers and childcare to professional day-care facilities. Even single, childless professionals today are so harried that they have no time to seek out romance and must rely instead on matchmaker services.

What explains the irony—this decline in leisure despite increasing efficiency that new technologies have brought about? I agree that technology itself is the culprit. We use the additional free time that technology affords us not for leisure but rather for work. As computer technology enables greater and greater office productivity, it also raises our employers' expectations—or demands—for production. Further technological advances breed still greater efficiency and, in turn, expectations. Our spiraling workload is only exacerbated by the competitive business environment in which nearly all of us work today. Moreover, every technological advance demands our time and attention—in order to learn how to use the new technology. Time devoted to keeping pace with technology depletes time for leisure activities.

Yet, upon further reflection, this apparent irony does not seem so ironic after all. The final objectives of technology have little to do with affording us more leisure time. Rather, there are far more vital concerns that technology seeks to address. Advances in biotechnology can help cure and prevent diseases; advances in medical technology can allow for safer, less invasive diagnosis and treatment; advances in genetics can help prevent birth defects; advances in engineering and chemistry can improve the structural integrity of our buildings, roads, bridges, and vehicles; information technology enables education; and communications technology facilitates global participation in the democratic process.

In sum, the claim that the same technology that breeds efficiency also robs us of our leisure is simply wrongheaded. At the end of our hectic day, we have not been robbed at all. Instead, we've ultimately chosen our frantic pace—trading off leisure in pursuit of our health, our safety, our education, and our freedom.

SECTION 2
(ANALYSIS OF AN ARGUMENT)

Evaluate your Argument-Analysis essay on a scale of 1 to 6 (6 being the highest score) according to the following five criteria:

1. Does your essay identify the key features of the argument and analyzes each one in a thoughtful manner?

2. Does your essay support each point of its critique with insightful reasons and examples?

3. Does your essay develop its ideas in a clear, organized manner, with appropriate transitions to help connect ideas together?

4. Does your essay demonstrate proficiency, fluency, and maturity in its use of sentence structure, vocabulary, and idiom?

5. Does your essay demonstrate command of the elements of Standard Written English, including grammar, word usage, spelling, and punctuation?

To help you evaluate your essay in terms of criteria 1 and 2, here's a list of more specific guidelines for meeting these criteria:

- Does your essay analyze the argument's line of reasoning?

- Does your essay consider questionable assumptions underlying the argument?

- Does your essay consider the extent to which the evidence presented supports the argument's conclusion?

- Does your essay discuss what additional evidence would help strengthen or refute the argument?

- Does your essay discuss what additional information, if any, would help you to evaluate the argument's conclusion?

Following is my response to this Argument-Analysis question. As you read it, keep in mind:

- The response meets all the criteria for a top score of 6.

- The response is brief enough (460 words) to compose and type in 30 minutes. Nevertheless, a top-scoring Argument-Analysis essay need be as lengthy as mine.

- I didn't compose this response under time pressure, so don't worry if your essay isn't as finely tuned as mine. You can attain a top score of 6 with a less polished essay.

Sample response

The article's author claims that people with only four-year degrees are better off in their careers than people with advanced degrees. The argument rests on four key assumptions—about Urbanville University (UU), its student body, and the types of jobs these students find. The argument is unconvincing as it stands because all four assumptions are dubious at best.

First of all, the argument relies on statistics about graduates from only one university. It is unreasonable to draw any conclusions about graduates of all colleges and universities from this one single example. Moreover, this single sample may be biased. It is entirely possible, for instance, that the UU undergraduate student body is particularly outstanding academically—perhaps because admission standards are very high—while admission standards for UU's graduate programs is especially low compared to those of other graduate programs.

Secondly, the argument relies on the poor assumption that the jobs people find within six months of obtaining an undergraduate degree will serve to advance their careers. In fact this might not generally be the case; jobs that new college graduates find easily and quickly are often ones that offer little or no potential for career advancement. Without ruling out this possibility, the article's author cannot confidently conclude that a person with only a four-year degree is better off in his or her career than a person with an advanced degree.

Thirdly, the excerpt fails to support the tenuous assumption that if a person with a graduate degree does not find employment in his or her specialty soon after obtaining the degree then that person will be at a career disadvantage. This might not be the case. It is entirely possible, for instance, that many of these people find positions outside their specialty that nevertheless are lucrative and offer career advancement potential. Without eliminating this possibility, the argument that people with graduate degrees are worse off in their careers than those with only four-year degrees is unconvincing at best.

Finally, the argument unfairly assumes that what is true in the short term will continue to be true in the long term. However, when it comes to a lifelong career, this notion runs contrary to experience and to common sense. In other words, a brief six-month period is hardly sufficient to draw any firm conclusions about the next thirty years.

In sum, the argument rests on a series of unfounded assumptions. To strengthen the argument the article's author should provide evidence that UU graduates are representative of all graduates and that the first six months after graduation provides a reliable indication of one's career prospects. Moreover, to better evaluate the argument, we would need more information about the types of jobs that UU graduates find within six months after obtaining a degree.

Day 26

Practice Test, Section 3: Quantitative Ability

Today's Topics:

Today you take a full-length practice test on Quantitative Ability. After completing the test, check your answers with the quick answer guide at the end of this lesson.

PRACTICE TEST

Number of questions: 37
Time allowed: 75 minutes

> **Directions:** If you are not already familiar with the directions and assumptions for Problem Solving and Data Sufficiency questions, review the relevant materials (Day 6). Tomorrow you assess your performance and review the explanations for this practice test.

1. Which of the following equations is equivalent to
   $x = \sqrt{10xy - 25y^2}$?

   (A) $x = 5y + 1$

   (B) $x = 5y$

   (C) $x = 5y\sqrt{y} - 2$

   (D) $x = \dfrac{2y}{5}$

   (E) $x = \dfrac{\sqrt{5}}{2y}$

2. The sum of Alan's age and Bob's age is 40. The sum of Bob's age and Carl's age is 34. The sum of Alan's age and Carl's age is 42. How old is Bob?

   (A) 12

   (B) 16

   (C) 18

   (D) 20

   (E) 24

3. If x and y are integers, is $x + y - 1$ divisible by 3?

   (1) When x is divided by 3, the remainder is 2.
   (2) When y is divided by 6, the remainder is 5.

   (A) Statement 1 ALONE is sufficient, but statement 2 alone is not sufficient to answer the question asked.

   (B) Statement 2 ALONE is sufficient, but statement 1 alone is not sufficient to answer the question asked.

   (C) BOTH statements 1 and 2 TOGETHER are sufficient to answer the question asked; but NEITHER statement ALONE is sufficient.

(D) EACH statement ALONE is sufficient to answer the question asked.

(E) Statements 1 and 2 TOGETHER are NOT sufficient to answer the question asked, and additional data specific to the problem are needed.

4. Four billboards—A, B, C, and D— appear in that order along a straight length of highway. Does the distance from billboard B to billboard D equal the distance from billboard A to billboard B?

   (1) The distance from billboard C to billboard A is less than the distance from billboard D to billboard B.

   (2) The distance from billboard D to billboard A is twice that from billboard C to billboard D.

   (A) Statement 1 ALONE is sufficient, but statement 2 alone is not sufficient to answer the question asked.

   (B) Statement 2 ALONE is sufficient, but statement 1 alone is not sufficient to answer the question asked.

   (C) BOTH statements 1 and 2 TOGETHER are sufficient to answer the question asked; but NEITHER statement ALONE is sufficient.

   (D) EACH statement ALONE is sufficient to answer the question asked.

   (E) Statements 1 and 2 TOGETHER are NOT sufficient to answer the question asked, and additional data specific to the problem are needed.

5. At the beginning of a five-day trading week, the price of a certain stock was $10 per share. During the week, four of the five closing prices of the stock exceeded $10. Did the average closing price of the stock during the week exceed its price at the beginning of the week?

   (1) The stock's closing price on Tuesday was the same as its closing price on Thursday.

   (2) The sum of the stock's highest and lowest closing prices during the week was 20.

(A) Statement 1 ALONE is sufficient, but statement 2 alone is not sufficient to answer the question asked.

(B) Statement 2 ALONE is sufficient, but statement 1 alone is not sufficient to answer the question asked.

(C) BOTH statements 1 and 2 TOGETHER are sufficient to answer the question asked; but NEITHER statement ALONE is sufficient.

(D) EACH statement ALONE is sufficient to answer the question asked.

(E) Statements 1 and 2 TOGETHER are NOT sufficient to answer the question asked, and additional data specific to the problem are needed.

6. What is the value of x?

   (1) $4x^2 - 4x = -1$

   (2) $2x^2 + 9x = 5$

   (A) Statement 1 ALONE is sufficient, but statement 2 alone is not sufficient to answer the question asked.

   (B) Statement 2 ALONE is sufficient, but statement 1 alone is not sufficient to answer the question asked.

   (C) BOTH statements 1 and 2 TOGETHER are sufficient to answer the question asked; but NEITHER statement ALONE is sufficient.

   (D) EACH statement ALONE is sufficient to answer the question asked.

   (E) Statements 1 and 2 TOGETHER are NOT sufficient to answer the question asked, and additional data specific to the problem are needed.

AREA OF WAREHOUSE UNITS A–D

Unit	Percent of total warehouse footage	Square feet
A	7	
B	10.5	
C		
D		19,000

7. Based on the table above, if the total area of the warehouse is 560,000 square feet, and if the four units listed account for 25% of this total area, by approximately how many square feet does Unit A exceed Unit C in size?

(A) 13,000

(B) 15,500

(C) 17,000

(D) 18,500

(E) 22,500

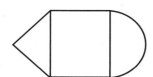

8. Three carpet pieces—in the shapes of a square, a triangle, and a semicircle—are attached to one another, as shown in the figure above, to cover the floor of a room. If the area of the square is 144 and the perimeter of the triangle is 28, what is the perimeter of the room's floor?

(A) $32 + 6\pi$

(B) $40 + 6\pi$

(C) $34 + 12\pi$

(D) $52 + 6\pi$

(E) $52 + 12\pi$

9. What is the sum of $\sqrt{.49}$, $\frac{3}{4}$ and 80% ?

(A) 1.59

(B) 1.62

(C) 2.04

(D) 2.25

(E) 2.53

10. A family of two adults and two children are going together to the local zoo, which charges exactly twice as much for each adult admission ticket as for each child's admission ticket. If the total admission price for the family of four is $12.60, what is the price of a child's ticket?

(A) $1.60

(B) $2.10

(C) $3.20

(D) $3.30

(E) $4.20

11. If $(b*a*c)$ is defined as being equal to $ab - c$, what is the sum of $(4*3*5)$ and $(6*5*7)$?

(A) 6

(B) 11

(C) 15

(D) 30

(E) 40

12. Two ships leave from the same port at 11:30 a.m. If one sails due east at 24 miles per hour and the other due south at 10 miles per hour, how many miles apart are the ships at 2:30 p.m.?

(A) 45

(B) 62

(C) 68

(D) 78

(E) 84

13. Which of the following fractions is equal to $\frac{1}{4}$%?

(A) $\frac{1}{400}$

(B) $\frac{1}{40}$

(C) $\frac{1}{25}$

(D) $\frac{4}{25}$

(E) $\frac{1}{4}$

14. It takes Paul m minutes to mow the lawn. Assuming that he mows at a constant rate, after Paul mows for k minutes, what fraction of the lawn remains unmowed?

(A) $\dfrac{k}{m}$

(B) $\dfrac{m}{k}$

(C) $\dfrac{m-k}{k}$

(D) $\dfrac{k-m}{m}$

(E) $\dfrac{m-k}{m}$

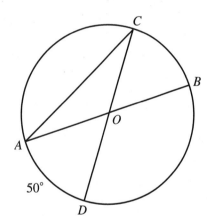

15. AB and CD are diameters of circle O. What is the number of degrees in angle CAB?

(A) $12\dfrac{1}{2}$

(B) 25

(C) 50

(D) 100

(E) 130

16. If $a = \sqrt{b}$, what is the value of $a - b$?

(1) $b = 3a$

(2) $ab = 27$

(A) Statement 1 ALONE is sufficient, but statement 2 alone is not sufficient to answer the question asked.

(B) Statement 2 ALONE is sufficient, but statement 1 alone is not sufficient to answer the question asked.

(C) BOTH statements 1 and 2 TOGETHER are sufficient to answer the question asked; but NEITHER statement ALONE is sufficient.

(D) EACH statement ALONE is sufficient to answer the question asked.

(E) Statements 1 and 2 TOGETHER are NOT sufficient to answer the question asked, and additional data specific to the problem are needed.

17. A county animal shelter houses two different types of animals: dogs and cats. If d represents the number of dogs, and if c represents the number of cats, which of the following expresses the portion of animals at the shelter that are dogs?

(A) $\dfrac{d+c}{d}$

(B) $\dfrac{d+c}{c}$

(C) $\dfrac{d}{c}$

(D) $\dfrac{c}{d}$

(E) $\dfrac{d}{d+c}$

18. If $\left(\dfrac{a}{b}\right)\left(\dfrac{b}{c}\right)\left(\dfrac{c}{d}\right)\left(\dfrac{d}{e}\right)(x) = 1$, then what must x equal?

(A) $\dfrac{a}{e}$

(B) $\dfrac{e}{a}$

(C) e

(D) $\dfrac{1}{a}$

(E) $\dfrac{be}{a}$

19. Two competitors battle each other in each match of a tournament with nine participants. What is the minimum number of matches that must occur for every competitor to battle every other competitor?

(A) 27

(B) 36

(C) 45

(D) 64

(E) 81

20. On the xy-coordinate plane, points A and B both lie on the circumference of a circle whose center is O, and the length of AB equals the circle's diameter. If the (x,y) coordinates of O are (2,1) and the (x,y) coordinates of B are (4,6), what are the (x,y) coordinates of A?

(A) (0, –3)

(B) (–1, –5)

(C) (0, –4)

(D) (–2, –3)

(E) (–1, –4)

21. If $a \neq 0$ or 1, which of the following fractions is equivalent to $\dfrac{\left(\frac{1}{a}\right)}{2-\frac{2}{a}}$?

(A) $\dfrac{1}{2a-2}$

(B) $\dfrac{2}{a-2}$

(C) $\dfrac{1}{a-2}$

(D) $\dfrac{1}{a}$

(E) $\dfrac{2}{2a-1}$

22. If a jewelry merchant bought a particular ring for $10,000 and sold the ring to Judith, how much did Judith pay for the ring?

(1) The merchant's profit from the sale was 50%.

(2) The amount that the merchant paid for the ring was two-thirds of the amount that Judith paid for the ring.

(A) Statement 1 ALONE is sufficient, but statement 2 alone is not sufficient to answer the question asked.

(B) Statement 2 ALONE is sufficient, but statement 1 alone is not sufficient to answer the question asked.

(C) BOTH statements 1 and 2 TOGETHER are sufficient to answer the question asked; but NEITHER statement ALONE is sufficient.

(D) EACH statement ALONE is sufficient to answer the question asked.

(E) Statements 1 and 2 TOGETHER are NOT sufficient to answer the question asked, and additional data specific to the problem are needed.

23. What is the value of the integer K?

(1) K is a prime number between 40 and 50.

(2) The integer $(K + 1)$ is divisible by exactly two different prime numbers.

(A) Statement 1 ALONE is sufficient, but statement 2 alone is not sufficient to answer the question asked.

(B) Statement 2 ALONE is sufficient, but statement 1 alone is not sufficient to answer the question asked.

(C) BOTH statements 1 and 2 TOGETHER are sufficient to answer the question asked; but NEITHER statement ALONE is sufficient.

(D) EACH statement ALONE is sufficient to answer the question asked.

(E) Statements 1 and 2 TOGETHER are NOT sufficient to answer the question asked, and additional data specific to the problem are needed.

24. A certain cylindrical tank set on its circular base is 7.5 feet in height. If the tank is filled with water, and if the water is then poured out of the tank into smaller cube-shaped tanks, how many cube-shaped tanks are required to hold all the water?

    (1) The length of a cube-shaped tank's side is equal to the radius of the cylindrical tank's circular base.

    (2) If three cube-shaped tanks are stacked on top of one another, the top of the third cube stacked is the same distance above the ground as the top of the cylindrical tank.

    (A) Statement 1 ALONE is sufficient, but statement 2 alone is not sufficient to answer the question asked.

    (B) Statement 2 ALONE is sufficient, but statement 1 alone is not sufficient to answer the question asked.

    (C) BOTH statements 1 and 2 TOGETHER are sufficient to answer the question asked; but NEITHER statement ALONE is sufficient.

    (D) EACH statement ALONE is sufficient to answer the question asked.

    (E) Statements 1 and 2 TOGETHER are NOT sufficient to answer the question asked, and additional data specific to the problem are needed.

25. Is $xyz < 0$?

    (1) $x^3y^2z < 0$

    (2) $z^3yx < 0$

    (A) Statement 1 ALONE is sufficient, but statement 2 alone is not sufficient to answer the question asked.

    (B) Statement 2 ALONE is sufficient, but statement 1 alone is not sufficient to answer the question asked.

    (C) BOTH statements 1 and 2 TOGETHER are sufficient to answer the question asked; but NEITHER statement ALONE is sufficient.

    (D) EACH statement ALONE is sufficient to answer the question asked.

    (E) Statements 1 and 2 TOGETHER are NOT sufficient to answer the question asked, and additional data specific to the problem are needed.

26. In a boat race between David and Jeff, when Jeff had covered half the 30-mile race distance, David was two miles ahead of Jeff. How long did it take David to travel the entire 30-mile distance?

    (1) David traveled the last 15 miles of the race distance in 40 minutes.

    (2) Jeff traveled the first 15 miles of the race distance in 45 minutes.

    (A) Statement 1 ALONE is sufficient, but statement 2 alone is not sufficient to answer the question asked.

    (B) Statement 2 ALONE is sufficient, but statement 1 alone is not sufficient to answer the question asked.

    (C) BOTH statements 1 and 2 TOGETHER are sufficient to answer the question asked; but NEITHER statement ALONE is sufficient.

    (D) EACH statement ALONE is sufficient to answer the question asked.

    (E) Statements 1 and 2 TOGETHER are NOT sufficient to answer the question asked, and additional data specific to the problem are needed.

27. During one complete revolution of a circular gear, a wheel driven directly by the gear completes $2\frac{1}{2}$ revolutions. After the wheel rolls across the ground 20 feet, how many revolutions has the gear completed?

    (1) The diameter of the gear is 10 inches.

    (2) The radius of the wheel is 12.5 inches.

    (A) Statement 1 ALONE is sufficient, but statement 2 alone is not sufficient to answer the question asked.

    (B) Statement 2 ALONE is sufficient, but statement 1 alone is not sufficient to answer the question asked.

    (C) BOTH statements 1 and 2 TOGETHER are sufficient to answer the question asked; but NEITHER statement ALONE is sufficient.

(D) EACH statement ALONE is sufficient to answer the question asked.

(E) Statements 1 and 2 TOGETHER are NOT sufficient to answer the question asked, and additional data specific to the problem are needed.

28. Code letters X, Y, and Z each represent one digit in the positive three-digit number XYZ. If X is a non-zero integer, and if Z is the only odd integer among the three digits, what is the number represented by XYZ?

(1) The sum of the three digits is 7.

(2) $X - Y > 4$

(A) Statement 1 ALONE is sufficient, but statement 2 alone is not sufficient to answer the question asked.

(B) Statement 2 ALONE is sufficient, but statement 1 alone is not sufficient to answer the question asked.

(C) BOTH statements 1 and 2 TOGETHER are sufficient to answer the question asked; but NEITHER statement ALONE is sufficient.

(D) EACH statement ALONE is sufficient to answer the question asked.

(E) Statements 1 and 2 TOGETHER are NOT sufficient to answer the question asked, and additional data specific to the problem are needed.

29. If q workers can paint a house in d days, how many days will it take $q + 2$ workers to paint the same house, assuming all workers paint at the same rate?

(A) $d + 2$

(B) $d - 2$

(C) $\dfrac{q+2}{qd}$

(D) $\dfrac{qd}{q+2}$

(E) $\dfrac{qd + 2d}{q}$

30. In an election between two candidates—Lange and Sobel—70% of the voters voted for Sobel. Of the election's voters, 60% were male. If 35% of the female voters voted for Lange, what percentage of the voters are males who voted for Sobel?

(A) 14

(B) 16

(C) 26

(D) 44

(E) 65

31. If a building b feet high casts a shadow f feet long, then, at the same time of day, a tree t feet high will cast a shadow how many feet long?

(A) $\dfrac{ft}{b}$

(B) $\dfrac{fb}{t}$

(C) $\dfrac{b}{ft}$

(D) $\dfrac{tb}{f}$

(E) $\dfrac{t}{fb}$

32. What is the difference between the sum of the integers 15 through 33, inclusive, and the sum of the integers 11 through 31, inclusive?

(A) 11

(B) 15

(C) 26

(D) 32

(E) 41

33. A solution of 60 ounces of sugar and water is 20% sugar. How much water must be added to make a solution that is 5% sugar?

(A) 180 ounces

(B) 120 ounces

(C) 100 ounces

(D) 80 ounces

(E) 20 ounces

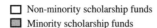

STATE SCHOLARSHIP FUNDS AWARDED (1980-95)

☐ Non-minority scholarship funds
■ Minority scholarship funds

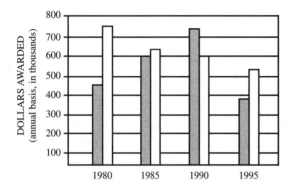

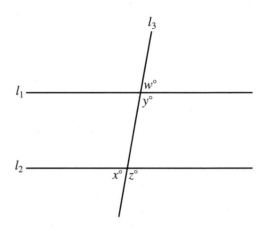

34. Based on the information in the graph above, during the greatest 10-year change in nonminority scholarship funds awarded, what is approximately the greatest five-year percentage change in minority scholarship funds awarded?

(A) 15
(B) 25
(C) 27
(D) 33
(E) 43

35. In the figure above, is l_1 parallel to l_2?

(1) $x + 90 = 270 - y$
(2) $z + w = 180$

(A) Statement 1 ALONE is sufficient, but statement 2 alone is not sufficient to answer the question asked.

(B) Statement 2 ALONE is sufficient, but statement 1 alone is not sufficient to answer the question asked.

(C) BOTH statements 1 and 2 TOGETHER are sufficient to answer the question asked; but NEITHER statement ALONE is sufficient.

(D) EACH statement ALONE is sufficient to answer the question asked.

(E) Statements 1 and 2 TOGETHER are NOT sufficient to answer the question asked, and additional data specific to the problem are needed.

36. If a total of 55 books were sold at a community book fair, and if each book was either hardback or paperback, how many hardback books were sold at the book fair?

    (1) The total proceeds from the sale of paperback books, each of which was sold for 75 cents, was $19.50.

    (2) The proceeds from the book fair totaled $48.50.

    (A) Statement 1 ALONE is sufficient, but statement 2 alone is not sufficient to answer the question asked.

    (B) Statement 2 ALONE is sufficient, but statement 1 alone is not sufficient to answer the question asked.

    (C) BOTH statements 1 and 2 TOGETHER are sufficient to answer the question asked; but NEITHER statement ALONE is sufficient.

    (D) EACH statement ALONE is sufficient to answer the question asked.

    (E) Statements 1 and 2 TOGETHER are NOT sufficient to answer the question asked, and additional data specific to the problem are needed.

37. If p pencils cost $2q$ dollars, how many pencils can be purchased for c cents? [Note: 1 dollar = 100 cents]

    (A) $\dfrac{pc}{2q}$

    (B) $\dfrac{pc}{200q}$

    (C) $\dfrac{50pc}{q}$

    (D) $\dfrac{2pq}{c}$

    (E) $200pcq$

Quick Answer Guide

Practice Test: Quantitative Ability

1. B	11. D	21. A	31. A
2. B	12. D	22. D	32. B
3. C	13. A	23. E	33. A
4. D	14. E	24. C	34. D
5. B	15. B	25. B	35. D
6. A	16. D	26. E	36. A
7. C	17. E	27. D	37. B
8. B	18. B	28. C	
9. D	19. B	29. D	
10. B	20. C	30. D	

Day 27

Practice Test: Review of Section 3 (Quantitative Ability)

Today's Topics:

Today you will review yesterday's Quantitative Ability practice test. Preceding each explanation, the question type and difficulty level are indicated.

1. The correct answer is (B). Quadratic equations (moderate).

To solve this problem, first remove the radical by squaring both sides of the equation. Then, set the result equal to 0. Simplify by factoring, and express x in terms of y:

$$x = \sqrt{10xy - 25y^2}$$
$$x^2 = 10xy - 25y^2$$
$$x^2 = 10xy + 25y^2 = 0$$
$$(x - 5y)^2 = 0$$
$$x - 5y = 0$$
$$x = 5y$$

2. The correct answer is (B). System of linear equations (moderate).

The question presents three equations:

$$A + B = 40$$
$$B + C = 34$$
$$A + C = 42$$

To solve for B, first subtract the second equation from the third equation. The result is $A - B = 8$. Then, subtract this resulting equation from the first equation. This result is $2B = 32$, or $B = 16$.

3. The correct answer is (C). Integers (easier).

Neither statement 1 nor 2 alone provides any information about the second variable or, in turn, about the value of $x + y - 1$. Thus, you can easily eliminate A, B, and D. Next, consider statements 1 and 2 together. Given a remainder of 2 when x is divided by 3, the value of x must be greater than a multiple of 3 by exactly 2: $x = \{5, 8, 11, 14 \dots\}$. Given a remainder of 5 when y is divided by 6, the value of y must be greater than a multiple of 6 by exactly 5: $y = \{11, 17, 23, 29 \dots\}$. Adding together any x-value and any y-value always results in a sum that exceeds a multiple of 3 by exactly 7 (or by exactly 1). Accordingly, subtracting 1 from that sum always results in a multiple of 3. Thus, given statements 1 and 2, $x + y - 1$ is divisible by 3.

4. The correct answer is (D). Linear ordering (easier).

Statement 1 alone suffices to answer the question. Given $AC < BD$, AB (which is smaller than AC) must be smaller than BD. $BD > AB$, and the answer to the question is no. Statement 2 also suffices alone to answer the question. Given $\frac{AD}{2}$ = CD, C bisects AD, and AC = CD. Thus, AB (which is smaller than AC) must be smaller than CD. Because CD is smaller than BD, AB < BD, and the answer to the question is no.

5. The correct answer is (B). Arithmetic mean (challenging).

Statement 1 provides no information about any of the closing prices relative to the stock's initial price of $10. Thus, statement 1 alone is insufficient to answer the question. Statement 2 establishes that the average of the highest and lowest closing prices during the week was $10. In other words, the lowest closing price was less than the stock's initial price by the same amount as the amount by which the highest closing price exceeded the stock's initial price. Given that the three remaining closing prices were all greater than $10, the average of all five closing prices must be greater than $10. Thus, statement 2 alone suffices to answer the question.

6. The correct answer is (A). Quadratic equations (moderate).

Both equations are quadratic. For each one, you can determine the possible values of x by setting the quadratic expression equal to 0 (zero) and factoring that expression. Considering statement 1 alone, solve for x:

$$4x^2 - 4x = -1$$
$$4x^2 - 4x + 1 = 0$$
$$(2x - 1)(2x - 1) = 0$$
$$(2x - 1)^2 = 0$$
$$2x - 1 = 0$$
$$x = \frac{1}{2}$$

Based on the equation given in statement 1, the only possible value of x is $\frac{1}{2}$. Thus, statement 1 alone suffices to answer the question. Considering statement 2, solve for x:

$$2x^2 + 9x = 5$$
$$2x^2 + 9x - 5 = 0$$
$$(x + 5)(2x - 1) = 0$$
$$x + 5 = 0 \text{ or } 2x - 1 = 0$$
$$x = -5 \text{ or } \frac{1}{2}$$

Based on the equation given in statement 2, there are two possible values of x: –5 and $\frac{1}{2}$. Thus, statement 2 alone is insufficient to answer the question.

7. The correct answer is (C). Data Interpretation (moderate).

Unit D (19,000 square feet) accounts for approximately 3.5% of the warehouse's 560,000 square feet. Together, Units A, B, and D account for approximately 21% of this total (7% + 10.5% + 3.5% = 21%). Since all four units together account for 25% of the total warehouse area, Unit C must account for approximately 4% of this area. Given that Unit A accounts for 7% of 560,000 square feet, Unit A must exceed Unit C in size by approximately 16,800 square feet (3% of 560,000). Of the five answer options, choice (C) comes closest to this approximation.

8. The correct answer is (B). Geometry: circles, quadrilaterals, triangles (moderate).

Each side of the square = 12. The length of the remaining two sides of the triangle totals 16. The perimeter of the semicircle = $\frac{1}{2}\pi d = \frac{1}{2}\pi(12) = 6\pi$. The length of the two sides of the square included in the overall perimeter totals 24. The total perimeter of the floor = $16 + 6\pi + 24 = 40 + 6\pi$.

9. The correct answer is (D). Percents/Roots/Decimals (easier).

Since the answer choices are expressed in decimal terms, convert all three terms in the question to decimals, and then add:

$$\sqrt{.49} = .7$$
$$\frac{3}{4} = .75$$
$$80\% = .8$$
$$.7 + .75 + .8 = 2.25$$

10. The correct answer is (B). Algebraic formulas: weighted average (moderate).

The price of two children's tickets together equals the price of one adult ticket. The total admission price is therefore equivalent to the price of three adult tickets.

$$3a = 12.60$$
$$a = 4.20$$

Price of a child's ticket = $\left(\frac{1}{2}\right)(4.20) = \$2.10$

11. The correct answer is (D). Hypothetical operations (easier).

$$(4*3*5) = 12 - 5 = 7$$
$$(6*5*7) = 30 - 7 = 23$$
$$7 + 23 = 30$$

12. The correct answer is (D). Geometry: triangles (moderate).

In three hours, one ship traveled 72 miles, while the other traveled 30 miles. The ratio of these two distances is 30:72 or 5:12, suggesting a 5:12:13 triangle in which the hypotenuse is the distance between the two ships at 2:30 p.m. That distance is 78 miles.

13. The correct answer is (A). Equivalent forms of numbers (easier).

$$\frac{1}{4}\% = \frac{\frac{1}{4}}{100} = \left(\frac{1}{4}\right)\left(\frac{1}{100}\right) = \frac{1}{400}$$

14. The correct answer is (E). Algebraic formulas: rate (challenging).

In k minutes, $\frac{k}{m}$ of the lawn is mowed. Still unmowed, then, is $(1 - \frac{k}{m})$ or $(\frac{m-k}{m})$.

15. The correct answer is (B). Geometry: circles (easier).

Given that arc $AD = 50°$; $\angle AOD = 50°$. $\angle AOC$ is supplementary; thus $\angle AOC = 130°$. Triangle AOC is isosceles (AO and CO are both radii). Therefore $\angle CAB = 25°$.

16. The correct answer is (D). System of equations (moderate).

To answer this question, it suffices to recognize that *either* statement 1 or 2, together with $a = \sqrt{b}$, establishes a system of two equations in two variables.

Because neither statement 1 nor 2 is equivalent to $a = \sqrt{b}$, either statement 1 or 2 suffices alone to solve for a and b and, in turn, to determine the value of $a - b$ ($a = 3, b = 9$).

17. The correct answer is (E). Proportion (easier).

The shelter houses $d + c$ animals altogether. Of these animals, d are dogs. You can express that portion as the fraction $\frac{d}{d+c}$.

18. The correct answer is (B). Operations on variables (easier).

$$\left(\frac{a}{b}\right)\left(\frac{b}{c}\right)\left(\frac{c}{d}\right)\left(\frac{d}{e}\right)(x) = 1$$
$$\left(\frac{a}{e}\right)(x) = 1$$
$$x = \frac{e}{a}$$

19. The correct answer is (B). Sets (moderate).

Competitor 1 must engage in eight matches. Competitor 2 must engage in seven matches not already accounted for (the match between competitors 1 and 2 has already been tabulated). Similarly, competitor 3 must engage in six matches other than those accounted for, and so on. The minimum number of total matches = $8 + 7 + 6 + 5 + 4 + 3 + 2 + 1 = 36$.

20. The correct answer is (C). Coordinate geometry (challenging).

Since AB is the circle's diameter, AB passes through point O, which is the midpoint of AB. Thus, the run (horizontal distance) and rise (vertical distance) from B to O are the same as from O to A (averaging the x-coordinates and averaging the y-coordinates). Those distances are 2 and 5, respectively. From O (2,1), move two units to the left and 5 units down, to (0,–4).

21. The correct answer is (A). Complex fractions (easier).

Simplify this complex fraction by multiplying *every* term by a:

$$\frac{\dfrac{a}{\dfrac{a}{2a - \dfrac{2a}{a}}}}{} = \frac{1}{2a - 2}$$

22. The correct answer is (D). Percent (easier).

Given that the merchant paid $10,000 for the ring, if the merchant earned a 50% profit from the sale to Judith, she paid $15,000 for the ring ($10,000 + 50% of $10,000). Statement 1 alone suffices to answer the question. If the merchant paid two-thirds what Judith paid, then $10,000 = ($\frac{2}{3}$)(Judith's price). Again, you can determine the price that Judith paid ($10,000 × $\frac{3}{2}$ = $15,000). Thus, statement 2 alone also suffices.

23. The correct answer is (E). Factors/Prime numbers (moderate).

Statement (1) alone establishes that K = 41, 43, or 47, and is therefore insufficient to answer the question.

Statement (2) alone is also insufficient to answer the question. For example, if K = 5, then $K + 1$ = 6. The integer 6 is divisible by exactly two different prime numbers: 2 and 3. If K = 9, then $K + 1$ = 10. The integer 10 is also divisible by exactly two different prime numbers: 2 and 5.

Consider statements (1) and (2) together by determining the prime factors of (41 + 1), (43 + 1), and (47 + 1):

42 = 2 × 3 × 7 (three different prime numbers)

44 = 2 × 2 × 11 (two different prime numbers)

48 = 2 × 2 × 2 × 2 × 3 (two different prime numbers)

Accordingly, K can equal either 43 or 47 while conforming to both statements (1) and (2). Thus, both statements together are still insufficient to answer the question.

24. The correct answer is (C). Geometry: solids (challenging).

To answer the question, you must determine the relative volumes of the cylindrical tank and a cube-shaped tank. Statement 1 fails to provide sufficient information to determine these volumes. The volume of the cylindrical tank is $7.5\pi r^2$, and, given statement 1, you can express the cube's volume as r^3. The ratio of the two volumes, then, is $7.5\pi r^2 : r^3$ or $7.5\pi : r$. Accordingly, the relative volumes of the containers vary depending on the value of r. Statement 2 is also insufficient to answer the question. Given statement 2, the length of a cube's side is 2.5 feet, and you can determine its volume (s^3). However, you cannot determine the cylindrical tank's volume, because the size of its circular base remains unknown. Statement 1 provides this missing information. Thus, statements 1 and 2 together suffice to answer the question. (Given statements 1 and 2, the ratio of V [cylinder] to V [cube] is $3\pi:1$, so 10 cube-shaped tanks are required.)

25. The correct answer is (B). Exponents (moderate).

Given $x^3 y^2 z < 0$, neither x, y, nor z can equal zero, and either all three terms (x^3, y^2, and z) are negative or exactly one of the three terms is negative [(−)(−)(−) < 0, (−)(+)(+) < 0]. However, whether y is negative or positive, y^2 is positive; thus, either x or z (but not both) must be negative. Accordingly, xyz could be either positive or negative, depending on the value of y. Statement 1 alone is insufficient to answer the question. Given $z^3 yx < 0$, either z, y, and x are all negative or exactly one of the three variable is negative. In either case, $xyz < 0$. Thus, statement 2 alone suffices to answer the question.

26. The correct answer is (E). Rate (moderate).

Statement 1 alone provides no information about how long it took David to travel the first 15 miles, and is therefore insufficient by itself to answer the question. Statement 2 alone provides even less information about how long it took David to travel the entire distance. Although you can determine from statement 2 that David traveled the first 17 miles in 45 minutes, you cannot determine how long it took David to travel the remaining 13 miles. Statement 1 and 2 together establish that David traveled 32 miles (17 + 15) in 85 minutes (45 + 40). However, 2 of the 32 miles are accounted for twice. Without knowing either the time that it took David to travel the 16th and 17th miles of the race or his average speed over those two miles, you cannot determine David's total time for the 30 mile race. Thus, statements 1 and 2 together are insufficient to answer the question.

27. The correct answer is (D). Geometry: circles, ratios (challenging).

Given that the wheel has rolled 20 feet, you must first determine the wheel's circumference to calculate the number of revolutions that the wheel has made and, in turn, the number of revolutions that the gear has made. Either statement provides sufficient information to determine the wheel's circumference. Given statement 1, the gear's circumference is 10π inches, and the wheel's circumference is 2.5 times that amount, or 25π inches. Given statement 2 (alone), the wheel's circumference, again, is 25π inches. To find the number of revolutions completed by the wheel after 20 feet, divide 20 feet by 25π inches. To find the corresponding number of gear revolutions; divide the result by $2\frac{1}{2}$.

28. The correct answer is (C). Integers/prime numbers (challenging).

Considering statement (1) alone, Z could be either 1, 3 or 5 (if Z were either 7 or 9, then the sum of the three digits would exceed 7, allowing for several possibilities—for example, 601 or 421). Statement (2) alone permits exactly three XY combinations (for each one Z can be either 1, 3, 5, 7, or 9): $60Z$, $80Z$, and $82Z$. Statements (1) and (2) together permit only the XY-combination, $60Z$, and thus XYZ must represent the number 601.

29. The correct answer is (D). Algebraic formulas: work (challenging).

The number of days (d) that it takes q workers to paint a house varies inversely with the number of days that it takes $q + 2$ workers to paint a house. You can express the relationship with the following equation: $(q)(d) = (q + 2)(x)$, where x = the number of days that it takes $q + 2$ workers to paint a house. You can solve for x as follows: $x = \frac{qd}{q+2}$.

30. The correct answer is (D). Proportion (moderate).

You can organize this problem's information in a table, as shown in this next figure.

	male	female	
Lange		14%	30%
Sobel	?		70%
	60%	40%	

Because 35% of 40% of the voters (female voters) voted for Lange, 14% ($.40 \times .35$) of all voters were females who voted for Lange. You can now fill in the entire table (the total of all four percentages must be 100%), as shown in the below figure.

	male	female	
Lange	16%	14%	30%
Sobel	44%	26%	70%
	60%	40%	

31. The correct answer is (A). Algebraic formulas: ratio (moderate).

The ratio of height to the shadow is constant. Thus, you can set the ratio of b to f equal to the ratio of t to x, where x represents the length of the tree's shadow:

$$\frac{b}{f} = \frac{t}{x}$$
$$bx = ft$$
$$x = \frac{ft}{b}$$

32. The correct answer is (B). Integers (easier).

You need not add all the terms of each sequence. Instead, notice that the two sequences have in common integers 15 through 31, inclusive. Thus, those terms cancel out, leaving 32 + 33 = 65 in the first sequence and 11 + 12 + 13 + 14 = 50 in the second sequence. The difference is 15.

33. The correct answer is (A). Algebraic formulas: wet mixture (challenging).

You can express the amount of sugar after you add water as .05(60 + x), where 60 + x represents the total amount of solution after you add the additional water. This amount of sugar is the same as (equal to) the original amount of sugar (20% of 60). Set up an equation, multiply both sides by 100 to remove the decimal point, and solve for x:

$$5(60 + x) = 1,200$$
$$300 + 5x = 1,200$$
$$5x = 900$$
$$x = 180$$

34. The correct answer is (D). Data interpretation (moderate).

The greatest 10-year change in nonminority scholarship funds awarded occurred from 1980 to 1990: $750,000 to $600,000 (approximately). During this period, the greatest change in funds awarded occurred from 1980 to 1985—an increase from $450,000 to $600,000 (approximately). This increase of approximately $150,000 is 33% of $450,000 (the amount in 1980).

35. The correct answer is (D). Geometry: lines and angles (easier).

You can express the equation in statement 1 as $x + y = 180$; thus, x and y are supplementary angles. This information suffices to establish that the angles created by the intersection of l_1 and l_3 are identical to those created by the intersection of l_2 and l_3. Accordingly, $l_1 \parallel l_2$, and statement 1 alone suffices to answer the question. Statement 2 establishes that $z = y$, because $w + y = 180$. This information suffices to es-

tablish that the degree measures of the angles created by the intersection of l_1 and l_3 are identical to those created by the intersection of l_2 and l_3. Accordingly, $l_1 \parallel l_2$, and statement 2 alone suffices to answer the question.

36. The correct answer is (A). Algebraic formulas: dry mixture (moderate).

Given statement 1, you can determine the total number of paperbacks sold: ($.75)(P) = $19.50, or P = 26. Given that 55 books were sold altogether, 29 hardback books were sold, and statement 1 alone suffices to answer the question. Statement 2 provides no information about the prices of either type of book, and is therefore insufficient to answer the question.

37. The correct answer is (B). Algebraic formulas: ratio (moderate).

Use a proportion comparing pencils to cents. Expressing 2q dollars as 200q cents, solve for the number of pencils (represented by x) that you can buy for c cents:

$$\frac{p}{200q} = \frac{x}{c}$$

$$\frac{pc}{200q} = x$$

Day 28

Practice Test, Section 4: Verbal Ability

Today's Topics:

Today you take a full-length Verbal Ability practice test. After completing the test, check your answers with the Quick Answer Guide at the end of this lesson.

PRACTICE TEST

Number of questions: 41
Time allowed: 75 minutes

Directions: If you are not already familiar with the directions for Sentence Correction, Critical Reasoning, and Reading Comprehension questions, review the introductory materials in the first lesson for each type (Days 9, 12, and 18, respectively). Tomorrow you will assess your performance and review the explanations for this test.

1. On this issue, this state's elected officials ignored the wishes of their electorate, which cannot reasonably be disputed in light of the legislative record.

   (A) On this issue, this state's elected officials ignored the wishes of their electorate, which

   (B) This state's elected officials, ignoring on this issue the wishes of their electorate,

   (C) That this state's elected officials ignored the wishes of their electorate

   (D) On this issue, the wishes of the electorate were ignored by this state's elected officials, and

   (E) That the wishes of the electorate on this issue were ignored by this state's elected officials

2. *The Reluctant Monarch, which Francis Craig wrote as her third* in a series of books about the British Monarchy.

   (A) *The Reluctant Monarch,* which Francis Craig wrote as her third

   (B) *The Reluctant Monarch,* written by Francis Craig, is her third

   (C) Written by Francis Craig, *The Reluctant Monarch,* which is her third book

   (D) Francis Craig wrote *The Reluctant Monarch,* which book is her third

   (E) *The Reluctant Monarch* is the third book written by Francis Craig

3. Either interest rates or the supply of <u>money can, along with the level of government spending, be factors contributing to</u> the amount of inflation.

(A) money can, along with the level of government spending, be factors contributing to

(B) money along with the level of government spending, can one or the other be contributing factors in

(C) money can, along with the level of government spending, contribute as factors to

(D) money can contribute, along with the level of government spending, to

(E) money can be a contributing factor to, along with the level of government spending

4. According to life-insurance company statistics, nine out of ten alcoholics die before the age of seventy-five, as opposed to seven out of ten non-alcoholics. A recent report issued by the State Medical Board recounts these statistics and concludes that alcohol addiction increases a person's susceptibility to certain life-threatening diseases, thereby reducing life expectancy.

The conclusion drawn by the State Medical Board depends on which of the following assumptions?

(A) People who are predisposed to life-threatening diseases are more likely than other people to become alcoholics.

(B) The statistics cited exclude deaths due to other alcohol-related events such as automobile accidents.

(C) Alcoholism does not also increase a person's susceptibility to diseases that are not life threatening.

(D) The life expectancy of the portion of the general population not characterized by alcoholism increases over time.

(E) The author of the report is not biased in his or her personal opinion about the morality of alcohol consumption.

5. Currently, the supply of office buildings in this state far exceeds demand, while demand for single-family housing far exceeds supply. As a result, real es-

tate developers have curtailed office building construction until demand meets supply and have stepped up construction of single-family housing. The state legislature recently enacted a law eliminating a state income tax on corporations whose primary place of business is this state. As a result, many large private employers from other states have already begun to relocate to this state, and according to a reliable study this trend will continue during the next five years.

If the statements above are all true, they best support which of the following assertions?

(A) During the next five years, the number of state residents working at home as opposed to working in office buildings will decrease.

(B) Five years from now, the available supply of single-family housing in the state will exceed demand.

(C) Five years from now, the per-capita income of the state's residents will exceed current levels.

(D) During the next five years, the cost of purchasing new single-family residential housing will decrease.

(E) During the next five years, fewer new office buildings than single-family houses will be constructed in the state.

Questions 6–8 refer to the following passage:

The arrival in a new location of a nonindigenous plant or animal species might be either intentional or unintentional. Rates of species movement driven by human transformations of natural
(5) environments as well as by human mobility—through commerce, tourism, and travel—dwarf natural rates by comparison. Although geographic distributions of species naturally expand or contract over historical time intervals
(10) (tens to hundreds of years), species' ranges rarely expand thousands of miles or across physical barriers such as oceans or mountains.

A number of factors confound quantitative evaluation of the relative importance of various
(15) entry pathways. Time lags often occur between

establishment of nonindigenous species and their detection, and tracing the pathway for a long-established species is difficult. Experts estimate that nonindigenous weeds are usually detected
(20) only after having been in the country for 30 years or having spread to at least 10,000 acres. In addition, federal port inspection, although a major source of information on nonindigenous species pathways, especially for agricultural pests, pro-
(25) vides data only when such species enter via scrutinized routes. Finally, some comparisons between pathways defy quantitative analysis—for example, which is more "important": the entry pathway of one very harmful species or one by
(30) which many but less harmful species enter the country?

6. Which of the following statements about species movement is best supported by the passage's information?

(A) Species movement is affected more by habitat modifications than by human mobility.

(B) Human-driven factors affect the rate at which species move more than they affect the long-term amount of such movements.

(C) Natural expansions in the geographic distribution of species account for less species movement than natural contractions do.

(D) Natural environments created by commerce, tourism, and travel contribute significantly to species movement.

(E) Movement of a species within a continent depends largely on the geographic extent of human mobility within the continent.

7. Which of the following best expresses the second paragraph's primary purpose?

(A) to identify the problems in assessing the relative significance of various entry pathways for nonindigenous species

(B) to describe the events usually leading to the detection of a nonindigenous species

(C) to discuss the role that time lags and geographic expansion of nonindigenous species play in species detection

(D) to point out the inadequacy of the federal port inspection system in detecting the entry of nonindigenous species

(E) to explain why it is difficult to trace the entry pathways for long-established nonindigenous species

8. Based on the information in the passage, whether the entry pathway for a particular nonindigenous species can be determined is LEAST likely to depend on which of the following?

(A) whether the species is considered to be a pest

(B) whether the species gains entry through a scrutinized route

(C) the rate at which the species expands geographically

(D) how long the species has been established

(E) the size of the average member of the species

9. The atmospheric study reported last month in the *Journal of the Environment* would not <u>have been taken seriously by the scientific community if they were</u> cognizant of the questionable methodology employed.

(A) have been taken seriously by the scientific community if they were

(B) be taken seriously by the scientific community in the event that it had become

(C) have been taken seriously by the scientific community were they

(D) have been taken seriously by the scientific community when the scientific community became

(E) have been taken seriously by the scientific community had scientists been

10. A recent study of this state's prison system indicates that prisoners participating in the weekend furlough program are less likely to become repeat offenders after they are released than prisoners who do not participate in the program. Hence, the weekend furlough program must be an effective means of reducing crime.

Which of the following, if true, would cast the most serious doubt on the conclusion drawn above?

(A) Among prisoners not involved in the furlough program, a minority become repeat offenders after their release.

(B) The crime rate in other states with similar furlough programs is lower overall than the crime rate in states without furlough programs.

(C) Whether the weekend furlough program is effective depends on how greatly one values the reform of any one prisoner.

(D) The furlough program was available only to prisoners who had demonstrated good behavior while in prison.

(E) Among the prisoners studied less than half participated in the furlough program.

11. More airplane accidents are caused by pilot error than any other single factor. The military recently stopped requiring its pilots to obtain immunization shots against chemical warfare agents. These shots are known to cause unpredictable dizzy spells, which can result in pilot error. Since many military pilots also pilot commercial passenger airliners, the reason for the military's decision must have been to reduce the number of commercial airline accidents.

Which of the following, if true, provides most support for the conclusion drawn above?

(A) Recently, more pilots have been volunteering for the immunization shots.

(B) All commercial airline flights are piloted by two copilots, whereas military flights are usually piloted by only one.

(C) Chemical warfare is likely to escalate in the future.

(D) Military pilots are choosing to resign rather than obtain the immunization shots.

(E) Recently, the number of military pilots also piloting commercial airliners has declined.

12. The rules of etiquette for formal dinner parties with foreign diplomats require <u>citizens from both the host and from the diplomat's countries to be seated across from each other</u>.

(A) citizens from both the host and from the diplomat's countries to be seated across from each other

(B) citizens of the host country and of the diplomat's country to sit opposite each other

(C) that the host country and diplomat's country seat their citizens opposite one another

(D) that citizens of the host country be seated opposite those of the diplomat's country

(E) the host country's citizens to be seated opposite to the diplomat's country's citizens

13. Health professionals widely concur that, beyond a certain point, the benefits that an individual can expect to derive <u>by further exercise is negligible</u>.

(A) by further exercise is negligible

(B) from further exercise are negligible

(C) in furthering exercise are negligible

(D) by exercising further would be negligible

(E) by exercising even more would be negligible

14. <u>After bounty hunters turn over their captives to the authorities, they often are denied due process of law.</u>

(A) After bounty hunters turn over their captives to the authorities, they often are denied due process of law.

(B) After turning over bounty hunters' captives to the authorities, the authorities often deny them due process of law.

(C) The authorities often deny captives due process of law after bounty hunters turn the captives over to the authorities.

(D) Bounty hunters turn over their captives to the authorities, often being denied due process of law.

(E) A captive, when turned over by bounty hunters to the authorities, is often denied due process of law.

Questions 15–17 refer to the following passage:

Scientists in the post-1917 Soviet Union occupied an ambiguous position. While the government encouraged and generally supported scientific research, it simultaneously thwarted the scientific
(5) community's ideal: freedom from geographic and political boundaries. A strong nationalistic emphasis on science led at times to the dismissal of all non-Russian scientific work as irrelevant to Soviet science. A 1973 article in *Literatunaya*
(10) *Gazeta*, a Soviet publication, insisted: "World science is based upon national schools, so the weakening of one or another national school inevitably leads to stagnation in the development of world science." According to the Soviet re-
(15) gime, socialist science was to be consistent with, and in fact grow out of, the Marxism-Leninism political ideology. Toward this end, some scientific theories or fields, such as relativity and genetics, were abolished. Where scientific work
(20) conflicted with political criteria, the work was often disrupted. During the Stalinist purges of the 1930s, many Soviet scientists simply disappeared. In the 1970s, Soviet scientists who were part of the refusenik movement lost their jobs
(25) and were barred from access to scientific resources. Nazi Germany during the 1930s and, more recently, Argentina, imposed strikingly similar, though briefer, constraints on scientific research.

15. Which of the following best characterizes the "ambiguous position" (line 2) in which Soviet scientists were placed during the decades that followed the Bolshevik Revolution?

(A) The Soviet government demanded that their research result in scientific progress, although funding was insufficient to accomplish this goal.

(B) They were exhorted to strive toward scientific advancements, while at the same time the freedoms necessary to make such advancements were restricted.

(C) While required to direct their research entirely toward military defense, most advancements in this field were being made by non-Soviet scientists with whom the Soviet scientists were prohibited contact.

(D) They were encouraged to collaborate with Soviet colleagues but were prohibited from any discourse with scientists from other countries.

(E) The Soviet government failed to identify those areas of research that it deemed most worthwhile, but punished those scientists with whose work it was not satisfied.

16. The author quotes an article from *Literatunaya Gazeta* most probably to

(A) illustrate the general sentiment among members of the international scientific community during the time period

(B) underscore the point that the Soviet government sanctioned only those notions about science that conformed to the Marxist-Leninist ideal

(C) show the disparity of views within the Soviet intellectual community regarding the proper role of science

(D) underscore the Soviet emphasis on the notion of a national science

(E) support the author's assertion that the Marxist-Leninist impact on Soviet scientific freedom continued through the decade of the 1970s

17. Which of the following best expresses the author's primary purpose in the passage?

    (A) to examine the events leading up to the suppression of the Soviet refusenik movement of the 1970s

    (B) to define and dispel the notion of a national science as promulgated by the post-revolution Soviet regime

    (C) to describe specific attempts by the modern Soviet regime to suppress scientific freedom

    (D) to examine the major Twentieth Century challenges to the normative assumption that science requires freedom and that it is inherently international

    (E) to point out the similarities and distinctions between scientific freedom and scientific internationalism in the context of the Soviet Union

18. In a one-year experiment involving addicted cigarette smokers, each subject was unknowingly administered either the new drug Nico-Gone or a placebo. During the one-year period less than a third of the subjects who were administered Nico-Gone reported that they had stopped smoking and not resumed smoking, whereas more than two thirds of the subjects who were administered the placebo reported that they had not stopped smoking.

    Based on the statements above, any claim that Nico-Gone is effective in curing addiction to cigarette smoking would be most seriously undermined if which of the following were true?

    (A) During the year of the experiment, some of the subjects received other treatment to help them avoid cigarette smoking.

    (B) Other reliable studies indicate that cigarette smokers rarely inform others falsely that they are not smokers.

    (C) During the year following the experiment, cigarettes were readily available to all of the subjects.

    (D) At the conclusion of the experiment, the total number of subjects who were cigarette smokers was less than the number who were smokers one year prior to the experiment.

    (E) One year after the experiment, the percentage of the experiment's subjects who were cigarette smokers was greater than the percentage of the general population who were smokers.

19. *John:* If a person believes in the inevitability of success, then that person will surely succeed.

    Jolanda: I disagree. According to a recent magazine article entitled "The 100 Most Successful Women in History," most of these 100 women did not believe they would ever become successful.

    Which of the following would be John's most logically convincing rebuttal to Jolanda's counter-argument above?

    (A) Successful people are often viewed by others as unsuccessful.

    (B) Success does not depend on whether a person believes in its inevitability.

    (C) Success is inevitable for some people but not for others.

    (D) Society's definition of success might have changed throughout history.

    (E) None of the successful people listed in the magazine article were men.

20. Vining University's teacher credential program should be credited for the high grade point averages of high school students who enroll in classes taught by Vining graduates. More new graduates of Vining's credential program accept entry-level positions at Franklin High School than at any other high school. But just prior to the current academic year, many of Franklin's teachers transferred to Valley View High School, and since then the median grade point average of Franklin students has declined while at Valley View it has increased.

    The argument above depends on which of the following assumptions?

(A) The two high schools employ differing methods of computing student grade point averages.

(B) Neither high school has a peer-tutoring program that would afford the school an advantage over the other in terms of student academic performance.

(C) Just prior to last year more teachers transferred from Franklin to Valley View than from Valley View to Franklin.

(D) The teachers who transferred from Franklin to Valley View last year were graduates of Vining's teacher credential program.

(E) The teachers who transferred from Franklin to Valley View were replaced with teachers who are also graduates of Vining University's teacher credential program.

21. Equipment used by private biotechnology research firms becomes obsolete more quickly than any other business equipment, simply because biotechnology advances so rapidly. A proposed tax law would provide significant tax incentives for businesses in every industry to replace their old equipment with new equipment. Obviously, political lobbyists for the biotechnology industry were the instigators of this tax proposal.

Which of the following statements, if true, would provide strongest support for the claim above that biotechnology industry lobbyists are responsible for the tax proposal?

(A) The monetary value of the equipment used in the biotechnology industry is greater than in any other industry.

(B) Biotechnology firms expect biotechnology advances to outpace those in other industries for the foreseeable future.

(C) The legislator introducing the proposed law used to work in the biotechnology industry.

(D) Other industries have not lobbied for the proposed law.

(E) Unless a biotechnology firm replaces its obsolete equipment, it will be driven out of business by competing firms.

22. <u>Who the terrorists are and at whom their</u> recent terrorist activities were aimed are currently under investigation by the bureau.

(A) Who the terrorists are and at whom their

(B) Whom the terrorists are and at whom their

(C) Who are the terrorists and at whom their

(D) Who they are and who the

(E) Who the terrorists are and to whom their

23. Despite his admiration of the great jazz musicians that preceded him, Blakey opposed <u>them trivializing the popular genre</u>.

(A) them trivializing the popular genre

(B) their trivializing of the popular genre

(C) their trivializing the popular genre

(D) the popular genre being trivialized by them

(E) them when trivializing the popular genre

24. <u>Even for high school freshmen and sophomores, theories concerning the psychology of death and dying among the elderly can hold considerable significance and interest for many such students.</u>

(A) Even for high school freshmen and sophomores, theories concerning the psychology of death and dying among the elderly can hold considerable significance and interest for many such students.

(B) Even as high school freshmen and sophomore students with considerable interest in theories concerning the psychology of death and dying among the elderly, these theories can hold considerable significance.

(C) Theories concerning the psychology of death and dying among the elderly, for many students, even high school freshmen and sophomores, can hold considerable significance and interest.

(D) Theories concerning the psychology of death and dying among the elderly can hold considerable significance and interest even for high school freshmen and sophomore students.

(E) Considerable significance and interest for even high school freshmen and sophomores is held in theories concerning the psychology of death and dying among the elderly.

25. Newspaper publishers earn their profits primarily from advertising revenue, and potential advertisers are more likely to advertise in newspapers with a wide circulation—a large number of subscribers and other readers—than with other newspapers. But the circulation of the newspaper that is currently the most profitable one in this city has steadily declined during the last two years, while the circulation of one of its competitors has steadily increased.

Each of the following, if true, would help explain the apparent discrepancy between the two statements above EXCEPT:

(A) Advertisers generally switch from the most widely circulated newspaper to another one only when the other one becomes the most widely circulated newspaper instead.

(B) Advertising rates charged by the most profitable newspaper in the city are significantly higher than those charged by its competitors.

(C) The most profitable newspaper in the city receives revenue from its subscribers as well from advertisers.

(D) The circulation of the most profitable newspaper in the city is still greater than of any of its competitors.

(E) The number of newspapers competing viably with the most profitable newspaper in the city has increased during the last two years.

26. The emission of fluorocarbons into the Earth's atmosphere has been shown to deplete the ozone layer in the atmosphere. Therefore, if we were to eliminate all sources of fluorocarbon emission, we could successfully halt ozone layer depletion.

Which of the following demonstrates a pattern of reasoning that is most similar to the flawed reasoning in the argument above?

(A) When challenged to prove their psychic abilities, several of the world's most celebrated so-called psychics were unable

to do so, clearly proving that the psychic phenomenon is fiction rather than fact.

(B) The theory that the Earth's temperature is cyclical is a convincing one, in light of the fact that changes in the Earth's temperature resulted in the extinction of dinosaurs.

(C) Flag burning is ultimately in the state's interest as well as the individual's interest, because the First Amendment right to free expression was created for the purpose of preserving our democratic way of life.

(D) Any person suffering from phlebitis must take the drug Anatol in order to prevent the condition from worsening, as evidenced be the fact that doctors have used Anatol successful for many years to treat and control phlebitis.

(E) Autopsies of the residents of Huiki Island killed by a recent volcanic eruption have shown excessive bone deterioration, which leads to my conclusion that the Huikan culture encourages a diet that promotes bone marrow disease.

27. The pesticide Azocide, introduced to central valley farms three summers ago, has proven ineffective because other pesticides' chemical compositions already in wide use neutralizing its desired effect.

(A) because other pesticides' chemical compositions already in wide use

(B) because of the chemical compositions of the pesticides already in wide use

(C) due to other pesticides already in wide use, whose chemical compositions have been

(D) since, due to the chemical compositions of other pesticides already in use, those pesticides have been

(E) because of other pesticides and their chemical compositions already in use, which have been

Questions 28–30 refer to the following passage:

The 35-millimeter (mm) format for movie production became a *de facto* standard around 1913. The mid-1920s through the mid-1930s, however, saw a resurgence of wide-film formats. During
(5) this time period, formats used by studios ranged in gauge from 55mm to 70mm. Research and development then slackened until the 1950s, when wide-screen film-making came back in direct response to the erosion of box-office receipts
(10) because of the rising popularity of television. *This is Cinerama* (1952) is generally considered to mark the beginning of the modern era of wide-screen film-making, which saw another flurry of specialized formats, such as Cinemascope. In 1956,
(15) Panavision developed Camera 65 for MGM Studios; it was first used during the filming of *Raintree Country*. Panavision soon contributed another key technical advance by developing spherical 65mm lenses, which eliminated the "fat
(20) faces" syndrome that had plagued earlier CinemaScope films.

Some forty "roadshow" films were filmed in wide-screen formats during this period. But wide-screen formats floundered due to expense,
(25) unwieldy cameras, and slow film stocks and lenses. After the invention of a set of 35mm anamorphic lenses which could be used in conjunction with much more mobile cameras to squeeze a wide-screen image onto theatrical
(30) screens, film technology improved to the point where quality 70mm prints could be blown up from 35mm negatives.

28. It can be inferred from the passage's information that wide-film formats were

(A) in use before 1913

(B) not used during the 1940s

(C) more widely used during the 1920s than during the 1930s

(D) not used after 1956

(E) more widely used for some types of movies than for others

29. The passage mentions all the following as factors contributing to the increased use of wide-film formats for moviemaking EXCEPT:

(A) spherical camera lenses

(B) Panavision's Camera 65

(C) television

(D) anamorphic camera lenses

(E) movie theater revenues

30. Which of the following statements is most strongly supported by the passage's information?

(A) If a movie does not suffer from the "fat faces" syndrome, then it was not produced in a wide-film format.

(B) Prior to the invention of the 35mm anamorphic lens, quality larger prints could not be made from smaller negatives.

(C) The same factors that contributed to the resurgence of wide-film formats in the 1950s also led to the subsequent decline in their use.

(D) The most significant developments in 35mm technology occurred after the release of *Raintree Country*.

(E) Movie-theater revenues are not significantly affected by whether the movies shown are in wide-screen format.

31. Which of the following provides the most logical completion of the passage below?

    More and more consumers are being attracted to sport utility vehicles because they are safer to drive than regular cars, and because of the feeling of power a person experiences when driving a sport utility vehicle. In its current advertising campaign, Novo Auto Company emphasizes the low price of its new sport utility vehicle compared to the price of other such vehicles. This marketing strategy is unwise because _____.

    (A) Novo's sport utility vehicle is not as safe as those produced by competing automobile manufacturers

    (B) if Novo reduces the price of its sport utility vehicle even further Novo would sell even more of these vehicles

    (C) consumers who purchase sport utility vehicles associate affordability with a lack of safety features

    (D) most consumers who purchase sport utility vehicles are also concerned about the reliability of their vehicle

    (E) the retail price of Novo's most expensive luxury car is less than that of its new sport utility vehicle

32. Last year two drownings occurred at a nearby lake, so this year the lake's owner added one more lifeguard to the lakefront staff. No drownings have occurred at the lake this year. But the new lifeguard has remained at home due to illness for nearly half the summer, so it appears that the new lifeguard was not needed after all.

    Which of the following, if true, would most seriously jeopardize the argument above?

    (A) This year the lake's owner posted a warning about swimming without a lifeguard present.

    (B) Drowning is not the lake owner's only safety concern.

    (C) The lake has been equally crowded with swimmers this year as last year.

    (D) Lake activities are safer in the presence of lifeguards.

    (E) The new lifeguard has never saved a person from drowning.

33. *Advertisement:* In a recent survey, nine out of ten people using Slim-Ease for two weeks as directed reported that they lost weight during this period. This fact surely proves that Slim-Ease is effective for anyone wanting to shed some unwanted pounds.

    The claim made in the advertisement above depends on which of the following assumptions?

    (A) The survey participants were not using Slim-Ease immediately prior to the two-week period.

    (B) The survey participants did not exercise during the two-week period.

    (C) The survey participants were overweight prior to the two-week period.

    (D) No other product is more effective than Slim-Ease to help lose weight.

    (E) During the two-week period, the survey participants did not change their prior dietary habits.

34. New theoretical models about electromagnetic waves have actually enhanced astronomers' understanding of the evolution of stars to a greater extent than <u>observational data</u>.

    (A) observational data

    (B) that of observational data

    (C) data that has been observed

    (D) have observational datum

    (E) observational data have

35. <u>Inventors have yet to learn</u> that something that does two things does one of them better.

    (A) Inventors have yet to learn

    (B) Having not yet learned, inventors need to learn

    (C) Inventors have not as of yet learned

    (D) Inventors as yet have to learn

    (E) Not having yet learned, inventors have to learn

36. *Connie:* This season's new episodes of my favorite television program are even more entertaining then previous episodes, so the program should be even more popular this season than last season.

Karl: I disagree. After all, we both know that the chief aim of television networks is to maximize advertising revenue by increasing the popularity of their programs. But this season the television networks that compete with the one that broadcasts your favorite program are broadcasting re-runs of old programs during the same time slot as new episodes of your favorite program.

Which of the following, if true, would provide most support for Karl's line of reasoning in response to Connie's argument?

(A) The most common reason for a network to rerun a television program is that a great number of television viewers request the re-run.

(B) Entertaining television shows are not necessarily popular as well.

(C) Television networks generally schedule their most popular shows during the same time slots as their competitors' most popular shows.

(D) Certain educational programs that are not generally considered entertaining are nevertheless among the most popular programs.

(E) What Connie considers entertaining does not necessarily coincide with what most television viewers consider entertaining.

Questions 37–39 refer to the following passage:

When Ralph Waldo Emerson pronounced America's declaration of cultural independence from Europe in his "American Scholar" address, he was actually articulating the transcendental
(5) assumptions of Jefferson's political independence. In the ideal new world envisioned by Emerson, America's becoming a perfect democracy of free and self-reliant individuals was within reach. Bringing Emerson's metaphysics
(10) down to earth, Henry David Thoreau's *Walden*

(1854) asserted that one can live without encumbrances. Emerson wanted to visualize Thoreau as the ideal scholar in action that he had called for in the "American Scholar," but in the end,
(15) Emerson regretted Thoreau's too-private individualism, which failed to signal the vibrant revolution in national consciousness that Emerson had prophesied.

For Emerson, what Thoreau lacked, Walt
(20) Whitman embodied in full. On reading *Leaves of Grass* (1855), Emerson saw in Whitman the "prophet of democracy" whom he had sought. Other American Renaissance writers were less sanguine than Emerson and Whitman about the
(25) fulfillment of the democratic ideal. In *The Scarlet Letter* (1850), Nathaniel Hawthorne concluded that antinomianism such as the "heroics" displayed by Hester Prynne leads to moral anarchy; and Herman Melville, who saw in his story of
(30) *Pierre* (1852) a metaphor for the misguided assumptions of democratic idealism, declared the transcendentalist dream unrealizable. Ironically, the literary vigor with which both Hawthorne and Melville explored the ideal showed their
(35) deep sympathy with it even as they dramatized its delusions.

37. The author of the passage seeks primarily to

(A) explore the impact of the American Renaissance writers on the literature of the late Eighteenth Century

(B) illustrate how American literature of the mid-Eighteenth Century differed in form from European literature of the same time period

(C) identify two schools of thought among American Renaissance writers regarding the democratic ideal

(D) point out how Emerson's democratic idealism was mirrored by the works of the American Renaissance writers

(E) explain why the writers of the American Renaissance believed that an ideal world was forming in America

38. Based on the passage's information, Emerson might be characterized as any of the following EXCEPT:

    (A) a transcendentalist

    (B) an American Renaissance writer

    (C) a public speaker

    (D) a political prophet

    (E) a literary critic

39. With which of the following statements about Melville and Hawthorne would the author most likely agree?

    (A) Both men were disillusioned transcendentalists.

    (B) Hawthorne sympathized with the transcendental dream more so than Melville.

    (C) They agreed as to what the transcendentalist dream would ultimately lead to.

    (D) Both men believed the idealists to be misguided.

    (E) Hawthorne politicized the transcendental ideal, whereas Melville personalized it.

40. A certain species of wild bird known as the kiki bird breeds more effectively in certain temperatures than other temperatures. During the period from 1985 to 1990 the kiki bird population in the Gugana region declined, despite ideal breeding temperatures during the period. During the period from 1991 to 1995 the kiki bird population in the region increased, despite a moratorium, or official ban, on the hunting and killing of the kiki bird's chief predator throughout this period.

    Which of the following, if true, best explains why the kiki bird population declined during the period from 1985 to 1990, then increased during the period from 1991 to 1995?

    (A) During the period from 1990 to 1995, temperatures in the Gugana region were ideally suited for kiki bird breeding.

    (B) The moratorium is enforced during times when kiki bird breeding conditions are ideal, but not during other times.

    (C) Ideal breeding temperatures for the kiki bird's chief predator differ from those for the kiki bird.

    (D) During the period from 1985 to 1990 the population of the kiki bird's chief predator increased throughout the Gugana region.

    (E) Many kiki birds immigrated to the Gugana region from other regions during the period from 1991 to 1995.

41. While few truly great artists consider themselves visionary, many lesser talents boast about their own destiny to lead the way to higher artistic ground.

    (A) While few truly great artists consider themselves visionary, many lesser talents boast about their own destiny to lead the way to higher artistic ground.

    (B) While many lesser talents boast about their own destinies to lead the way to higher ground, few truly great artists consider themselves as visionary.

    (C) Many lesser talents boast about their own destiny to lead the way to higher artistic ground, while few truly great artists consider themselves as being visionary.

    (D) Few truly great artists consider himself or herself a visionary while many lesser talents boast about their own destinies to lead the way to higher artistic ground.

    (E) While many lesser talents boast about their own destiny, few truly great artists consider themselves visionary, to lead the way to higher artistic ground.

Quick Answer Guide

Practice Test: Verbal Ability

1. C	12. D	23. C	34. E
2. B	13. B	24. D	35. A
3. D	14. C	25. E	36. A
4. B	15. B	26. D	37. C
5. E	16. D	27. C	38. E
6. E	17. C	28. A	39. D
7. A	18. A	29. D	40. B
8. E	19. B	30. B	41. A
9. E	20. D	31. C	
10. D	21. B	32. C	
11. C	22. A	33. E	

Day 29

Practice Test: Review of Section 4 (Verbal Ability)

Today's Topics:

Today you will review yesterday's Verbal Ability practice test. Preceding each explanation, the question type and difficulty level are indicated.

EXPLANATIONS

1. The correct answer is (C). Sentence correction (easier).

The original sentence, choice (A), includes a misplaced modifying phrase (following the second comma). The sentence's construction suggests that it is the *electorate* that cannot reasonably be disputed, although this makes little sense in the context of the sentence as a whole.

Choice (B) suffers from a confusing syntax. It appears from the sentence's construction that the elected officials—rather than the fact that they ignored their electorate's wishes—cannot be disputed. Choice (B) also misplaces the prepositional phrases "on this issue" between the gerund "ignoring" and the object of that gerund, "the wishes of the electorate."

Choice (C) remedies the underlined phrase's faulty construction by rephrasing it as a noun clause.

Choice (D) improperly uses a comma between two clauses that do not constitute independent sentences on their own. Choice (D) also sets up a paral-lel between "were ignored . . . " and "cannot reasonably." Both phrases seem to refer to "the wishes of the electorate," although this is probably not the intended meaning.

Choice (E) is faulty in its use of the passive voice rather than the preferred active voice.

2. The correct answer is (B). Sentence correction (challenging).

The original sentence, choice (A), is a long sentence fragment with no predicate.

Choice (B) completes the sentence by reconstructing it.

Choice (C), like choice (A), is a long sentence fragment.

Choice (D) uses the idiomatically incorrect "which book is"; that phrase should exclude the word "book."

Choice (E) is unclear as to whether Francis Craig wrote all the books in the series or just the first three books.

3.The correct answer is (D). Sentence correction (moderate).

The original sentence, choice (A), is faulty in two respects. First, the sentence treats the compound subject ("interest rates" and "the supply of money") as singular by using "either . . . or"; the predicate should agree by also referring to the subject in the singular form, using "a factor" rather than "factors." Second, the verb phrase "can . . . be" is improperly split. Third, the phrase "can . . . be factors contributing to" is redundant and wordy.

Choice (B) is faulty in two respects. Choice (B) improperly separates the components of the progressive verb "can be." Also, the phrase "one or the other" duplicates the earlier phrase "either . . . or," resulting in redundancy and unnecessary wordiness.

Choice (C) improperly splits the progressive verb "can contribute," and also separates that verb from its modifying prepositional phrase "to the amount . . . "

Choice (D) remedies all the original sentence problems by uniting the verb parts, rewording the predicate to agree in form with the subject, and removing the redundant language.

Choice (E) improperly separates the preposition "to" and its object "the amount of . . . ," thereby confusing the meaning of the sentence (the improper construction suggests that interest rates and the supply of money contribute to the level of government spending).

4. The correct answer is (B). Assumption (moderate).

The argument relies on the unstated assumption that alcoholics die relatively young only because alcoholism increases a person's susceptibility to life-threatening diseases, and not for other reasons as well. Choice (C) provides explicitly that those other possible reasons were ruled out in compiling the insurance statistics cited in the report.

Choice (A) need not be assumed for the argument's conclusion to be inferable. In fact, choice (A) actually *weakens* the argument, by reversing the causal connection (between alcoholism and susceptibility to life-threatening diseases) upon which the argument relies.

Choice (C) need not be assumed for the argument's conclusion to be inferable. Even if alcoholism *does* increase a person's susceptibility to non-life-threatening diseases, this fact would have no effect on the causal connection between alcoholism and life-threatening diseases upon which the argument relies.

Choice (D) need not be assumed for the argument's conclusion to be inferable. Even if the reverse of choice (D) were true—that is, life expectancy of the non-alcoholic population *decreases* over time—it is still entirely possible that alcoholism serves to reduce life expectancy.

Choice (E) need not be assumed for the argument's conclusion to be inferable. Even if the report's author is biased about the morality of alcoholism, that bias would serve to undermine the argument only if the bias effected the report itself. Yet, the argument provides no evidence that this was the case.

5. The correct answer is (E). Probable-inference (challenging).

The passage indicates that developers have curtailed construction of new office buildings until demand grows to meet supply, while stepping up construction of single-family houses. This evidence in itself strongly supports choice (E). Admittedly, it is quite possible that an influx of businesses from other states will quickly deplete the current oversupply of office buildings and in fact create sufficient demand for new ones. Nevertheless, common sense informs us that for every new office building the demand for single-family housing increases manifold. Thus, on balance, choice (E) is the best of the five choices.

Choice (A) is not readily inferable from the passage. Although it is possible that the large corporations relocating to the state will employ many residents and thereby reduce the number of residents who work at home, the passage provides insufficient information to show that this will be the case. It is just as likely, for example, that most residents who work at home would continue to do so and that the number of self-employed residents who work at home will remain at current levels or perhaps even increase.

Choice (B) is not readily inferable from the passage. First of all, it is entirely possible that businesses relocating to the state due to the favorable tax climate will bring their employees with them, in which case increasing demand for single-family housing might very well continue to outpace the rate at which developers construct new housing. Secondly, choice (B) assumes that the population of the state will not increase for some other reason.

Choice (C) is not readily inferable. It is possible the large employers relocating to the state provide jobs whose compensation is low relative to the current average income. Also, other factors unrelated to the information in the passage might affect average income of state residents in the future. For example, an influx of retired persons might significantly increase the state's population while decreasing average income.

Choice (D) is not strongly inferable. Admittedly, an increase in supply will exert downward pressure on price. However, choice (D) involves the cost of *new* housing, and other factors—including the costs of building materials and labor as well as the price and availability of older housing—can also affect the price of a new house. Without considering these factors, it is unfair to conclude that the price of new single-family houses will decline. Moreover, corporations relocating to the state will in all likelihood bring their employees with them, and demand for single-family housing might very well continue to outpace supply as a result. In this event, the price of new homes might increase, not decrease.

6. The correct answer is (E). Interpretation (moderate).

Choice (E) is the best response. Choice (E) restates the author's point in the first paragraph that rates of species movement driven by human transformation of the natural environment and by human mobility dwarf natural rates by comparison.

The passage does not support choice (A). Although the author compares natural species movement to human-driven movement, the passage makes no such comparison between human modification of habitats and human mobility.

The passage also fails to support choice (B). The author makes no attempt to compare rate (interpreted either as frequency or speed) of species movement to total amounts of movement (distance).

The passage does not support choice (C). The author makes no attempt to compare natural expansions to natural contractions.

Choice (D) is nonsensical. Human mobility (commerce, tourism, and travel) do not create "natural" environments. It is human mobility itself, not the "natural environment" created by it, that contributes significantly to species movement.

7. The correct answer is (A). Interpretation (moderate).

Choice (A) is the best response. In the second paragraph's first sentence, the author claims that "[a] number of factors confound quantitative evaluation of the relative importance of various entry pathways." In the remainder of the paragraph, the author identifies three such problems: the difficulty of early detection, the inadequacy of port inspection, and the inherent subjectivity in determining the "importance" of a pathway.

Choice (B) is off focus and too narrow. Although the author does mention that a species is usually not detected until it spreads to at least 10,000 acres, the author mentions this single "event" leading to detection as part of the broader point that the unlikelihood of early detection contributes to the problem of quantifying the relative importance of entry pathways.

Choice (C) is off focus. Although the author mentions these factors, the passage does not discuss them in any detail, as choice (C) suggests. Also, the second paragraph's primary concern is not with identifying the factors affecting species detection but instead with identifying the problems in quantifying the relative importance of various entry pathways.

Choice (D) is too narrow. The author is concerned with identifying other problems as well as in determining the relative importance of various entry pathways.

Choice (E) is off focus. Although the author asserts that it is difficult to trace an entry pathway once a species is well established, the author does not explain why this is so.

8. The correct answer is (E). Explicit detail (easier).

Choice (E) is the best response. Nowhere in the passage does the author either state or imply that the physical size of a species' members affects whether the entry pathway for the species can be determined.

Choice (A) is the second-best response. Unlike choices (B), (C), and (D), choice (A) is not supported explicitly by the passage. However, the author mentions in the final paragraph that federal port inspection is "a major source of information on nonindigenous species pathways, especially for agricultural pests." Accordingly, whether a species is an agricultural pest might have some bearing on whether port inspectors detect its entry.

The second paragraph explicitly mentions choices (B), (C), and (D) as factors affecting how precisely the entry pathways of a species can be determined.

9. The correct answer is (E). Sentence correction (easier).

The original sentence, choice (A), confuses the subjunctive verb form (which deals with possibilities rather than facts) and past-perfect tense. Choice (A) also includes a disagreement in pronoun reference; "scientific community" is singular in form, calling for the singular pronoun "it" rather than "they."

Choice (B) includes a disagreement in verb tense. The progressive verb "would not be" is in the present-perfect tense, whereas the verb "had . . . become" is in the past-perfect tense. Moreover, in the context of the sentence as a whole, neither tense is appropriate; the subjunctive verb form should be used instead.

Choice (C) properly uses the subjunctive form ("were") but fails to remedy the incorrect pronoun reference ("they") in the original sentence.

Choice (D) improperly expresses the idea to be conveyed in the past tense ("when the scientific community became") rather than in the appropriate subjunctive verb form.

Choice (E) remedies both problems in the original sentence. It uses the subjunctive form consistently—at both the beginning and end of the phrase.

It also replaces the incorrect plural pronoun "they" with "scientists."

10. The correct answer is (D). Weakening-evidence (easier).

The argument relies on the assumption that the furlough program is responsible for, or at least contributes to, a prisoner's refraining from committing crimes after release. One effective way of weakening the argument is to refute this assumption, by providing evidence that the program does *not* contribute to the reform of prisoners. Choice (D) provides such evidence. Specifically, choice (D) strongly suggests that program participants would have been less likely than non-participants to commit crimes after being released whether or not they participated in the program.

Choice (A) provides no useful information to determine whether or not the program is effective.

Choice (B) actually tends to *support* the argument by providing additional evidence, albeit weak, that furlough programs are effective in reducing crime.

Choice (C) provides insufficient information to assess either the strength or weakness of the argument.

Choice (E) raises the possibility that the percentage of prisoners participating in the program *might* not be large enough to allow one to assess its effectiveness with a high degree of certainty. If the percentage is very low (for example, 5 percent) then choice (E) would significantly weaken the argument; but as this percentage approaches 50 percent, choice (E) would actually tend to strengthen the argument. Thus, without additional information about the percent of prisoners participating in the program, choice (E) accomplishes little toward either weakening or supporting the argument.

11. The correct answer is (C). Supporting-evidence (challenging).

The argument concludes that the reason for the military's decision was to reduce pilot error during commercial flights. Choice (C) is the only answer choice that supports this conclusion. Given that chemical warfare is likely to escalate in the future, it would seem that the military would *continue* to require immunization shots. But the military stopped requiring the shots. So, the military's decision must have been based on some factor outweighing the potential danger of chemical warfare to pilots. One possible such factor is the increased danger of commercial airline accidents resulting from the immunization shots.

Choice (A) weakens the argument, by providing a plausible alternative reason why the military decided to no longer require the shots.

Choice (B) weakens the argument. Choice (B) provides evidence that pilot error is more critical during military flights than commercial flights. Accordingly, choice (B) shows that the reason for the military's decision to no longer require shots is that it endangers pilots during *military* flights, not commercial flights.

Choice (D) weakens the argument, by providing a plausible alternative reason why the military decided to no longer require the shots. Specifically, the military wished to prevent more pilots from resigning.

Choice (E) weakens the argument, by providing evidence that the danger that the immunization program poses for commercial airliners is less significant than it would be otherwise. This in turn makes it less likely that the military's decision was based on a concern for the safety of commercial flights.

12. The correct answer is (D). Sentence correction (challenging).

The original sentence, choice (A), suffers from faulty parallelism. The second occurrence of "from" should be deleted to restore the proper parallelism between the phrases "the host" and "the diplomat's." At the same time, the word "both" in choice (A) is redundant in light of the words "the other" at the end of the sentence, thereby confusing the meaning of the sentence.

Choice (B) remedies the original sentence's problems but presents a usage problem. The phrase "each other" properly refers to only two persons or things. Because the potential number of "citizens" (guests) might exceed two, "one another" should be used instead.

Choice (C) suggests a nonsensical meaning—that the *country* itself (rather than a person) seats its citizens. The construction also creates ambiguity as to what the rules require.

Choice (D) remedies the original sentence's faulty parallelism by reconstructing the phrase, using the subjunctive form ("that . . . be").

Choice (E) is faulty in two respects. It includes the word "to" twice; the second occurrence is redundant and should be excluded. Also, the use of double possessive adjectives—"diplomat's" and "country's"—is improper.

13. The correct answer is (B). Sentence correction (easier).

Choice (A) is faulty because the plural subject "benefits" is followed by the singular verb "is."

Choice (B) remedies the original sentence's problem by using the plural "are," which agrees with "benefits."

Choice (C) improperly uses the word "furthering," suggesting that exercise is a benefit or goal that is being furthered.

Choice (D) improperly uses the subjunctive verb form ("would be") instead of the more appropriate present tense ("are").

Choice (E) improperly uses the subjunctive verb form ("would be") instead of the more appropriate present tense ("are").

14. The correct answer is (C). Sentence correction (moderate).

The original statement, choice (A), includes an ambiguous pronoun reference. It is unclear whether "they" refers to the bounty hunters, their captives, or the authorities.

Choice (B) is illogically constructed. It appears from choice (B) that the authorities turn over captives to themselves. Also, the antecedent of "them" is unclear.

Choice (C) remedies the original sentence's ambiguous pronoun reference by reconstructing the sentence.

Choice (D) is ambiguous and confusing. It is unclear whether the modifying phrase following the comma refers to bounty hunters, their captives, or the authorities.

Choice (E) is faulty in two respects. First, it is awkwardly constructed; the modifying phrase (set off by commas) belongs at the beginning of the sentence so that the other two (related) parts of the sentence are closer to each other. Second, the plural "bounty hunters" disagrees with the singular "captive," thereby confusing the sentence's meaning.

15. The correct answer is (B). Interpretation (easier).

Choice (B) is the best response. According to the passage, the ambiguous position of Soviet scientists was that the Soviet government encouraged and generally supported scientific research, while at the same time it imposed significant restrictions on its scientists. Choice (B) restates this idea.

The passage does not support choice (A). The author neither states nor suggests that the Soviets lacked sufficient funding; moreover, although choice (A), if true, would indicate an ambiguous position for scientists, it is not the nature of the ambiguity to which the passage refers.

Choice (C) is wholly unsupported. The author neither states nor suggests either assertion made in statement choice (C).

The passage supports choice (D) (albeit, not explicitly) and, if choice (D) is true, it presents an ambiguous position for Soviet scientists. However, the ambiguity to which choice (D) refers fails to reflect the nature of the ambiguity to which the passage refers.

The passage does not support choice (E). Although the government indeed punished some Soviet scientists, the author neither states nor implies that the government failed to identify those areas of research that it deemed most worthwhile. Moreover, although choice (E), if true, would indicate an ambiguous position for scientists, it is not the nature of the ambiguity to which the passage refers.

16. The correct answer is (D). Purpose of detail (moderate).

Choice (D) is the best response. This part of the passage is concerned exclusively with pointing out evidence of the Soviet emphasis on a national science;

given the content of the excerpt from *Literatunaya Gazeta*, you can reasonably infer that the author is quoting this article as one such piece of evidence.

Choice (B) is the second-best response. The quoted article does indeed reflect the Marxist-Leninist ideal (at least as interpreted and promulgated by the government) and might in fact have been published only because the Soviet government sanctioned it. However, choice (B) is not likely to be the author's purpose in quoting the article, because this conclusion would require speculation and because the quoted excerpt does not mention government approval or disapproval of certain scientific notions.

Choice (A) distorts the nature of the quoted article and runs contrary to the passage. The article illustrates the official Soviet position and possibly the sentiment among some members of the Soviet intellectual or scientific community. However, the article does not necessarily reflect the views of scientists from other countries.

Choice (C) is not likely to be the author's purpose in quoting the article, because the author does not discuss disagreement and debate among Soviet intellectuals.

Choice (E) is not likely to be the author's purpose in quoting the article. Although the assertion mentioned in choice (E) might in fact be true and indeed be supported by the passage's information, the author gives no indication as to when the article was written or published; thus, the article itself lends no support to the assertion mentioned in choice (E).

17. The correct answer is (C). Primary purpose (moderate).

Choice (C) is the best response. The passage as a whole is indeed concerned with describing Soviet attempts to suppress scientific freedom.

Choice (D) is the second-best response. Although the last paragraph briefly discusses other attempts at suppression of scientific freedom in the 20th Century, the passage does not examine these attempts; thus, choice (D) is too broad.

Choice (A) is off focus and far too narrow; moreover, the author does not actually discuss any specific events that might have caused the suppression of the refusenik movement; rather, the passage mentions this historical phenomenon simply as another example of the Soviet regime's long-term pattern of suppression.

Choice (B) is off focus and misses the author's attitude. Although the author does define the concept of national science, the passage makes no attempt to dispel or disprove the concept.

Choice (E) is too narrow and is off focus. Although the author does imply that scientific freedom and scientific internationalism are related, the passage makes no attempt to examine their differences; moreover, the author's broader concern is quite different than to examine the relationship between these two types of scientific freedoms.

18. The correct answer is (A). Weakening-evidence (easier).

The claim relies on the assumption that no factor other than Nico-Gone could have been responsible for the results reported by the participants who were administered Nico-Gone. Choice (A) refutes this assumption by providing evidence that another treatment might have been responsible for the decline in the number of smokers among those participants.

Choice (B) actually *supports* the claim, by providing evidence that the results as reported by the subjects themselves are likely to be reliable.

Choice (C) actually *strengthens* the claim, by asserting the factuality of another assumption on which the claim depends. (If cigarettes were unavailable to some of the subjects during the year, this fact would be the primary explanation for any decrease in the number of smokers among the subjects.)

Choice (D) depends on additional unknown evidence for it to weaken the claim. Specifically, choice (D) fails to distinguish between the subjects receiving Nico-Gone and those receiving the placebo. Choice (D) also fails to account for the possibility that the number of subjects who smoked changed during the year immediately preceding the experiment (and fails to compare the amount and direction of any such change as between participants who were administered Nico-Gone and those who were administered the placebo).

Choice (E) is not directly relevant to the argument, which seeks to explain changes in smoking habits *only* among two groups of study participants.

19. The correct answer is (B). Necessary-inference (moderate).

John's statement does *not* logically infer, as Jolanda seems to think, that a person must believe in the inevitability of success in order to be successful. Choice (B) is an effective rebuttal for John because it points out this possible error in Jolanda's reasoning.

Choice (A) would not be an effective rebuttal. Neither John's argument nor Jolanda's response suggests that they disagree about the definition of success (specifically, whether one's success is defined by oneself or by others).

Choice (C) would not be an effective rebuttal. Considered along with John's original statement, choice (C) would merely add that some people believe in the inevitability of success. This assertion does not directly address Jolanda's point that some successful people did not consider that they might become successful.

Choice (D) would not be an effective rebuttal. Neither John nor Jolanda appear to disagree about the definition of success.

Choice (E) would not be an effective rebuttal. Choice (E) would help make the point that some successful people (especially, some successful men) might consider themselves successful. However, this is not John's point.

20. The correct answer is (D). Assumption (challenging).

The argument relies on two important but unstated assumptions. One is that the teachers who transferred from Franklin to Valley View were Vining graduates; the other is that teachers who transferred from Valley View to Franklin were not Vining graduates. If neither or only one were the case, then it would be unreasonable to conclude that Vining graduates are responsible for high academic performance. Admittedly, these assumptions involve a matter of degree; for example, the greater the percentage of Vining alumni among the teachers transferring from Franklin to Valley View, the stronger the argument's conclusion. And admittedly, choice (D) does not acknowledge this fact. Nevertheless, choice (D) provides the essence of one of these two crucial assumptions.

Choice (A) is irrelevant to the argument. The argument provides no evidence to suggest that the transferring teachers use any grading system other than the one used by all other teachers at their current school. Whether the schools differ in their grading methods is irrelevant, as long as each school has continued to use the same system consistently.

Choice (B) is not a necessary assumption. Admittedly, if true, choice (B) would lend support to the argument, by ruling out one alternative explanation for the decrease in median GPA at one school and increase in median GPA at the other school. However, choice (B) rules out only this one single explanation, leaving available many other possible explanations. (For example, perhaps Valley View received significantly more funding than Franklin School last year, allowing Valley View to improved its computer lab, which in turn enhanced the median GPA of its students.)

Choice (C) is not a necessary assumption. If true, choice (C) would appear to lend support to an argument that the teachers who transferred from Franklin are more effective teachers than those who transferred from Valley View to Franklin. However, we are not informed what percentage of the teachers who transferred in each direction were Vining graduates. Without this information, it is impossible to determine the extent to which Vining's credential program can be credited with high academic performance of its alumni's students.

Choice (E) can easily be ruled out as a necessary assumption because it actually serves to *weaken* the argument, by providing evidence that Vining University contributes to *lower* grade point averages among its graduate's students.

21. The correct answer is (B). Supporting-evidence (moderate).

Choice (B) is needed in order to conclude that biotechnology firms will in fact continue to replace equipment more frequently than other businesses will, and therefore will stand to benefit from the proposed law more than other businesses. (Unless the biotechnology industry is likely to benefit from the proposed law more than other industries, the argument's claim that the biotechnology lobbyists are the ones behind the proposal is untenable.)

Choice (A) also supports the claim by showing that biotechnology firms stand more to gain from the proposed tax law than any other industry. However, choice (A) is not a necessary assumption. As long as biotechnology equipment will be replaced more quickly than other business equipment, biotechnology firms will stand more to gain from the proposed law even if their equipment is worth no more than other business equipment.

Choice (C) also supports the claim, by showing that the biotechnology industry has enough political clout to instigate the proposal. However, choice (C) is not a necessary assumption. Absent evidence to the contrary, the biotechnology industry does not necessarily require a political operative inside the legislature in order for this industry to be the catalyst for the proposal.

Choice (D) also supports the claim, by ruling out certain other possible catalysts for the proposal. Absent more information, however, choice (D) does not rule out a myriad of other possible catalysts—for example, non-profit health organizations, government economic advisors, or the legislators themselves.

Choice (E) provides no support for the claim, which is that biotechnology companies, as opposed to companies from other industries, are behind the proposal.

22. The correct answer is (A). Sentence correction (moderate).

The original sentence, choice (A), includes a compound subject, expressed as a noun clause (the first part of the sentence through "aimed"). Choice (A) properly uses "who" as one of the sentence's subjects and properly uses "whom" as an indirect object.

Choice (B) incorrectly uses "whom" as one of the sentence's subjects.

Choice (C) is awkwardly constructed. "Who are the terrorists" poses a question and does not parallel the other subject ("at whom . . . aimed").

Choice (D) omits the preposition "at," resulting in a nonsensical phrase. Also, choice (D) is vague as to whom the pronoun "they" refers.

Choice (E) improperly uses the preposition "to" instead of "at," suggesting that the terrorists' activities were aimed *to* a particular target.

23. The correct answer is (C). Sentence correction (challenging).

The original sentence, choice (A), is faulty in its use of the pronoun *them* instead of the possessive *their* where the object of a verb ("opposed") is a verbal noun ("idealizing") that is not the musicians themselves but instead their actions or traits.

Choice (B) improperly adds the word "of." A person is said to trivialize something (direct object), not trivialize *of* something.

Choice (C) corrects the improper use of "them," replacing it with the possessive "their," which properly precedes the gerund noun "trivializing."

Choice (D) employs the awkward passive voice instead of the preferred active voice.

Choice (E) is awkward and confusing. It is unclear whether the modifying phrase beginning with "when" refers to Blakey or earlier jazz musicians.

24. The correct answer is (D). Sentence correction (moderate).

In the original statement, choice (A), the phrase "Even for high school freshmen and sophomores" and the phrase "for many such students" are redundant.

Choice (B) is constructed in a way that confuses the meaning as well as nonsensically equating "high school students" with "theories."

Choice (C) inserts the modifying phrase "for many high school freshmen and sophomores" between two closely related ideas. The author should connect those ideas syntactically by moving the modifying phrase to either the beginning or the end of the sentence.

Choice (D) moves the initial prepositional phrase to the end of the sentence and eliminates the redundancy.

Choice (E) employs improper diction. It is awkward to speak of a person's interest as "held in" a particular subject.

25. The correct answer is (E). Probable-inference (challenging).

Assuming the number of viable competitors has increased during the last two years, the likely result would be to draw circulation away from preexisting newspapers, including the most profitable one. Given that profitability depends primarily on advertising revenues and therefore on circulation, choice (E) actually exacerbates the discrepancy between the two statements.

Choices (A) and (D) help explain why the most profitable newspaper remains most profitable even though its circulation is declining: advertisers have not yet begun to switch because the most profitable newspaper is still the most widely circulated.

Choice (B) helps explain the discrepancy. Although the argument provides that advertisers are more likely to advertise with widely circulated newspapers than with others, it is entirely possible that other factors, such as advertising rates charged by the newspaper, also affect which newspapers advertisers choose.

Choice (C) helps explain the discrepancy, by identifying another source of revenue and therefore another means of enhancing profitability. Simply stated, the more sources of revenue, the more profitable a newspaper is likely to be. This in turn helps explain why the most profitable newspaper in the city remains the most profitable one, despite declining circulation. Admittedly, as circulation decreases so does subscriber revenue, and thus overall profitability. Yet, the newspaper's profitability is still greater than it would be without revenue from its subscribers.

26. The correct answer is (D). Parallel-argument (moderate).

Here is the argument's essential reasoning:

Premise: If fluorocarbons are emitted, then ozone depletion will occur.

Conclusion: If fluorocarbons are not emitted, then ozone depletion will not occur.

It is useful to express this reasoning symbolically as follows:

    Premise: If A, then B.

    Conclusion: If not A, then not B.

The reasoning is fallacious, because it fails to account for other possible causes of ozone depletion. (B might occur whether or not A occurs.)

Choice (D) is the only answer choice the demonstrates the same essential pattern of flawed reasoning:

    Premise: If a person with phlebitis takes Anatol, the phlebitis will be controlled.

    Conclusion: If a person does not take Anatol, the phlebitis will not be controlled.

Note that choice (D) begins with the conclusion, whereas the original argument begins with the premise. This fact makes no difference, however, in assessing the reasoning itself.

27. The correct answer is (C). Sentence correction (moderate).

The original sentence, choice (A), is faulty in two respects. First, it improperly uses "because" instead of "because of." Second, the construction leaves it unclear as to whether the modifying phrase "already in wide use" refers to "other pesticides" or to "chemical compositions."

Choice (B) misuses the phrase "because of." The author should follow this prepositional phrase with a modifying clause by inserting a comma followed by "which" after "in wide use" ("in wide use, which ... ").

Choice (C) corrects the misuse of "because" by replacing it with "due to." Choice (C) also changes the sentence's structure to clarify its meaning.

Choice (D) is redundant in its use of both "since" and "due to." This redundancy results, in turn, in an awkward construction.

Choice (E) misplaces the adverbial clause "already in use," which is intended to refer not to "chemical compositions" but rather to "other pesticides."

28. The correct answer is (A). Inference (moderate).

Choice (A) is the best response. The passage refers to the establishment of a *de facto* 35mm standard around 1913, followed by a "resurgence" of wide-film formats (in the mid-1920s to the mid-1930s). This resurgence suggests that wide-film formats were not new because they had been used before the 35mm standard was established—that is, before 1913.

Choice (B) distorts the passage's information. The passage does indicate that research and development slackened between the mid-1930s and the beginning of the modern era of wide-screen moviemaking (the early 1950s). However, the author neither states nor implies that wide-film formats fell into complete disuse during this interim period.

Choice (C) distorts the passage's information. The author makes no comparison between the 1920s and the 1930s in terms of the extent to which wide-film formats were used. The passage indicates only that "[t]he mid-1920s through the mid-1930s saw a resurgence of wide-film formats."

The passage does not strongly support choice (D), but suggests only that the 25mm format began again to dominate film-making after 1956.

Choice (E) alludes to information that the passage does not discuss. Nowhere in the passage does the author either state or imply that wide-film formats were used more commonly for some types of movies than for others.

29. The correct answer is (D). Explicit detail (easier).

Choice (D) is the best response. According to the passage's last sentence, anamorphic lenses, used with more mobile cameras, made it possible to create quality 70mm prints from 35mm negatives. In this respect, the invention of the anamorphic camera lens contributed to the demise (not the increased use) of wide-film moviemaking.

The passage discusses choice (A) as a key technical advance in wide-film format technology. The spherical 65mm lens eliminated the "fat faces" syndrome (presumably, wide-film images were thereby made to appear more realistic). Accordingly, this new type of lens contributed to the increased use of the wide-film format.

The author indirectly refers to choice (B) as a key technical advance in wide-film format technology. In mentioning that "Panavision soon contributed another key technical advance," the author implies that Camera 65 was also a key technical advance.

The second paragraph's first sentence mentions choice (C) as one of two factors that prompted the resurgence in the 1950s of the wide-film format.

The same sentence mentions choice (E) as one of two factors that prompted the resurgence in the 1950s of the wide-film format.

30. The correct answer is (B). Interpretation (moderate).

Choice (B) is the best response. The passage's final sentence states that after the invention of the 35mm anamorphic lens, quality 70mm (larger) prints could be made from 35mm (smaller) negatives. It is reasonable to assume that larger prints could not be made from smaller negatives prior to that invention.

Choice (A) calls for an illogical inference that contradicts the passage's information. The author states that the invention of the spherical 65mm lens "eliminated the 'fat faces' syndrome that had plagued earlier CinemaScope films." CinemaScope was one of the specialized wide-film formats. Thus, if a particular movie does not suffer from the "fat faces" syndrome, it could very well have been produced in wide-film format with a spherical 65mm lens.

Choice (C) runs contrary to the passage's information. According to the passage, the advent of television and the resulting decline in box-office revenues prompted the resurgence of wide-film formats in the 1950s. The author identifies several factors as contributing to the subsequent demise of wide-film formats: expenses, unwieldy cameras, slow film stocks and lenses, the invention of the anamorphic lenses, and mobile cameras. However, the passage does not mention the popularity of television or box-office receipts among those factors.

Choice (D) distorts the passage's information. The only post-*Raintree Country* technological developments that the passage mentions are the invention of anamorphic lenses and more mobile cameras. Although such developments were probably significant in the development of 35mm technology, to suggest that these innovations were the most significant

developments in 35mm technology (as choice (D) suggests) exaggerates the author's point.

Choice (E) runs contrary to the passage's information. The information in the second paragraph suggests that it was in response to eroding box-office revenues that the movie industry stepped up its efforts to improve wide-screen technology. Moreover, based on the author's discussion of the modern era of wide-screen filmmaking, these attempts apparently were successful, at least until other problems (such as expense, unwieldy cameras, and slow film stocks and lenses) made continued use of wide-film format unfeasible.

31. The correct answer is (C). Supporting-evidence (easier).

The passage boils down to the following:
Premise: People buy sport utility vehicles because they believe these vehicles are safe.
Conclusion: To sell a vehicle a manufacturer should not emphasize affordability.
Choice (C) provides the unstated assumption needed to render the argument logically convincing:
Premise: People buy sport utility vehicles because they believe these vehicles are safe.
Premise (C): People do not believe that affordable vehicles are safe.
Conclusion: To sell a sport utility vehicle a manufacturer should not emphasize its affordability.
Choice (A) provides a reason not to emphasize safety, but does not provide a reason not to emphasize affordability.

Choice (B) provides merely that Novo's sport utility vehicle would be even more attractive were it priced lower; choice (B) is accomplishes nothing toward explaining why Novo should not emphasize affordability.

Choice (D) provides a reason to emphasize reliability, but not a reason to de-emphasize affordability. It is possible, for example, that consumers are equally concerned about these two factors.

Choice (E) provides a reason for Novo to de-emphasize the price of its sport utility vehicle compared to the price of its luxury car, not compared to other sport utility vehicles.

32. The correct answer is (C). Weakening-evidence (moderate).

The argument's conclusion is that the new lifeguard was *not* a factor in the declining number of deaths from last year to this year. Choice (C) rules out one other possible explanation for the decline in the number of drownings, in turn rendering it more likely that the additional lifeguard *did* contribute to the decline. Here's the effect of choice (C) on the argument, in a nutshell:

Premise: There have been fewer drownings this year than last year.

Premise (C): The number of swimmers doesn't explain the decline in the number of drownings.

Conclusion: The additional lifeguard more likely accounts for the decline.

Choice (A) actually *strengthens* the argument, by providing evidence that swimmers might have been more cautious this year because of the posted warning, and therefore lifeguards were not as necessary as they would have been otherwise.

Choice (B) is not directly relevant to the argument, which seeks to evaluate the new lifeguard's effectiveness only with respect to drowning.

Choice (D) provides no useful information, as it stands. In order to evaluate the effect of choice (D) on the argument, we would need more specific information—about the degree of safety afforded by one additional lifeguard.

Choice (E) actually *strengthens* the argument in two respects. First, choice (E) provides some evidence that the new lifeguard is ineffective (and therefore that *this particular lifeguard* was not needed). Second, even if the lifeguard would be effective in saving swimmers from drowning if given the chance, choice (E) provides evidence that the lifeguard was not needed this year anyway.

33. The correct answer is (E). Assumption (moderate).

The advertisement's claim relies on the unstated assumption that all other factors known to cause weight loss—such as exercise and dietary habits—remained unchanged from prior to the two-week period through the two-week period.

Choice (A) is not a necessary assumption; whether the survey participants were already using Slim-Ease is irrelevant in determining whether the product was effective during the two-week period.

Choice (B) is not a necessary assumption. Even if the survey participants did exercise during the period, and even if exercise contributed to their weight loss, it is entirely possible that Slim-Ease also contributed to the weight loss. Also, it is entirely possible that exercise would not have contributed to weight loss in any event, depending on the amount and type of exercise.

Choice (C) is not a necessary assumption. Without evidence to the contrary, whether a person is overweight to begin with is irrelevant to whether a particular product causes weight loss.

Choice (D) is not a necessary assumption. The advertisement does not make any claims about the effectiveness of Slim-Ease compared to that of any other product. The advertisement merely claims that Slim-Ease causes weight loss.

34. The correct answer is (E). Sentence correction (challenging).

The original sentence, choice (A), makes an illogical comparison between "the evolution of stars" and "observational data."

Choice (B) makes an illogical comparison between "that of observational data" and "electromagnetic waves." The word "that" does not logically refer to anything and should be excluded.

Choice (C) fails to remedy the original sentence's flaw.

Choice (D) improperly uses the distinctively singular noun "datum" along with the plural verb "have."

Choice (E) establishes the logical comparison between "new theoretical models" and "observational data" by including the verb "have." The noun "data" is plural, so the verb "have" is proper here.

35. The correct answer is (A). Sentence correction (easier).

The original sentence, choice (A), is correct in its use of the idiomatic phrase "have yet to."

Choice (B) is redundant and awkward; "having not yet learned" and "need to learn" convey essentially the same idea. Also, it is unclear what inventors have not yet learned.

Choice (C) uses the improper "as of yet."

Choice (D) shifts perspective (tense) in midsentence from the present ("as yet") to the future ("have to learn").

Choice (E) is redundant and awkward in a manner similar to choice (B).

36. The correct answer is (A). Supporting-evidence (challenging).

Karl's rebuttal relies on two alternative but interrelated assumptions: (1) the reruns are likely to be popular enough to compete with Connie's favorite program, and (2) Connie's favorite program will not in fact be popular. (A) provides evidence that helps affirm both of these assumptions, by suggesting that the reruns might very well be popular enough to draw the viewing audience away from Connie's favorite program, thus rendering it less popular. Admittedly, choice (A) would provide even greater support if it explicitly indicated that one popular program can draw viewers away from another. Nevertheless, choice (A) is the best among the five answer choices.

Choice (B) provides *some* evidence that Connie's favorite *might* not be popular, thereby weakening Connie's argument that because the program is entertaining it will be popular. However, choice (B) allows for the possibility that Connie's favorite program will nevertheless be popular.

Choice (C) would strengthen Karl's rebuttal only under the assumption that reruns are likely to be popular. In other words, choice (C) relies on the evidence provided by choice (A).

Choice (D) would help support Karl's rebuttal only if the reruns to which Karl refers are educational programs that were very popular when originally aired and are likely to be popular as reruns. Yet, we are not informed that this is the case. Thus, choice (D) is ineffective as it stands in supporting Karl's rebuttal.

Choice (E) does admittedly serve to weaken Connie's argument. However, Connie's statement is vague as to whether her favorite program is entertaining just to her or to many other people as well. If the latter is the case, choice (E) would provide no useful information to evaluate either Connie's argument or Karl's rebuttal. Moreover, we are not informed whether entertaining shows are necessarily popular. Without this additional information, choice (E) is not useful to evaluate either Connie's argument or Karl's rebuttal. Finally, while choice (E) tends to weaken Connie's argument, it fails to provide *affirmative* support Karl's rebuttal.

37. The correct answer is (C). Primary purpose (moderate).

Choice (C) is the best response. The passage describes an imaginary debate over the American democratic ideal among the writers of the American Renaissance, in which Emerson, Thoreau, and Whitman are grouped together in one school of thought while Hawthorne and Melville are paired in another.

The passage does not support choice (A). The author does not "explore" the impact of the American Renaissance writers to any extent.

The passage also fails to support choice (B). The author makes no further attempt to distinguish American forms from European forms.

Choice (D) is the second-best response. Admittedly, Emerson's idealism was reflected in the works of Thoreau and Whitman insofar as they too shared the transcendentalists' dream. However, choice (D) distorts the passage's information. The author actually points out that Thoreau's "too-private individualism" was not in accord with what Emerson hoped for. In this sense, the author is pointing out how Thoreau's *Walden* failed to accurately mirror Emerson's idealism. In addition, although the passage does strongly suggest that, through his works, Whitman fully reflected Emerson's ideal American scholar, the passage does not discuss how Whitman's works serve this end. Thus, the passage does not support choice (D) as well as choice (C).

Choice (E) distorts the passage's information. The only event that the passage mentions that might have contributed to the idealist mind set of the times was Jefferson's declaration of political independence. However, the author does not actually claim that it was because of Jefferson (in whole or in part) that the writers of the American Renaissance believed that an ideal world was forming in America. Moreover, the passage does not discuss any other reasons that the American Renaissance writers might have believed as they did.

38. The correct answer is (E). Interpretation (moderate).

Choice (E) is the best response. Although in criticizing Thoreau's *Walden* (a literary work), Emerson could be viewed as playing the role of literary critic, this suggestion is a bit attenuated. Moreover, the passage supports all other answer choices more strongly.

The assertion that Emerson "was actually articulating the transcendental assumptions of Jefferson's political independence" implies choice (A).

The statement that "the other writers of the American Renaissance were less sanguine than Emerson and Whitman about the fulfillment of the democratic ideal" implies choice (B).

The passage's first sentence implies choice (C), referring to Emerson's "American Scholar" address. The word "address" suggests a public speech, and it was Emerson himself who was the speaker (he "pronounced").

The passage supports choice (D). The author asserts that Thoreau "failed to signal the vibrant revolution in national consciousness that Emerson had prophesied." Also, the passage supports the idea that Emerson anticipated and predicted that America would become "a perfect democracy of free and self-reliant individuals."

39. The correct answer is (D). Interpretation (challenging).

Choice (D) is the best response. According to the passage, Melville, through his story of *Pierre*, conveyed the notion that democratic idealism was based on "misguided assumptions." Although the author is not so explicit that Hawthorne also believed idealists to be misguided, Hawthorne's conclusion that transcendental freedom leads to moral anarchy can reasonably be interpreted as such.

Choice (A) is the second-best response. According to the passage, both men sympathized with the democratic ideal, which was part of the transcendental dream. In this respect, it can be argued that both men were transcendentalists at heart. Also, Hawthorne concluded that transcendental freedom would lead to moral anarchy, whereas Melville declared the dream unrealizable. In this sense, then, both men were disillusioned with the transcendental dream. However, the author states that for Emerson—a transcendentalist—the democratic ideal seemed "within reach," whereas for Hawthorne and Melville, the ideal was clearly not within reach. Accordingly, to categorize them as transcendentalists would contradict the author's description of the transcendental viewpoint.

The passage does not support choice (B). The passage states that both men sympathized with the transcendental dream. However, the author neither states nor implies that one of these two men sympathized with the transcendental dream more than the other.

The passage also fails to support choice (C). According to the passage, Hawthorne believed that personal "heroics" lead to moral anarchy, whereas Melville believed that the transcendental dream was unrealizable. This information suggests neither agreement nor disagreement between the two men as to what the transcendental dream would ultimately lead to.

Choice (E) confuses the passage's information. The passage suggests just the opposite. It can be argued that Melville politicized transcendentalism in that, through his metaphorical story of *Pierre*, he revealed the problems of democratic idealism. At the same time, Hawthorne personalized transcendentalism through the actions of an individual character (Hester Prynne) in *The Scarlet Letter*.

40. The correct answer is (B). Probable-inference (moderate).

Given the information provided in choice (B), along with the fact that kiki bird breeding temperatures were ideal from 1985 to 1990, the moratorium must have been enforced during that period. The moratorium would tend to stabilize and perhaps even result in an increase in the population of the kiki bird's chief predator, thereby explaining the decreasing kiki bird population during the period. Conversely, from 1991 to 1995, since the moratorium was enforced breeding conditions must have been ideal, which helps explain the increase in the kiki bird population during that period.

Choice (A) explains why the kiki bird population increased from 1991 to 1995, but not why the kiki bird population declined from 1985 and 1990.

Choice (C) actually contributes to the paradox presented in the passage, by providing another reason why the kiki bird population should have *increased* during the period from 1985 to 1990.

Choice (D) explains why the kiki bird population decreased from 1985 to 1990, but not why the kiki bird population increased from 1991 to 1995.

Choice (E) explains why the kiki bird population increased during the period from 1991 to 1995, but not why the kiki bird population decreased during the period from 1985 to 1990.

41. The correct answer is (A). Sentence correction (challenging).

Choice (A) is the best response. The original sentence contains no grammatical errors, ambiguous references, or idiomatically improper words or phrases. The word "visionary," used as an adjective here, is proper, although you could use the word "visionaries" (a noun) instead.

Choice (B) incorrectly uses the plural "destinies" to describe a singular idea. The word "as" in choice (B) is idiomatically incorrect and should either be deleted or replaced with the infinitive "to be."

In choice (C) the phrase "as being" is idiomatically improper here and should either be removed or replaced with the infinitive "to be."

Choice (D) is faulty in two respects. In the first part of the sentence, the subject and verb disagree in number: "few" suggests plurality, whereas "himself or herself" suggests singularity (as does "a visionary"). Choice (D), like choice (B), incorrectly uses the plural "destinies" to describe a singular idea.

Choice (E) is faulty in that the phrase following the second comma is separated from the term to which it refers ("destiny"). This misplaced modifier results in a confusing overall syntax that obscures the sentence's meaning.

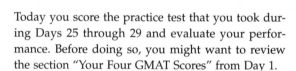

Day 30

Evaluating Your Practice Test Scores

Today's Topics:

1.   Determining your Analytical Writing Assessment (AWA) score
2.   Determining your Verbal, Quantitative, and total scaled scores
3.   Interpreting your scaled scores

Today you score the practice test that you took during Days 25 through 29 and evaluate your performance. Before doing so, you might want to review the section "Your Four GMAT Scores" from Day 1.

DETERMINING YOUR ANALYTICAL WRITING ASSESSMENT (AWA) SCORE

To evaluate your performance on the AWA practice test that you took on Day 24, refer to the AWA scoring criteria from Day 3, pages 22–23, and Day 4, page 30. Score each of your two essays on a scale of 0 to 6, based on the scoring guide. Your final AWA score (0 to 6) is simply the average of these two individual scores, rounded to the nearest one-half point.

DETERMINING YOUR VERBAL, QUANTITATIVE, AND TOTAL SCALED SCORES

To determine your scaled score for either the Quantitative or Verbal section of the practice test, follow these steps:

1.   Determine your total number of correct responses for the section, based on the answer keys. This is your *raw score*.

2.   Subtract one-quarter point from that total for each *incorrect* response; round off this number to the nearest integer. The result is your *corrected raw score*. (This is how the pencil-and-paper GMAT penalizes test-takers for incorrect responses. Recall from Day 2, however, that the computer-adaptive GMAT penalizes you for an incorrect response by posing easier subsequent questions, for which correct responses add fewer points to your score than do correct responses for more difficult questions.)

CONVERSION TABLE A:
VERBAL AND
QUANTITATIVE SCORES
(0-60)

CORRECTED RAW SCORE	VERBAL	QUANTITATIVE	CORRECTED RAW SCORE	VERBAL	QUANTITATIVE
41	52	—	19	27	31
40	51	—	18	25	30
39	50	—	17	24	28
38	48	—	16	23	27
37	47	53	15	22	25
36	46	52	14	21	24
35	45	51	13	20	23
34	44	50	12	19	22
33	43	49	11	18	21
32	42	48	10	17	20
31	41	47	9	16	18
30	39	45	8	15	17
29	38	44	7	14	16
28	37	43	6	13	14
27	36	41	5	12	13
26	35	40	4	11	12
25	33	38	3	10	11
24	32	37	2	9	10
23	31	36	1	8	9
22	30	34	0	7	8
21	29	33			
20	28	32			

CONVERSION TABLE B: TOTAL SCORE (200-800)

CORRECTED RAW SCORE	TOTAL SCALED SCORE	CORRECTED RAW SCORE	TOTAL SCALED SCORE	CORRECTED RAW SCORE	TOTAL SCALED SCORE
63 and up	800	41	580	19	370
62	790	40	570	18	360
61	780	39	560	17	350
60	770	38	550	16	340
59	760	37	540	15	330
58	750	36	530	14	330
57	740	35	530	13	320
56	730	34	520	12	310
55	720	33	510	11	300
54	710	32	500	10	290
53	700	31	490	9	280
52	690	30	480	8	270
51	680	29	470	7	260
50	670	28	460	6	250
49	660	27	450	5	240
48	650	26	440	4	230
47	640	25	430	3	220
46	630	24	420	2	310
45	620	23	410	0-1	200
44	610	22	400		
43	600	21	390		
42	590	20	380		

Percentile Rankings

Total Scaled Score	Percentage Below
740	99
720	99
700	98
680	97
660	95
640	93
620	89
600	85
580	80
560	74
540	68
520	61
500	53
480	46
460	39
440	32
420	26
400	20
380	15
360	11
340	8
320	6
300	4
280	2
260	1
240	1
220	0

Verbal and Quantitative Scores		
	Percentages Below	
Scaled Scores	**Verbal**	**Quantitative**
50	99	99
48	99	99
46	99	97
44	98	95
42	95	91
40	92	87
38	87	82
36	82	75
34	75	68
32	67	60
30	59	52
28	50	43
26	42	34
24	34	27
22	26	20
20	20	14
18	15	9
16	10	5
14	7	3
12	4	1
10	2	0
8	1	0
6	0	0

3. Refer to the appropriate column in the conversion table shown on the next page to convert your corrected raw score to the appropriate *scaled score* (0–60).

4. To determine your total scaled score, add your two corrected raw scores together and convert the total corrected raw score to a scaled score (200–800) using the conversion table shown in this next figure.

INTERPRETING YOUR SCALED SCORES

Understanding Scaled Scores

The figures in conversion tables A and B are average conversion figures based on several previously ad-ministered exams. Nevertheless, your scaled score on the practice test as determined by the two conversion tables should approximate the scores that you would attain on your GMAT CAT. As these tables illustrate, extremely high scaled scores (approaching 60 and 800) and extremely low scaled scores (approaching 0 and 200) are rare.

Understanding Percentile Rankings

Your GMAT score report indicates not only your scaled scores but also your percentile ranking (0 to 99%) based on your Verbal, Quantitative, and total scaled scores. These three percentile rankings indicate how you performed relative to all others taking the GMAT over a recent multiyear period. A percentile ranking of 60%, for example, indicates that you scored higher than 60% of all other test-takers (and lower than 40% of all other test-takers). (Note: The testing service reports only the scaled scores, not percentile rankings, to the business schools.) Refer to this next figure's percentile ranking conversion chart to determine your rankings for the practice test.

Note the following observations about scaled-score/percentile-ranking conversions:

- You don't have to attain the highest possible Quantitative or Verbal score or a "perfect" total score of 800 to rank in the 99th percentile. Conversely, your scaled scores don't have to be as low as possible to rank among the lowest percentile.

- Assuming that you responded to all 78 multiple-choice questions, if you responded correctly to 40 of those questions (plus or minus one), you've performed better than about one out of every two test-takers!

IF YOU HAVE MORE TIME TODAY

Go back to the practice test answer keys to determine your particular strengths and weaknesses. If you performed particularly poorly in one area (geometry questions, for example), review the lessons pertaining to those questions.

Notes

Notes

Notes

Notes

Notes

Notes

Notes

Notes

Notes

Notes

Build the skills you need for test success!

Students turn to **ARCO**® for a complete library of targeted test-prep handbooks that have helped thousands of test-takers reach—and even exceed—their score goals. Don't miss these exceptional resources:

GRE Answers to Real Essay Questions
Instructional tips and detailed review for 251 essay questions that have frequently appeared on the exam.
$14.95

More GRE CAT prep from **ARCO**!

GRE/LSAT Logic Workbook
In-depth practice for building critical skills for the analytical section of the exam.
$10.95

ARCO
™
THOMSON LEARNING

www.petersons.com AOL Keyword: Peterson's

GRE/LSAT/GMAT/MCAT Reading Comprehension Workbook
A targeted handbook packed with all types of reading passages that you'll encounter on the exam.
$10.95

Visit your local bookstore or call to order: **800-338-3282**. To order online, go to **www.petersons.com** and head for the bookstore!